鳥　山　明

Ah, we're finally at the 30th volume! Son Goku, who used to be a little kid, is now a father! The main reason I've been able to keep drawing this manga for so long is due to the support of all you readers. Thank you very much! Thank you so, so much! I'm also amazed with myself because I usually get bored with things very quickly, so it's pretty unusual that I've been able to do the same manga for over seven years.

—Akira Toriyama, 1992

Widely known all over the world for his playful, innovative storytelling and humorous, distinctive art style, **Dragon Ball** creator Akira Toriyama is also known in his native Japan for the wildly popular **Dr. Slump**, his previous manga series about the adventures of a mad scientist and his android "daughter." His hit series **Dragon Ball** ran from 1984 to 1995 in Shueisha's **Weekly Shonen Jump** magazine. He is also known for his design work on video games such as **Dragon Warrior**, **Chrono Trigger** and **Tobal No. 1**. His recent manga works include **Cowa!**, **Kajika**, **Sand Land**, **Neko Majin**, and a children's book, **Toccio the Angel**. He lives with his family in Japan.

DRAGON BALL Z VOL. 14
SHONEN JUMP Manga Edition

STORY AND ART BY
AKIRA TORIYAMA

English Adaptation/Gerard Jones
Translation/Lillian Olsen
Touch-Up Art & Lettering/Wayne Truman
Cover & Graphics Design/Sean Lee
Senior Editor/Jason Thompson

In the original Japanese edition, DRAGON BALL and DRAGON BALL Z
are known collectively as the 42-volume series DRAGON BALL. The
English DRAGON BALL Z was originally volumes 17–42 of the Japanese
DRAGON BALL.

Printed in Canada

Published by VIZ Media, LLC
P.O. Box 77010
San Francisco, CA 94107

11
First printing, December 2003
Eleventh printing, April 2018

SHONEN JUMP MANGA

DRAGON BALL Z

Vol. 14

DB: 30 of 42

STORY AND ART BY
AKIRA TORIYAMA

THE MAIN CHARACTERS

Bulma

Goku's oldest friend, Bulma is a scientific genius. She met Goku while on a quest for the seven magical Dragon Balls which, when gathered together, can grant any wish.

Son Goku

The greatest martial artist on Earth, he owes his strength to the training of Kame-Sen'nin and Kaiô-sama, and the fact that he's an alien Saiyan. To get even stronger, he has trained under 100 times Earth's gravity.

Dr. Gero

The mad scientist who built the androids to kill Goku. He even turned himself into a cyborg, and refers to himself as android #20.

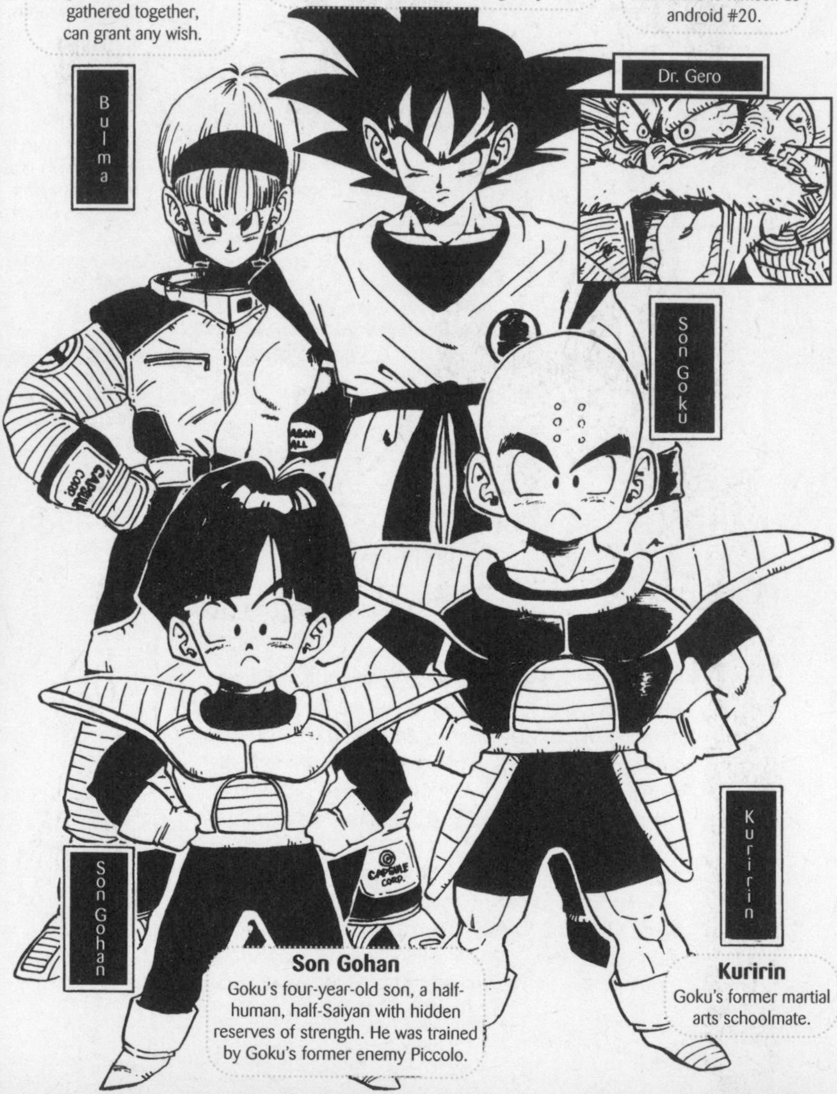

Bulma
Dr. Gero
Son Goku
Son Gohan
Kuririn

Son Gohan

Goku's four-year-old son, a half-human, half-Saiyan with hidden reserves of strength. He was trained by Goku's former enemy Piccolo.

Kuririn

Goku's former martial arts schoolmate.

Androids #16, #17 and #18
Incredibly strong androids—or are they cyborgs?—created by Dr. Gero.

Vegeta

Piccolo

Vegeta
The evil prince of the Saiyans, a powerful (but now almost extinct) alien race. He yearns to defeat Goku with his own hands.

Android #16

Piccolo
Goku's former arch-enemy, Piccolo is an alien from planet Namek—and the dark half of Kami-sama, the deity who created the Dragon Balls.

Trunks
The future son of Vegeta and Bulma, he is a half-human, half-Saiyan—and the second person, after Goku, able to become an all-powerful "Super Saiyan." In our heroes' current timeline, he's just a little baby.

#18

#17

Trunks

Son Goku was Earth's greatest hero, and the Dragon Balls—which can grant any wish—were Earth's greatest treasure. Three years ago, Earth was visited by Trunks, a time traveler from the future. Trunks warned Earth's martial artists that the world would soon be attacked by terrifying androids—and Goku would develop a deadly virus! With Goku sick, the other heroes were forced to fight androids #19 and #20 by themselves. They were winning, until Trunks returned from the future and told them that *these weren't the same androids he warned them about!* Now, the mad Dr. Gero has awakened #17 and #18, the *real* deadly androids from Trunks' future...

DRAGON BALL Z 14

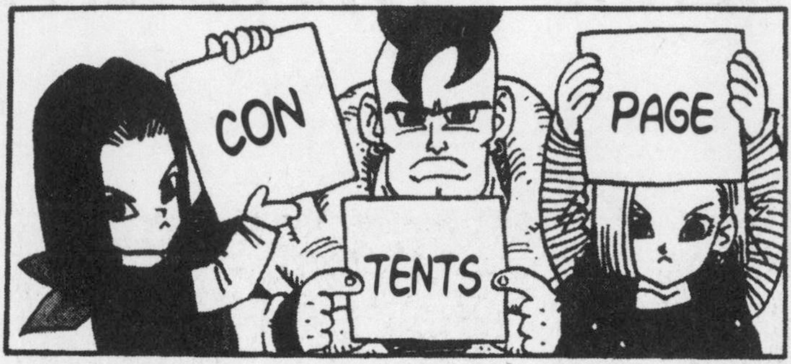
CON
TENTS
PAGE

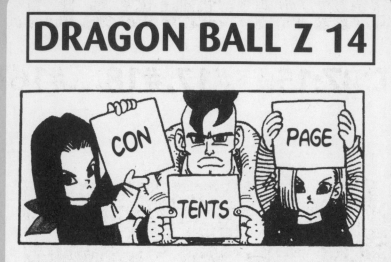

DRAGONBALL

DBZ:156 • #17, #18...#16?

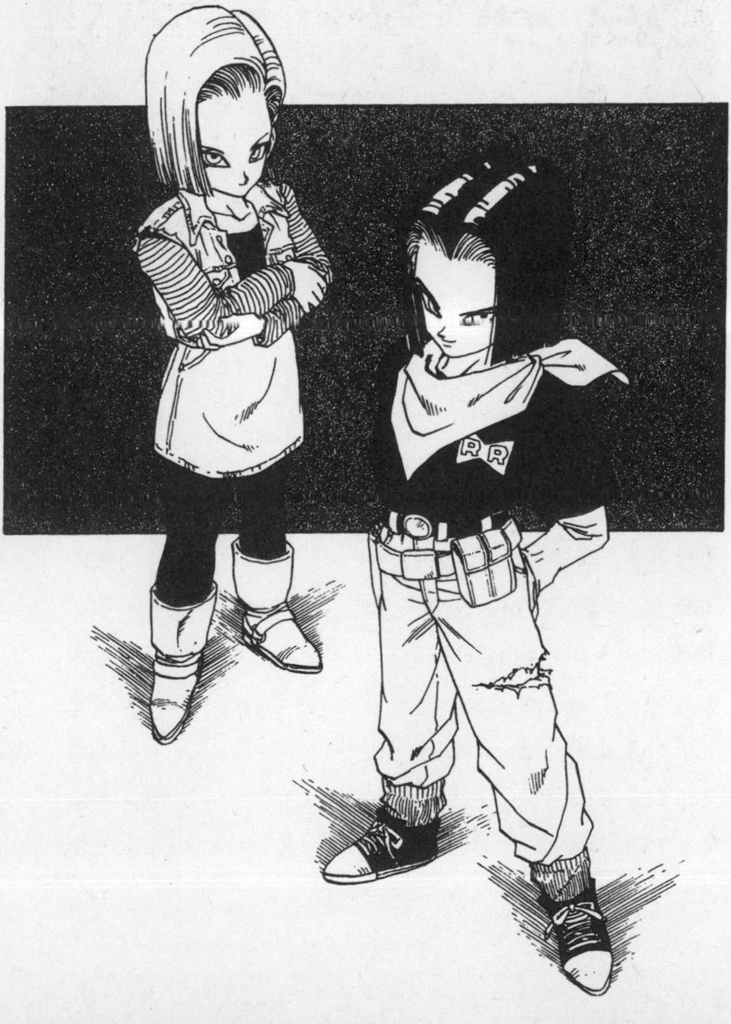

READ THIS WAY

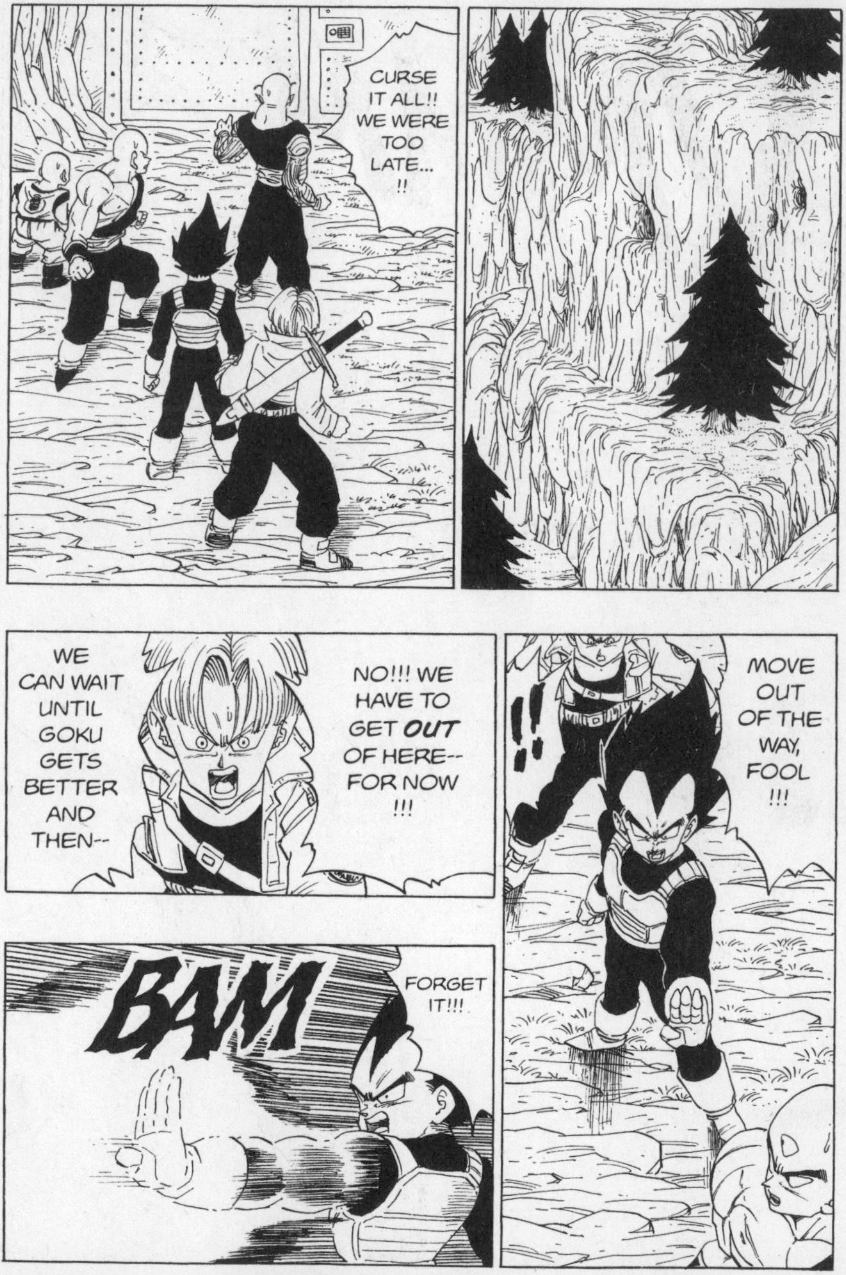
CURSE IT ALL!! WE WERE TOO LATE... !!
!!
MOVE OUT OF THE WAY, FOOL !!!
NO!!! WE HAVE TO GET OUT OF HERE-- FOR NOW !!!
WE CAN WAIT UNTIL GOKU GETS BETTER AND THEN--
FORGET IT!!!
BAM

READ THIS WAY

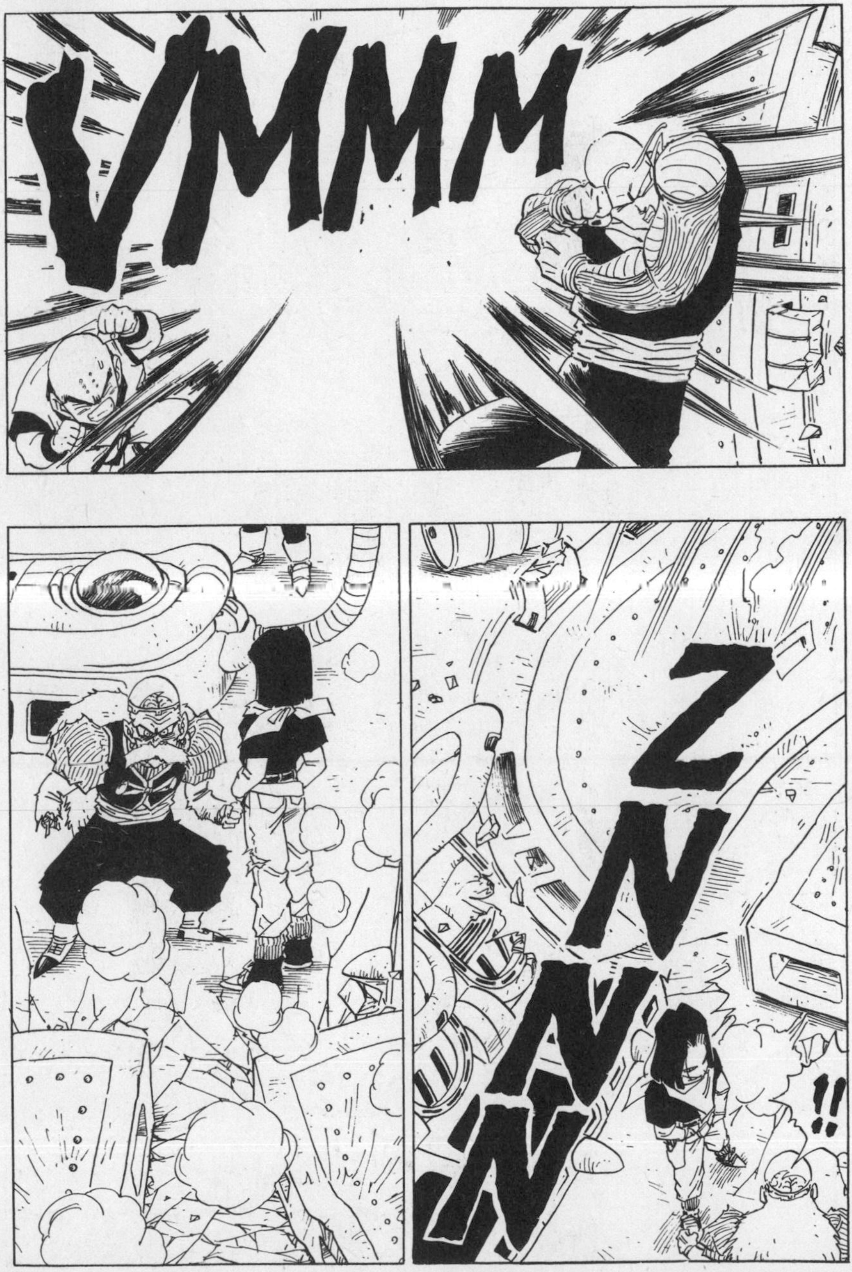
VMMM
ZNNN
!!

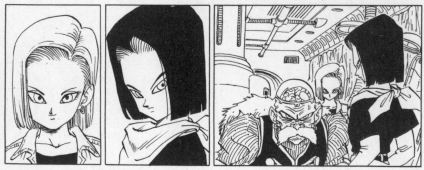

YES...
!!

IS THAT
THEM?
THEY
BETTER BE
THE RIGHT
ONES THIS
TIME.

READ THIS WAY

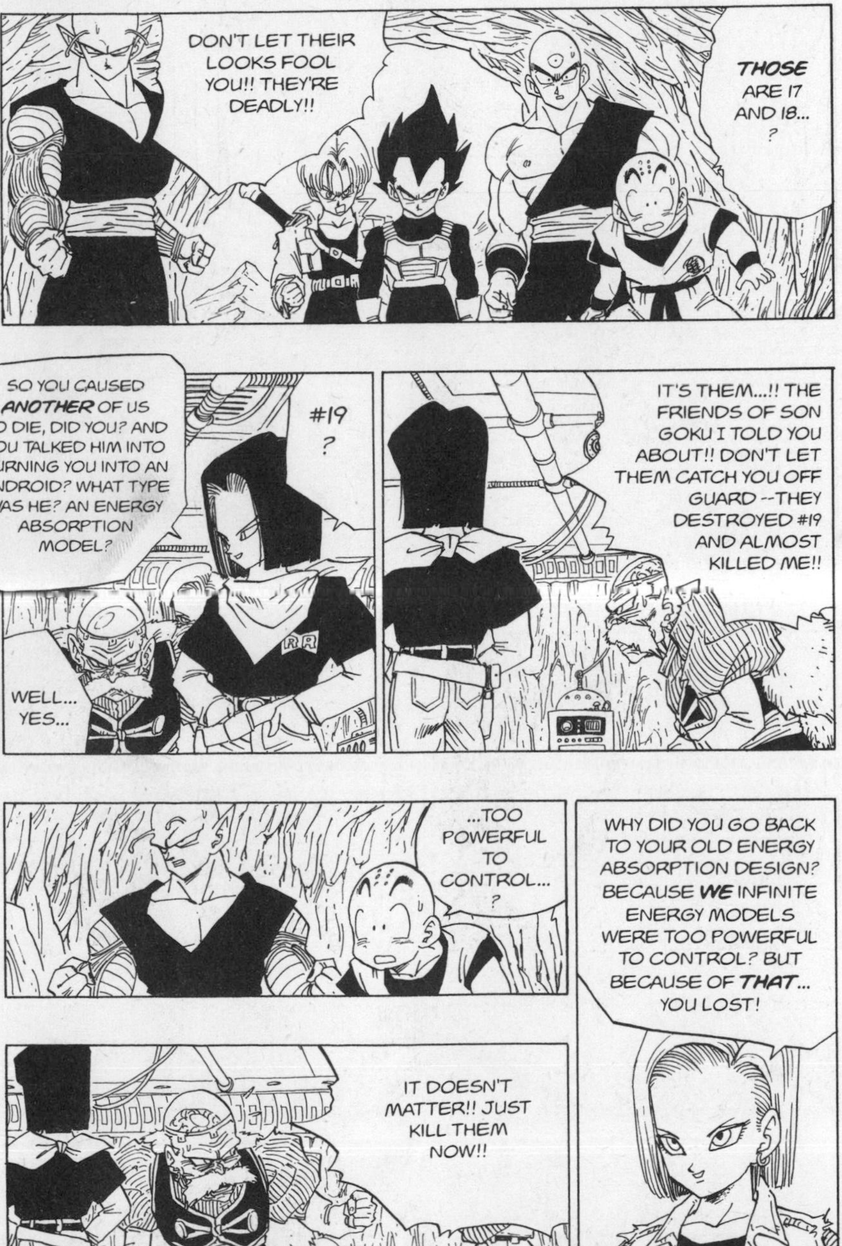
THOSE ARE 17 AND 18...?
DON'T LET THEIR LOOKS FOOL YOU!! THEY'RE DEADLY!!
IT'S THEM...!! THE FRIENDS OF SON GOKU I TOLD YOU ABOUT!! DON'T LET THEM CATCH YOU OFF GUARD --THEY DESTROYED #19 AND ALMOST KILLED ME!!
#19?
SO YOU CAUSED ANOTHER OF US TO DIE, DID YOU? AND YOU TALKED HIM INTO TURNING YOU INTO AN ANDROID? WHAT TYPE WAS HE? AN ENERGY ABSORPTION MODEL?
WELL... YES...
WHY DID YOU GO BACK TO YOUR OLD ENERGY ABSORPTION DESIGN? BECAUSE WE INFINITE ENERGY MODELS WERE TOO POWERFUL TO CONTROL? BUT BECAUSE OF THAT... YOU LOST!
...TOO POWERFUL TO CONTROL...?
IT DOESN'T MATTER!! JUST KILL THEM NOW!!

READ THIS WAY

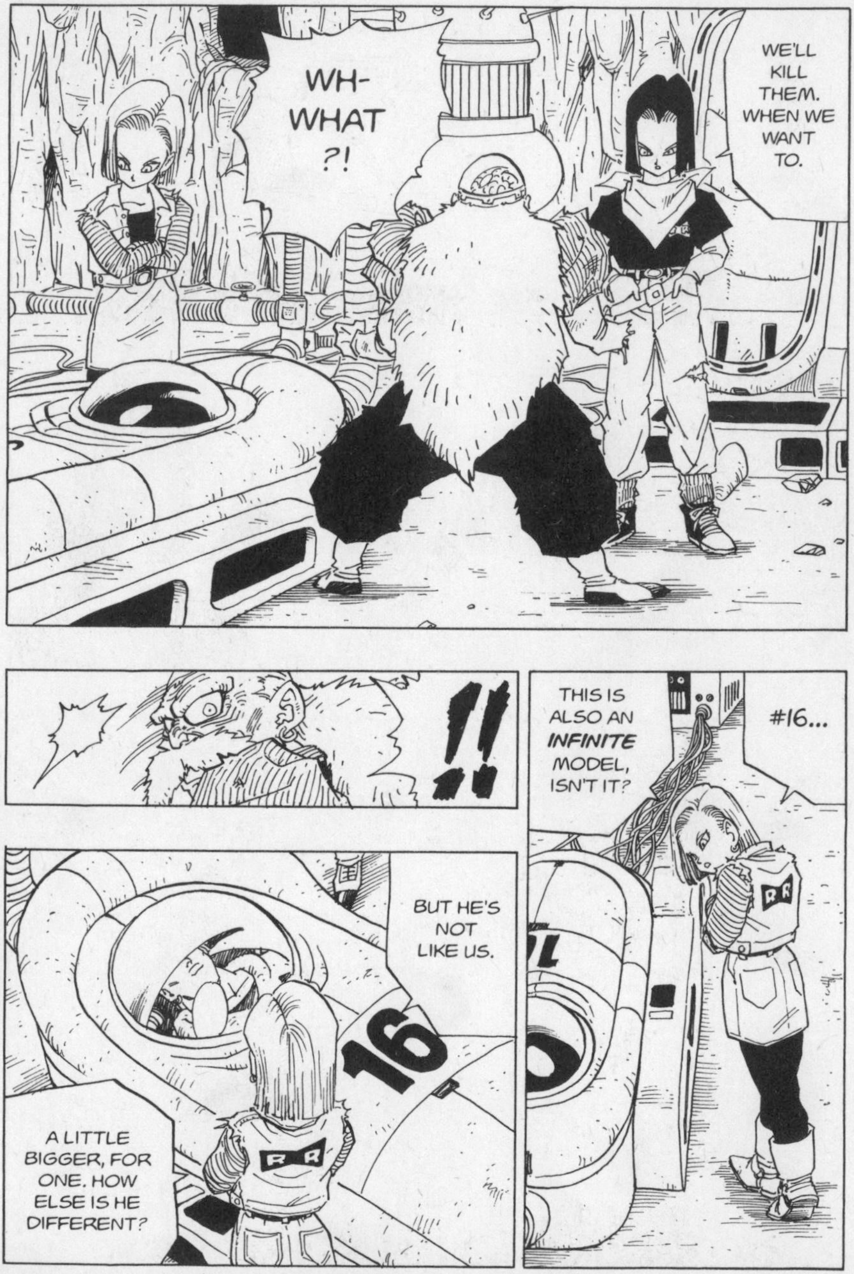

WE'LL KILL THEM. WHEN WE WANT TO.
WH-WHAT ?!
#16...
THIS IS ALSO AN INFINITE MODEL, ISN'T IT?
!!
BUT HE'S NOT LIKE US.
A LITTLE BIGGER, FOR ONE. HOW ELSE IS HE DIFFERENT?

READ THIS WAY

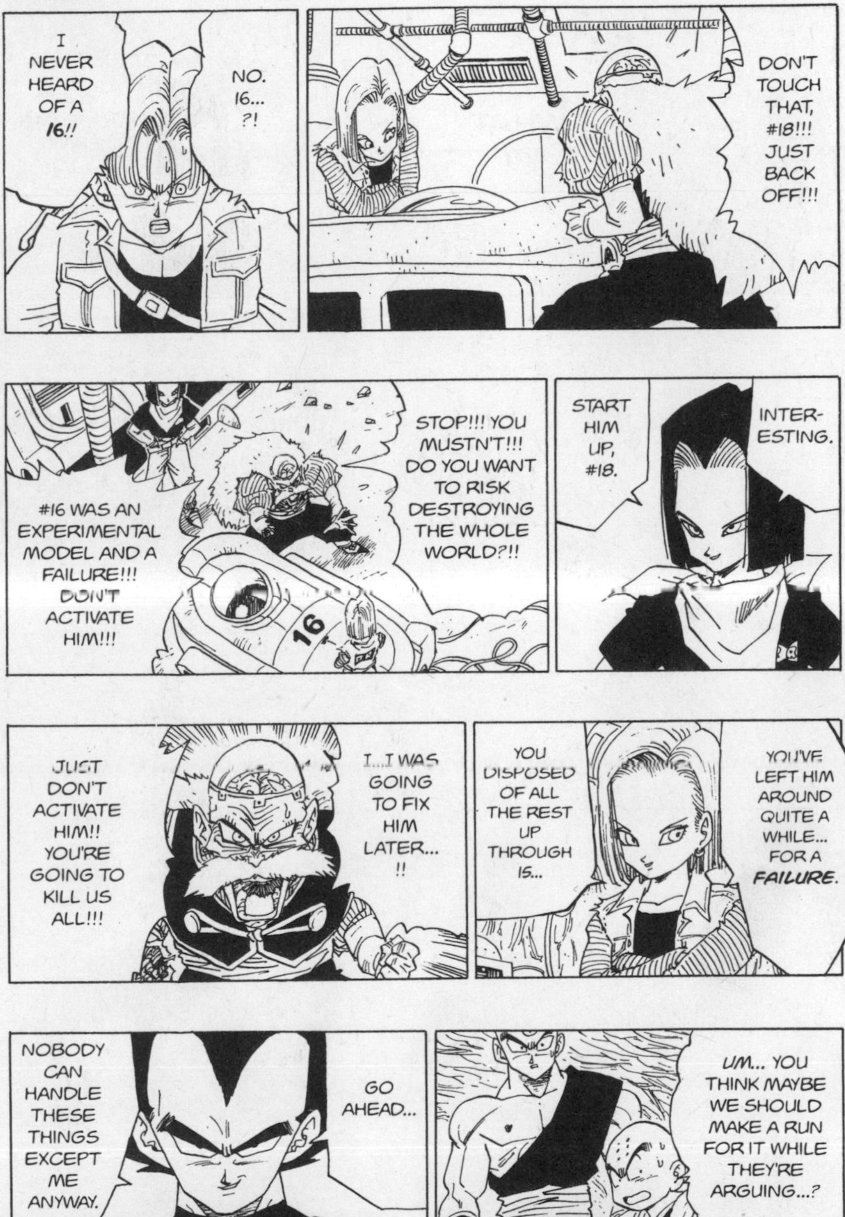
DON'T TOUCH THAT, #18!!! JUST BACK OFF!!!
NO. 16...?!
I NEVER HEARD OF A 16!!
INTER-ESTING.
START HIM UP, #18.
STOP!!! YOU MUSTN'T!!! DO YOU WANT TO RISK DESTROYING THE WHOLE WORLD?!!
#16 WAS AN EXPERIMENTAL MODEL AND A FAILURE!!! DON'T ACTIVATE HIM!!!
16
YOU'VE LEFT HIM AROUND QUITE A WHILE... FOR A *FAILURE*.
YOU DISPOSED OF ALL THE REST UP THROUGH 15...
I...I WAS GOING TO FIX HIM LATER...!!
JUST DON'T ACTIVATE HIM!! YOU'RE GOING TO KILL US ALL!!!
UM... YOU THINK MAYBE WE SHOULD MAKE A RUN FOR IT WHILE THEY'RE ARGUING...?
GO AHEAD...
NOBODY CAN HANDLE THESE THINGS EXCEPT ME ANYWAY.

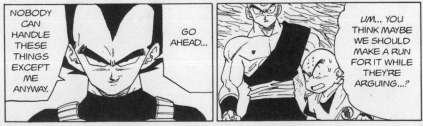

READ THIS WAY

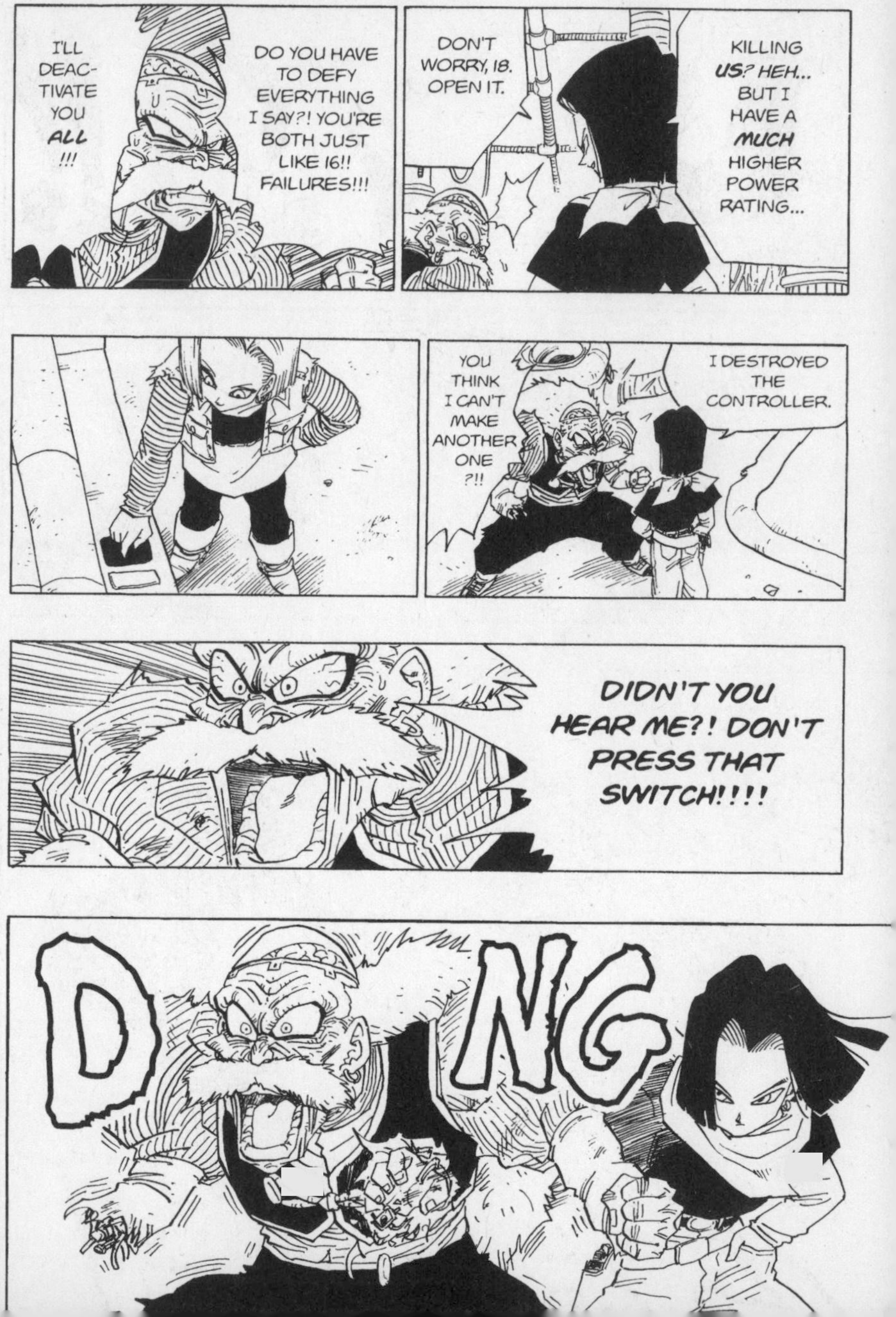
KILLING *US*? HEH... BUT I HAVE A *MUCH* HIGHER POWER RATING...
DON'T WORRY, 18. OPEN IT.
DO YOU HAVE TO DEFY EVERYTHING I SAY?! YOU'RE BOTH JUST LIKE 16!! FAILURES!!!
I'LL DEACTIVATE YOU *ALL* !!!
I DESTROYED THE CONTROLLER.
YOU THINK I CAN'T MAKE ANOTHER ONE ?!!
DIDN'T YOU HEAR ME?! DON'T PRESS THAT SWITCH!!!!
D NG

READ THIS WAY

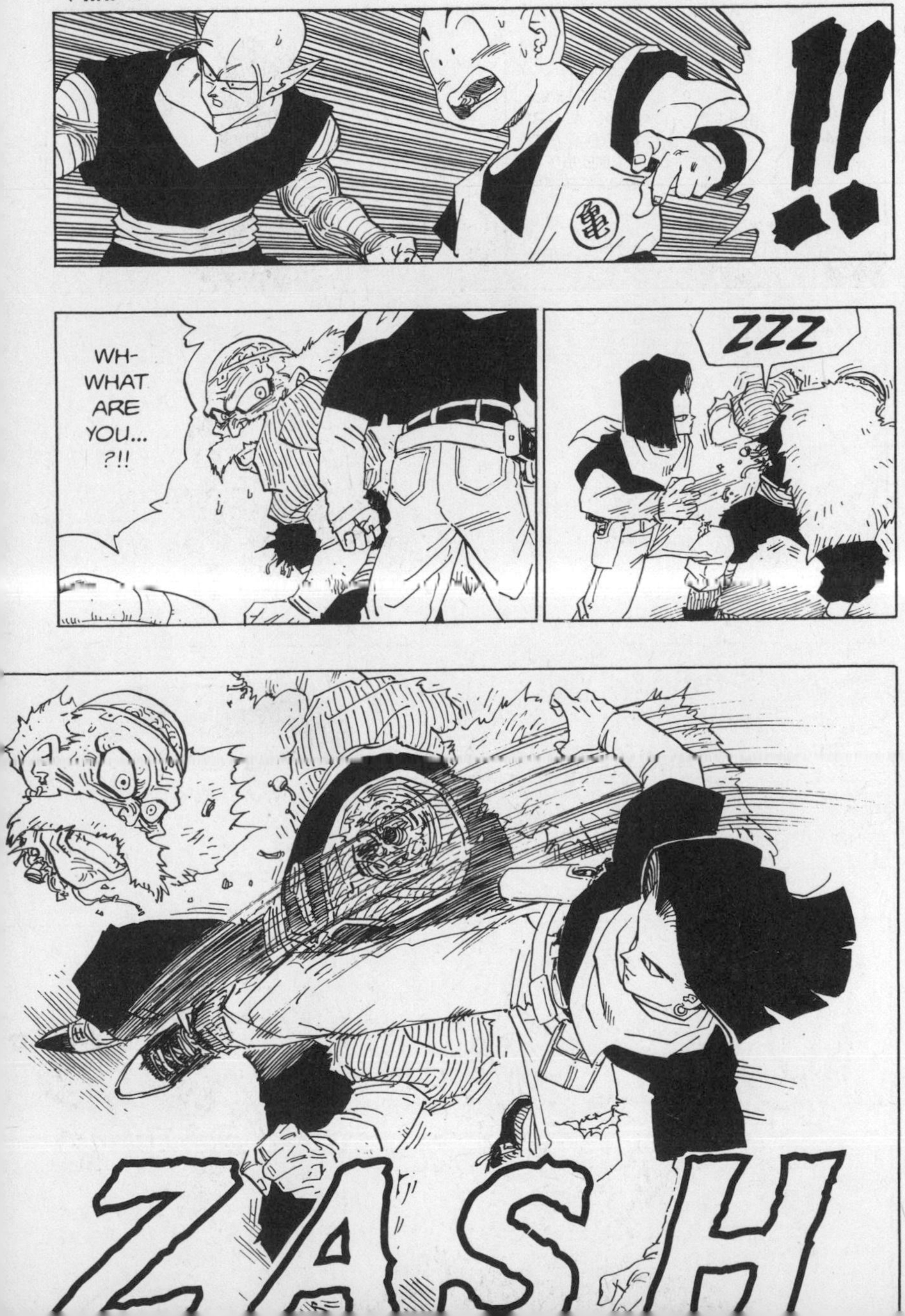
!!
ZZZ
WH- WHAT ARE YOU...?!!
ZASH

READ THIS WAY

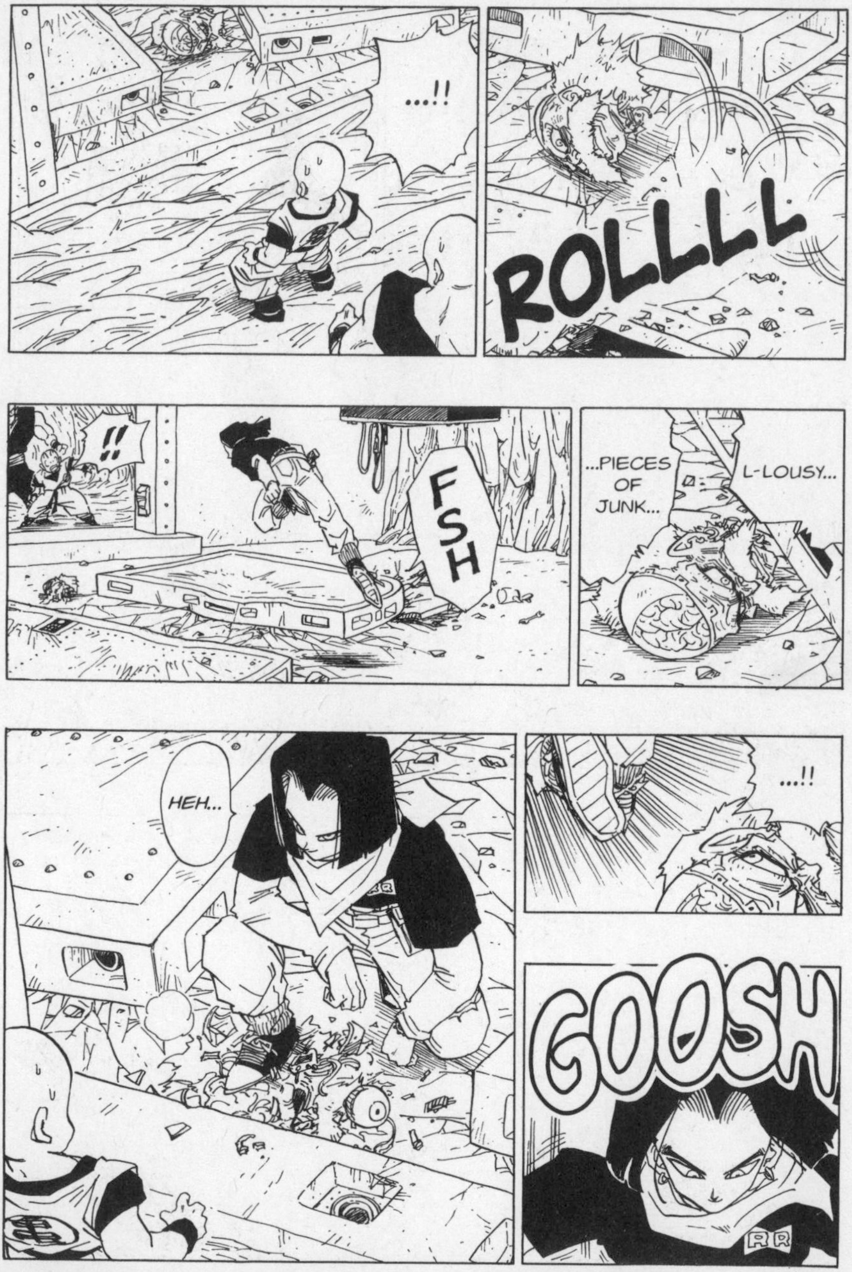
ROLLLL
...!!
L-LOUSY...
...PIECES OF JUNK...
FSH
!!
...!!
GOOSH
HEH...

READ THIS WAY

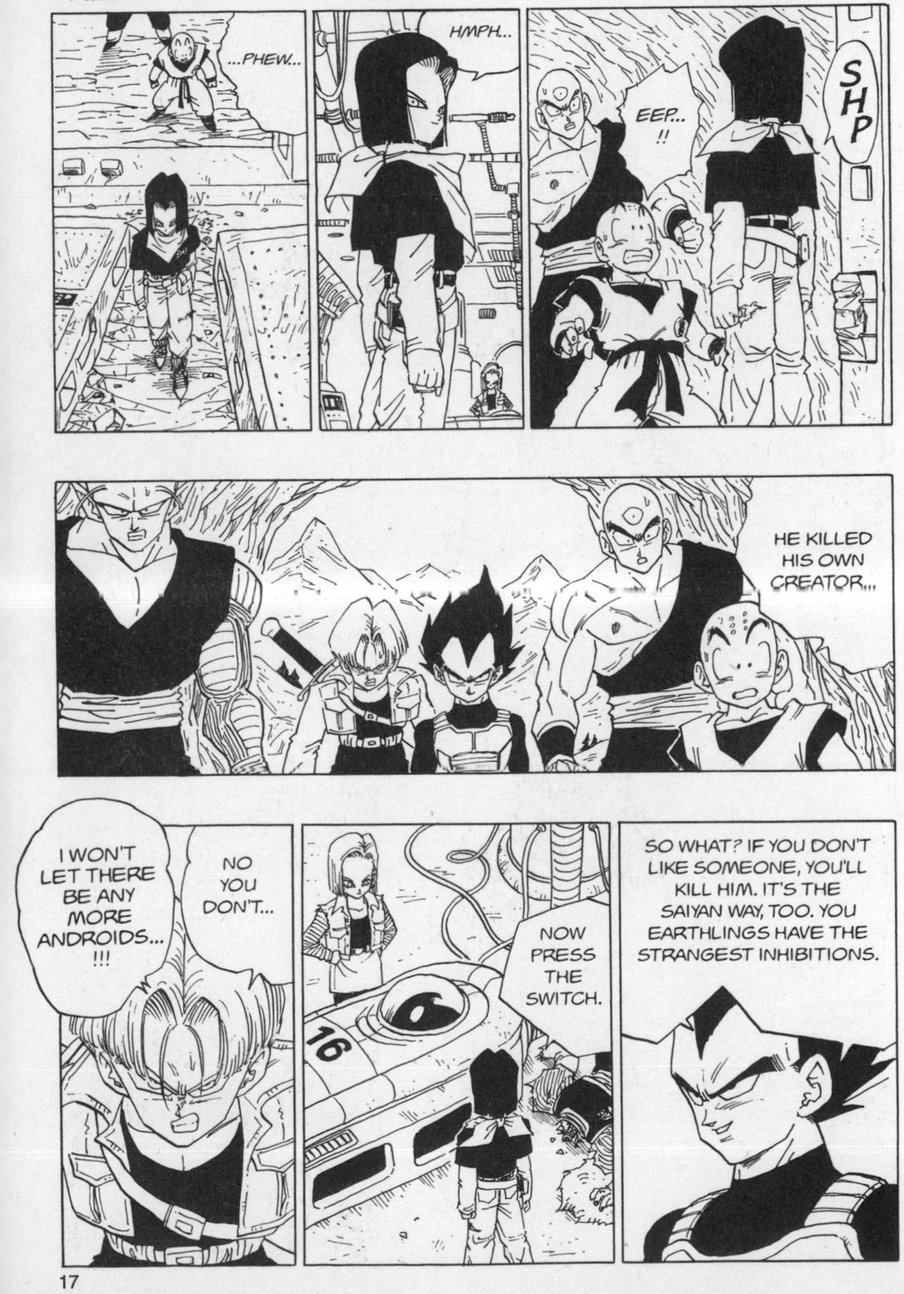
SHP
EEP... !!
HMPH...
...PHEW...
HE KILLED HIS OWN CREATOR...
SO WHAT? IF YOU DON'T LIKE SOMEONE, YOU'LL KILL HIM. IT'S THE SAIYAN WAY, TOO. YOU EARTHLINGS HAVE THE STRANGEST INHIBITIONS.
NOW PRESS THE SWITCH.
NO YOU DON'T...
I WON'T LET THERE BE ANY MORE ANDROIDS... !!!
16

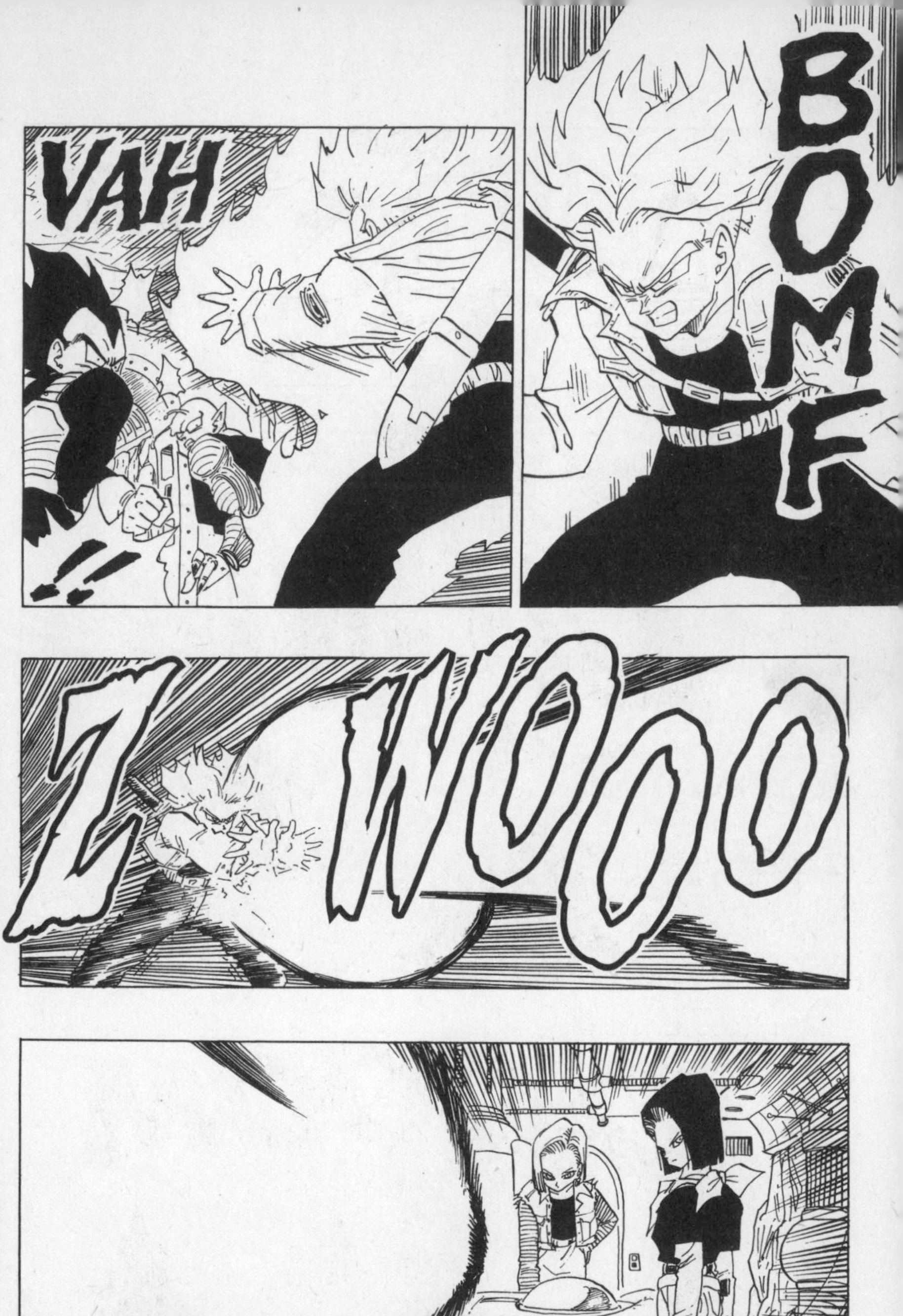
BOMF
VAH
!!
ZWOOO

READ THIS WAY

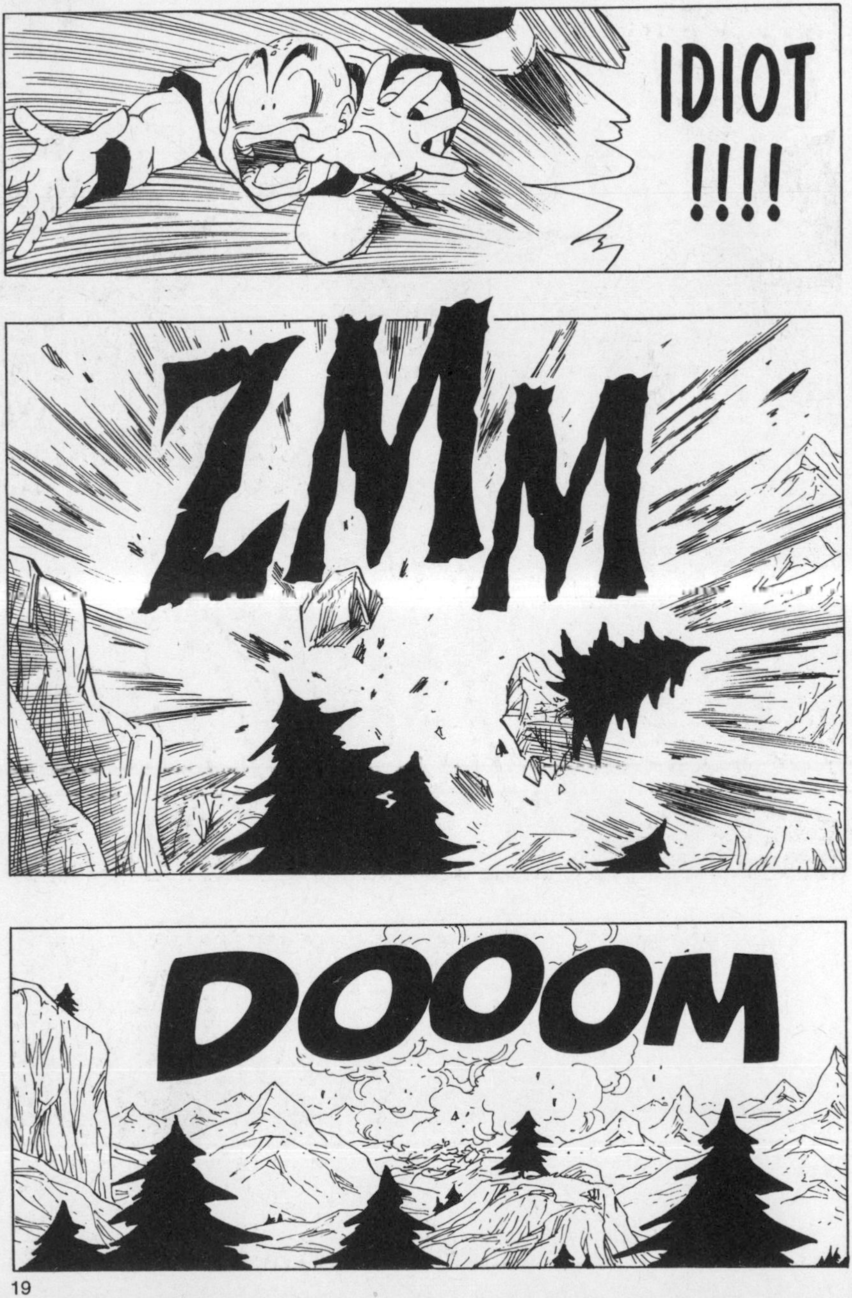
IDIOT !!!!
ZMM
DOOOM

READ THIS WAY

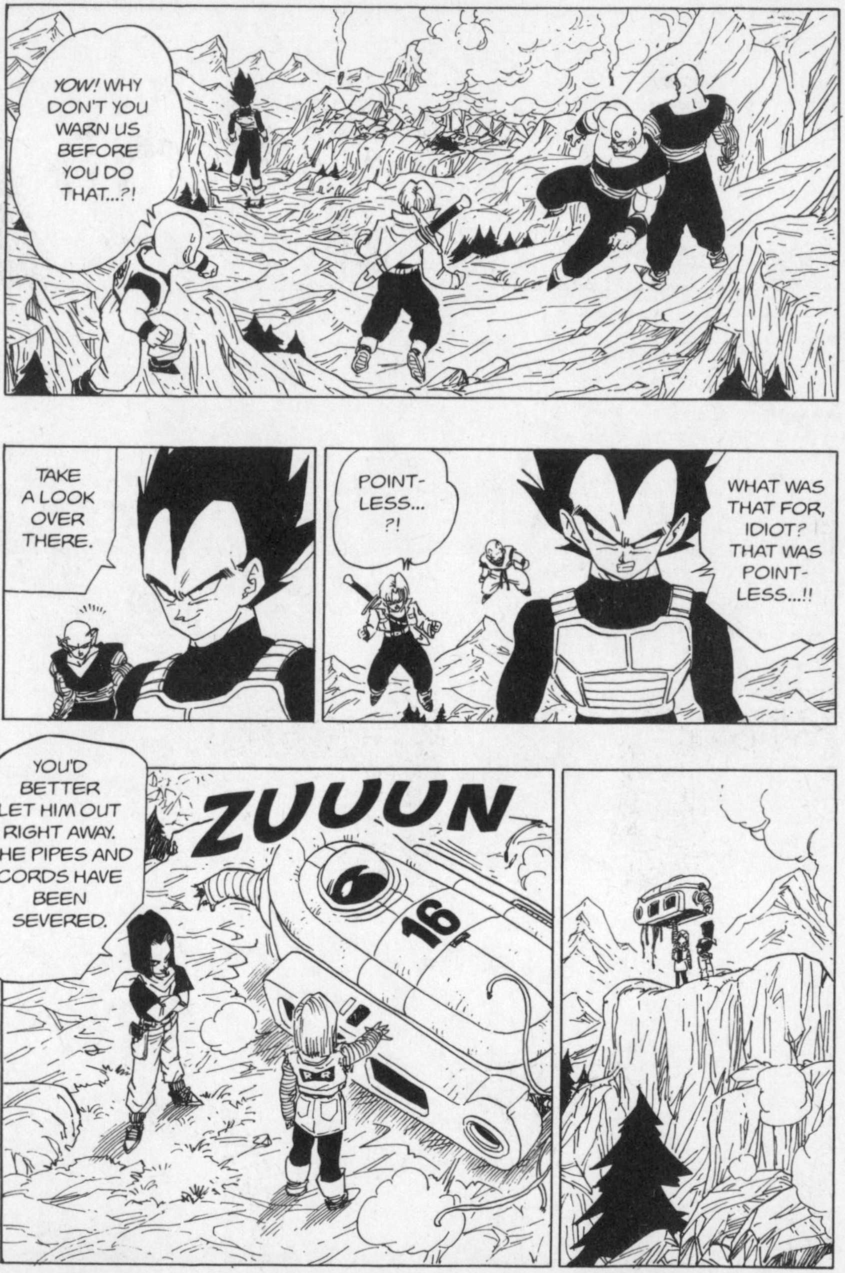
YOW! WHY DON'T YOU WARN US BEFORE YOU DO THAT...?!
WHAT WAS THAT FOR, IDIOT? THAT WAS POINT-LESS...!!
POINT-LESS...?!
TAKE A LOOK OVER THERE.
ZUUUN
YOU'D BETTER LET HIM OUT RIGHT AWAY. THE PIPES AND CORDS HAVE BEEN SEVERED.

READ THIS WAY

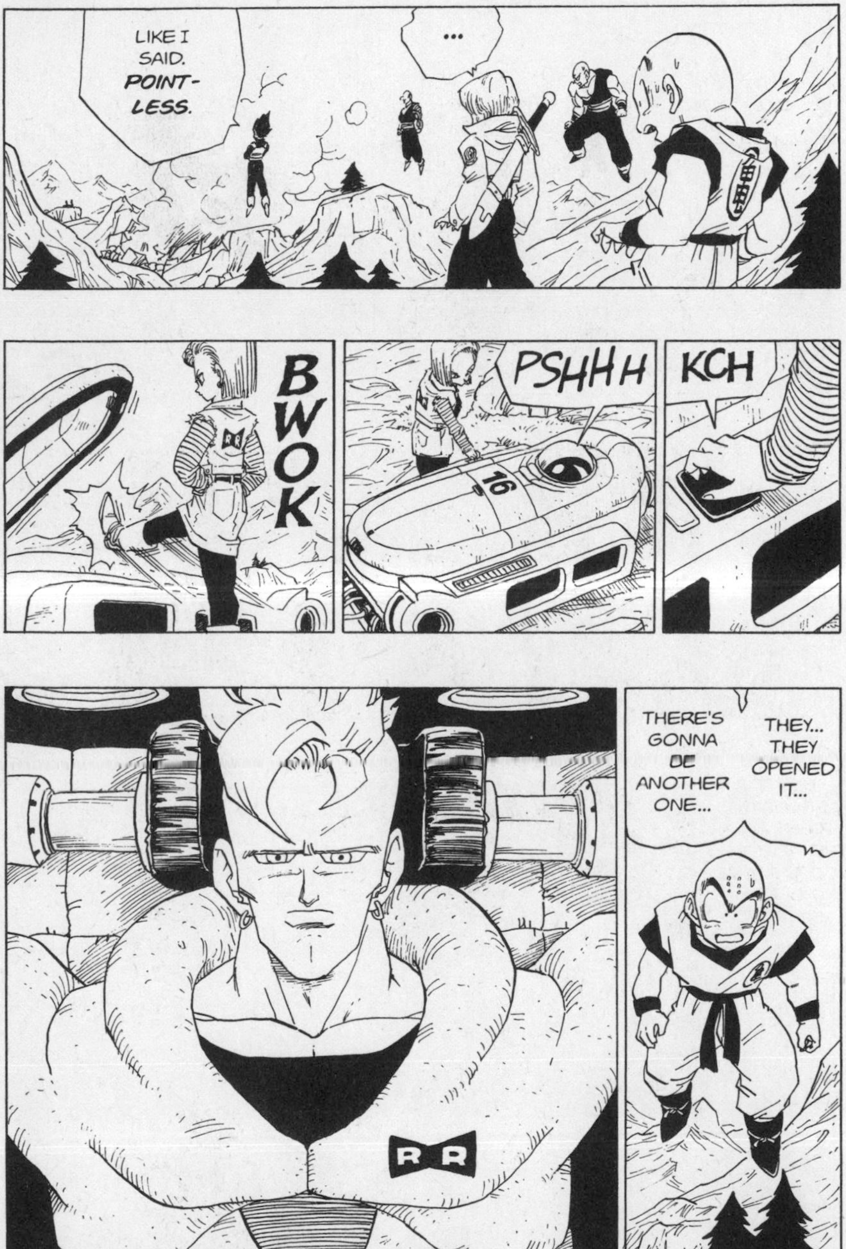
...
LIKE I SAID. POINT-LESS.
KCH
PSHHH
BWOK
THEY... THEY OPENED IT...
THERE'S GONNA BE ANOTHER ONE...

NEXT: The Mysterious #16

DBZ:157 • The Androids Walk Among Us

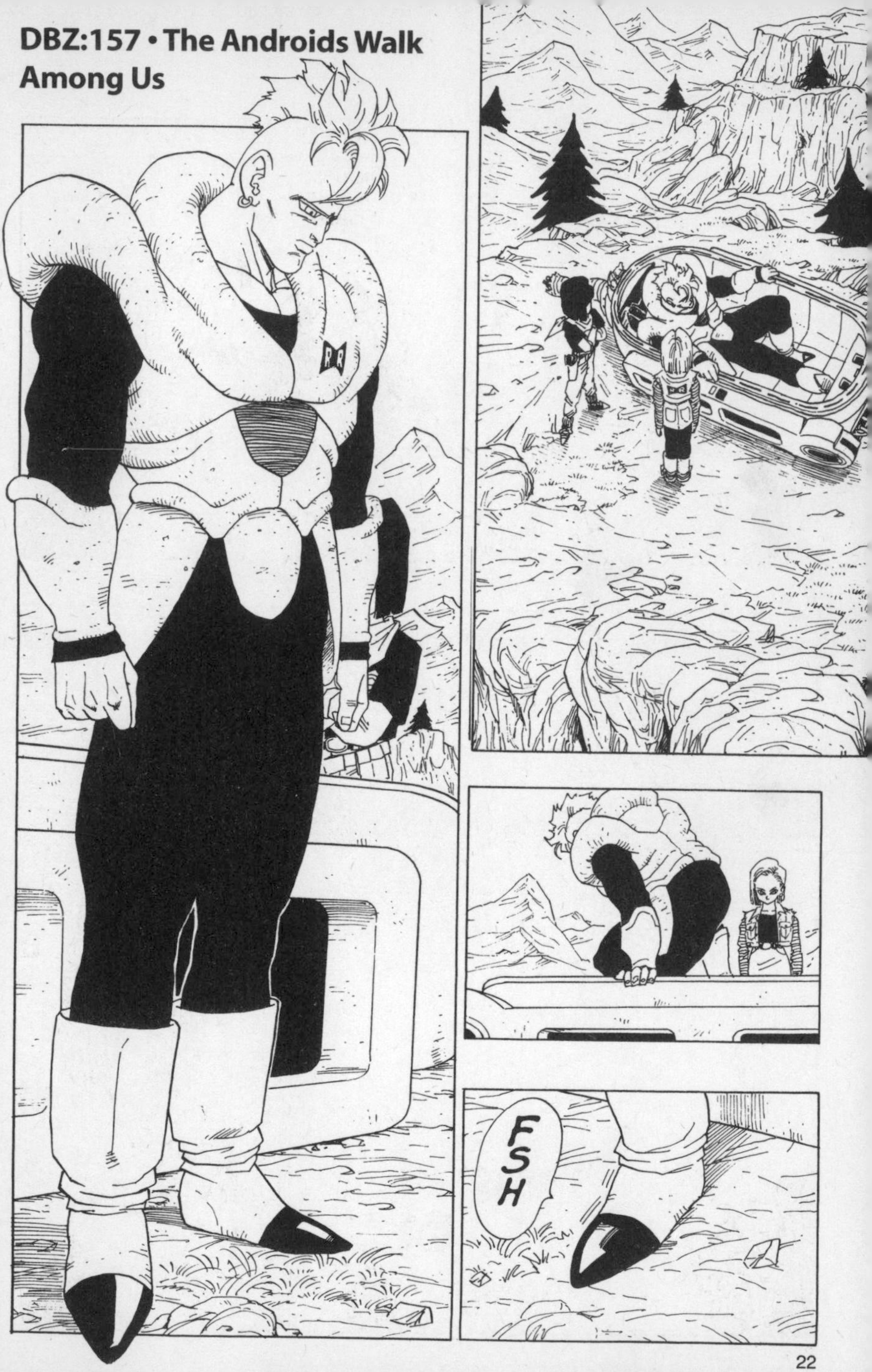
FSH

READ THIS WAY

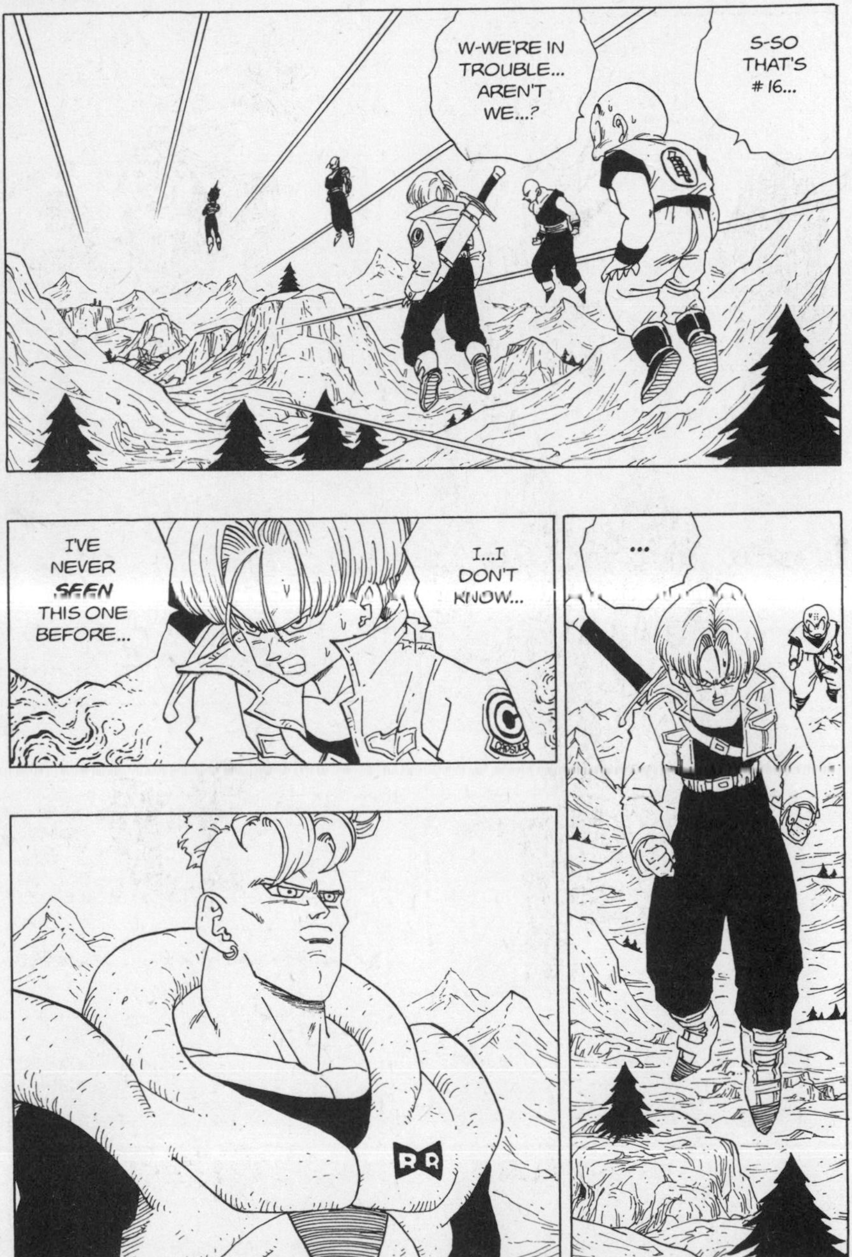

S-SO THAT'S # 16...
W-WE'RE IN TROUBLE... AREN'T WE...?
...
I...I DON'T KNOW...
I'VE NEVER SEEN THIS ONE BEFORE...

READ THIS WAY

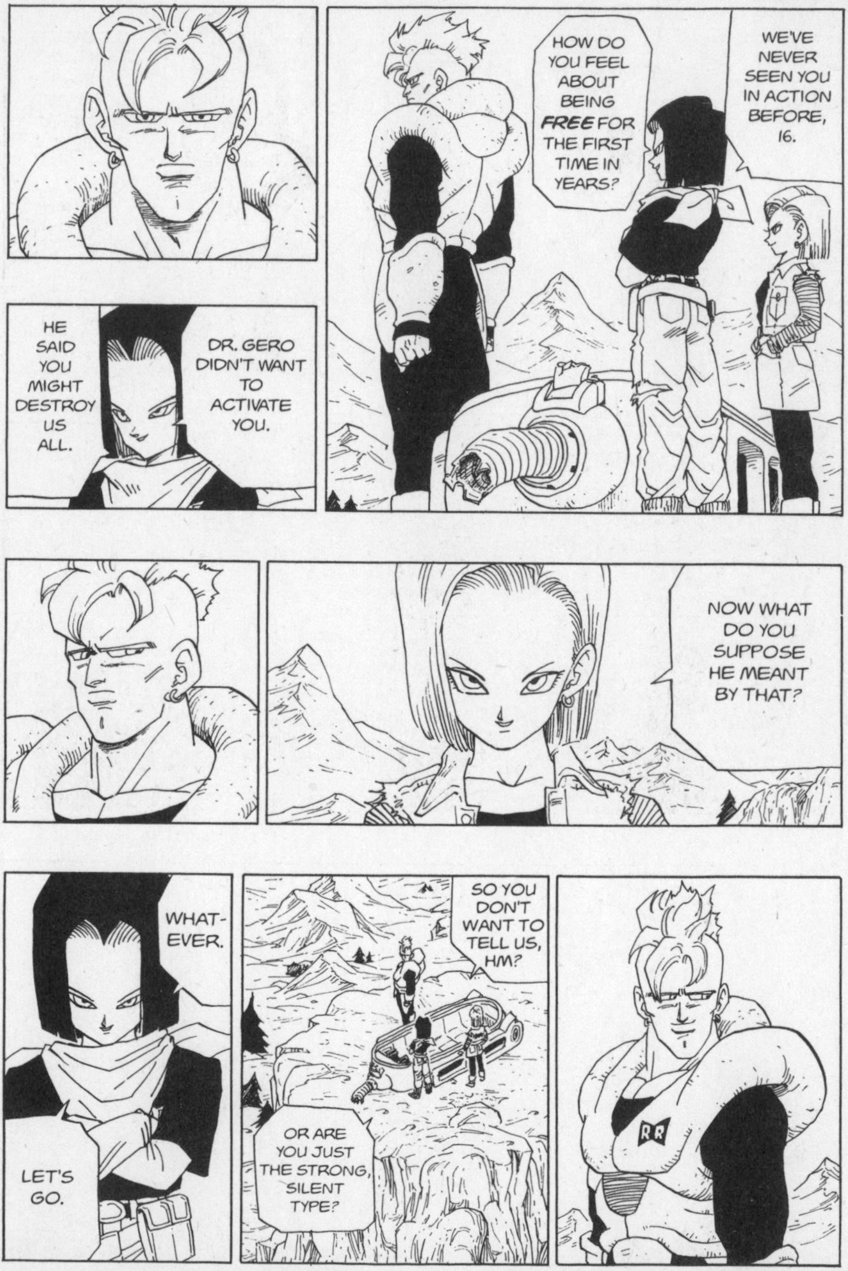
WE'VE NEVER SEEN YOU IN ACTION BEFORE, 16.
HOW DO YOU FEEL ABOUT BEING FREE FOR THE FIRST TIME IN YEARS?
DR. GERO DIDN'T WANT TO ACTIVATE YOU.
HE SAID YOU MIGHT DESTROY US ALL.
NOW WHAT DO YOU SUPPOSE HE MEANT BY THAT?
SO YOU DON'T WANT TO TELL US, HM?
OR ARE YOU JUST THE STRONG, SILENT TYPE?
WHAT-EVER.
LET'S GO.

READ THIS WAY

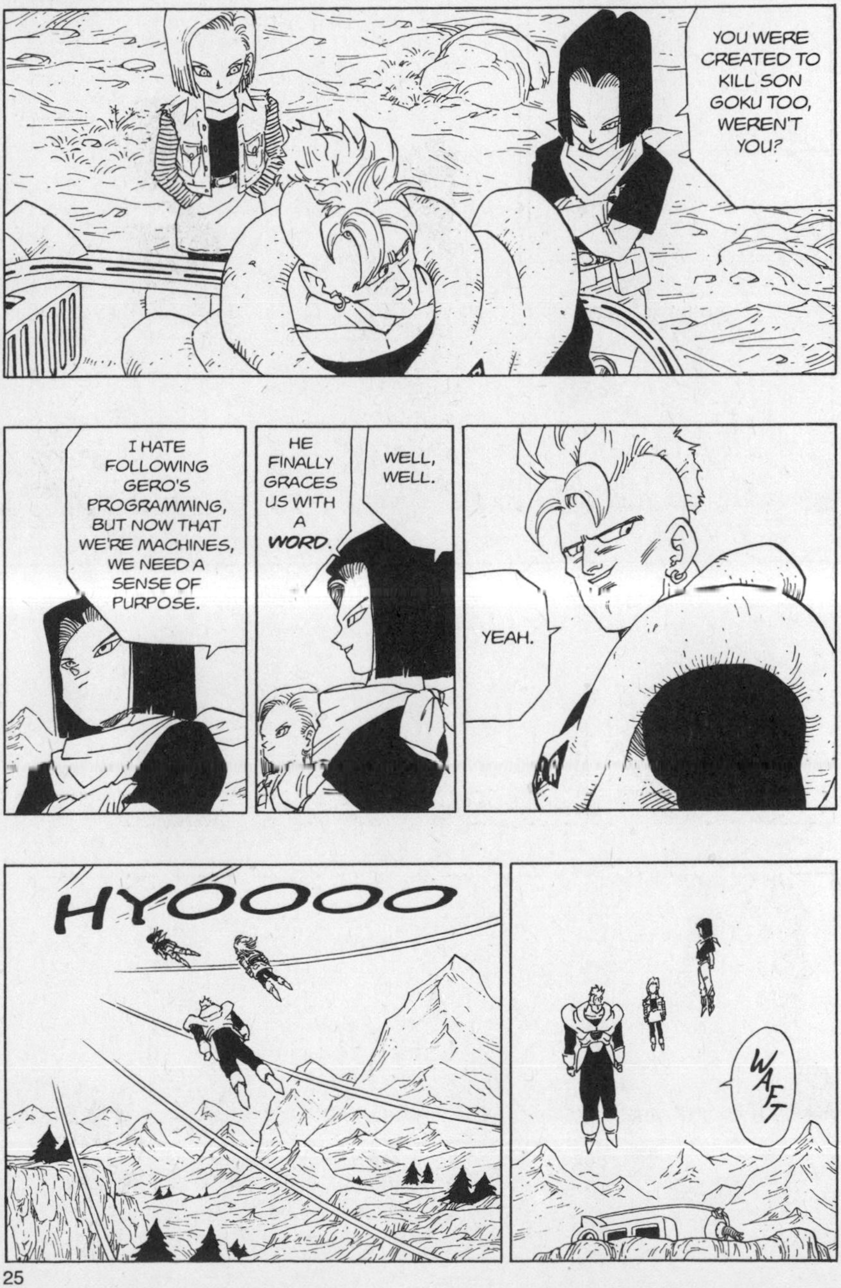
YOU WERE CREATED TO KILL SON GOKU TOO, WEREN'T YOU?
YEAH.
WELL, WELL.
HE FINALLY GRACES US WITH A **WORD**.
I HATE FOLLOWING GERO'S PROGRAMMING, BUT NOW THAT WE'RE MACHINES, WE NEED A SENSE OF PURPOSE.
WAFT
HYOOOO

READ THIS WAY

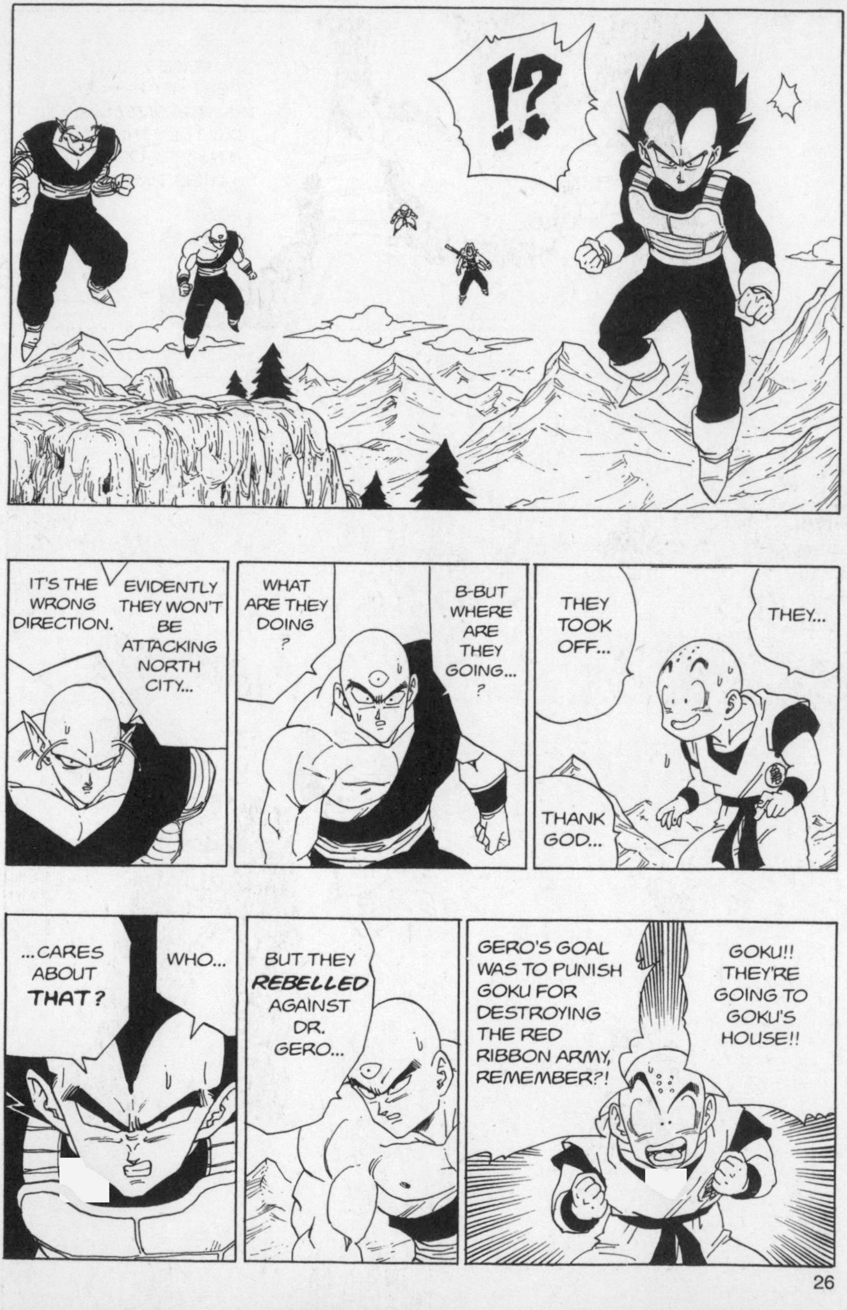
!?
THEY...
THEY TOOK OFF...
THANK GOD...
B-BUT WHERE ARE THEY GOING...?
WHAT ARE THEY DOING?
EVIDENTLY THEY WON'T BE ATTACKING NORTH CITY...
IT'S THE WRONG DIRECTION.
GOKU!! THEY'RE GOING TO GOKU'S HOUSE!!
GERO'S GOAL WAS TO PUNISH GOKU FOR DESTROYING THE RED RIBBON ARMY, REMEMBER?!
BUT THEY *REBELLED* AGAINST DR. GERO...
WHO...
...CARES ABOUT **THAT**?

READ THIS WAY

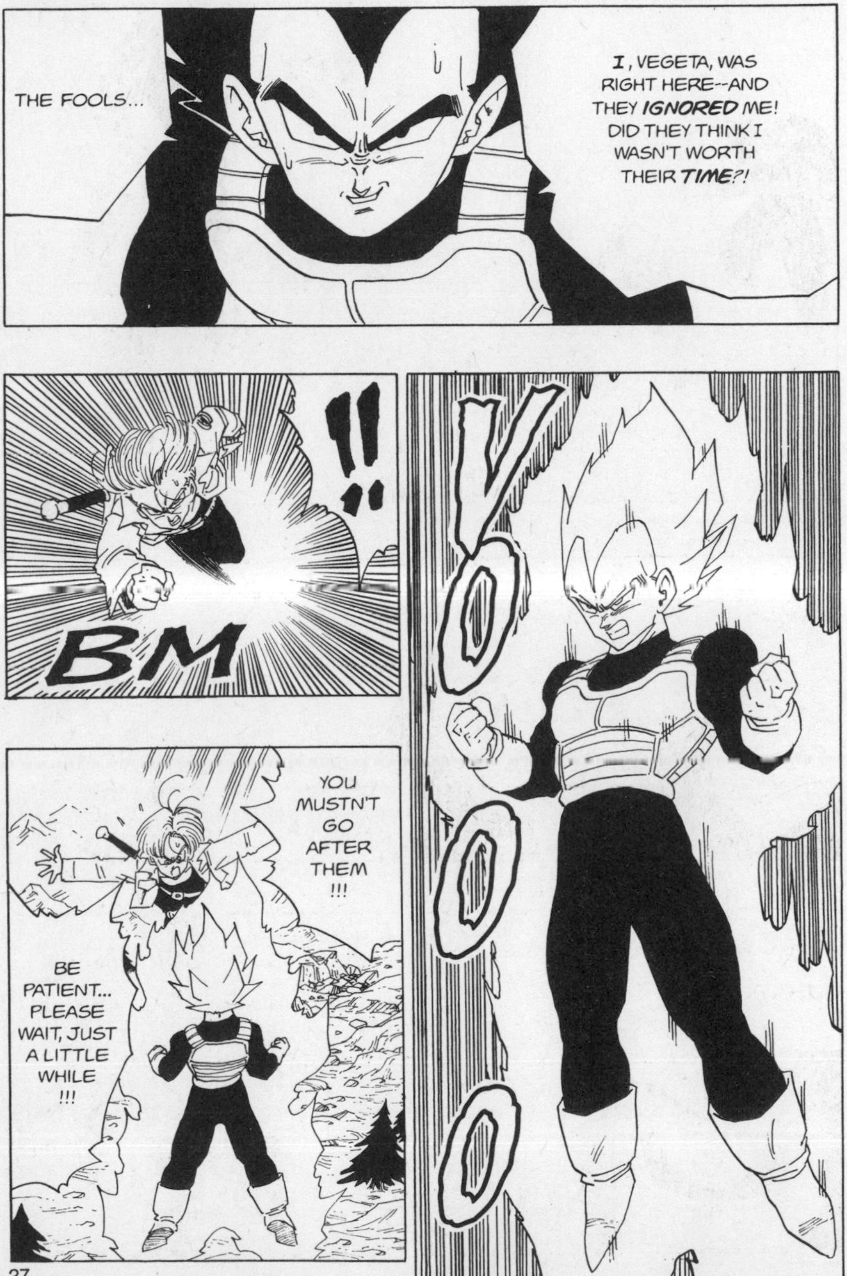
I, VEGETA, WAS RIGHT HERE--AND THEY IGNORED ME! DID THEY THINK I WASN'T WORTH THEIR TIME?!
THE FOOLS...
VOOOO
!!
BM
YOU MUSTN'T GO AFTER THEM !!!
BE PATIENT... PLEASE WAIT, JUST A LITTLE WHILE !!!

READ THIS WAY

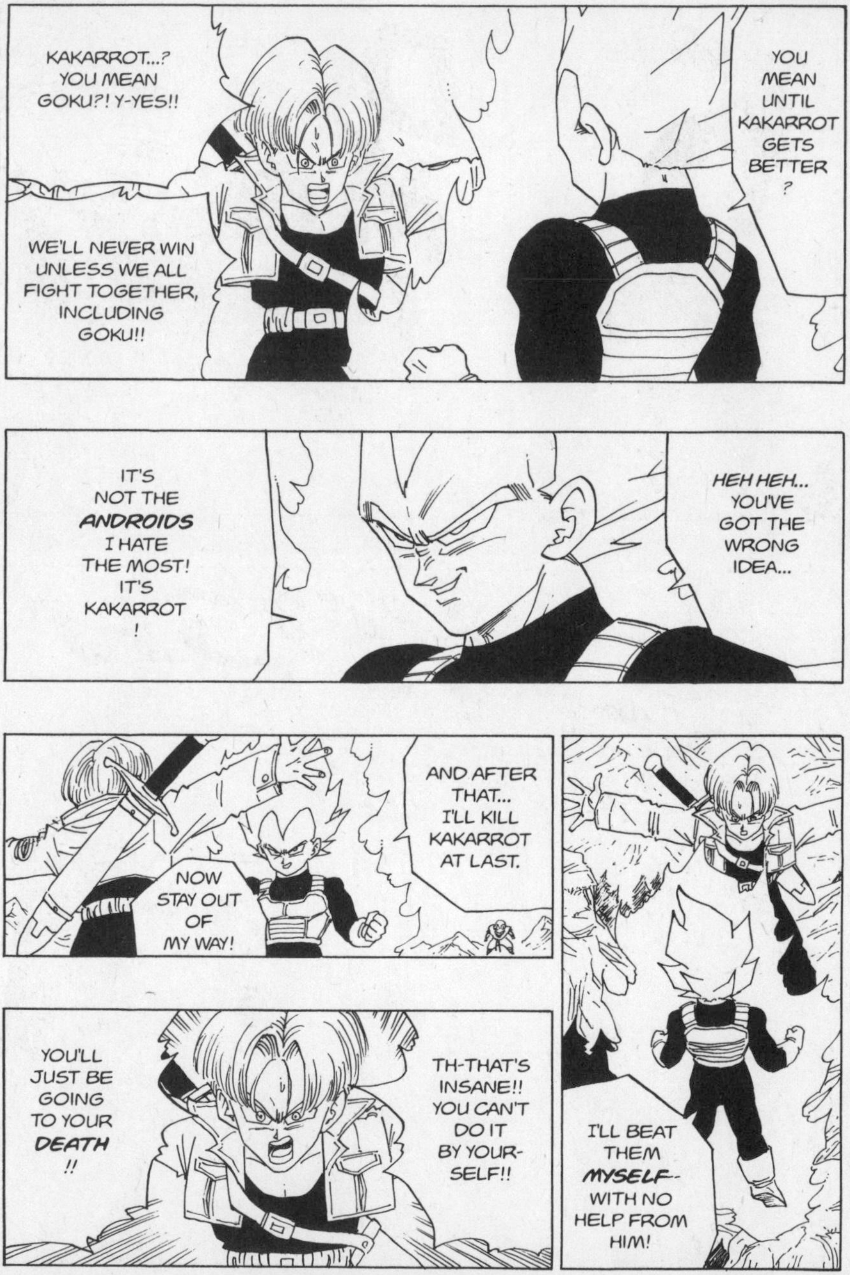
YOU MEAN UNTIL KAKARROT GETS BETTER?
KAKARROT...? YOU MEAN GOKU?! Y-YES!!
WE'LL NEVER WIN UNLESS WE ALL FIGHT TOGETHER, INCLUDING GOKU!!
HEH HEH... YOU'VE GOT THE WRONG IDEA...
IT'S NOT THE *ANDROIDS* I HATE THE MOST! IT'S KAKARROT!
I'LL BEAT THEM *MYSELF*-WITH NO HELP FROM HIM!
AND AFTER THAT... I'LL KILL KAKARROT AT LAST.
NOW STAY OUT OF MY WAY!
TH-THAT'S INSANE!! YOU CAN'T DO IT BY YOUR-SELF!!
YOU'LL JUST BE GOING TO YOUR *DEATH*!!

READ THIS WAY

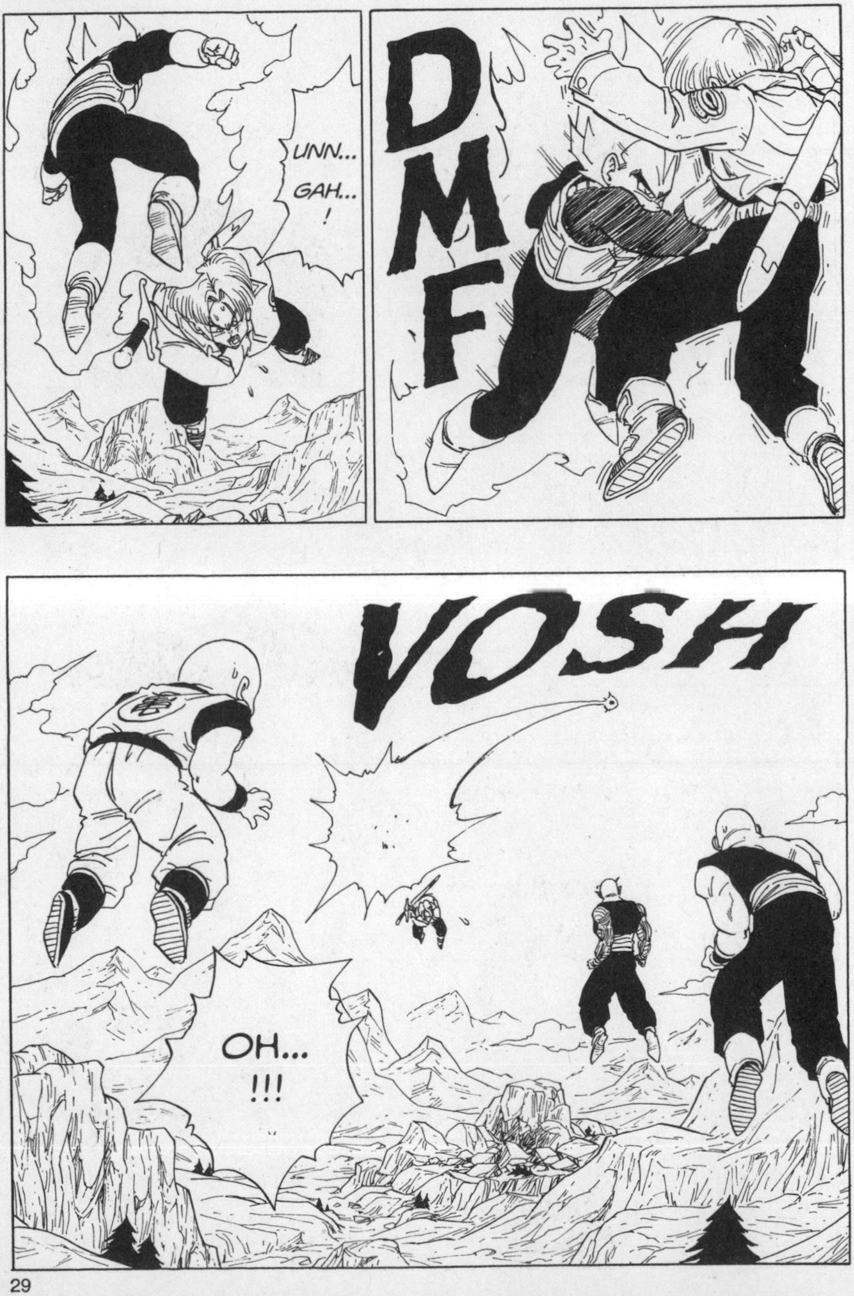
DMF
UNN... GAH... !
VOSH
OH... !!!

READ THIS WAY

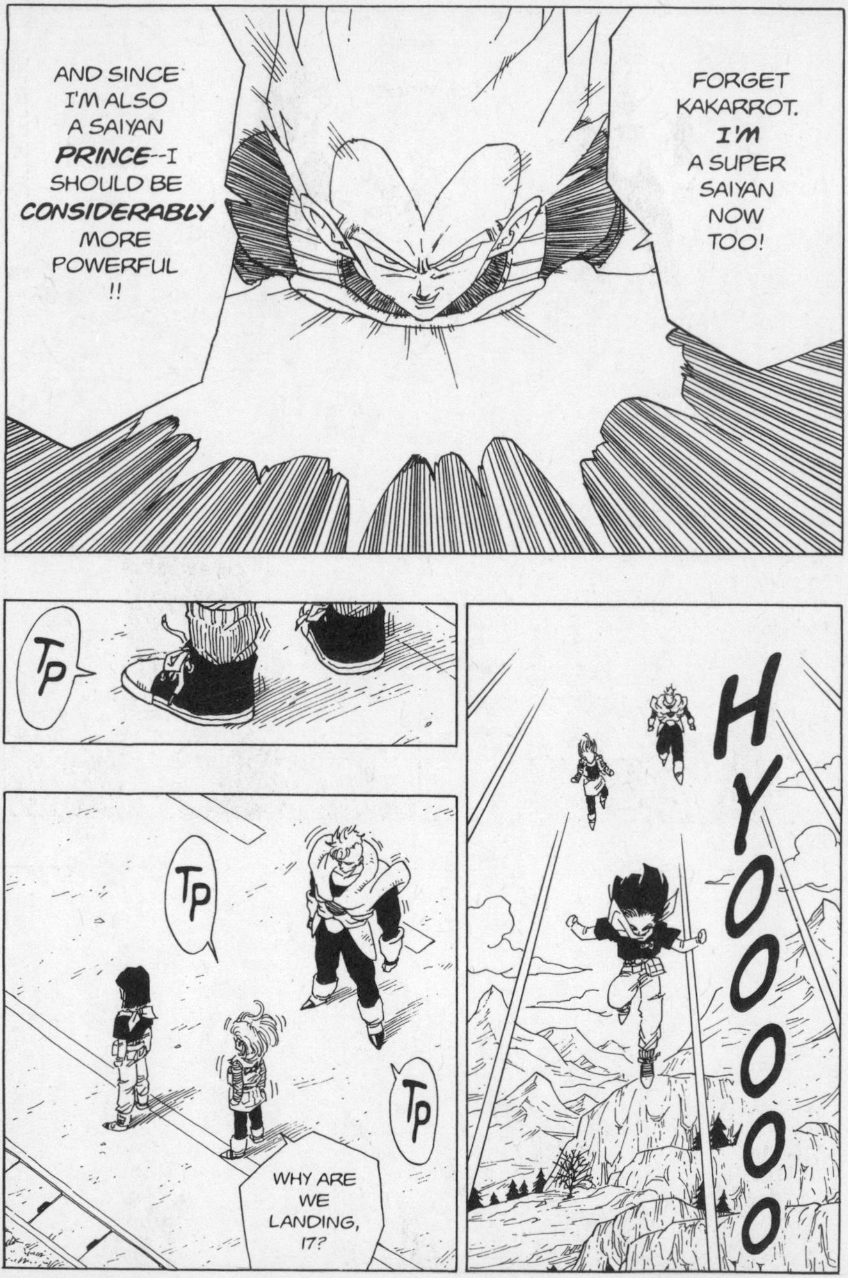
FORGET KAKARROT. I'M A SUPER SAIYAN NOW TOO!
AND SINCE I'M ALSO A SAIYAN PRINCE--I SHOULD BE CONSIDERABLY MORE POWERFUL!!
HYOOOOO
Tp
Tp
Tp
WHY ARE WE LANDING, 17?

READ THIS WAY

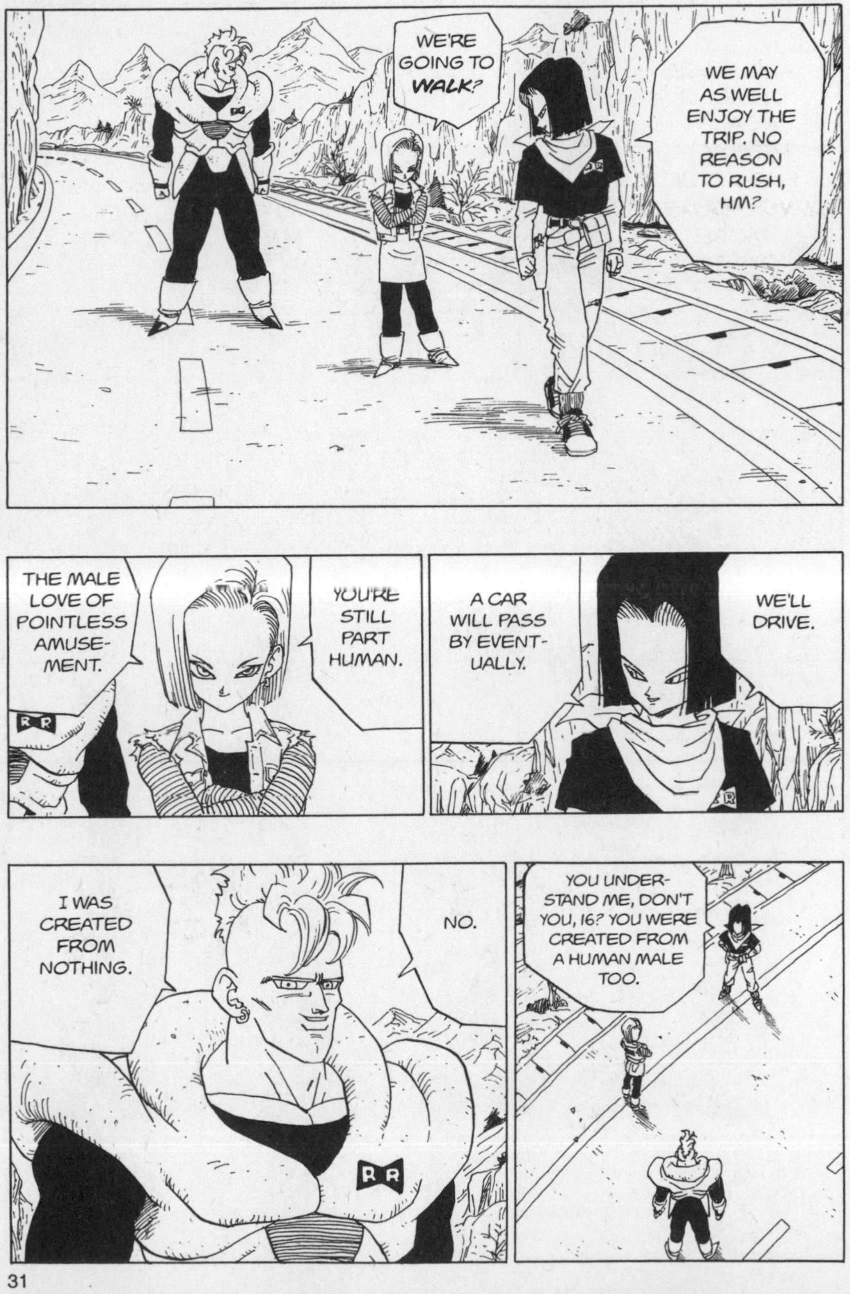
WE MAY AS WELL ENJOY THE TRIP. NO REASON TO RUSH, HM?
WE'RE GOING TO *WALK*?
WE'LL DRIVE.
A CAR WILL PASS BY EVENTUALLY.
YOU'RE STILL PART HUMAN.
THE MALE LOVE OF POINTLESS AMUSEMENT.
YOU UNDERSTAND ME, DON'T YOU, 16? YOU WERE CREATED FROM A HUMAN MALE TOO.
NO.
I WAS CREATED FROM NOTHING.

READ THIS WAY

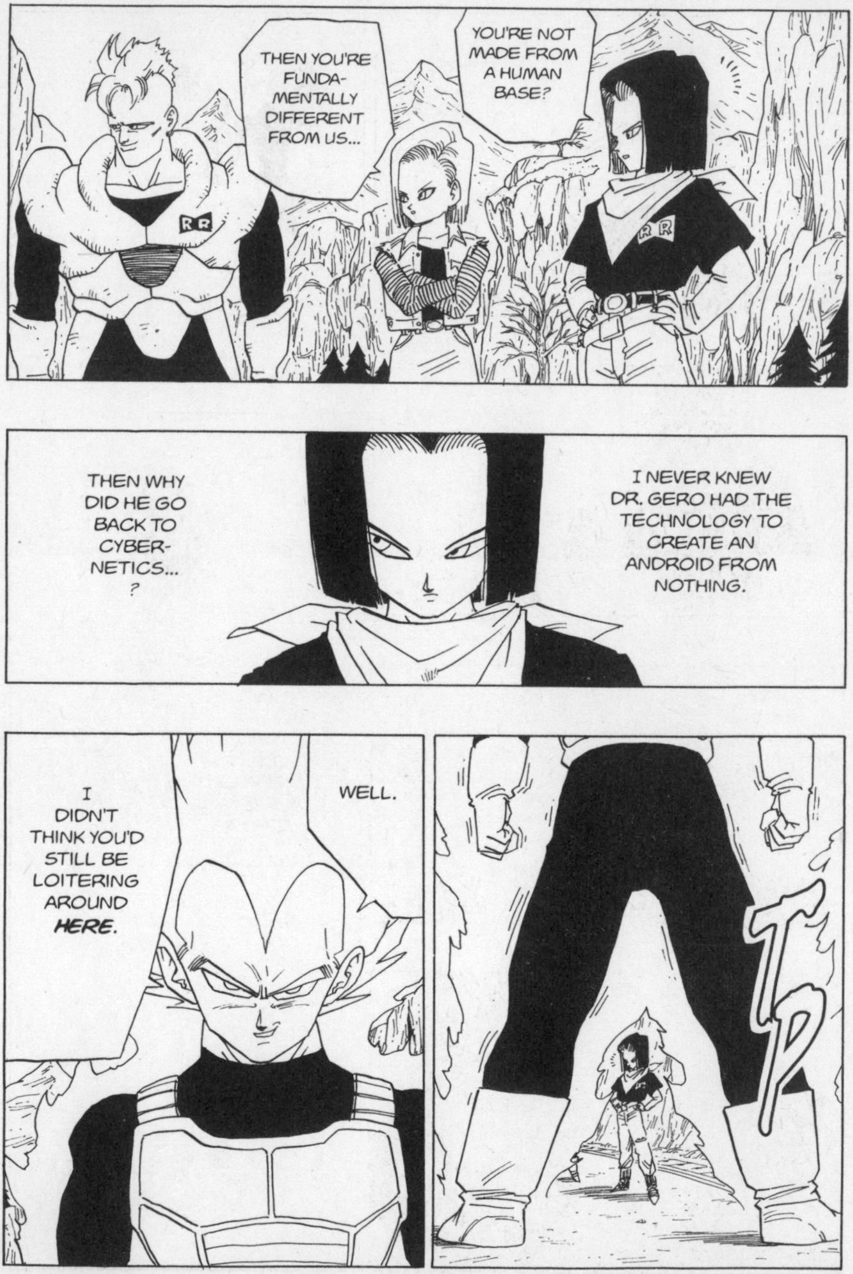
YOU'RE NOT MADE FROM A HUMAN BASE?
THEN YOU'RE FUNDA-MENTALLY DIFFERENT FROM US...
I NEVER KNEW DR. GERO HAD THE TECHNOLOGY TO CREATE AN ANDROID FROM NOTHING.
THEN WHY DID HE GO BACK TO CYBER-NETICS... ?
WELL.
I DIDN'T THINK YOU'D STILL BE LOITERING AROUND ***HERE***.

READ THIS WAY

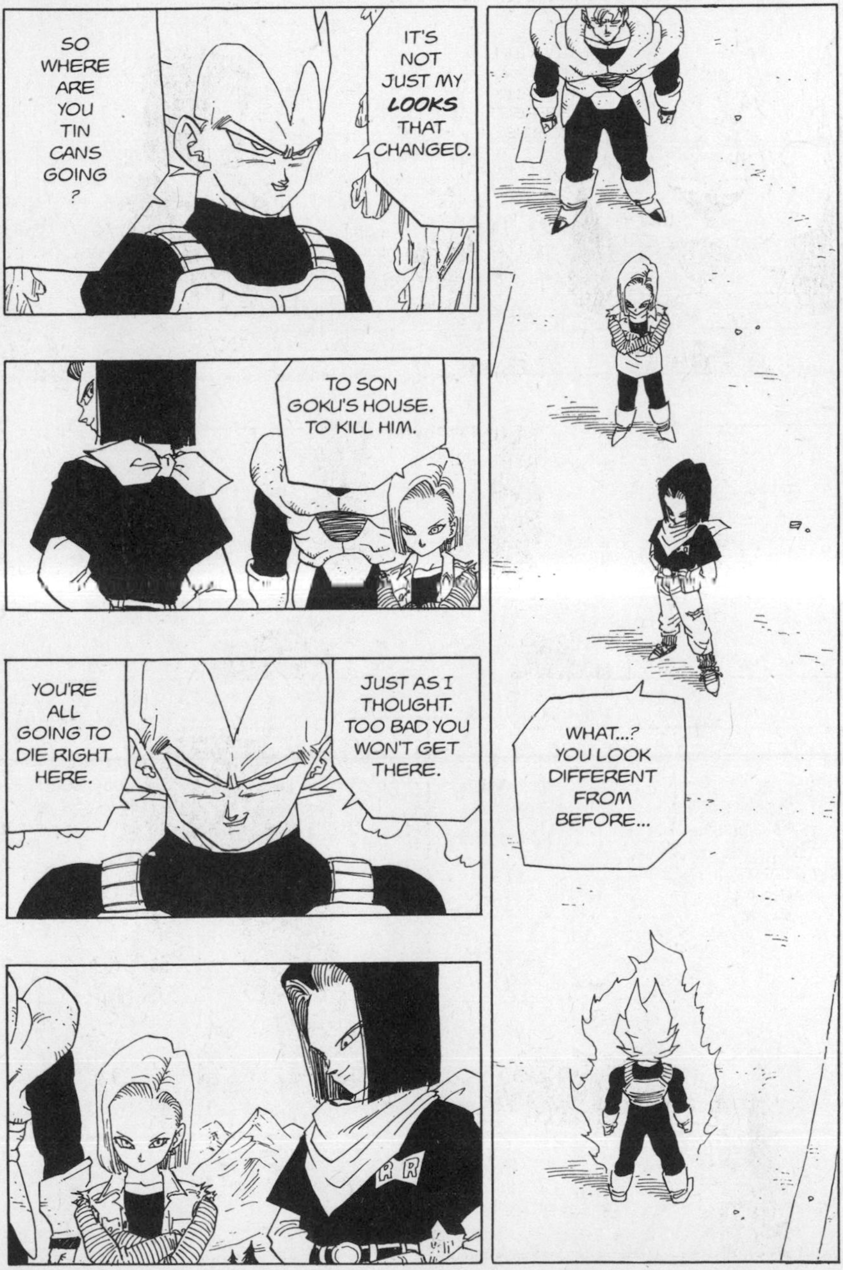

WHAT...? YOU LOOK DIFFERENT FROM BEFORE...
IT'S NOT JUST MY **LOOKS** THAT CHANGED.
SO WHERE ARE YOU TIN CANS GOING?
TO SON GOKU'S HOUSE. TO KILL HIM.
JUST AS I THOUGHT. TOO BAD YOU WON'T GET THERE.
YOU'RE ALL GOING TO DIE RIGHT HERE.

READ THIS WAY

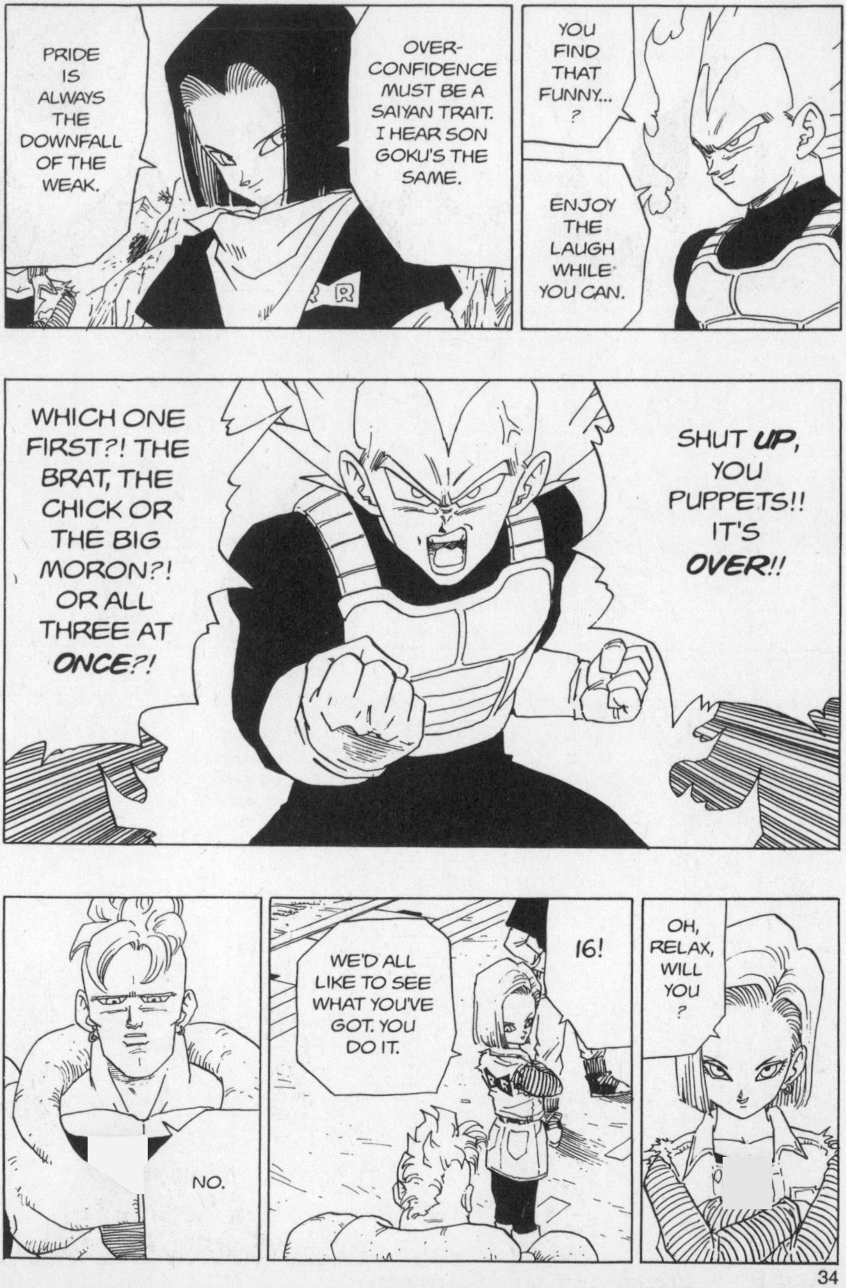

YOU FIND THAT FUNNY... ?
ENJOY THE LAUGH WHILE YOU CAN.
OVER-CONFIDENCE MUST BE A SAIYAN TRAIT. I HEAR SON GOKU'S THE SAME.
PRIDE IS ALWAYS THE DOWNFALL OF THE WEAK.
SHUT UP, YOU PUPPETS!! IT'S OVER!!
WHICH ONE FIRST?! THE BRAT, THE CHICK OR THE BIG MORON?! OR ALL THREE AT ONCE?!
OH, RELAX, WILL YOU ?
16!
WE'D ALL LIKE TO SEE WHAT YOU'VE GOT. YOU DO IT.
NO.

READ THIS WAY

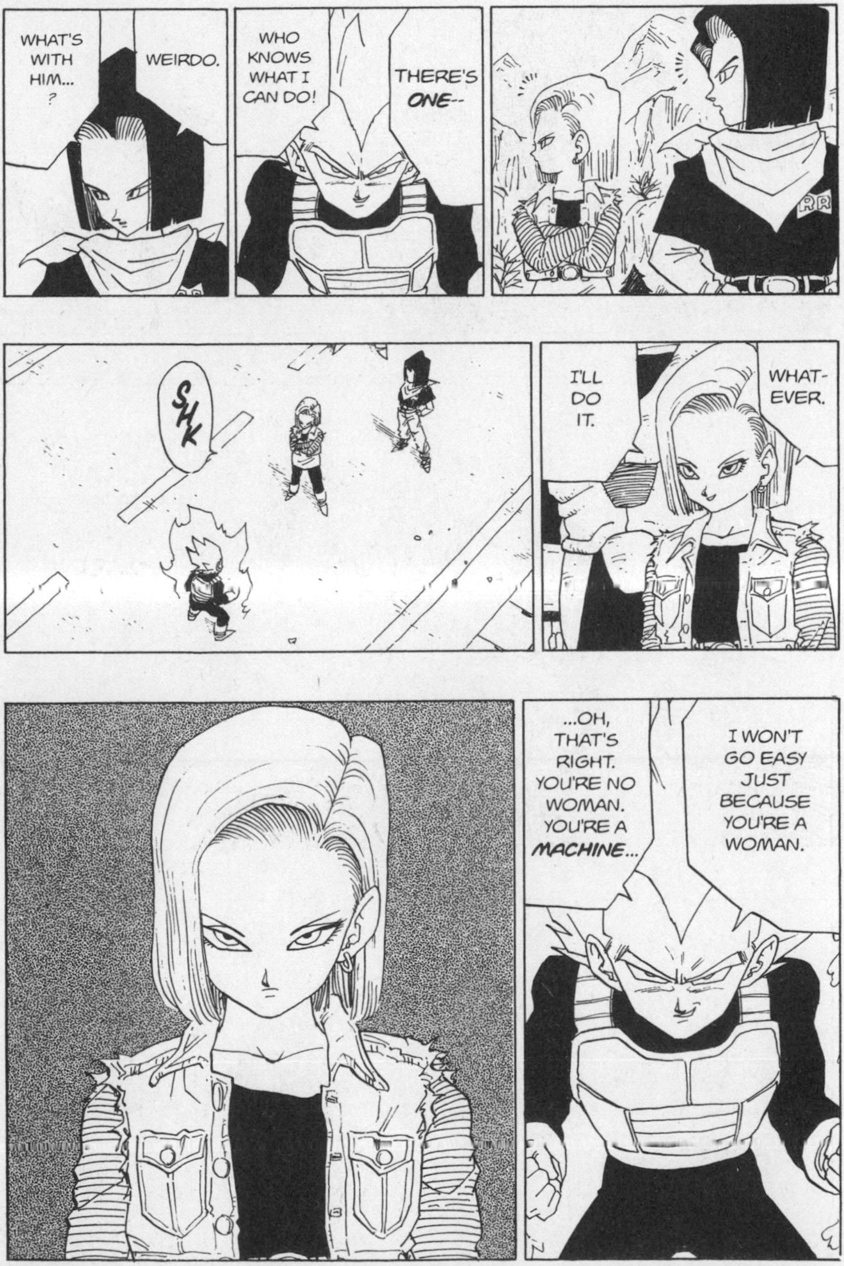

THERE'S ONE--
WHO KNOWS WHAT I CAN DO!
WEIRDO.
WHAT'S WITH HIM... ?
WHAT-EVER.
I'LL DO IT.
SHK
I WON'T GO EASY JUST BECAUSE YOU'RE A WOMAN.
...OH, THAT'S RIGHT. YOU'RE NO WOMAN. YOU'RE A MACHINE...

NEXT: Android vs. Saiyan

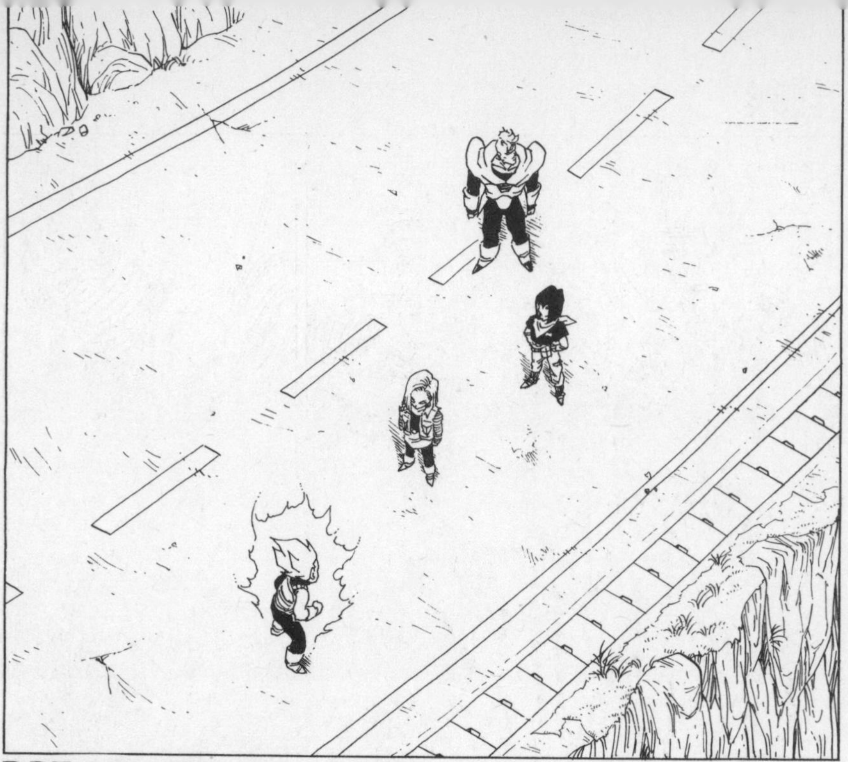

DBZ:158 • Vegeta vs. #18

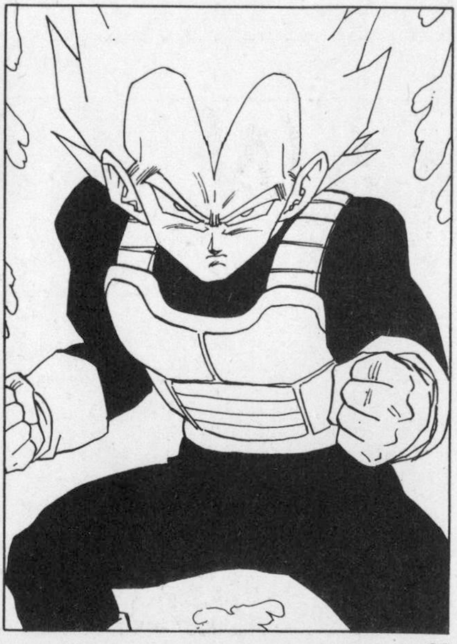

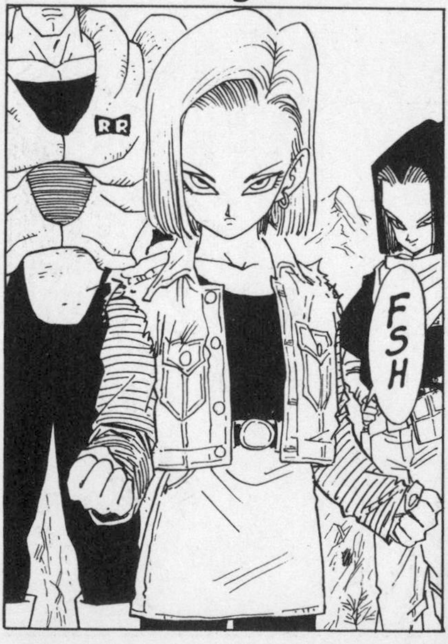
FSH

READ THIS WAY

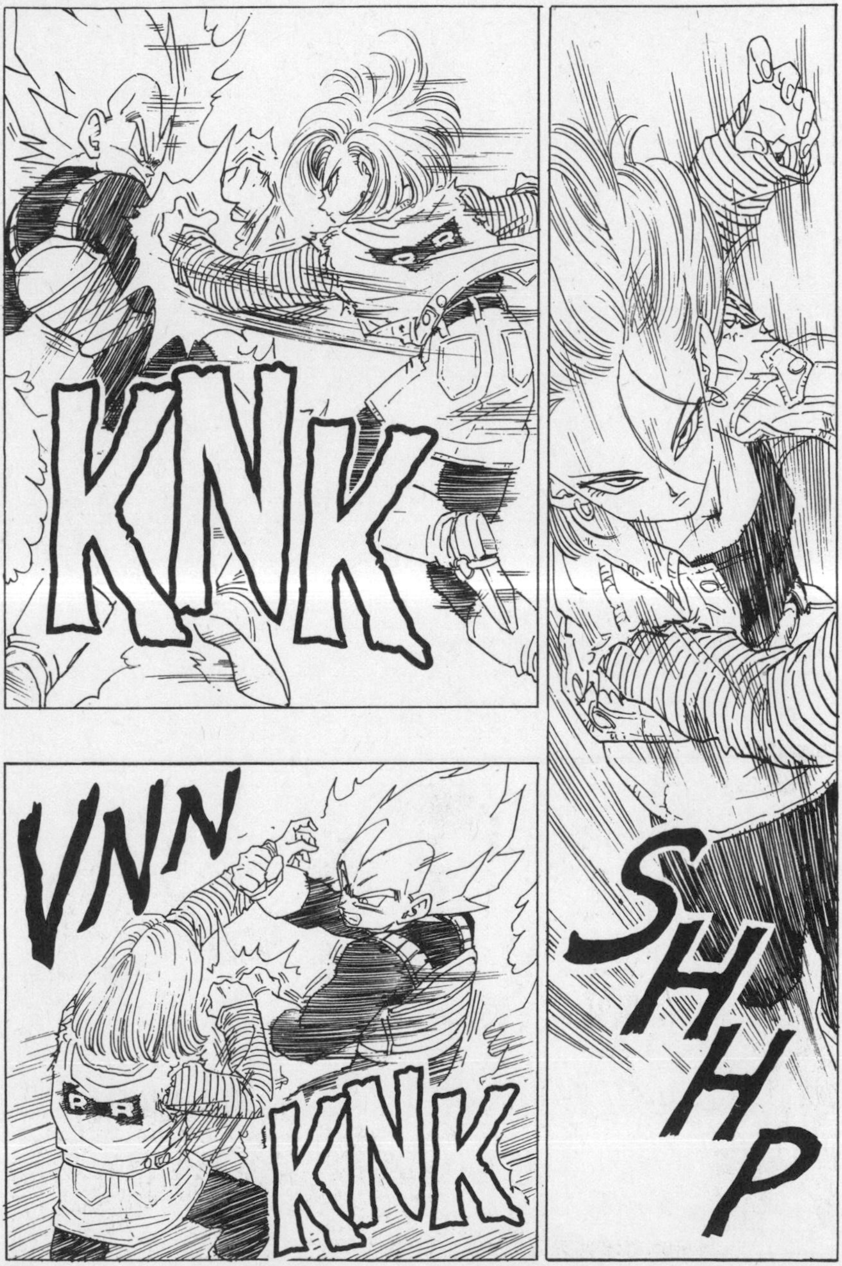
SHHP
KNK
VNN
KNK

READ THIS WAY

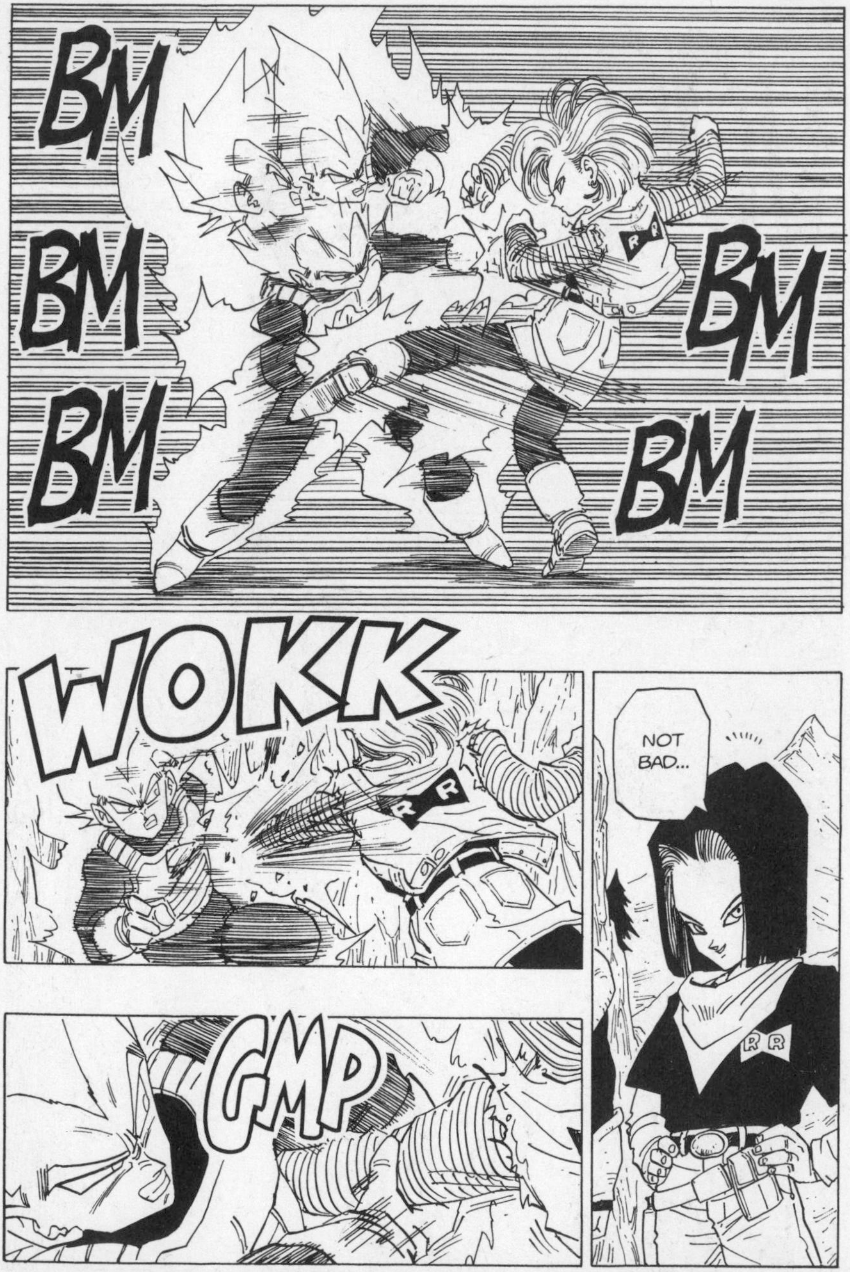
BM
BM
BM
BM
BM
NOT BAD...
WOKK
GMP

READ THIS WAY

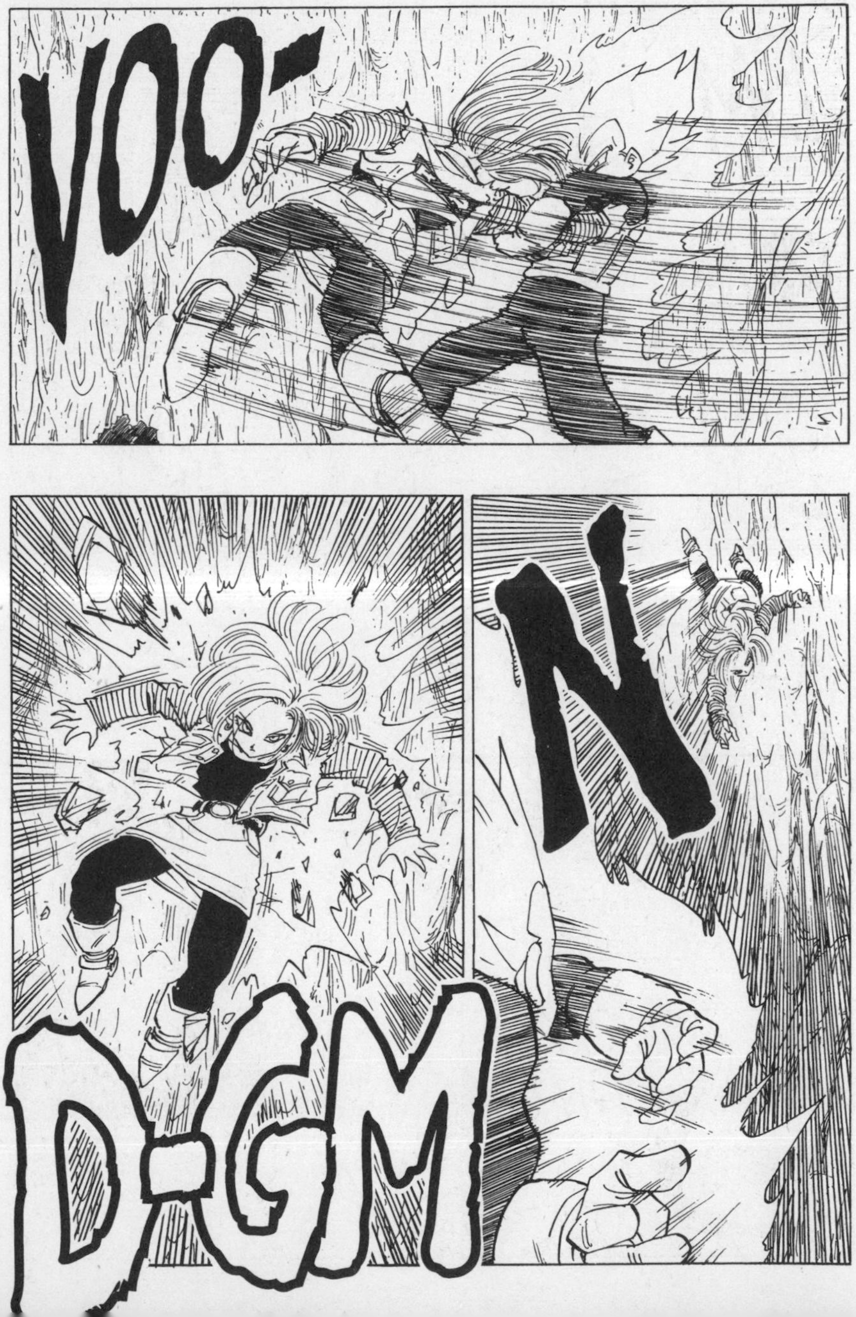
VOO-
N
D-GM

READ THIS WAY

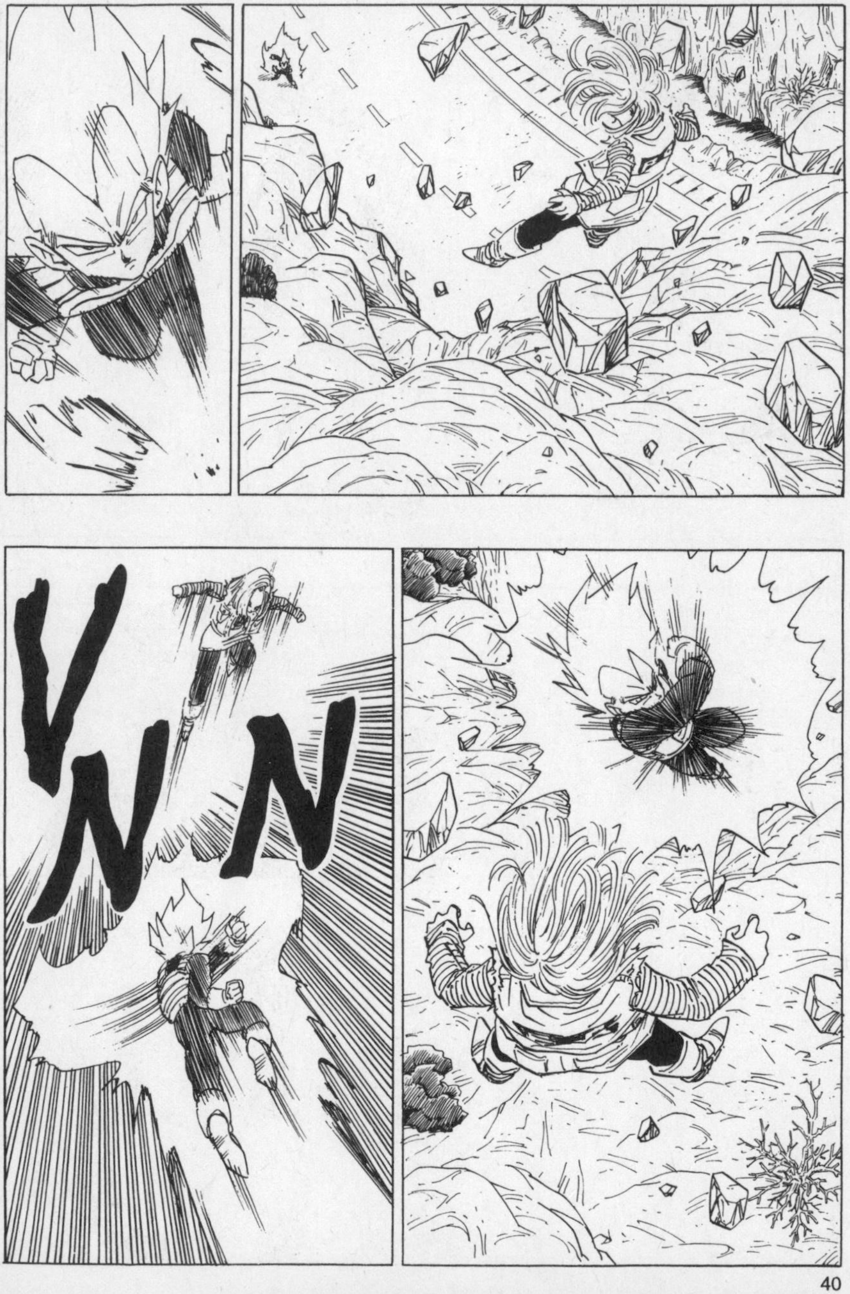
VNN

READ THIS WAY

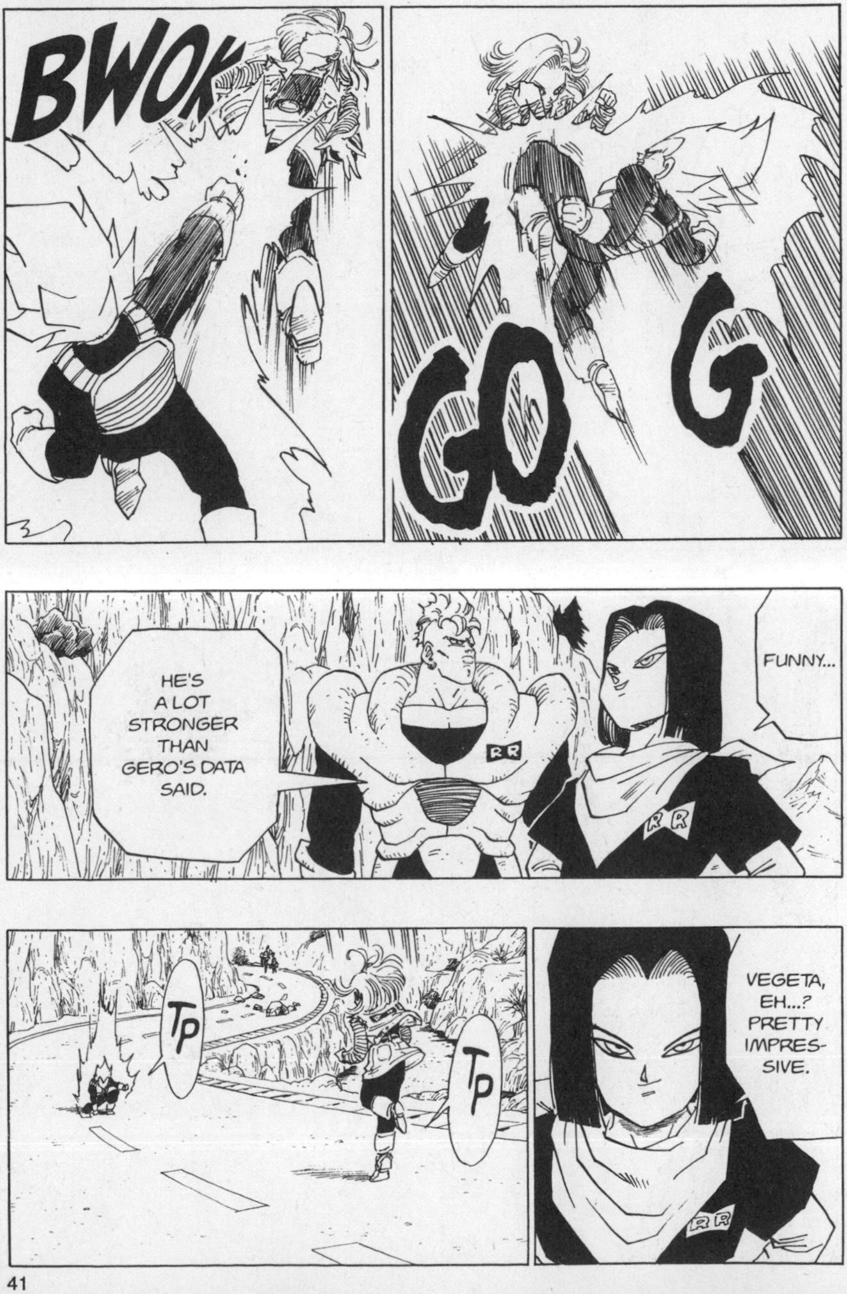
GO G
BWOK
FUNNY...
HE'S A LOT STRONGER THAN GERO'S DATA SAID.
VEGETA, EH...? PRETTY IMPRES-SIVE.
TP
TP

READ THIS WAY

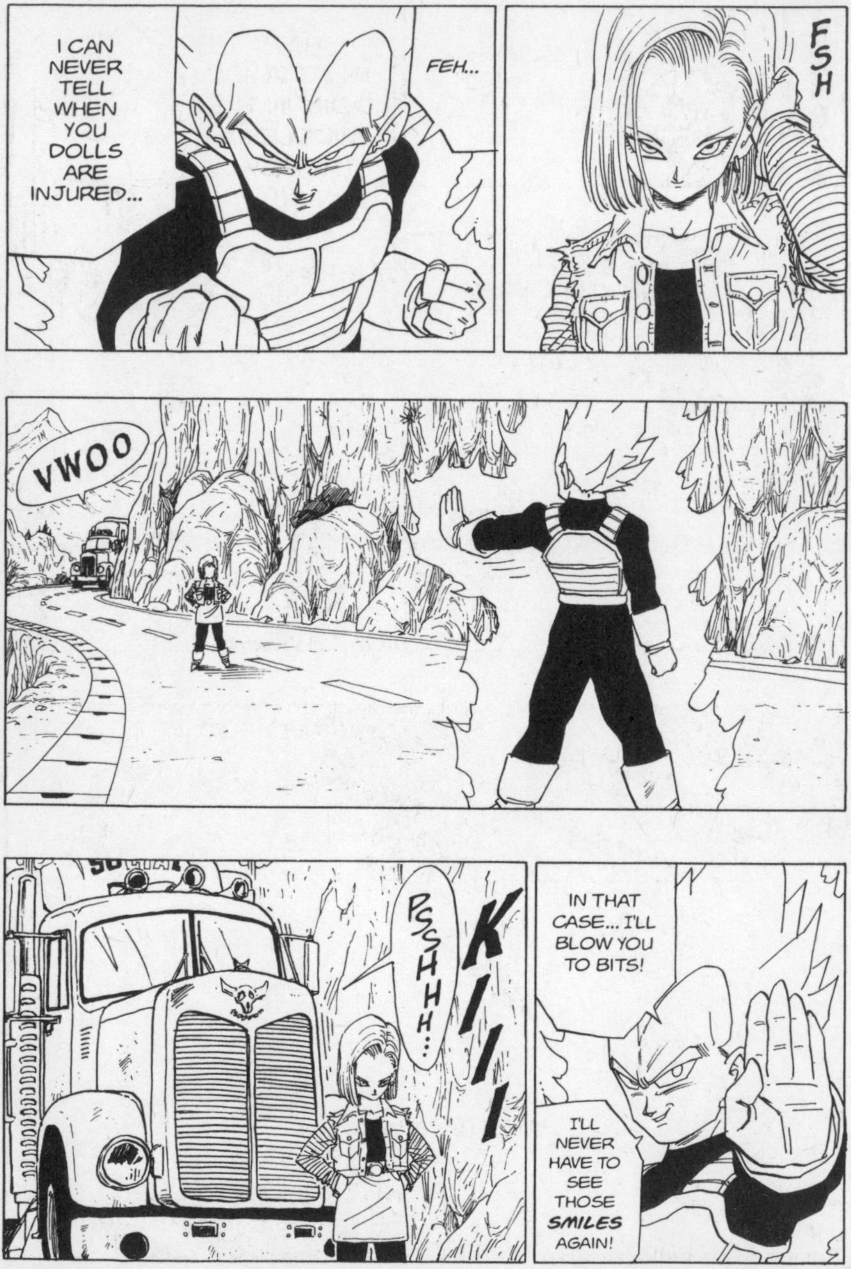

FSH
FEH...
I CAN NEVER TELL WHEN YOU DOLLS ARE INJURED...
VWOO
IN THAT CASE... I'LL BLOW YOU TO BITS!
I'LL NEVER HAVE TO SEE THOSE *SMILES* AGAIN!
KIIII
PSSHHH...

READ THIS WAY

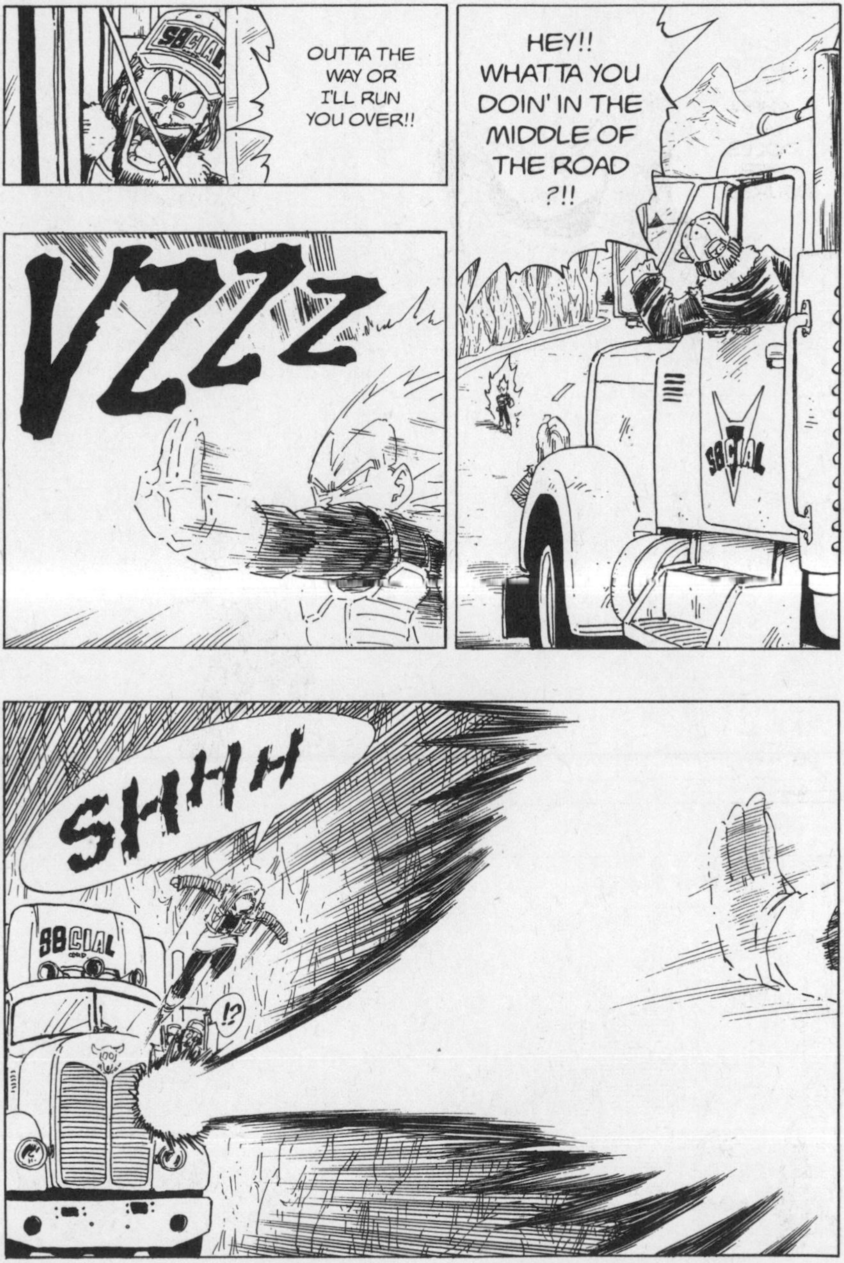
HEY!! WHATTA YOU DOIN' IN THE MIDDLE OF THE ROAD ?!!
OUTTA THE WAY OR I'LL RUN YOU OVER!!
VZZZ
SHHH
!?

READ THIS WAY

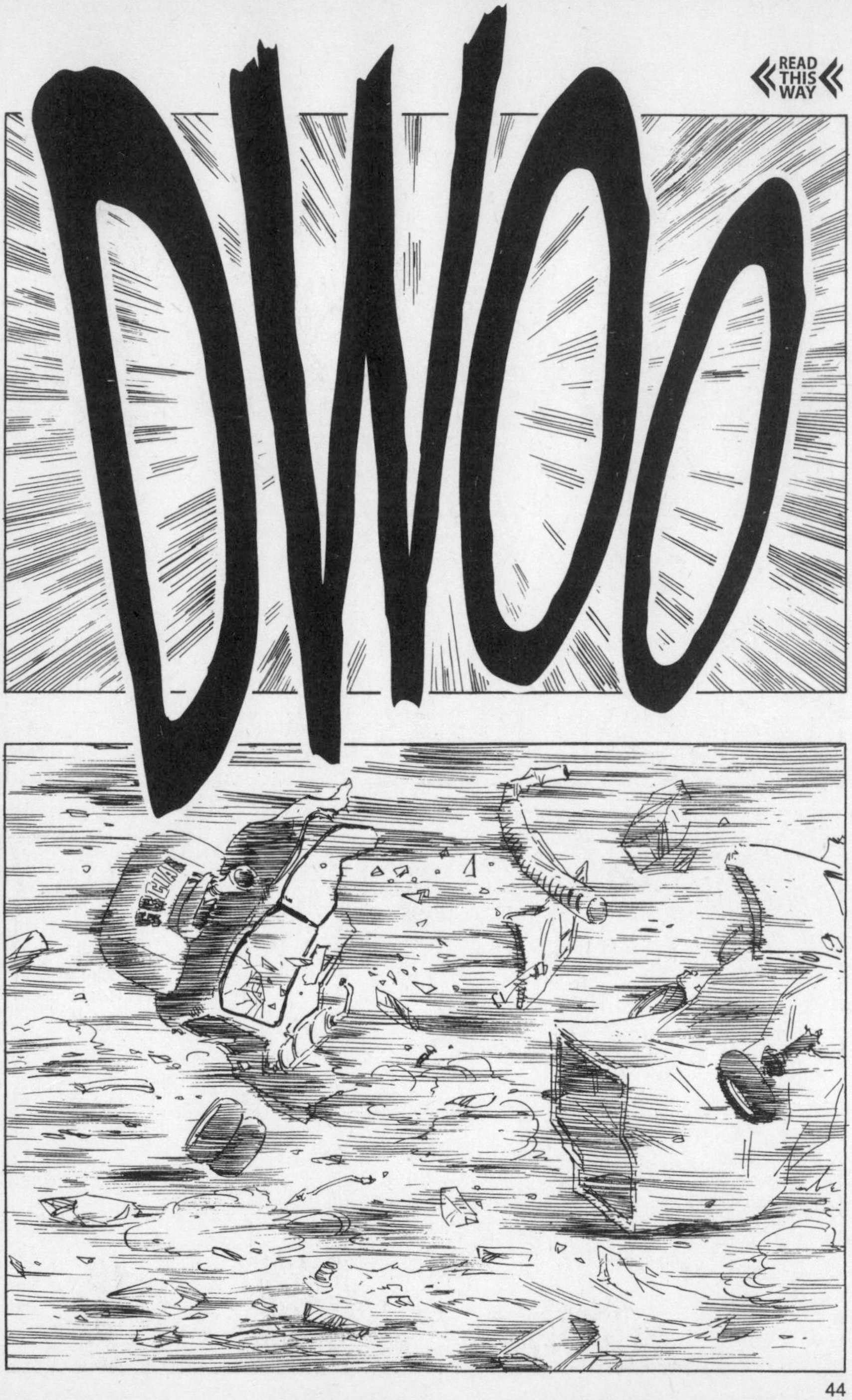
DWOO

READ THIS WAY

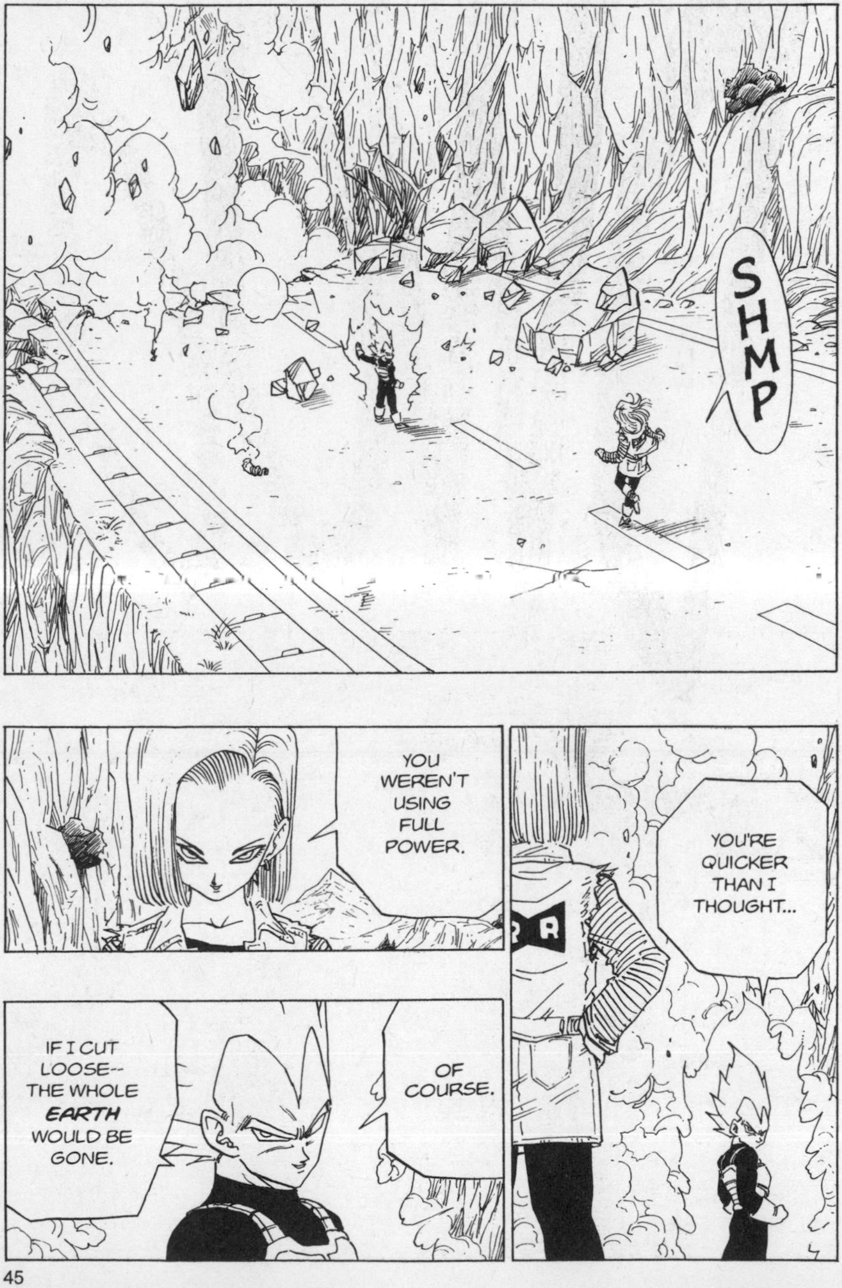
SHMP
YOU'RE QUICKER THAN I THOUGHT...
YOU WEREN'T USING FULL POWER.
OF COURSE.
IF I CUT LOOSE-- THE WHOLE *EARTH* WOULD BE GONE.

READ THIS WAY

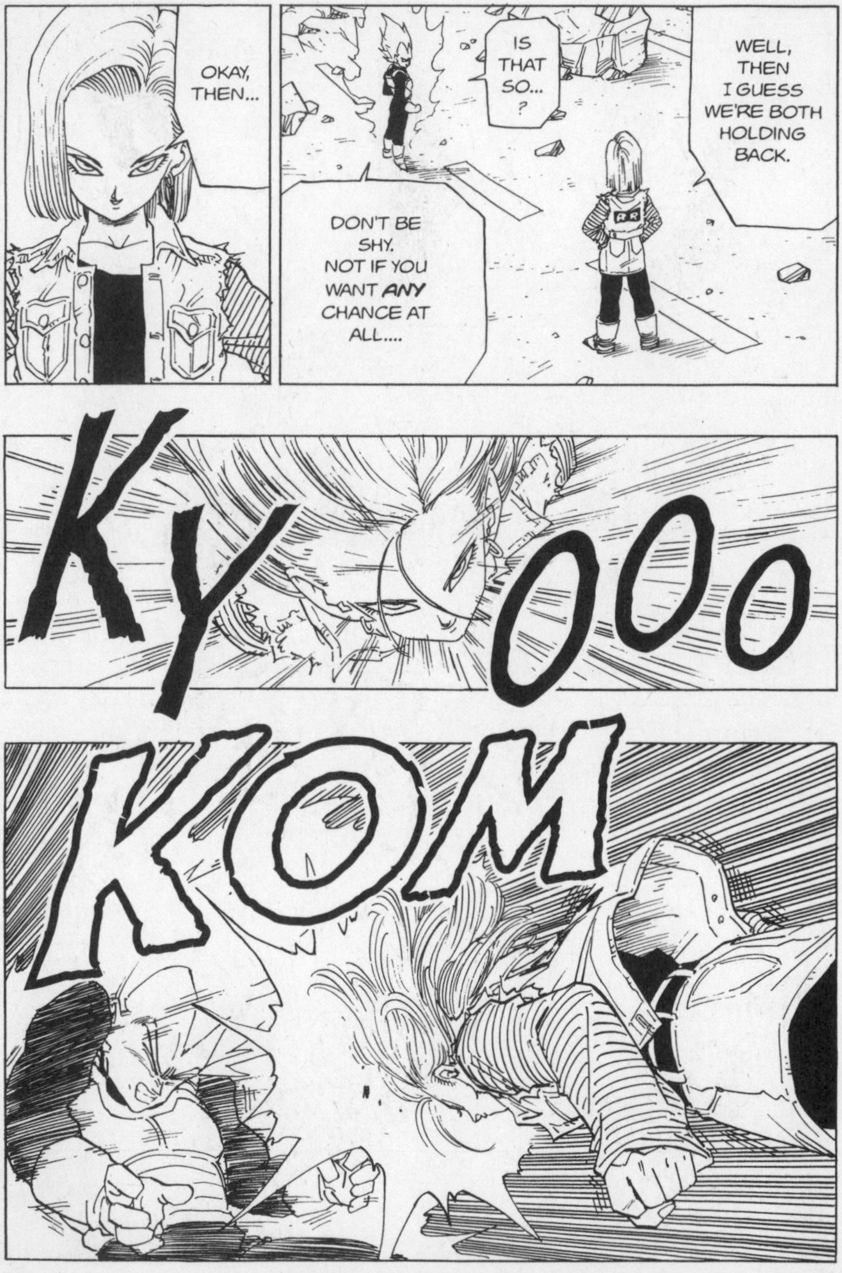
WELL, THEN I GUESS WE'RE BOTH HOLDING BACK.
IS THAT SO... ?
DON'T BE SHY. NOT IF YOU WANT **ANY** CHANCE AT ALL....
OKAY, THEN...
KYOOOO
KOM

READ THIS WAY

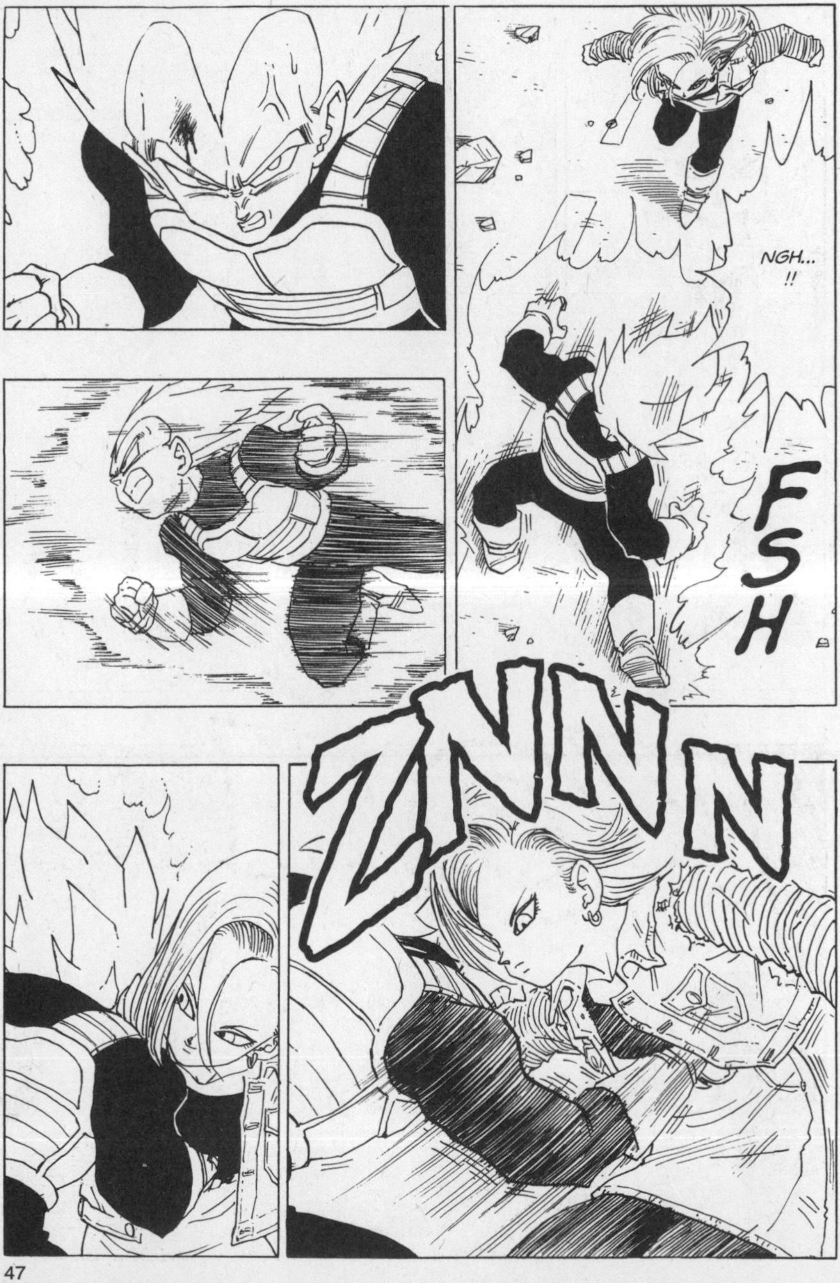
NGH... !!
FSH
ZNNN

READ THIS WAY

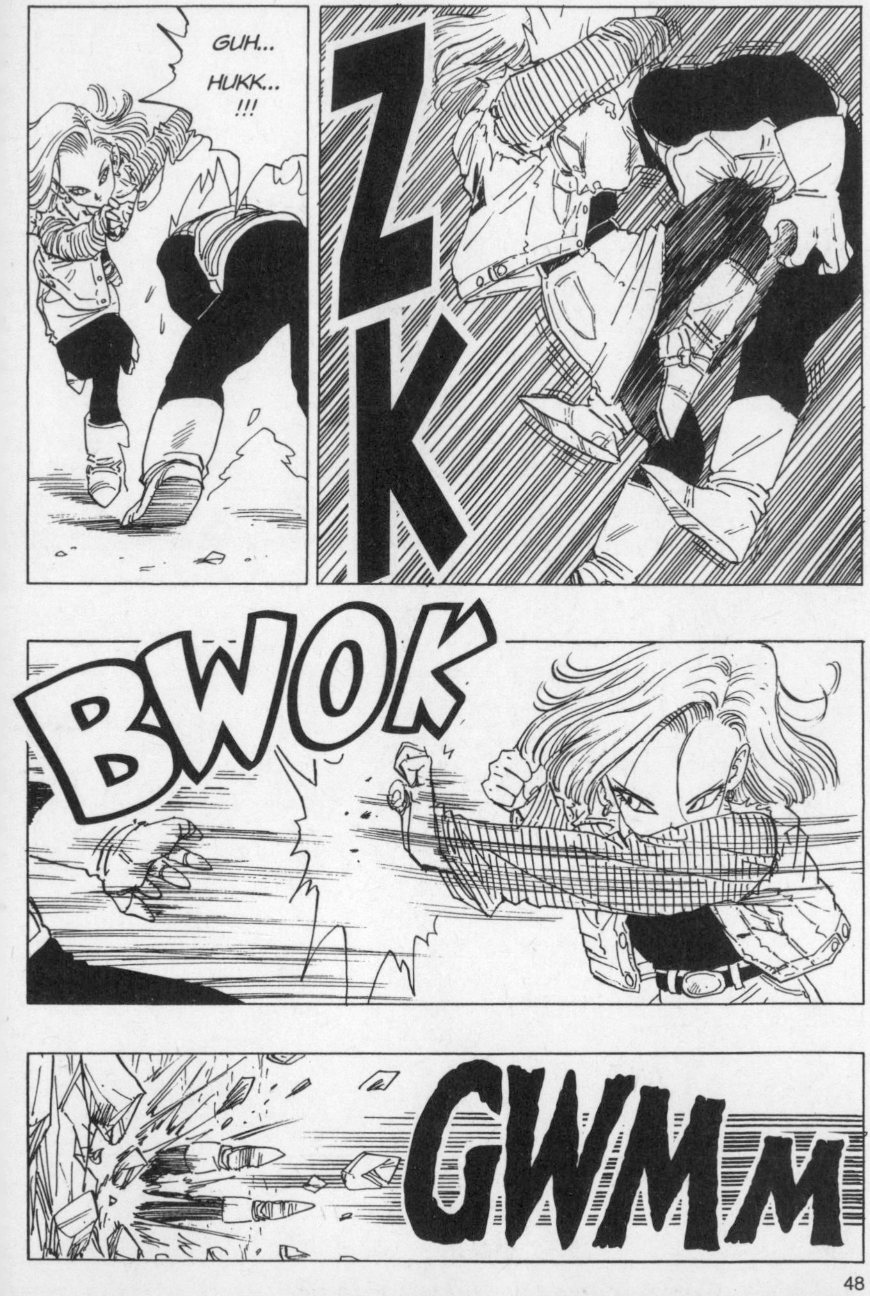
ZK
GUH...
HUKK...
!!!
BWOK
GWMM

READ THIS WAY

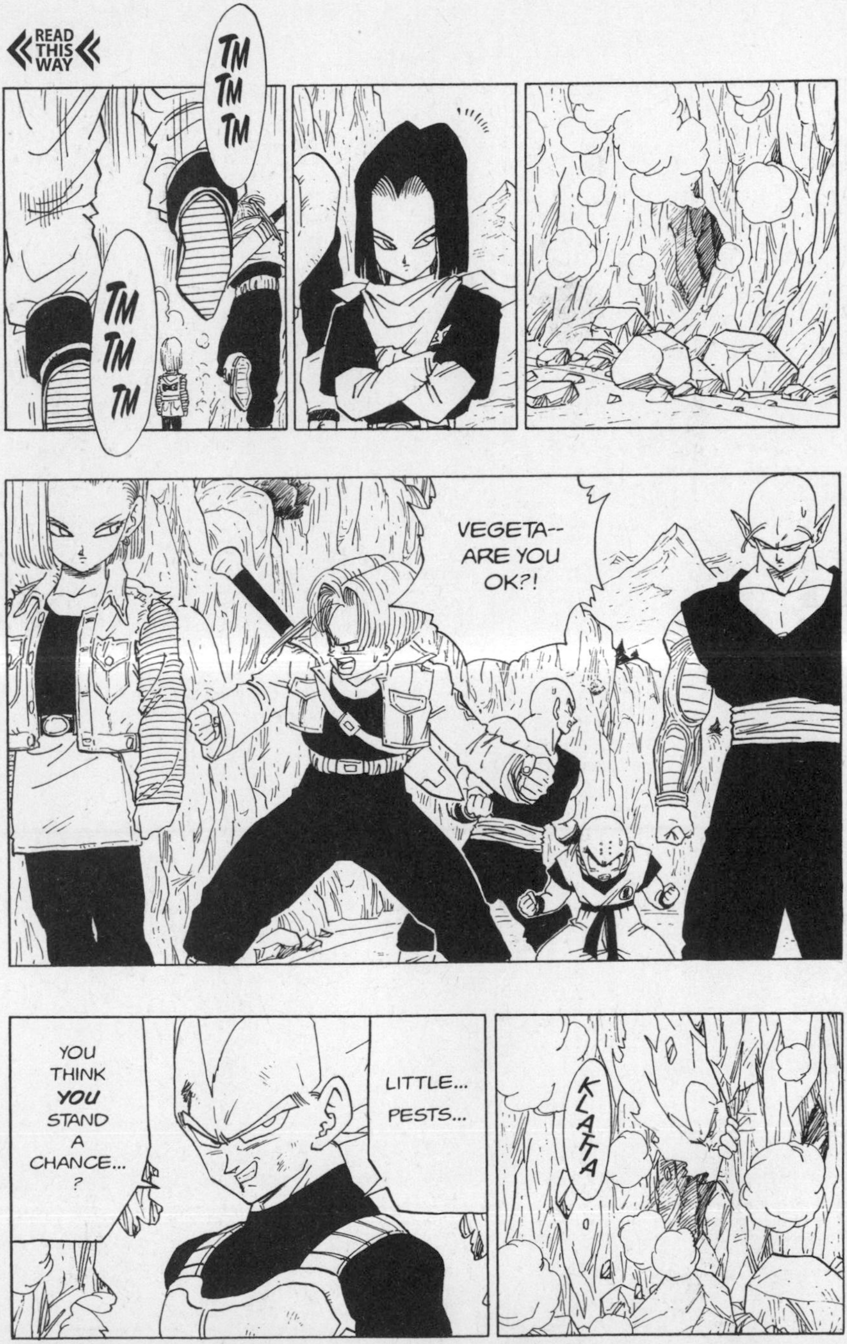
TM TM TM
TM TM TM
VEGETA-- ARE YOU OK?!
KLATTA
LITTLE... PESTS...
YOU THINK *YOU* STAND A CHANCE...?

NEXT: From Vegeta, What Else?

DBZ:159 • Vegeta vs. #18, Round Two

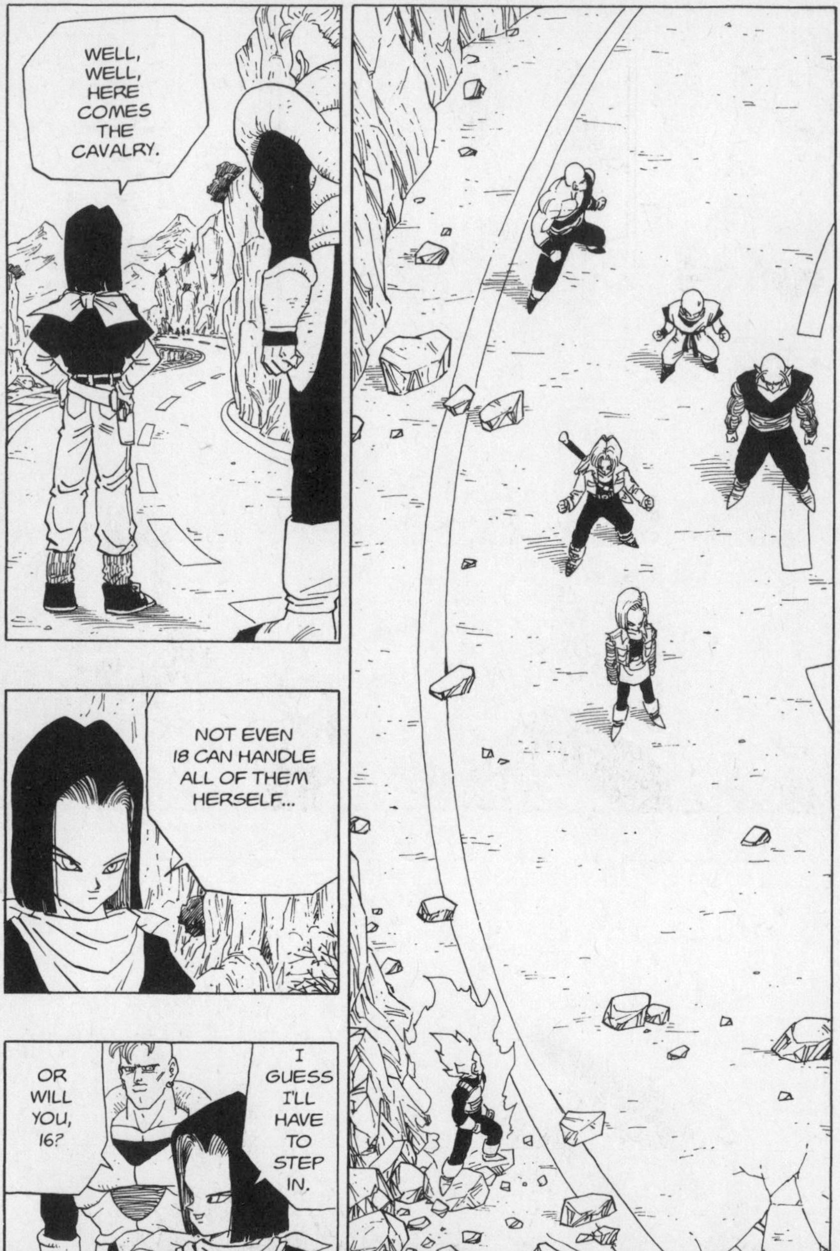

WELL, WELL, HERE COMES THE CAVALRY.
NOT EVEN 18 CAN HANDLE ALL OF THEM HERSELF...
I GUESS I'LL HAVE TO STEP IN.
OR WILL YOU, 16?

READ THIS WAY

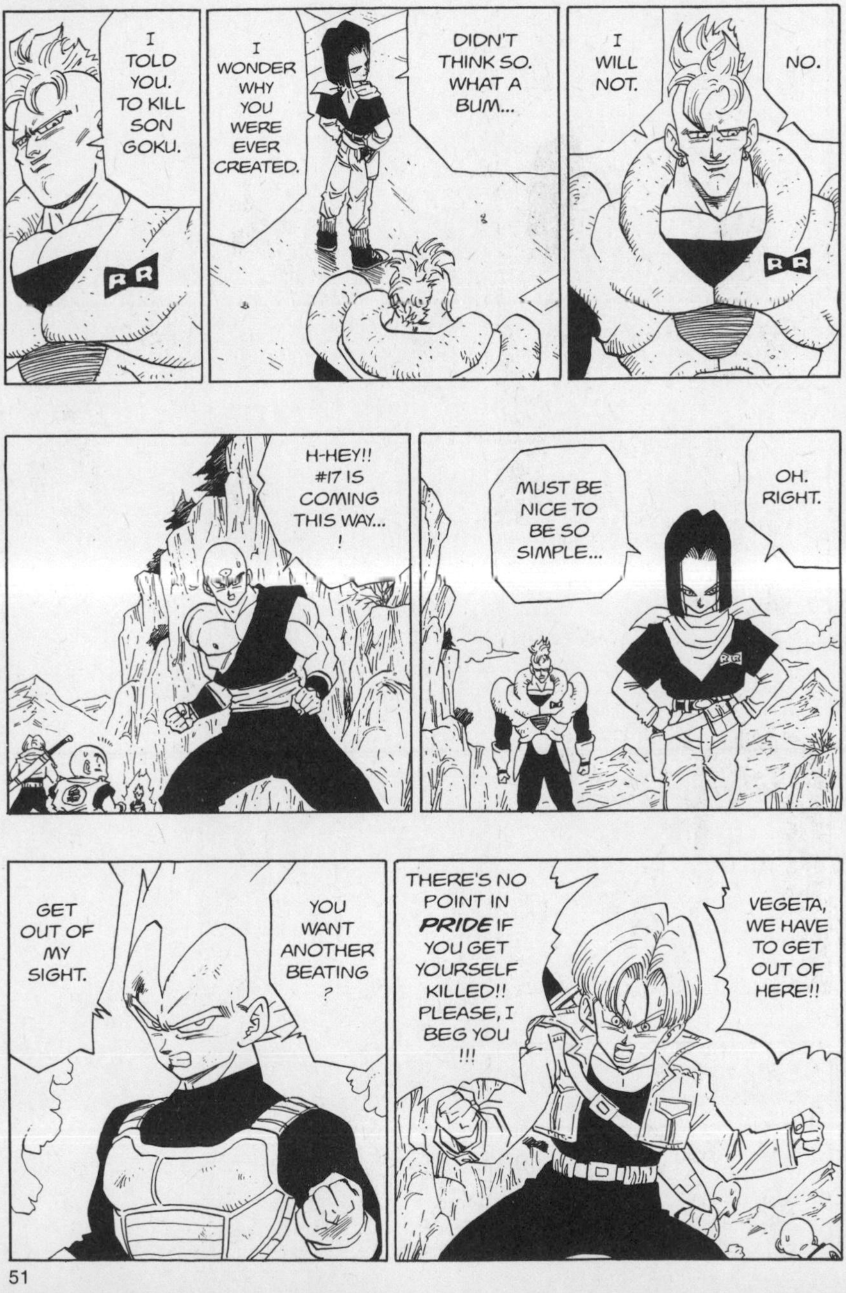
NO.
I WILL NOT.
DIDN'T THINK SO. WHAT A BUM...
I WONDER WHY YOU WERE EVER CREATED.
I TOLD YOU. TO KILL SON GOKU.
OH. RIGHT.
MUST BE NICE TO BE SO SIMPLE...
H-HEY!! #17 IS COMING THIS WAY... !
VEGETA, WE HAVE TO GET OUT OF HERE!!
THERE'S NO POINT IN PRIDE IF YOU GET YOURSELF KILLED!! PLEASE, I BEG YOU !!!
YOU WANT ANOTHER BEATING ?
GET OUT OF MY SIGHT.

READ THIS WAY

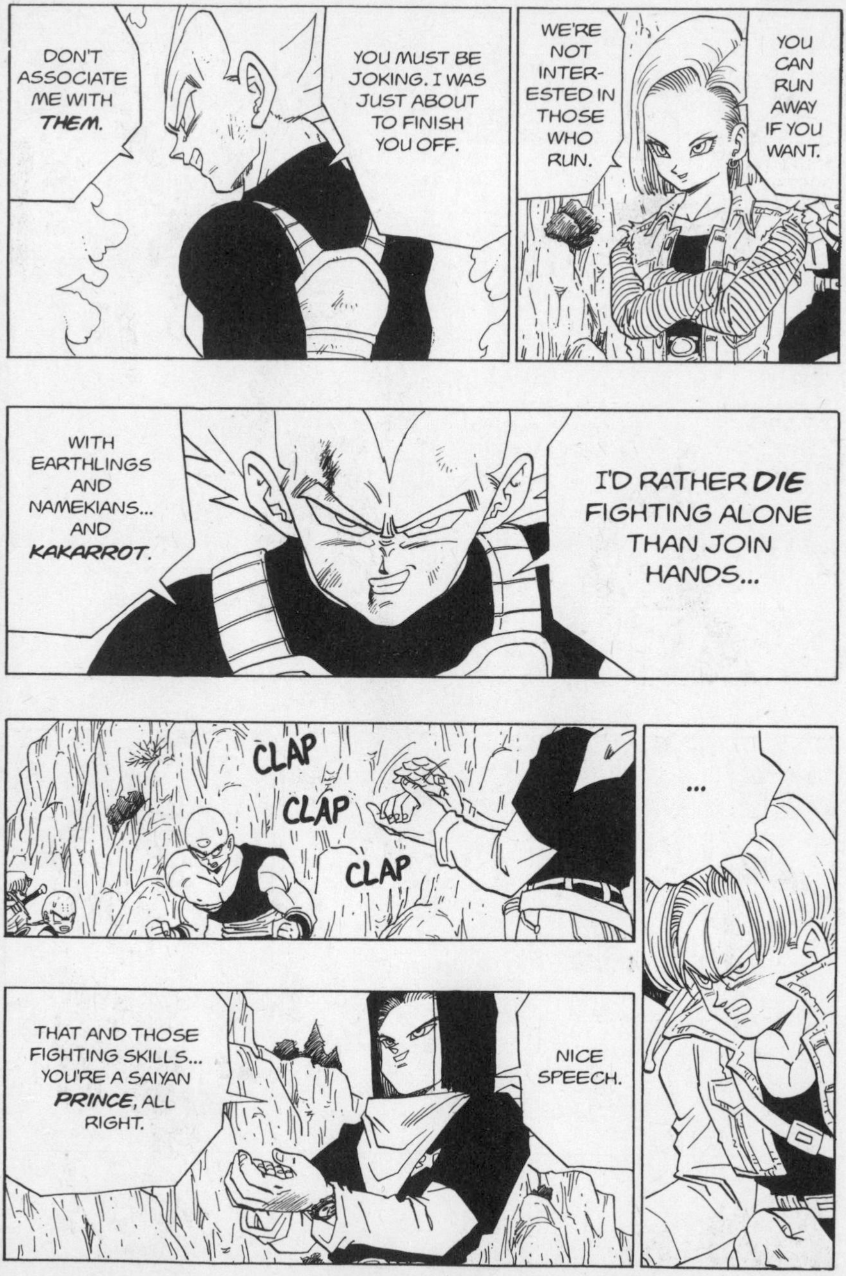
YOU CAN RUN AWAY IF YOU WANT.
WE'RE NOT INTER-ESTED IN THOSE WHO RUN.
YOU MUST BE JOKING. I WAS JUST ABOUT TO FINISH YOU OFF.
DON'T ASSOCIATE ME WITH *THEM*.
I'D RATHER ***DIE*** FIGHTING ALONE THAN JOIN HANDS...
WITH EARTHLINGS AND NAMEKIANS... AND ***KAKARROT***.
...
CLAP
CLAP
CLAP
NICE SPEECH.
THAT AND THOSE FIGHTING SKILLS... YOU'RE A SAIYAN ***PRINCE***, ALL RIGHT.

READ THIS WAY

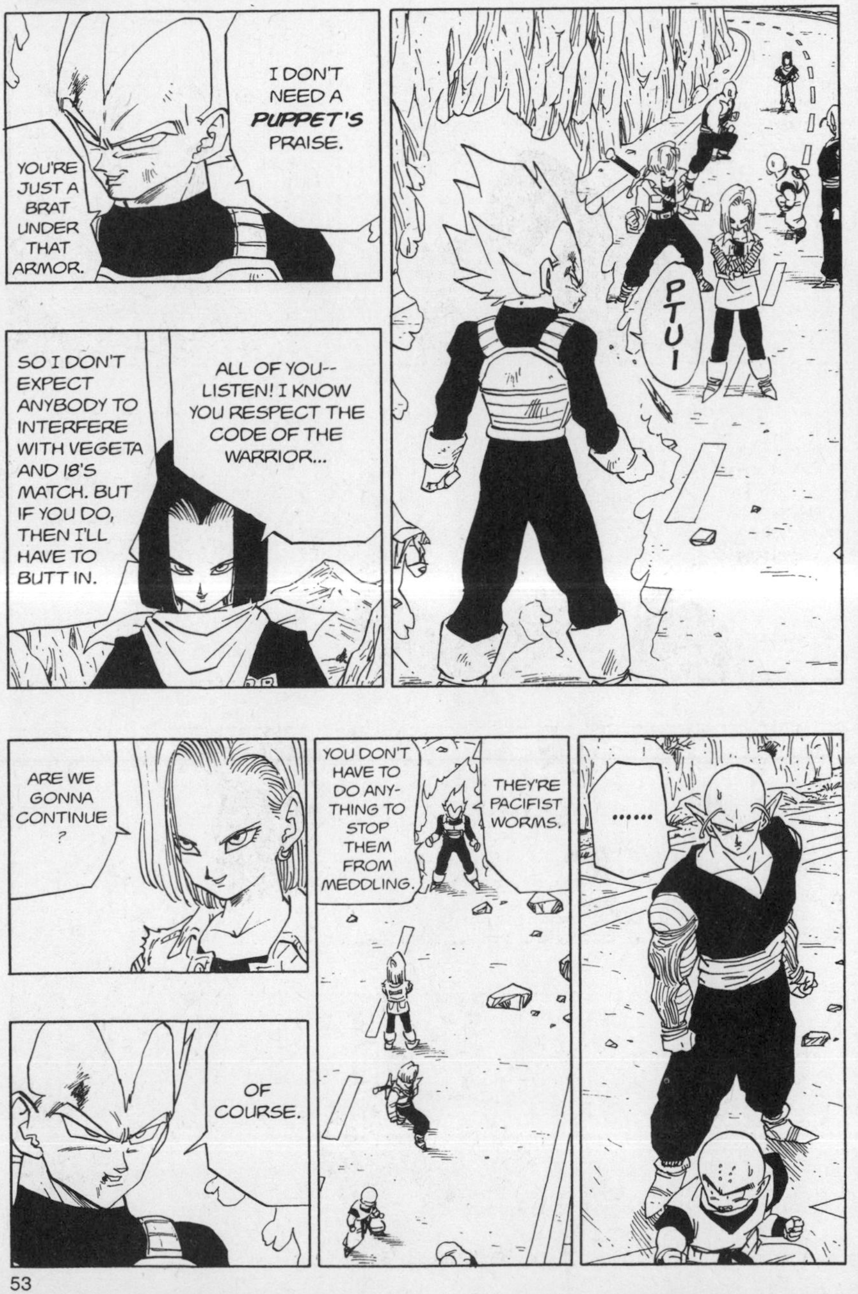
PTUI
I DON'T NEED A PUPPET'S PRAISE.
YOU'RE JUST A BRAT UNDER THAT ARMOR.
ALL OF YOU-- LISTEN! I KNOW YOU RESPECT THE CODE OF THE WARRIOR...
SO I DON'T EXPECT ANYBODY TO INTERFERE WITH VEGETA AND 18'S MATCH. BUT IF YOU DO, THEN I'LL HAVE TO BUTT IN.
....
THEY'RE PACIFIST WORMS.
YOU DON'T HAVE TO DO ANYTHING TO STOP THEM FROM MEDDLING.
ARE WE GONNA CONTINUE?
OF COURSE.

READ THIS WAY

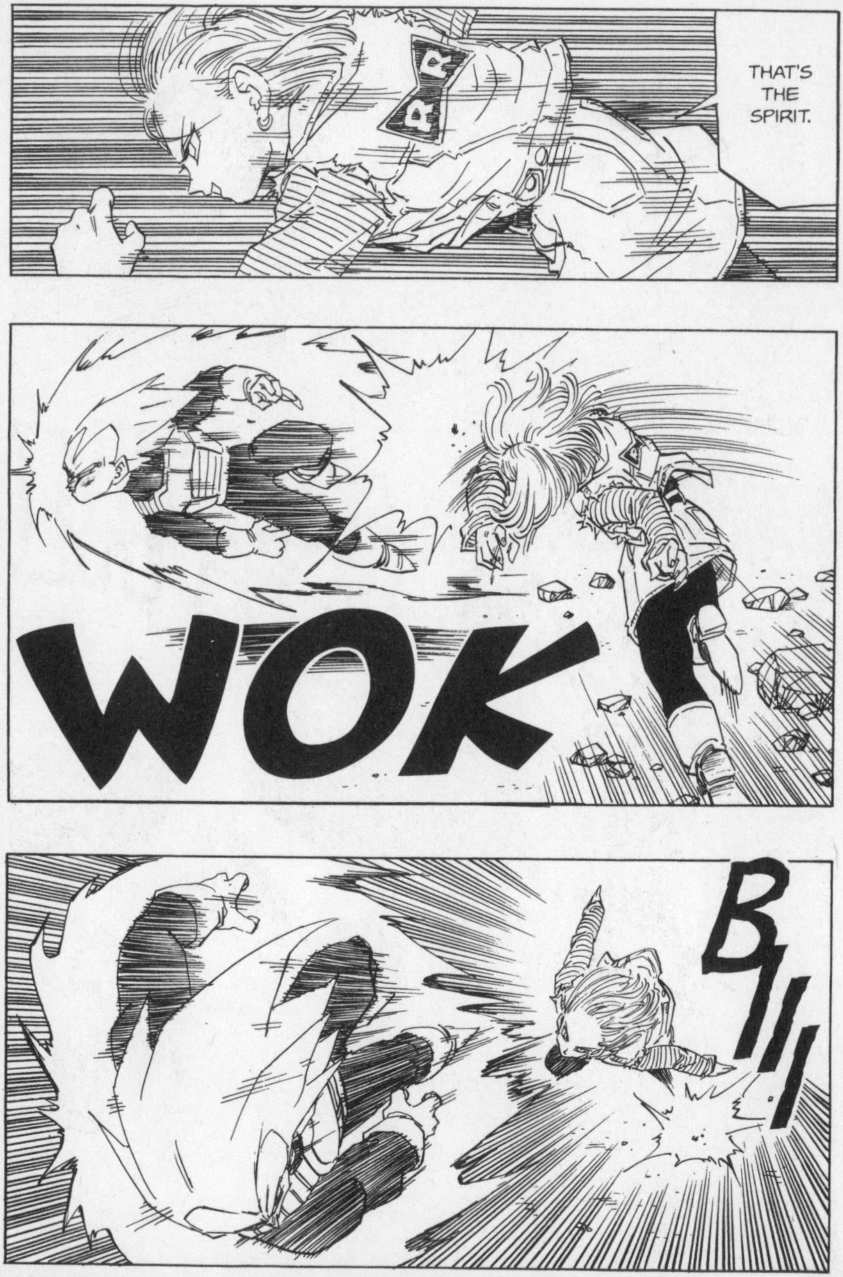
THAT'S THE SPIRIT.
WOK

READ THIS WAY

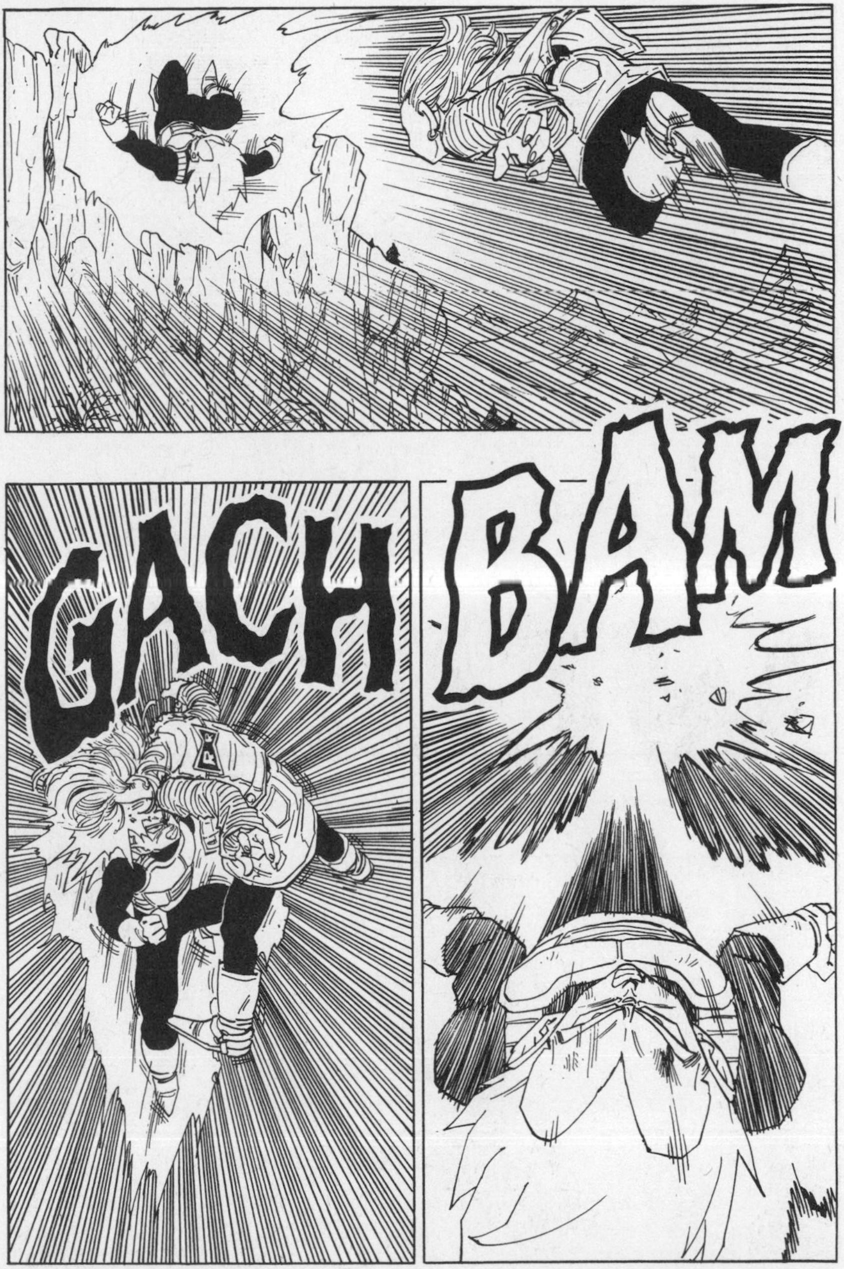
GACH BAM

READ THIS WAY

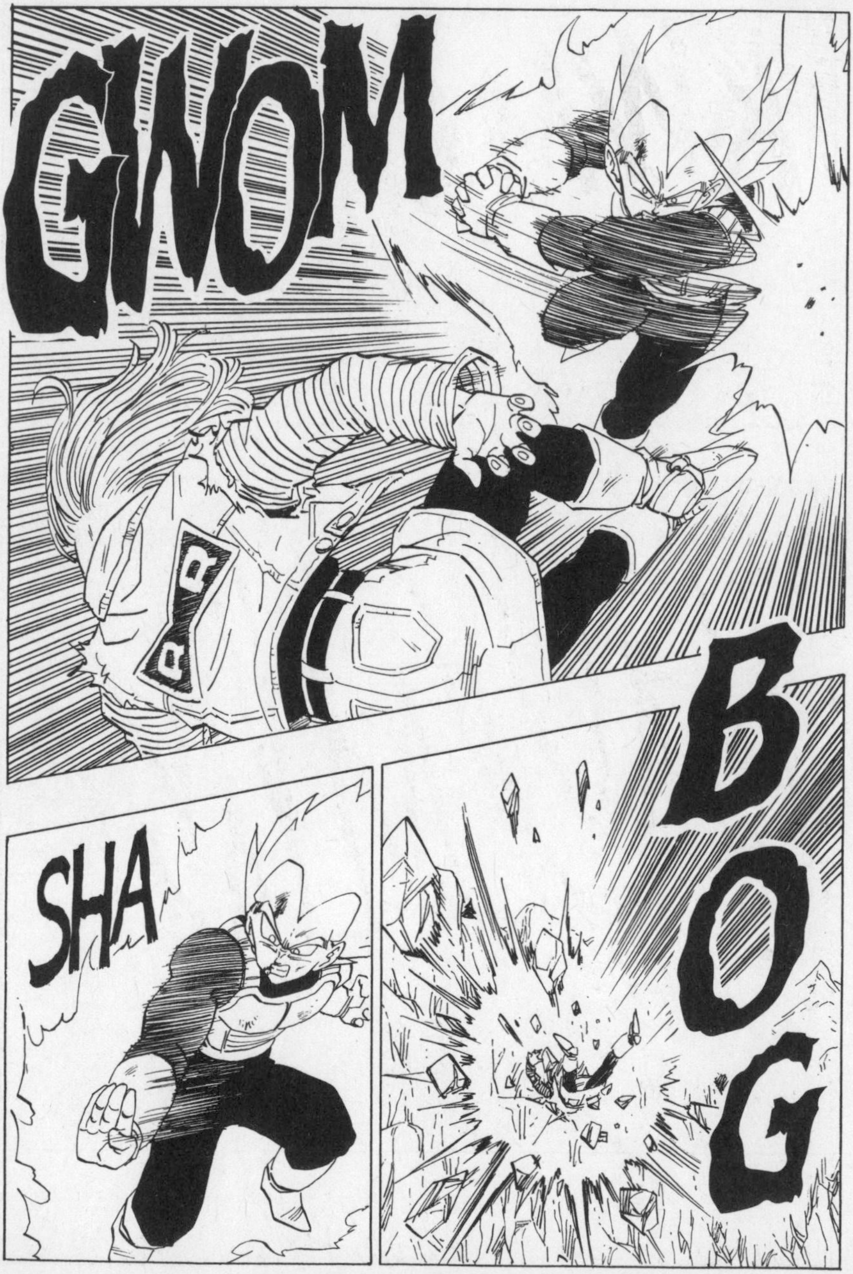

GNOM
BOG
SHA

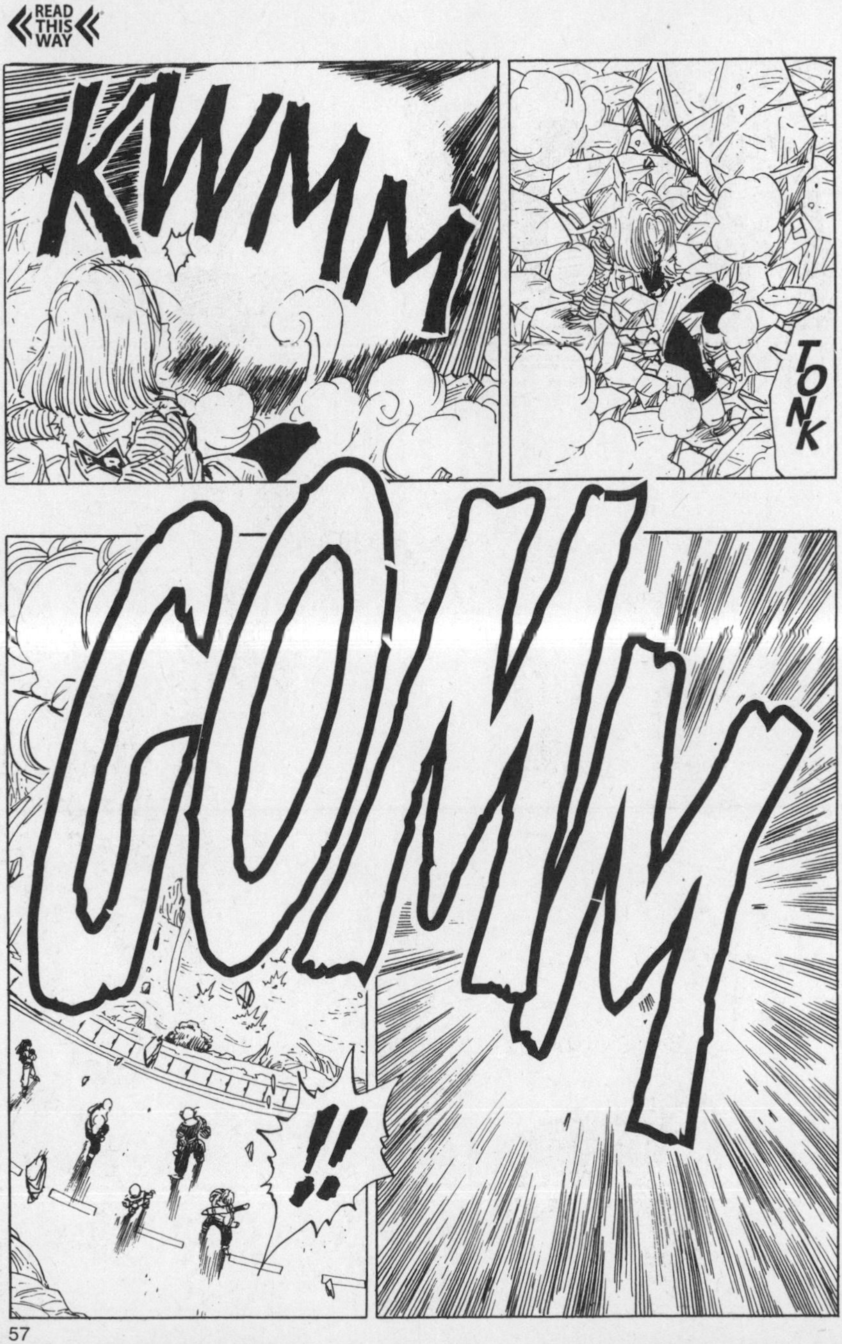
TONK
KWMM
!!

READ THIS WAY

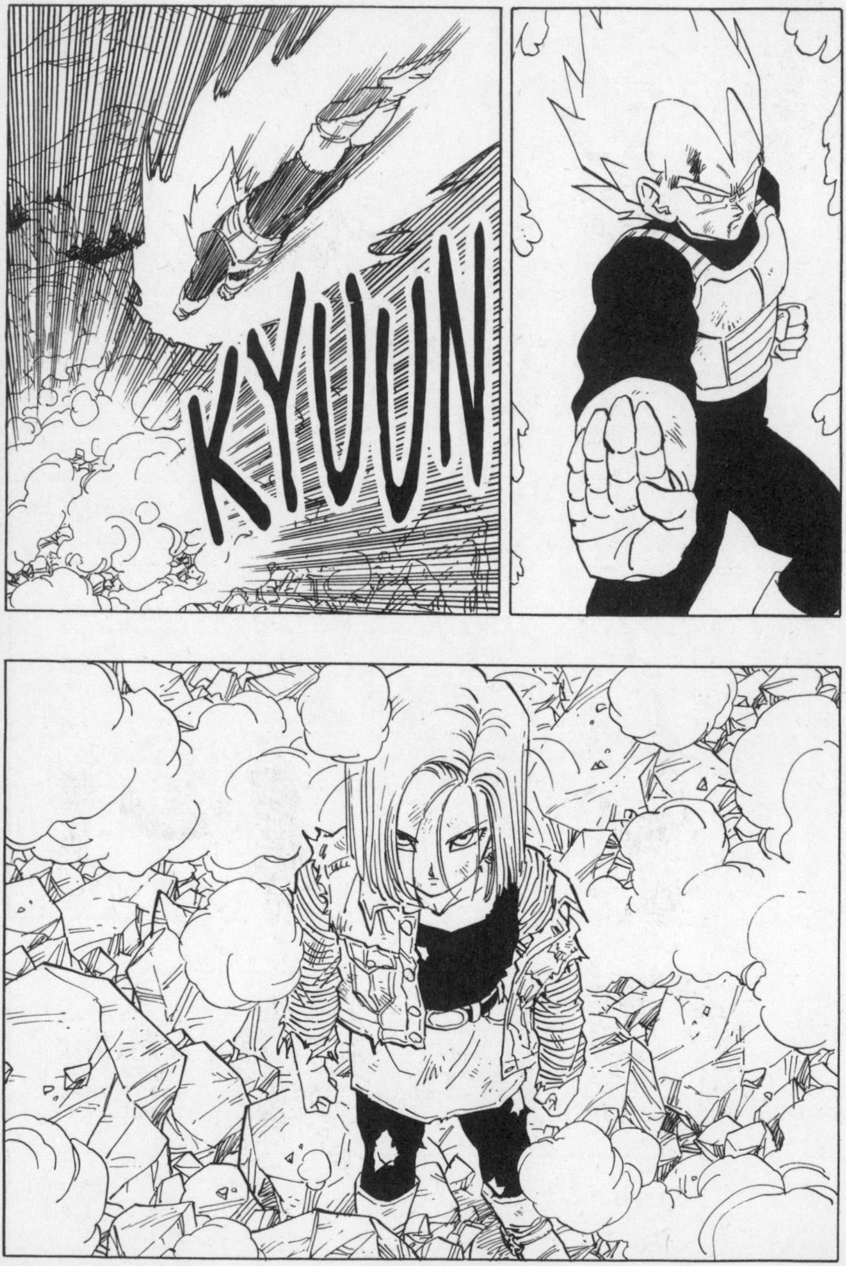
KYUUN

READ THIS WAY

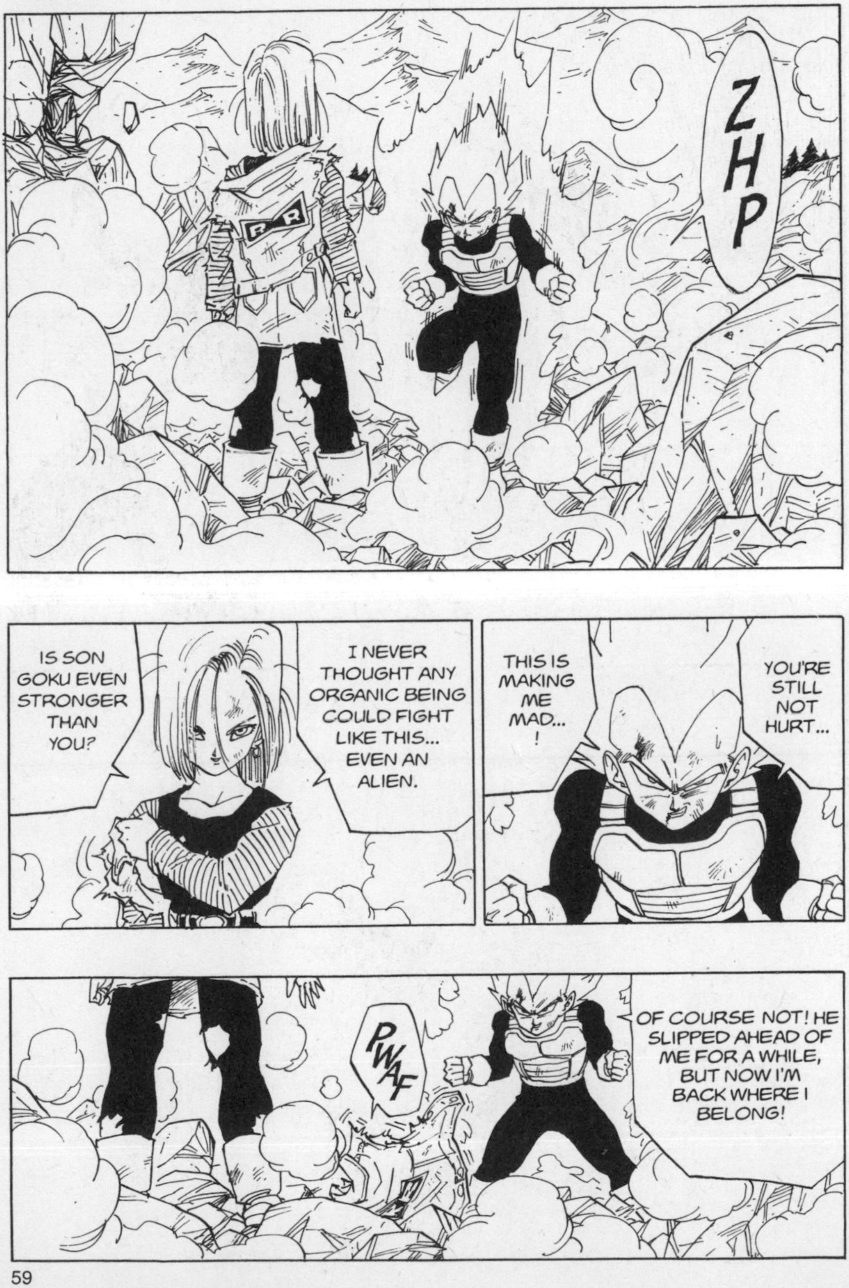
ZHP
YOU'RE STILL NOT HURT...
THIS IS MAKING ME MAD...!
I NEVER THOUGHT ANY ORGANIC BEING COULD FIGHT LIKE THIS... EVEN AN ALIEN.
IS SON GOKU EVEN STRONGER THAN YOU?
OF COURSE NOT! HE SLIPPED AHEAD OF ME FOR A WHILE, BUT NOW I'M BACK WHERE I BELONG!
PWAF

READ THIS WAY

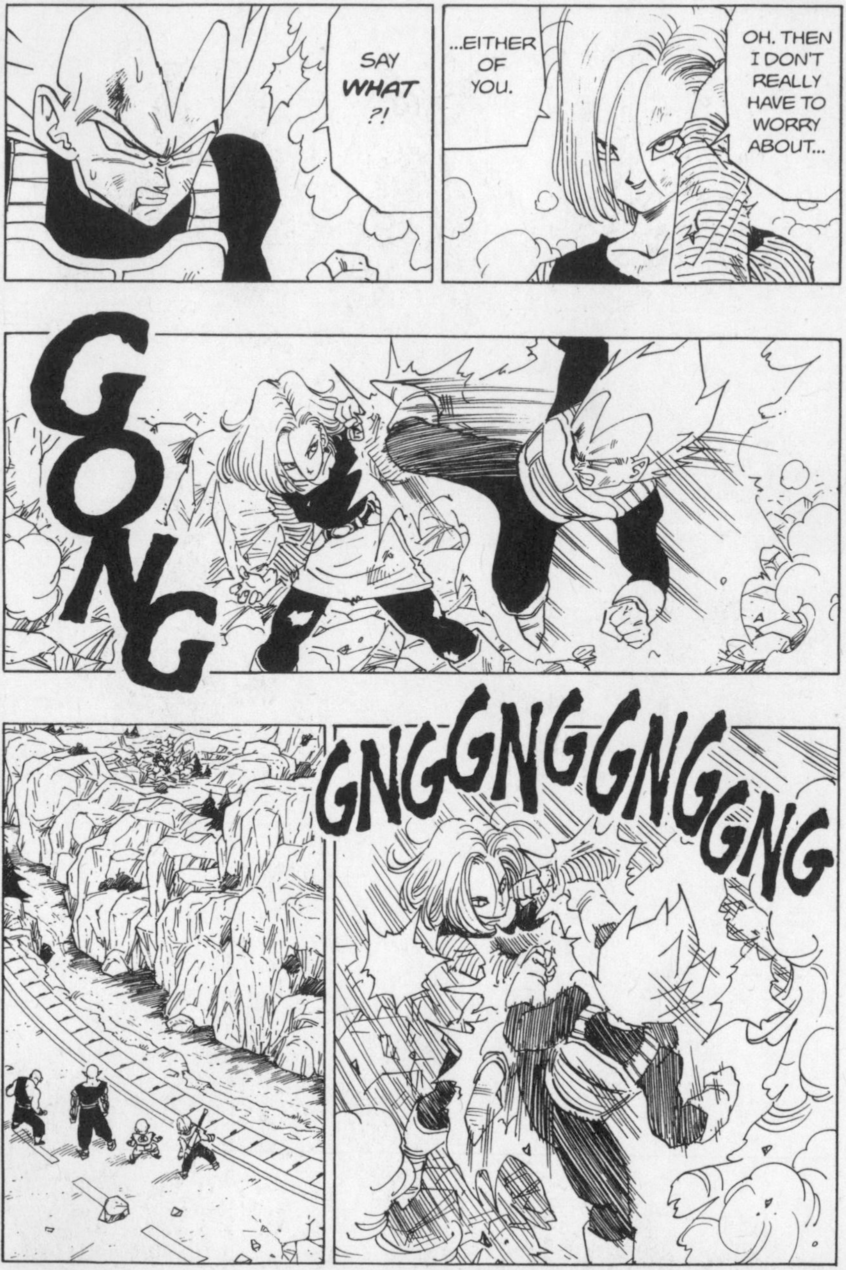

OH. THEN I DON'T REALLY HAVE TO WORRY ABOUT...
...EITHER OF YOU.
SAY WHAT?!
GONG
GNGGNGGNGGNG

READ THIS WAY

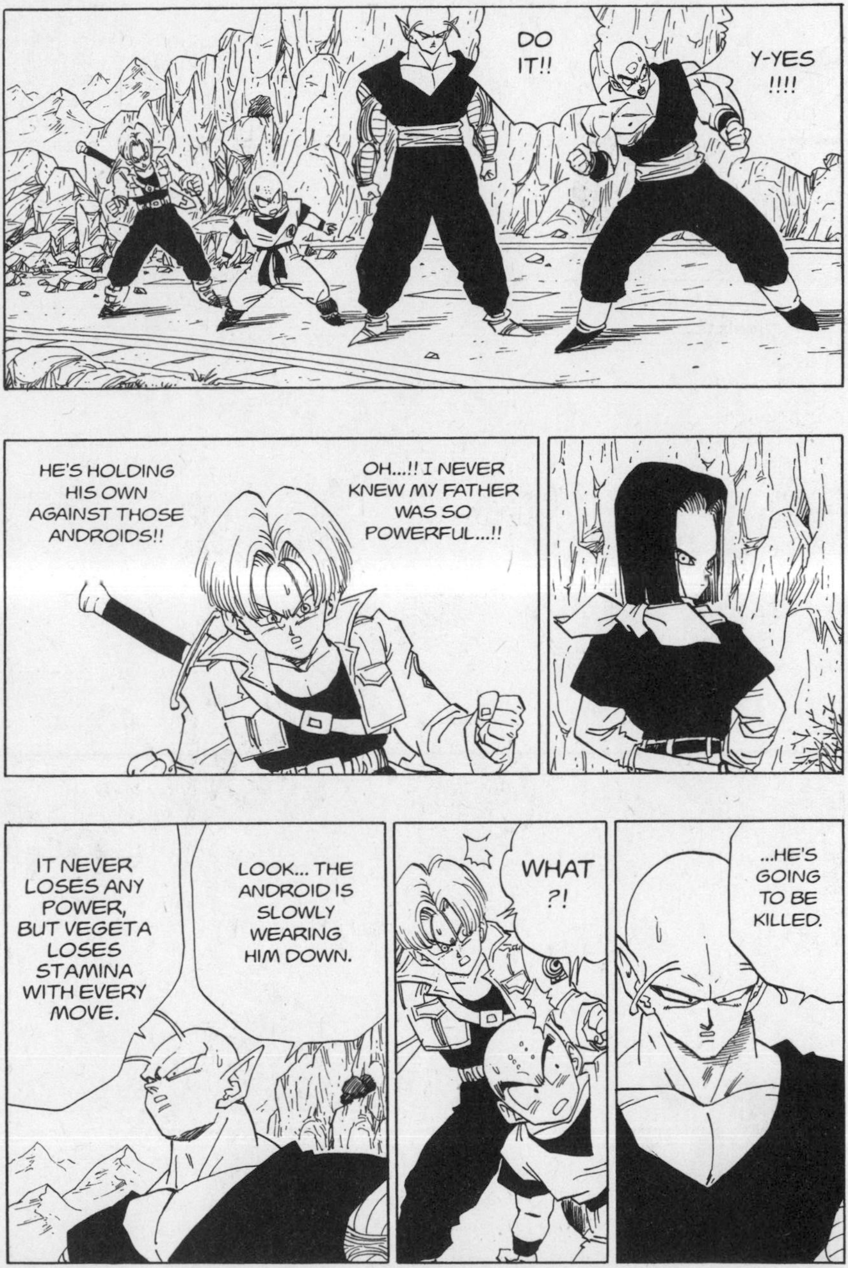
DO IT!!
Y-YES !!!!
OH...!! I NEVER KNEW MY FATHER WAS SO POWERFUL...!!
HE'S HOLDING HIS OWN AGAINST THOSE ANDROIDS!!
...HE'S GOING TO BE KILLED.
WHAT ?!
LOOK... THE ANDROID IS SLOWLY WEARING HIM DOWN.
IT NEVER LOSES ANY POWER, BUT VEGETA LOSES STAMINA WITH EVERY MOVE.

READ THIS WAY

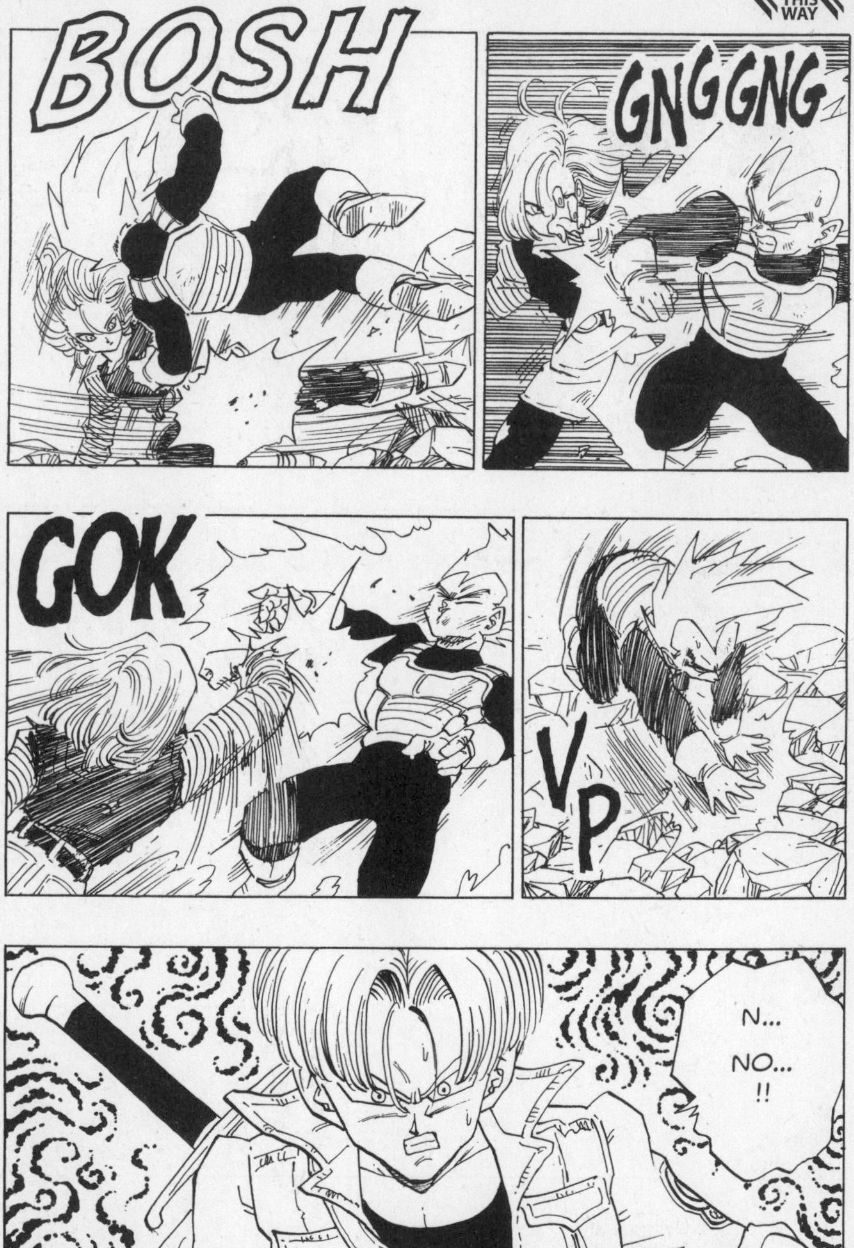
GNGGNG
BOSH
VP
GOK
N...
NO...
!!

READ THIS WAY

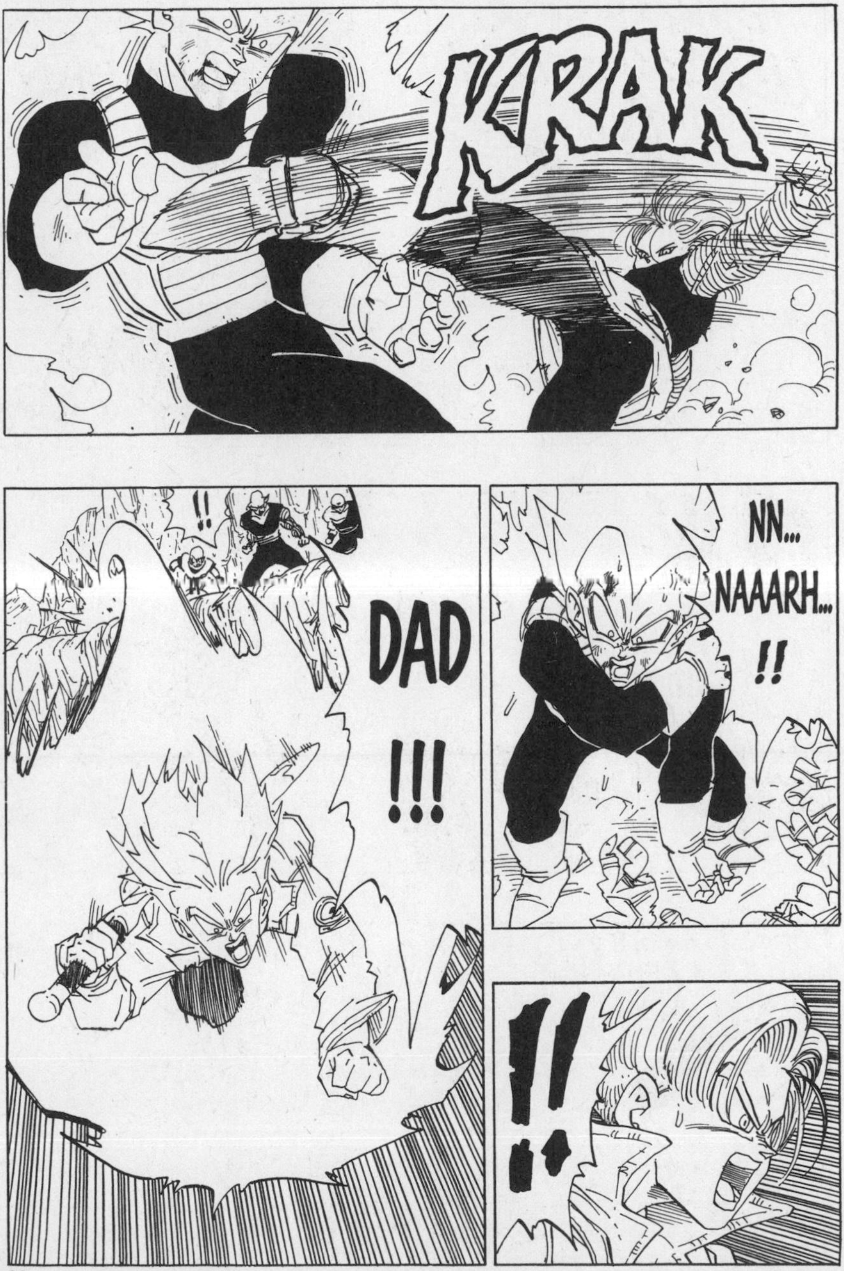
KRAK
NN... NAAARH... !!
!!
!!
DAD !!!

DBZ:160 • The Androids at Ease

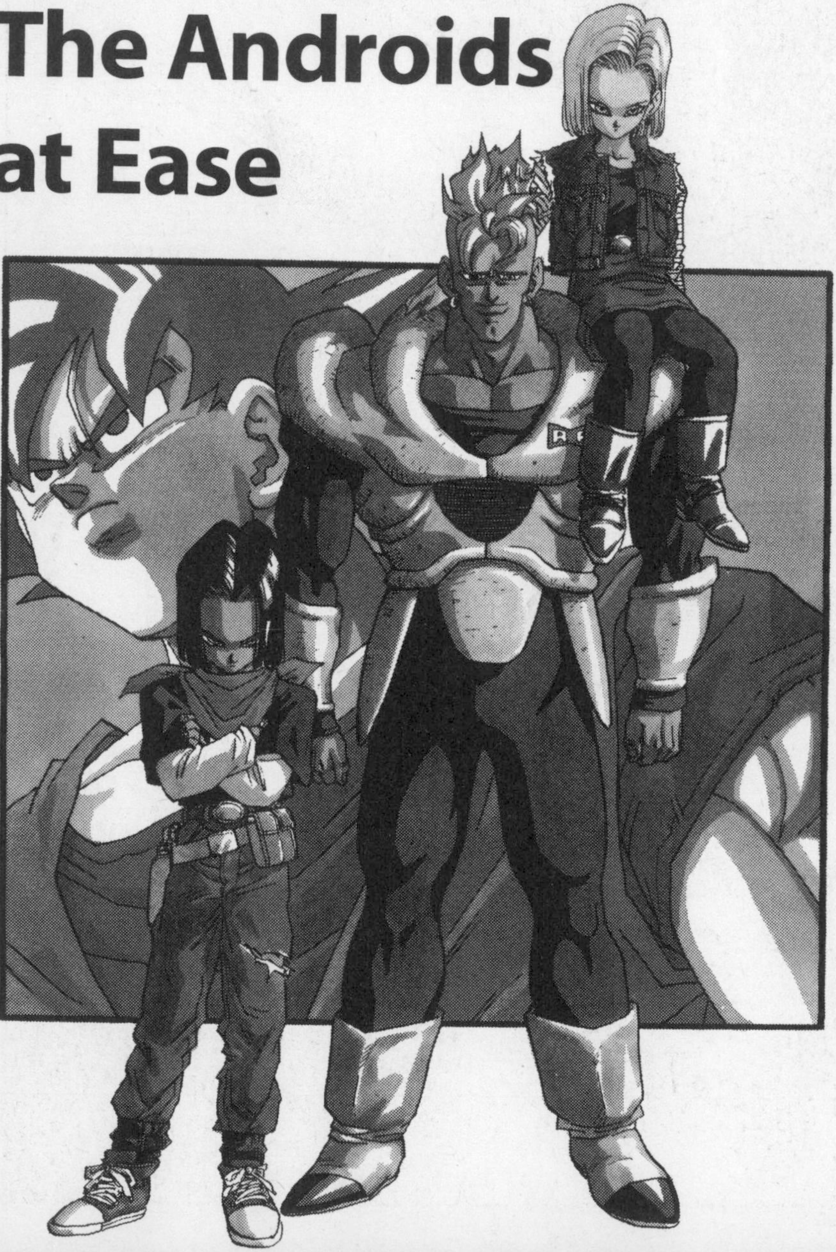

READ THIS WAY

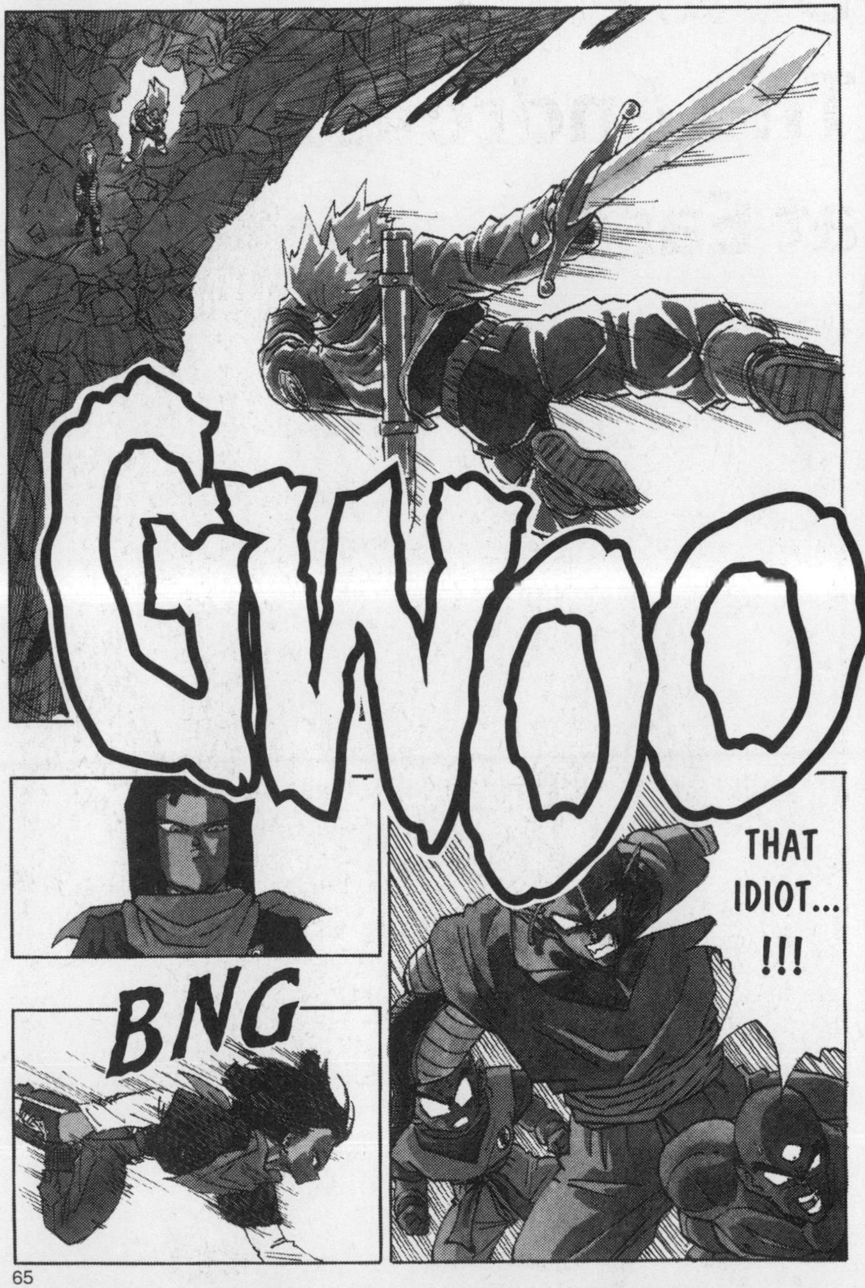
GWOO
THAT IDIOT... !!!
BNG

READ THIS WAY

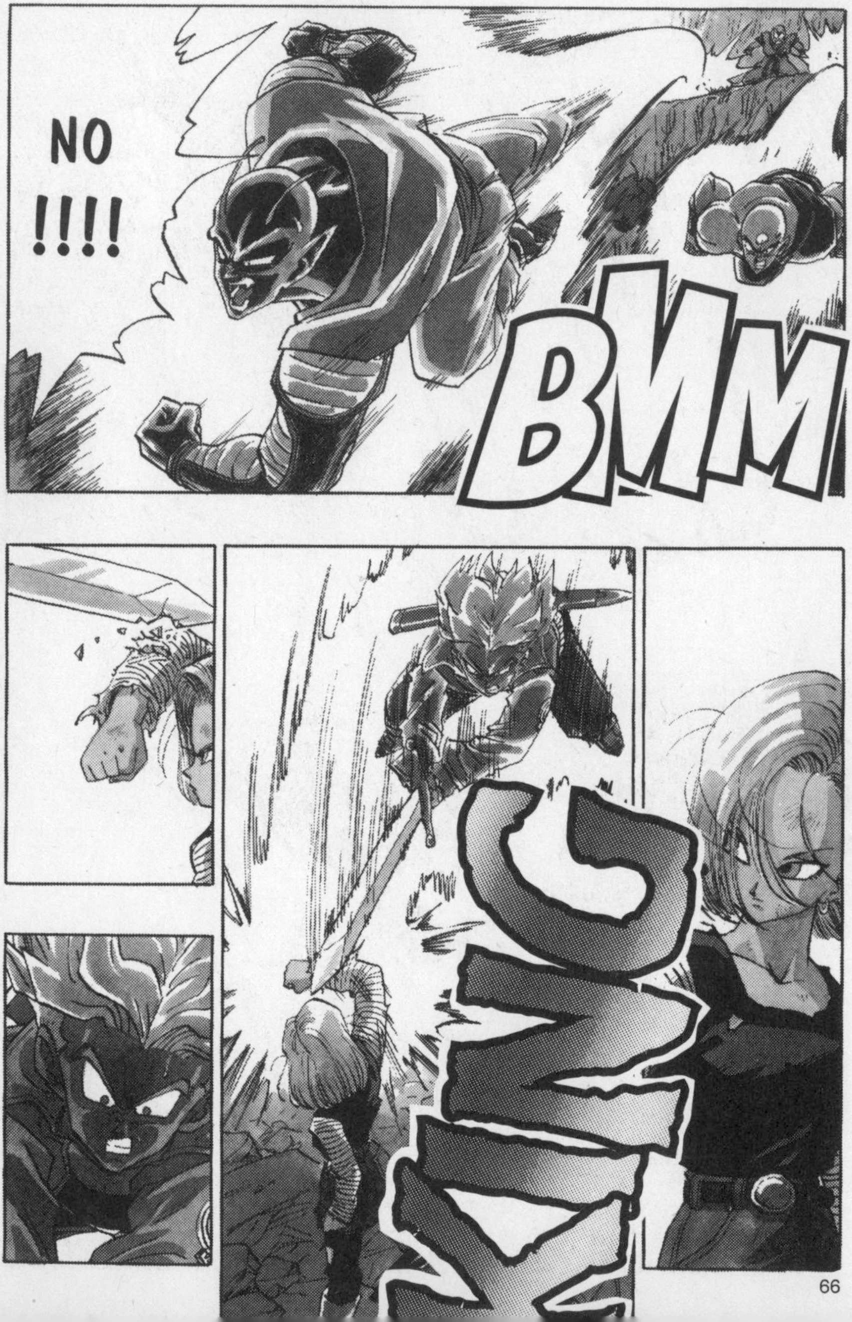
NO !!!!
BMM
CHING

READ THIS WAY

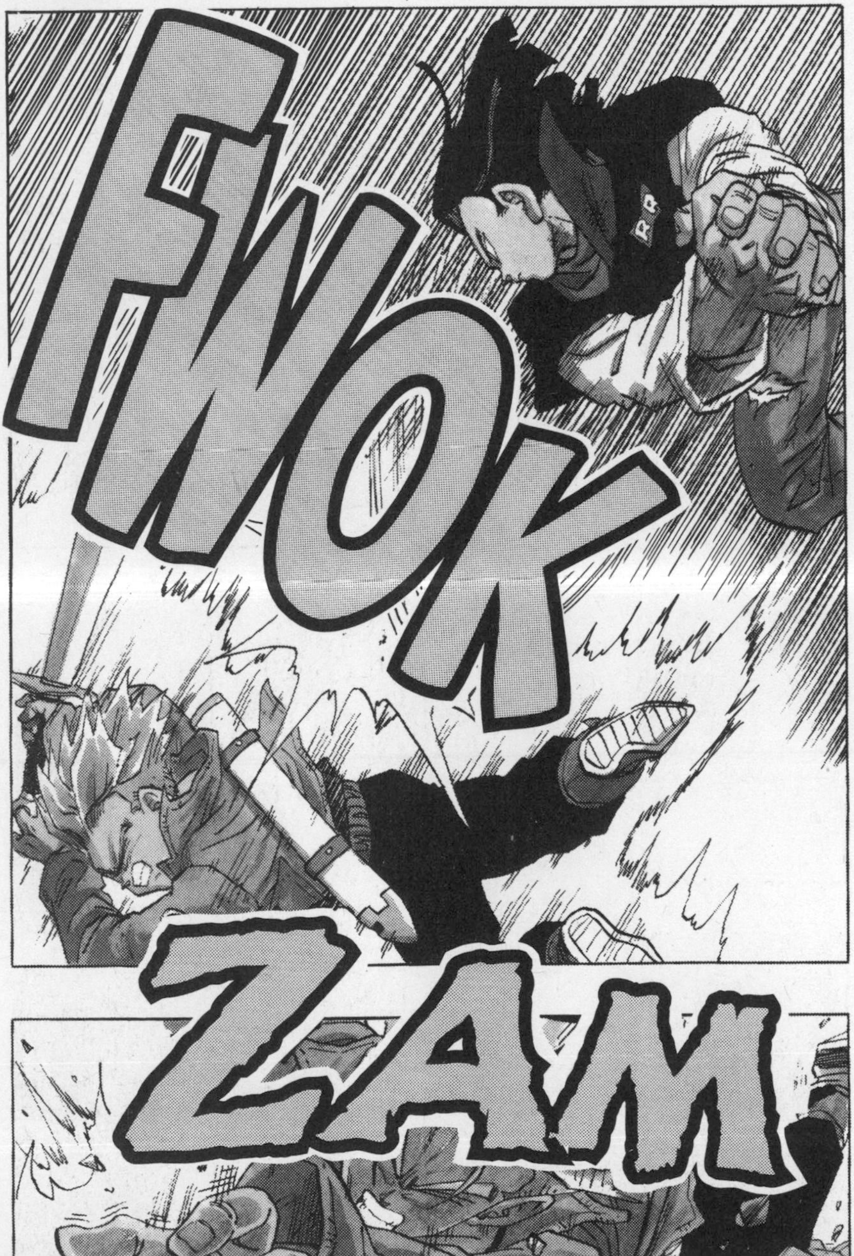
FWOK
ZAM

READ THIS WAY

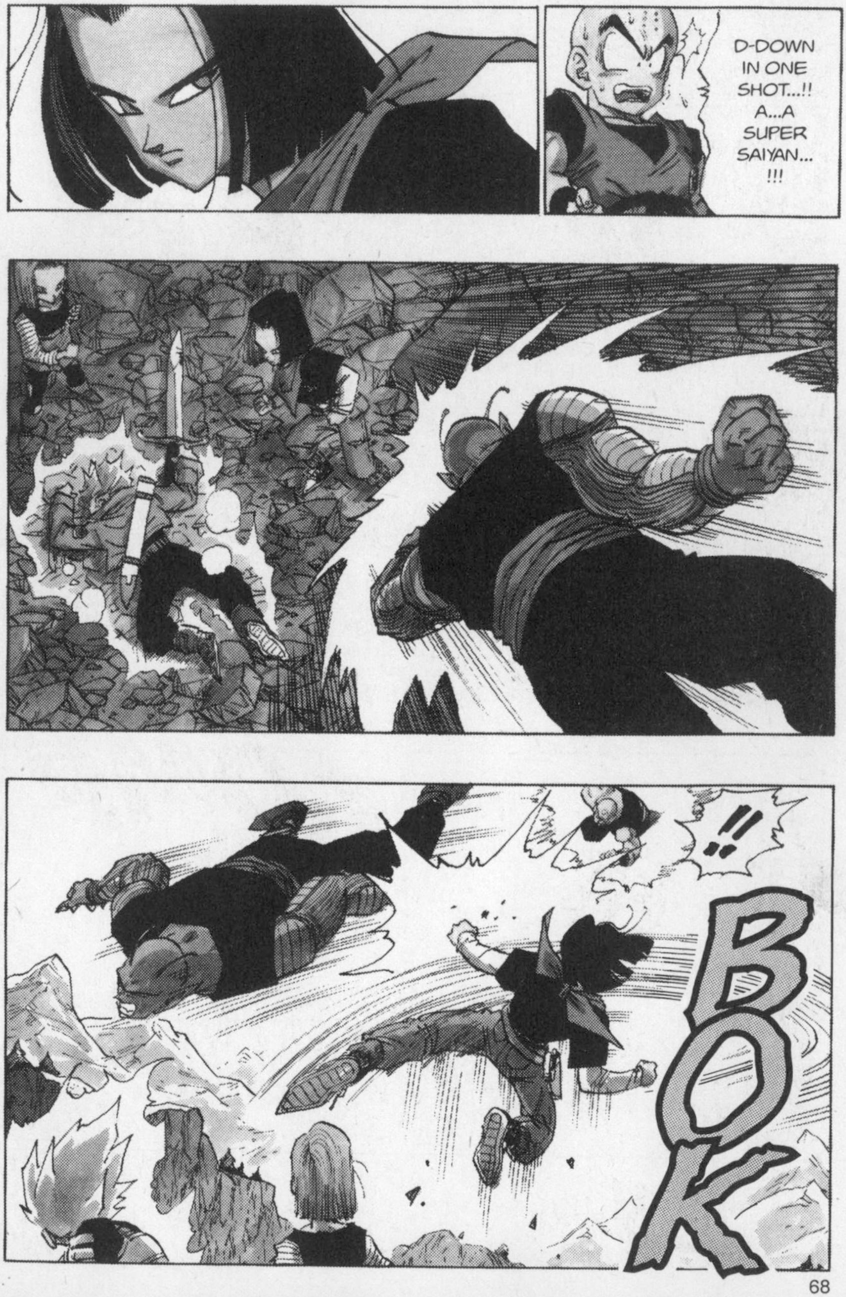
D-DOWN IN ONE SHOT...!! A...A SUPER SAIYAN... !!!
!!
BOK

READ THIS WAY

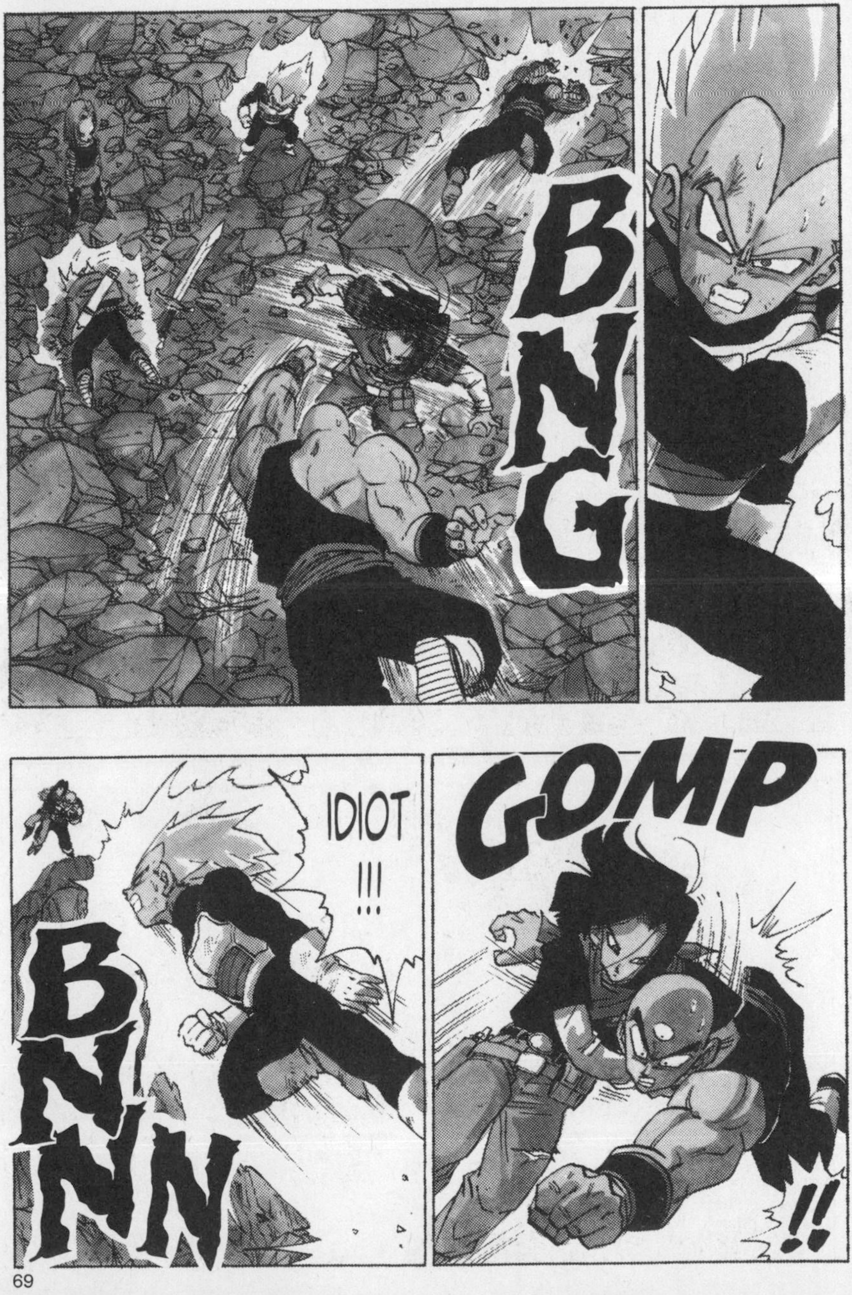
BNG
GOMP
!!
IDIOT
!!!
BNNN

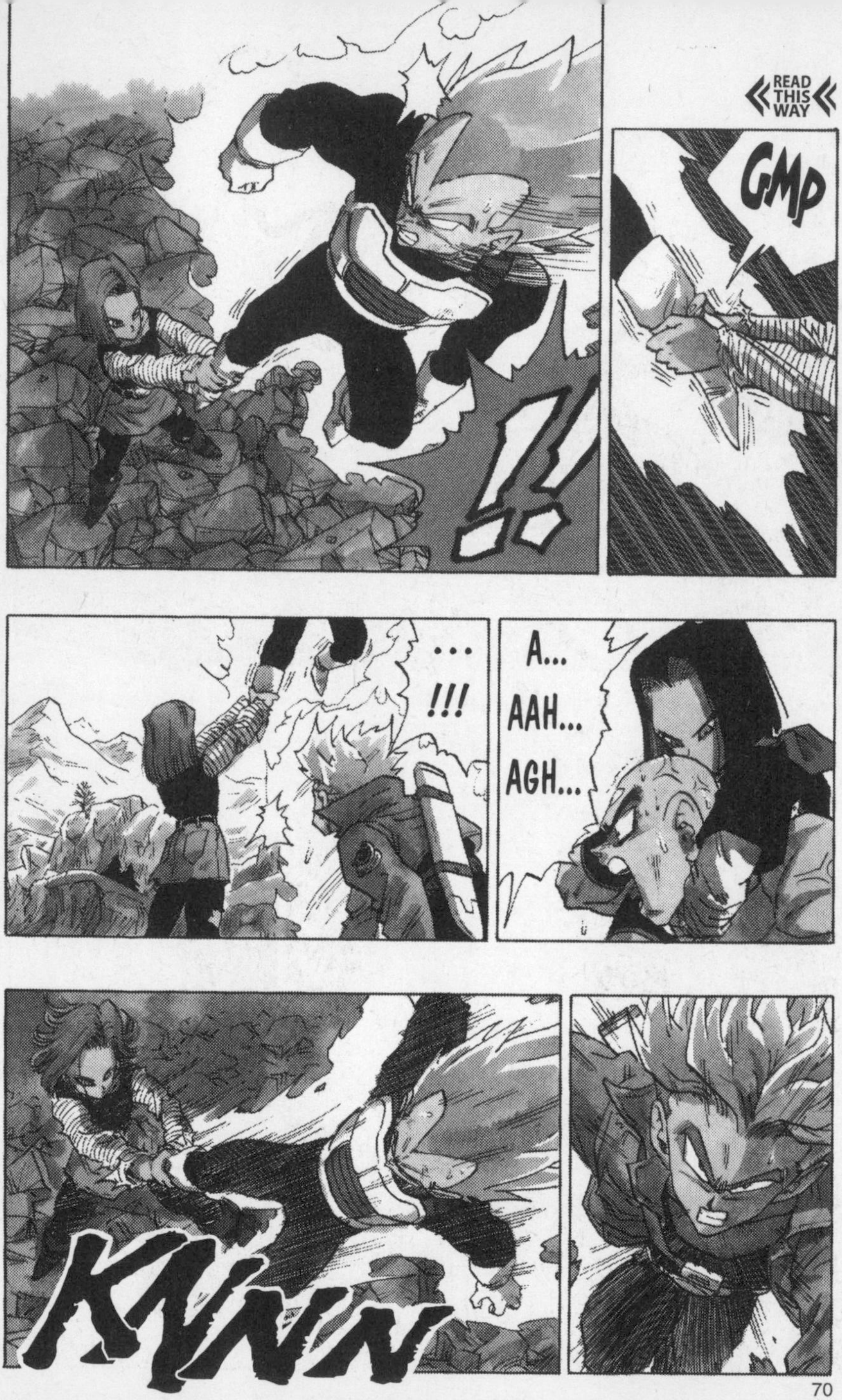
READ THIS WAY
GMP
A...
AAH...
AGH...
...
!!!
KNNN

READ THIS WAY

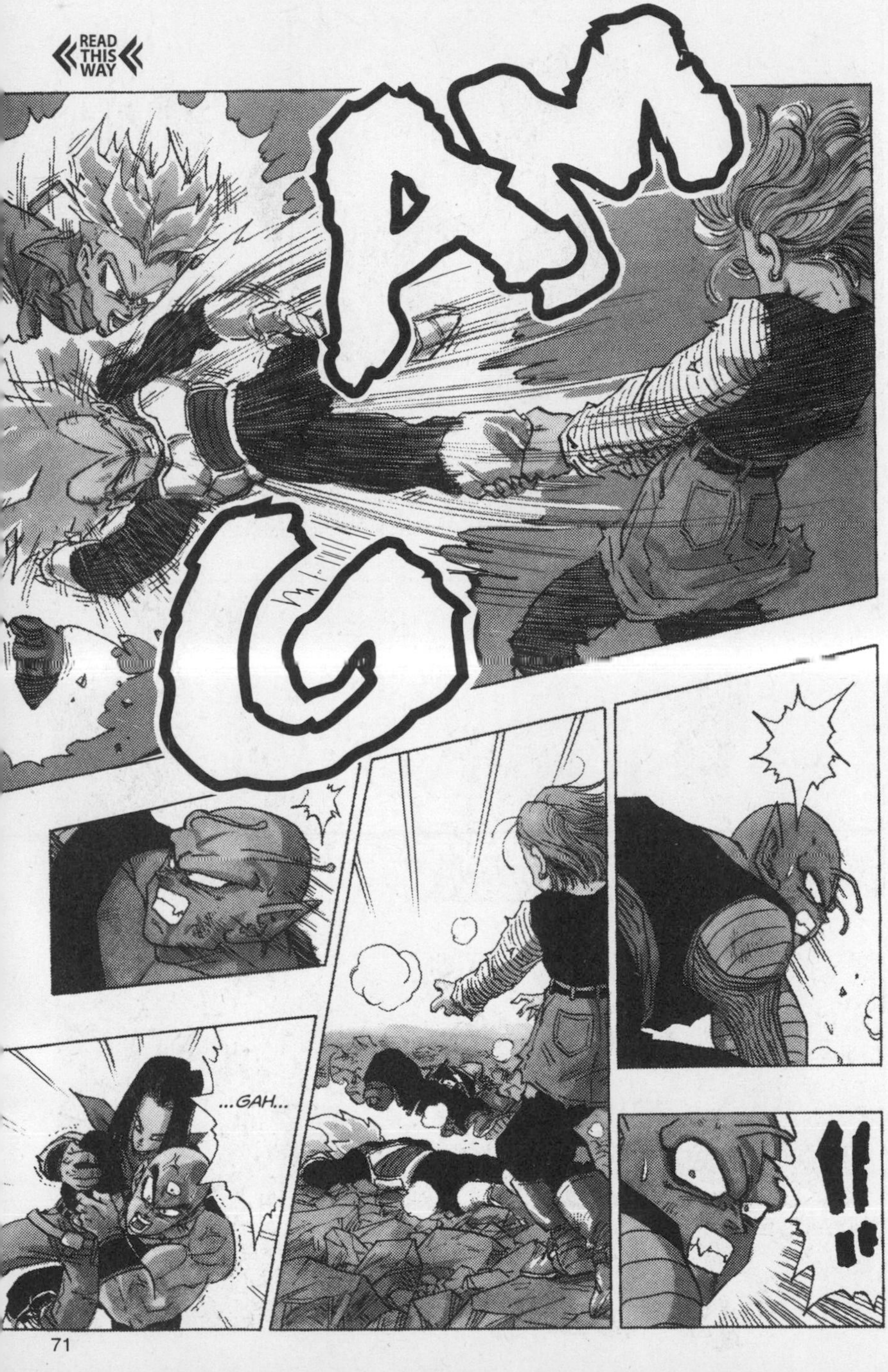

!!
...GAH...

READ THIS WAY

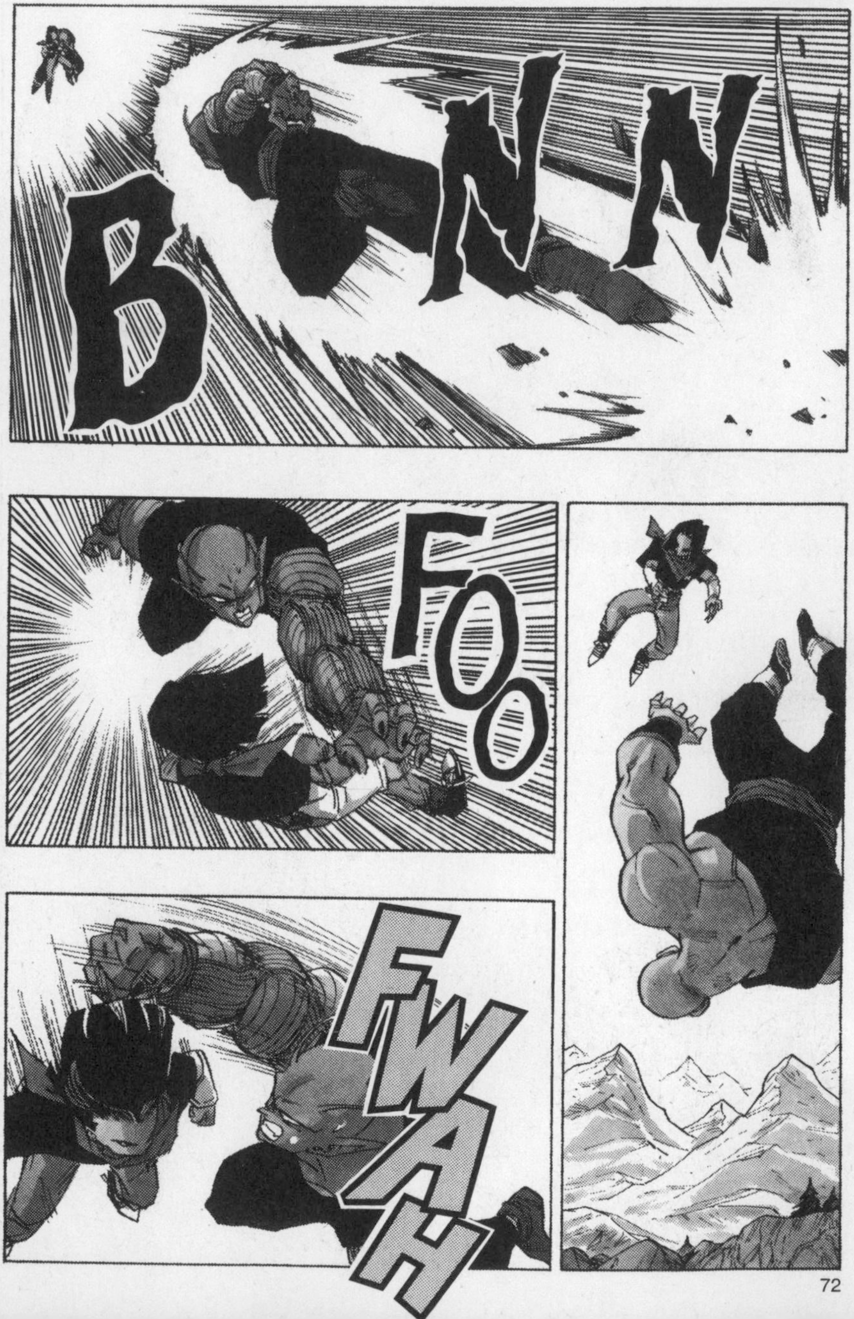
BNN
FOO
FWAH

READ THIS WAY

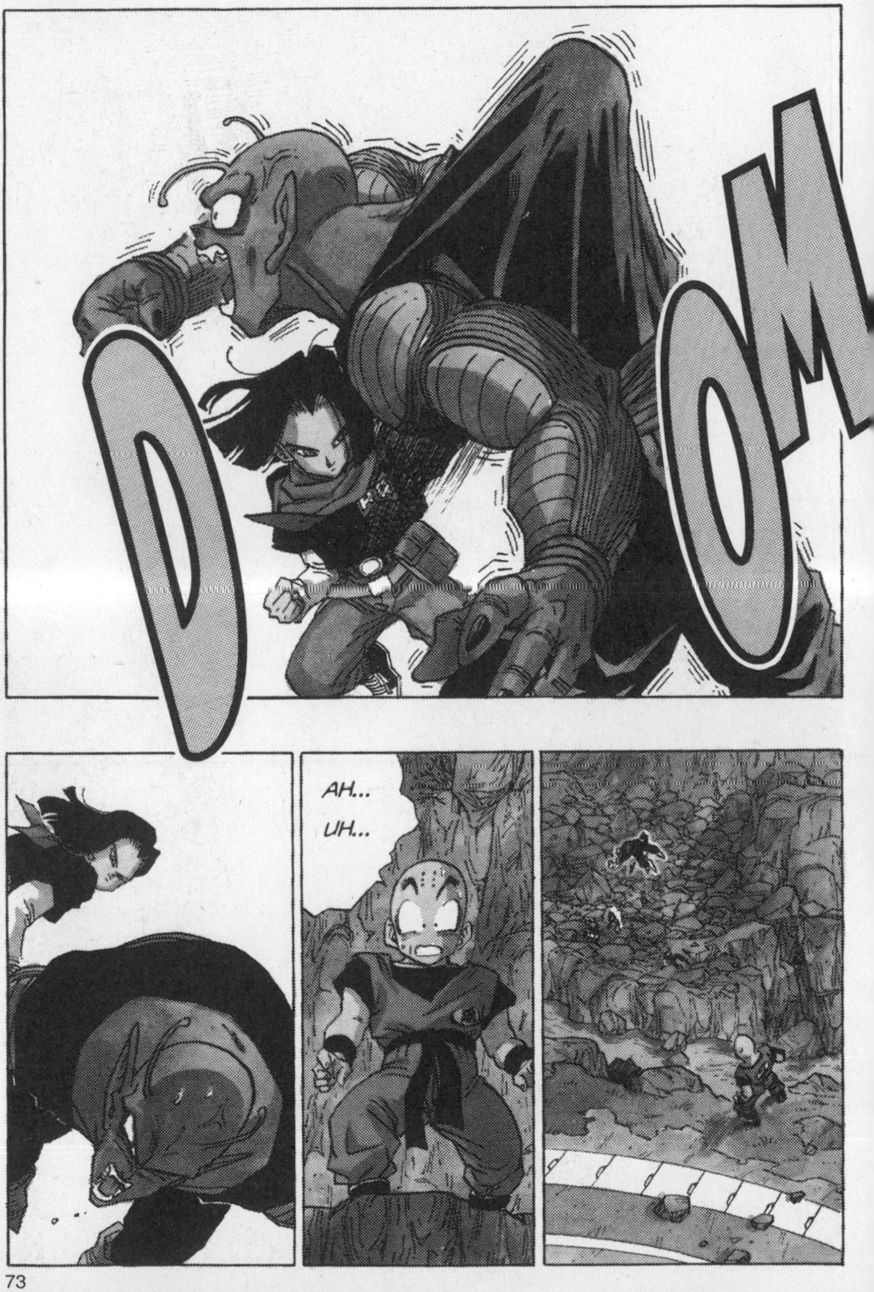
DOM
AH...
UH...

READ THIS WAY

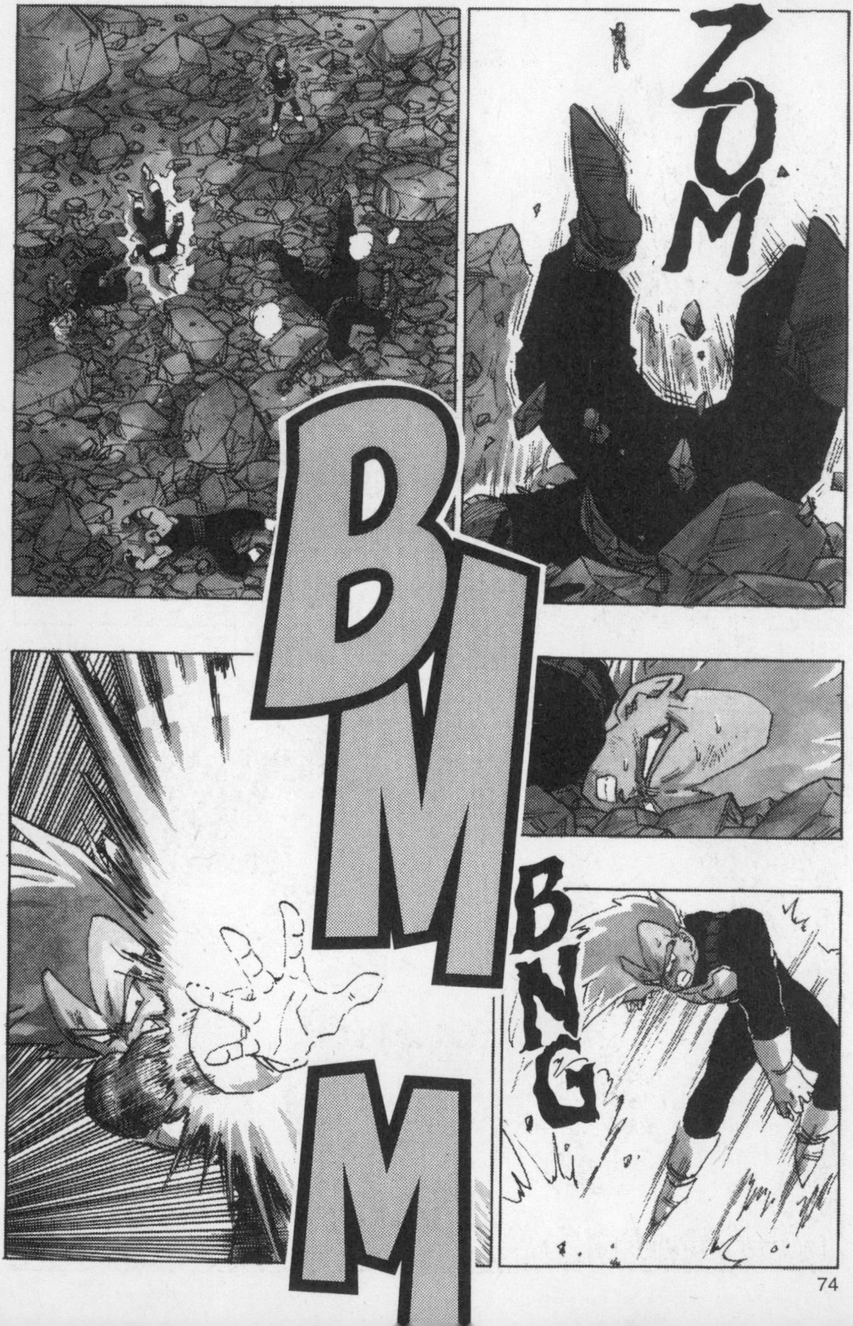
ZOM
BMM
BNG

READ THIS WAY

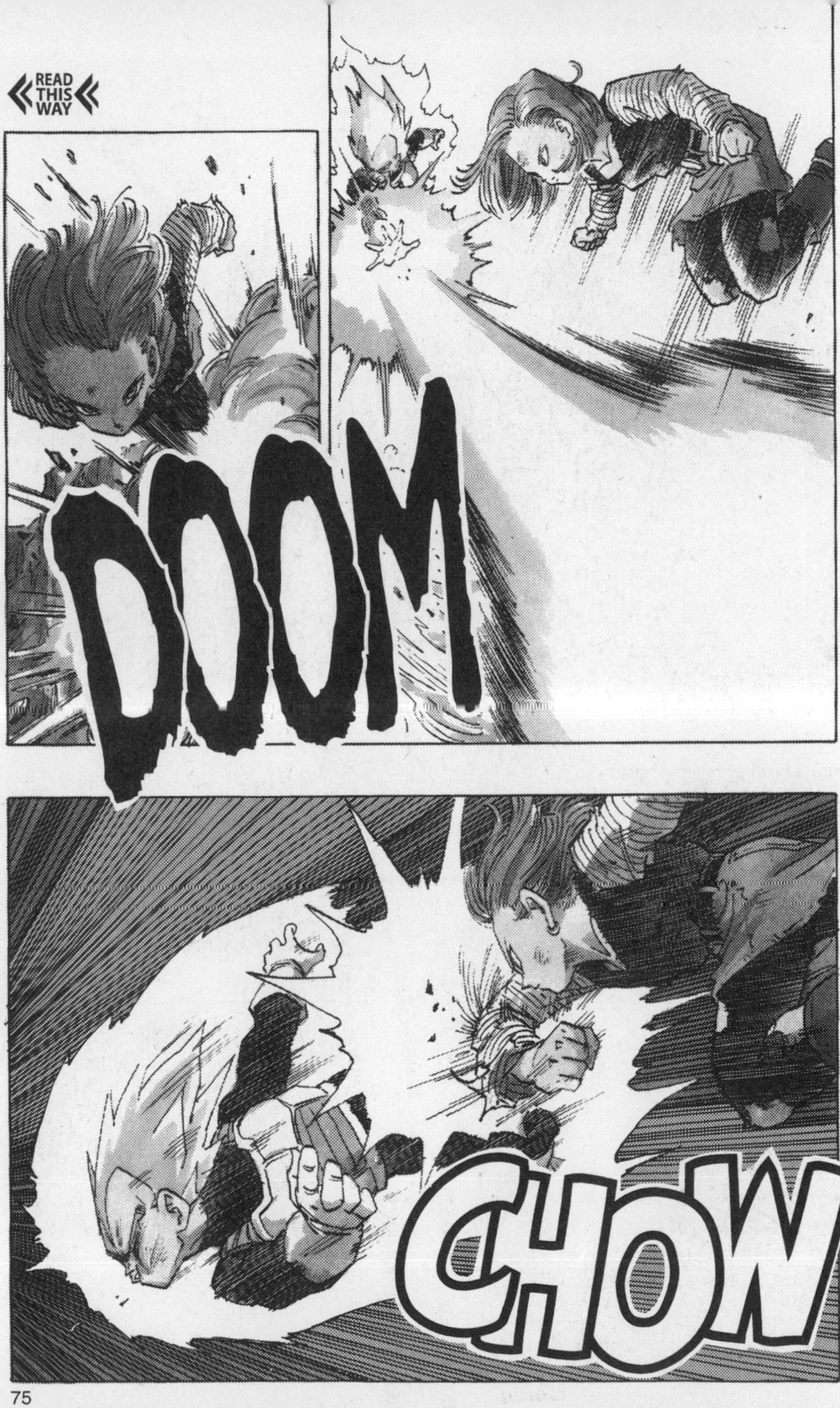
DOOM
CHOW

READ THIS WAY

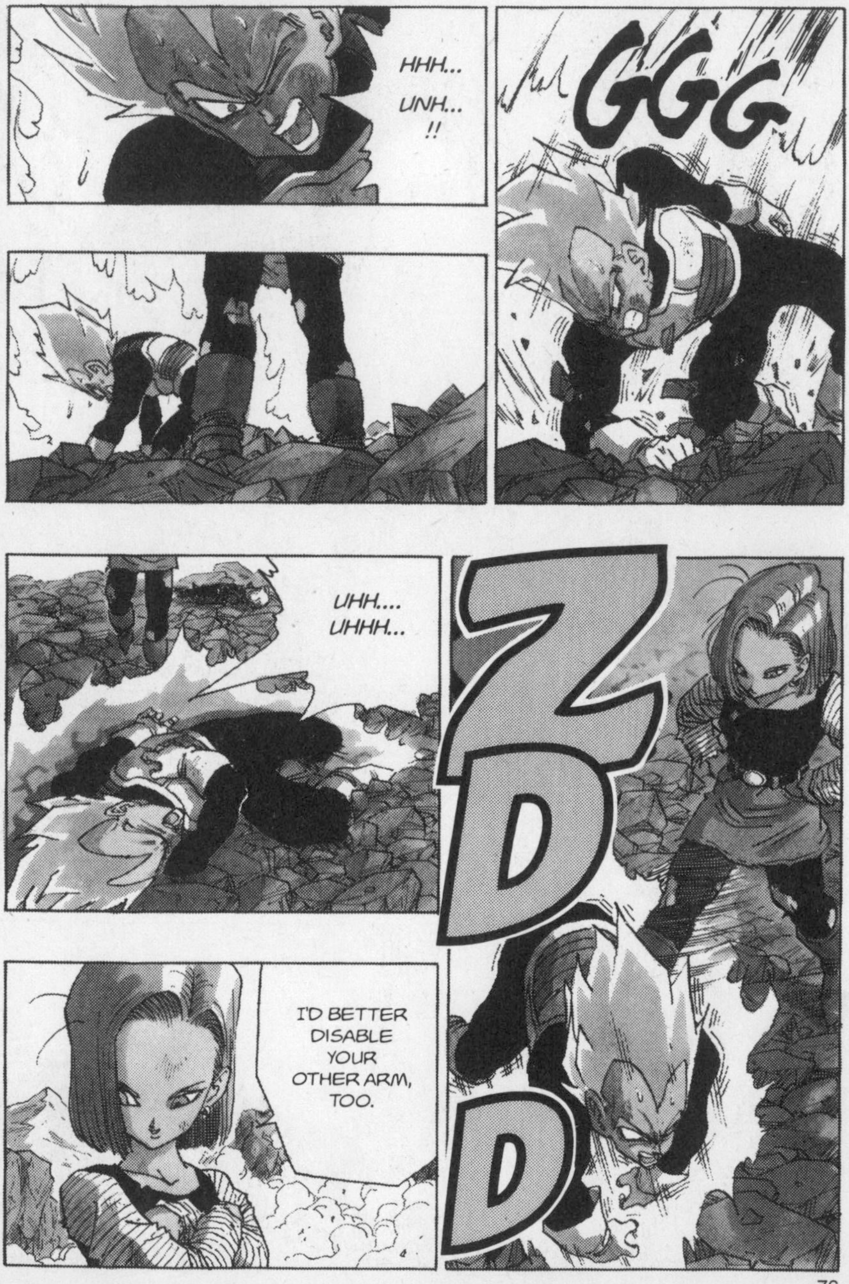

GGG
HHH...
UNH...
!!
ZDD
UHH....
UHHH...
I'D BETTER DISABLE YOUR OTHER ARM, TOO.

READ THIS WAY

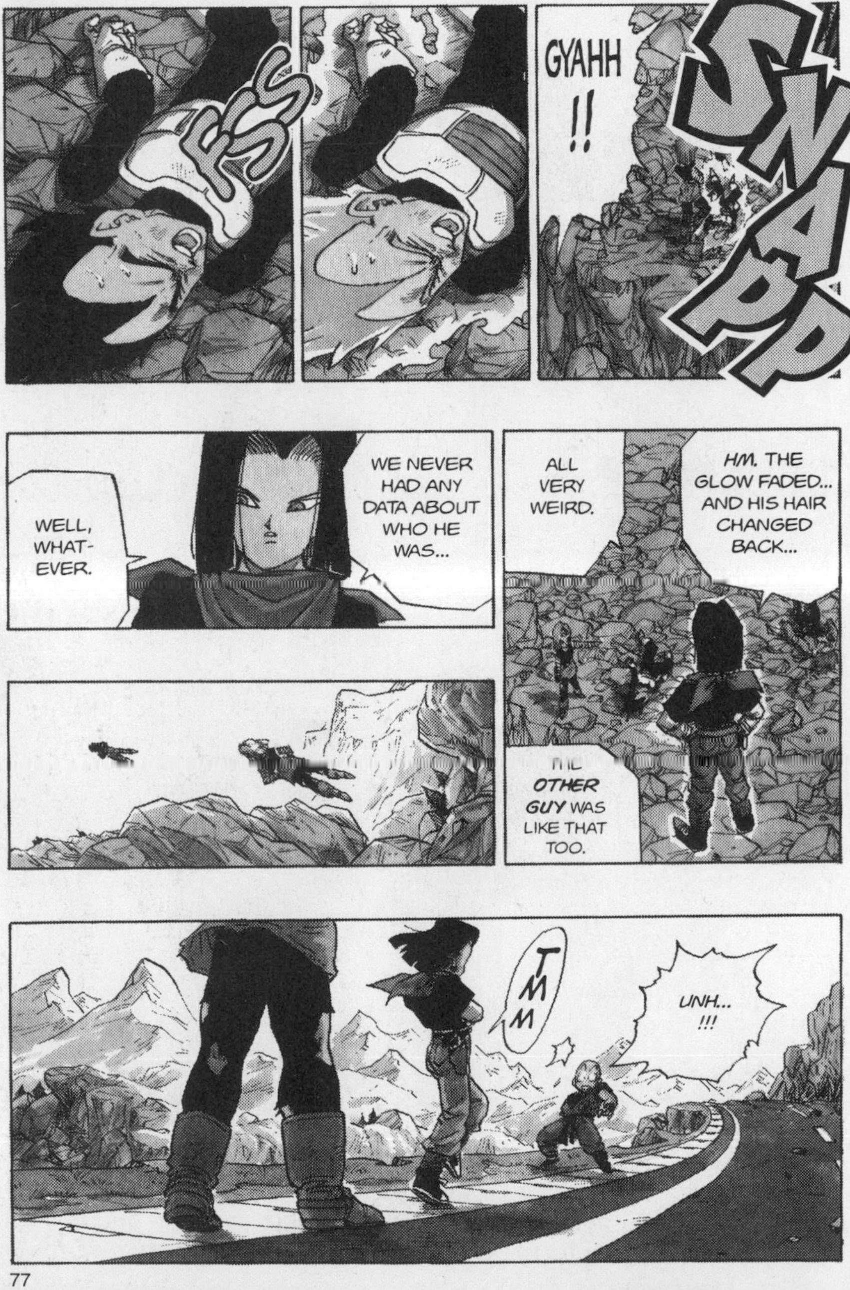
GYAHH !!
SNAPP
FSS
HM. THE GLOW FADED... AND HIS HAIR CHANGED BACK...
ALL VERY WEIRD.
THE OTHER GUY WAS LIKE THAT TOO.
WE NEVER HAD ANY DATA ABOUT WHO HE WAS...
WELL, WHAT-EVER.
UNH... !!!
TMM

READ THIS WAY

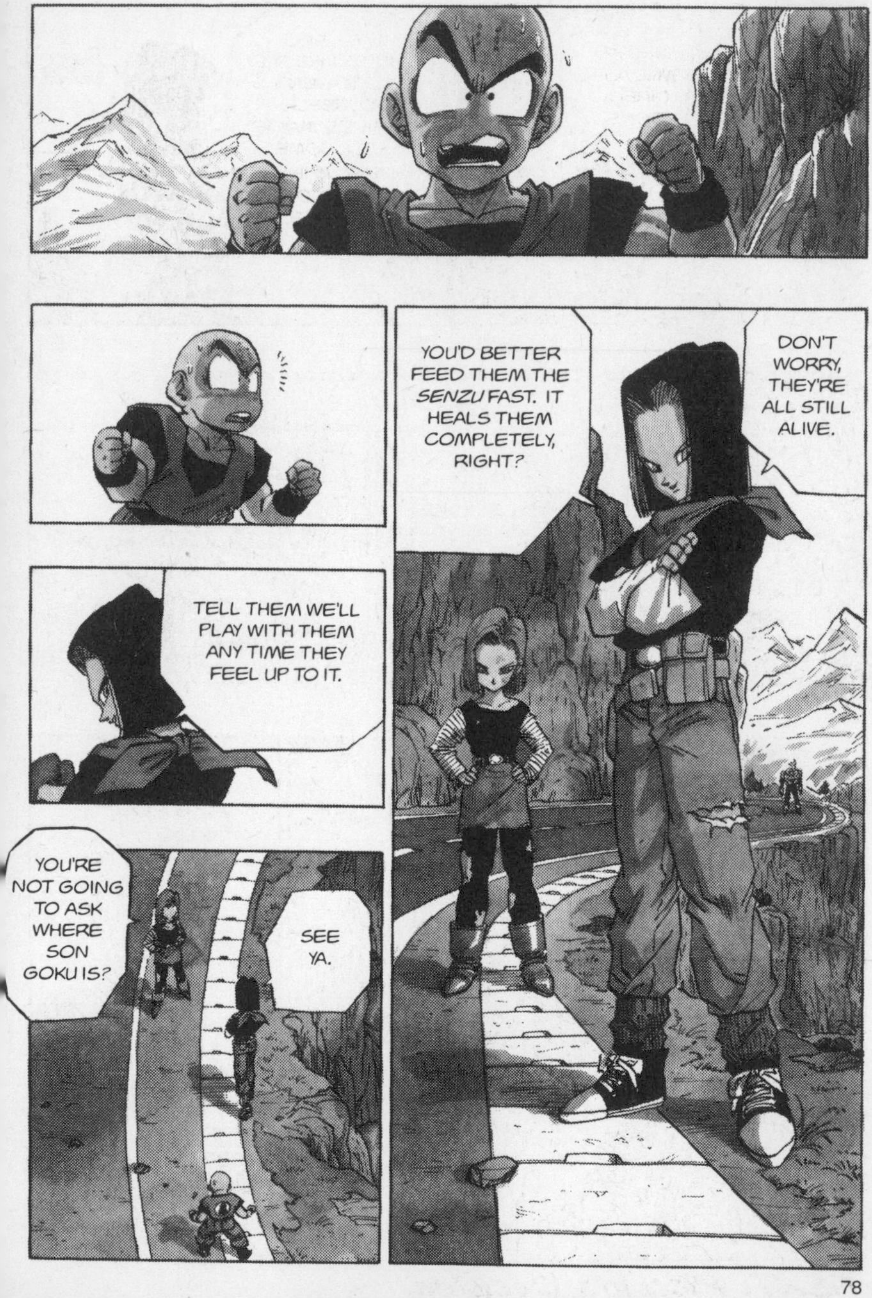

DON'T WORRY, THEY'RE ALL STILL ALIVE.
YOU'D BETTER FEED THEM THE *SENZU* FAST. IT HEALS THEM COMPLETELY, RIGHT?
TELL THEM WE'LL PLAY WITH THEM ANY TIME THEY FEEL UP TO IT.
SEE YA.
YOU'RE NOT GOING TO ASK WHERE SON GOKU IS?

READ THIS WAY

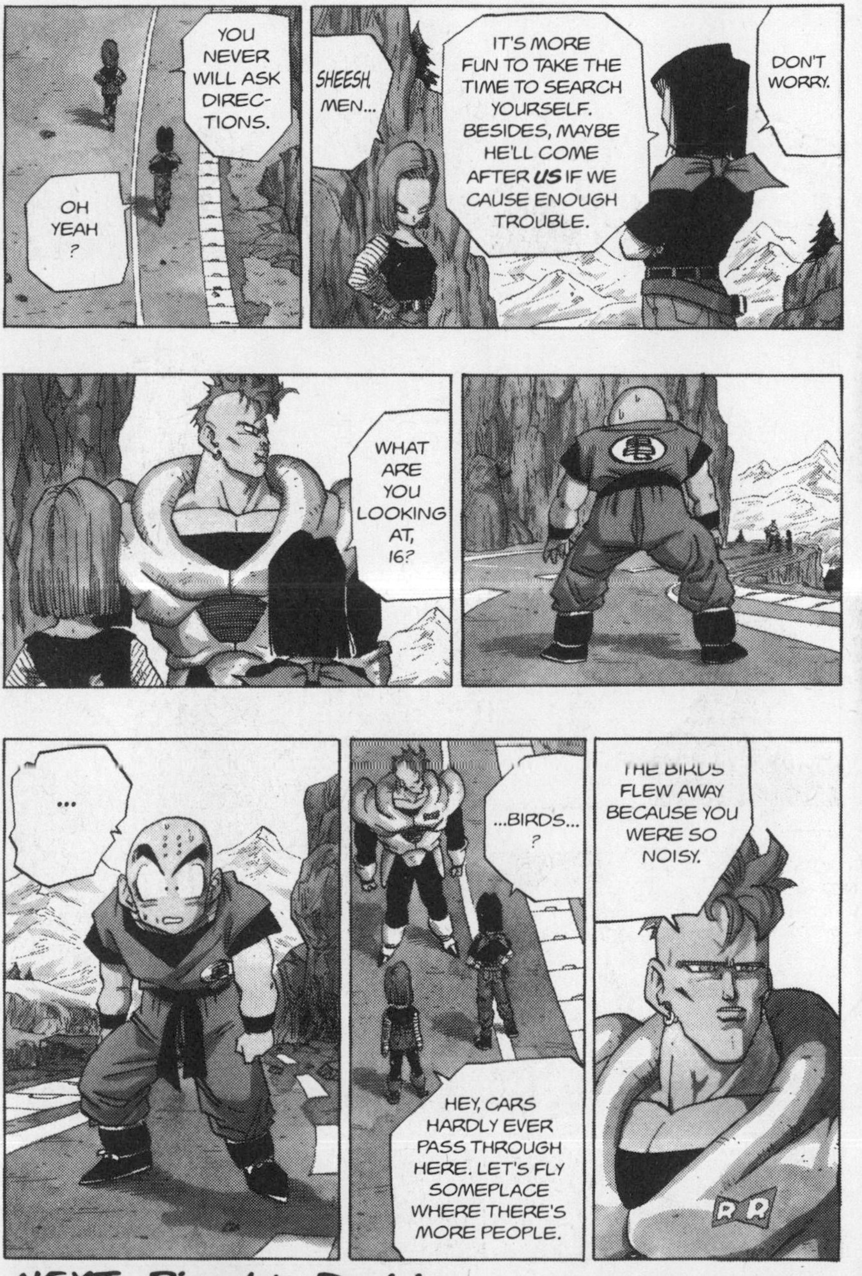
DON'T WORRY.
IT'S MORE FUN TO TAKE THE TIME TO SEARCH YOURSELF. BESIDES, MAYBE HE'LL COME AFTER *US* IF WE CAUSE ENOUGH TROUBLE.
SHEESH, MEN...
YOU NEVER WILL ASK DIRECTIONS.
OH YEAH ?
WHAT ARE YOU LOOKING AT, 16?
THE BIRDS FLEW AWAY BECAUSE YOU WERE SO NOISY.
...BIRDS... ?
HEY, CARS HARDLY EVER PASS THROUGH HERE. LET'S FLY SOMEPLACE WHERE THERE'S MORE PEOPLE.
...

NEXT: Piccolo's Decision

DBZ:161 • Retreat and Regroup

READ THIS WAY

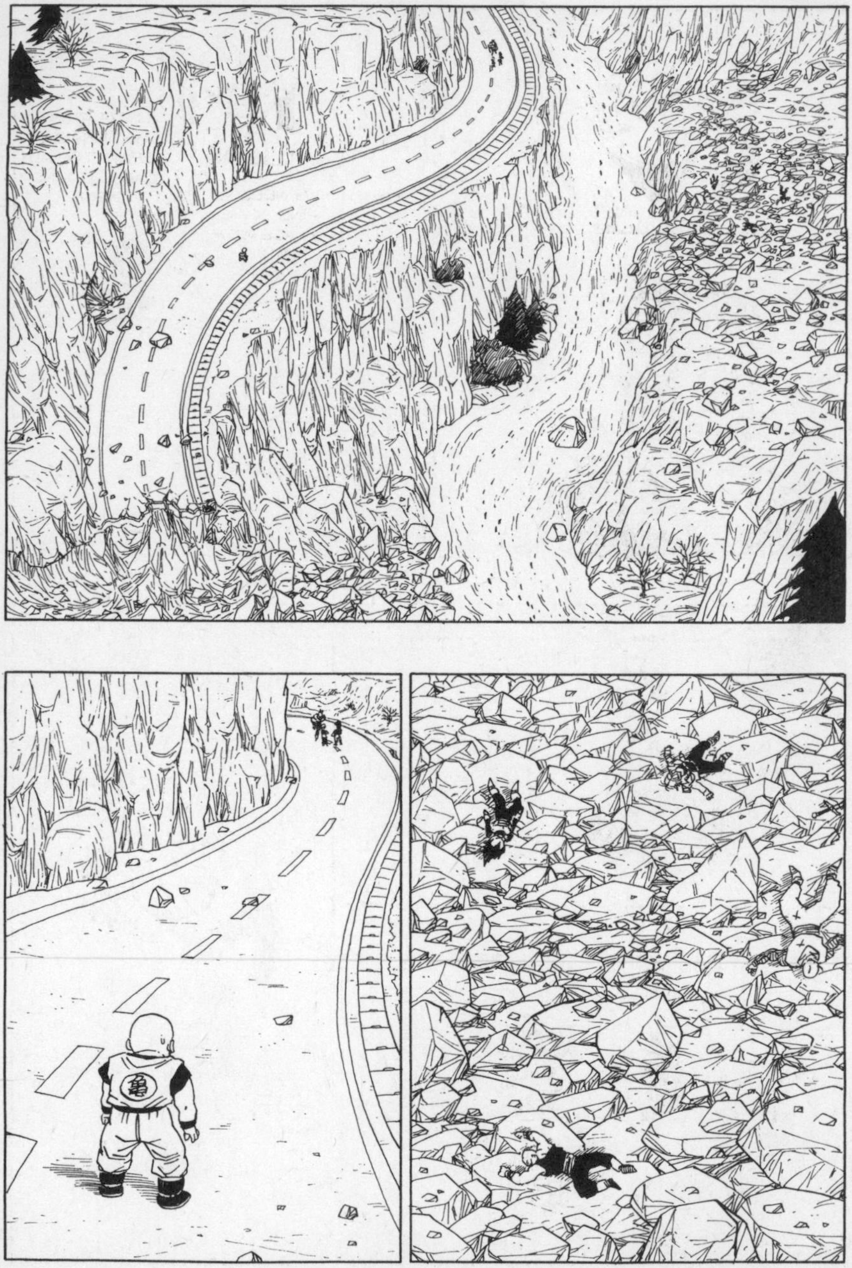

READ THIS WAY

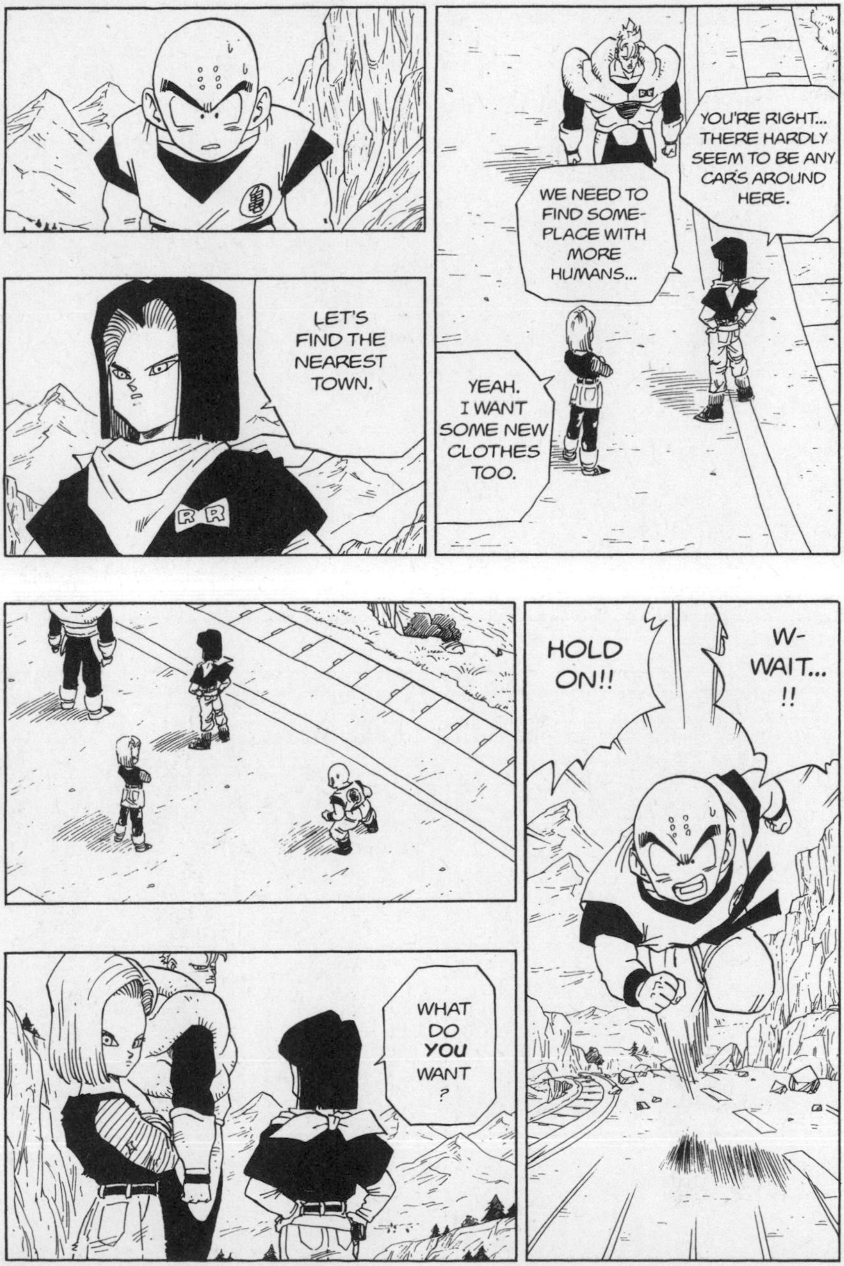

YOU'RE RIGHT... THERE HARDLY SEEM TO BE ANY CARS AROUND HERE.
WE NEED TO FIND SOME-PLACE WITH MORE HUMANS...
YEAH. I WANT SOME NEW CLOTHES TOO.
LET'S FIND THE NEAREST TOWN.
W- WAIT... !!
HOLD ON!!
WHAT DO YOU WANT ?

READ THIS WAY

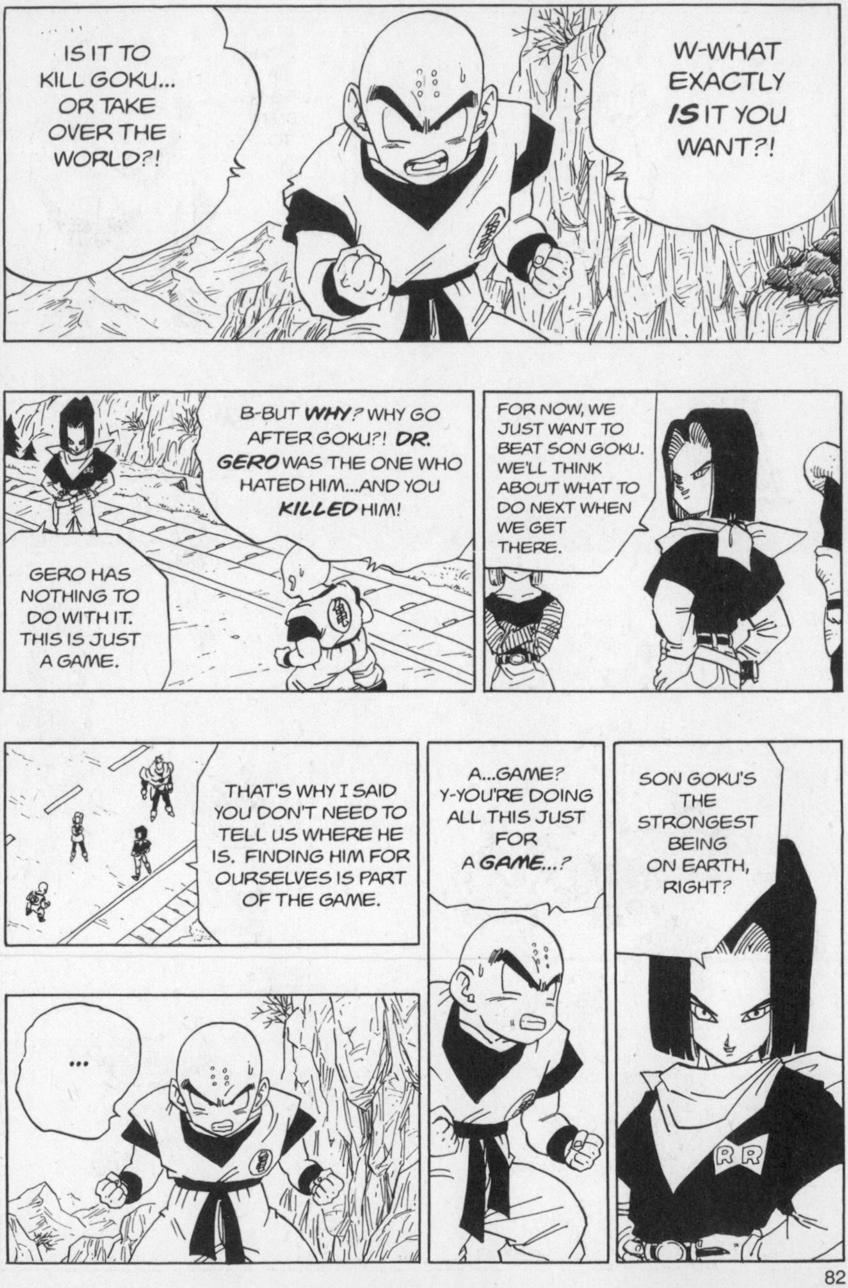
W-WHAT EXACTLY IS IT YOU WANT?!
IS IT TO KILL GOKU... OR TAKE OVER THE WORLD?!
FOR NOW, WE JUST WANT TO BEAT SON GOKU. WE'LL THINK ABOUT WHAT TO DO NEXT WHEN WE GET THERE.
B-BUT WHY? WHY GO AFTER GOKU?! DR. GERO WAS THE ONE WHO HATED HIM...AND YOU KILLED HIM!
GERO HAS NOTHING TO DO WITH IT. THIS IS JUST A GAME.
SON GOKU'S THE STRONGEST BEING ON EARTH, RIGHT?
A...GAME? Y-YOU'RE DOING ALL THIS JUST FOR A GAME...?
THAT'S WHY I SAID YOU DON'T NEED TO TELL US WHERE HE IS. FINDING HIM FOR OURSELVES IS PART OF THE GAME.
...

READ THIS WAY

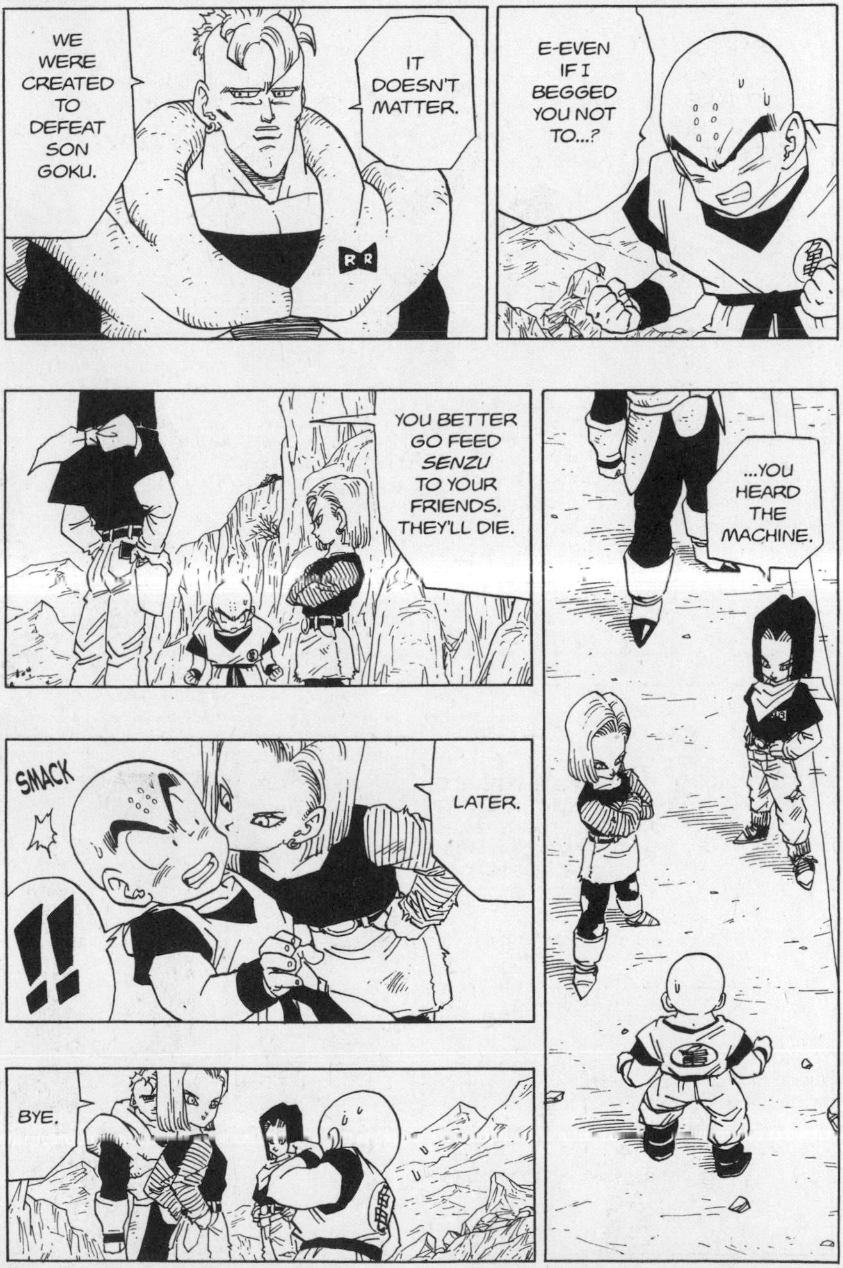
E-EVEN IF I BEGGED YOU NOT TO...?
IT DOESN'T MATTER.
WE WERE CREATED TO DEFEAT SON GOKU.
...YOU HEARD THE MACHINE.
YOU BETTER GO FEED *SENZU* TO YOUR FRIENDS. THEY'LL DIE.
LATER.
SMACK
!!
BYE.

READ THIS WAY

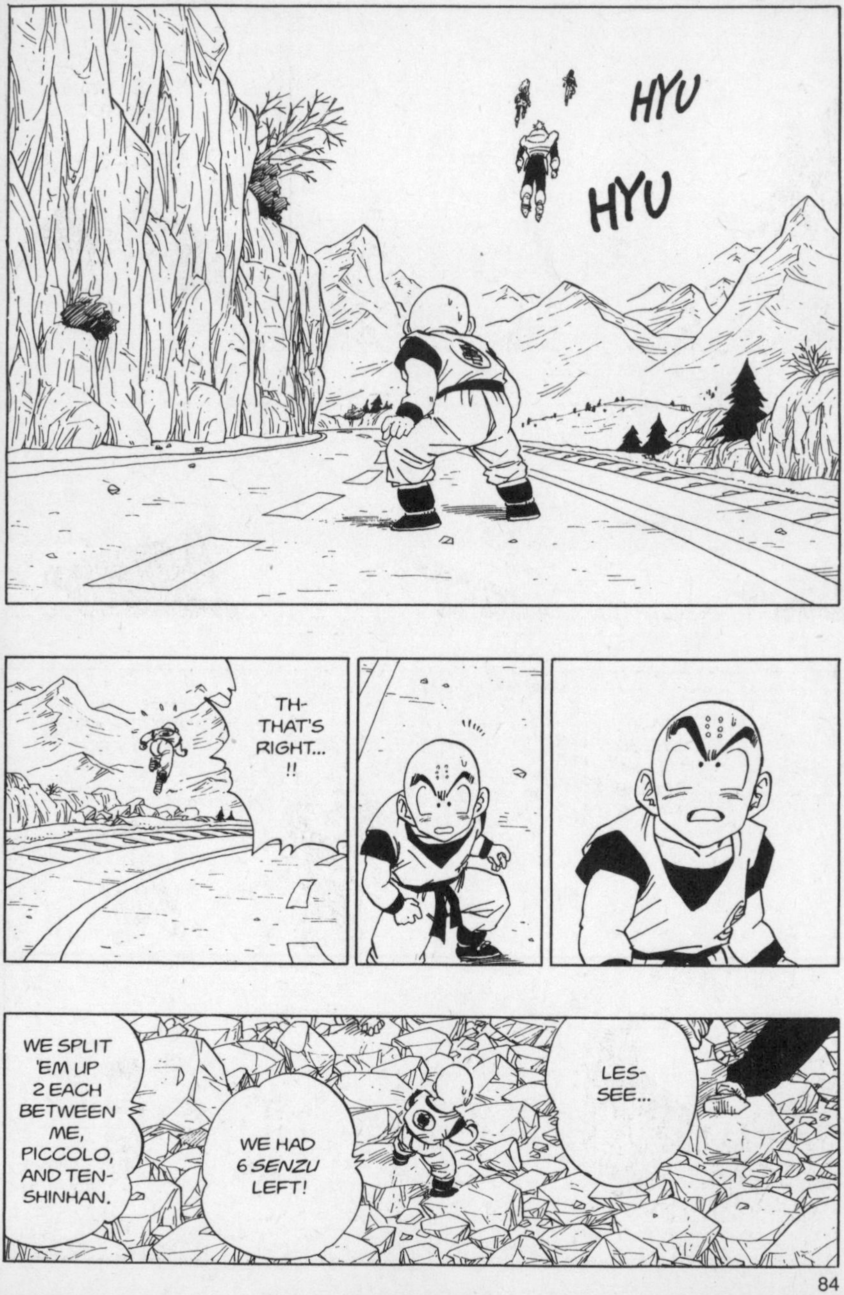

HYU
HYU
TH-THAT'S RIGHT...!!
LES-SEE...
WE HAD 6 SENZU LEFT!
WE SPLIT 'EM UP 2 EACH BETWEEN ME, PICCOLO, AND TEN-SHINHAN.

READ THIS WAY

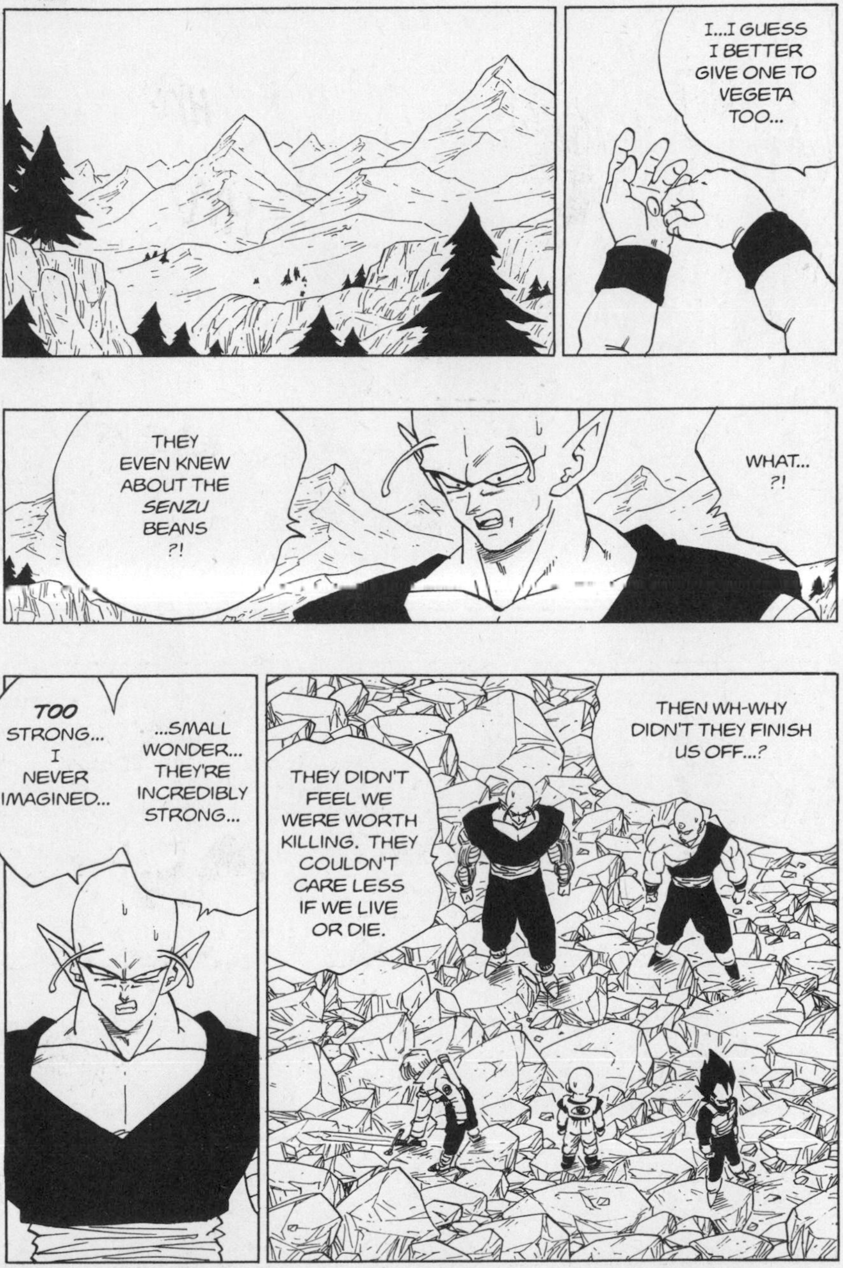
I...I GUESS I BETTER GIVE ONE TO VEGETA TOO...
WHAT...?!
THEY EVEN KNEW ABOUT THE *SENZU* BEANS?!
THEN WH-WHY DIDN'T THEY FINISH US OFF...?
THEY DIDN'T FEEL WE WERE WORTH KILLING. THEY COULDN'T CARE LESS IF WE LIVE OR DIE.
...SMALL WONDER... THEY'RE INCREDIBLY STRONG...
TOO STRONG... I NEVER IMAGINED...

READ THIS WAY

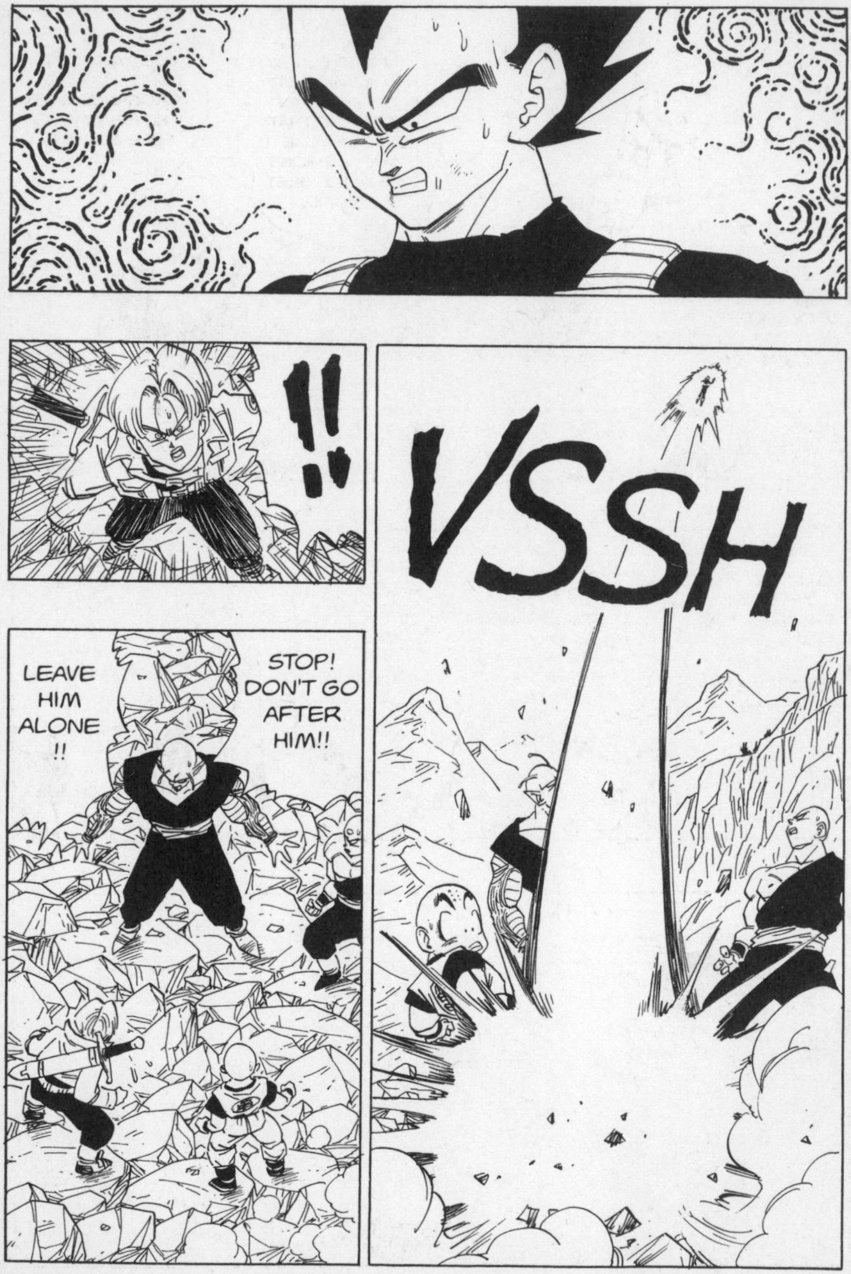
VSSH
!!
STOP! DON'T GO AFTER HIM!!
LEAVE HIM ALONE !!

READ THIS WAY

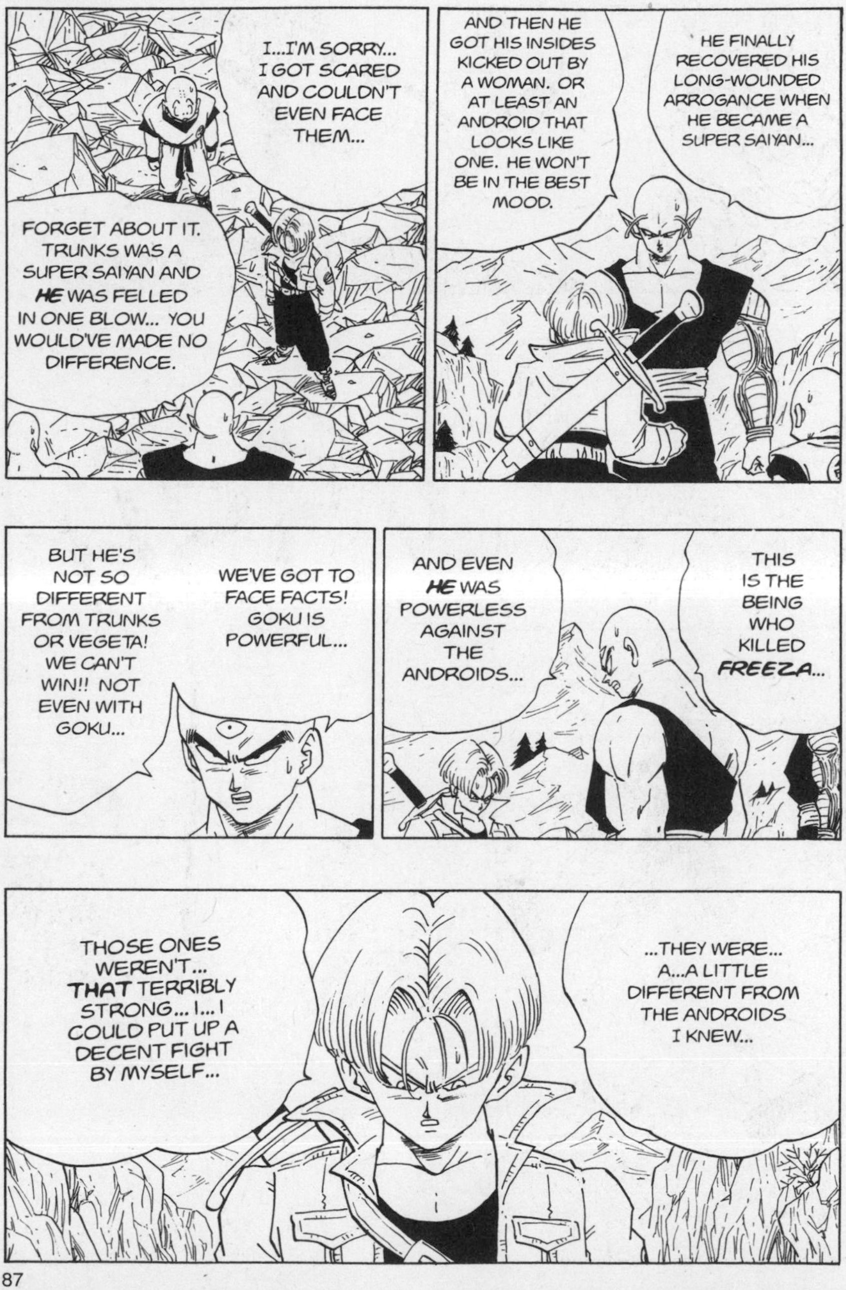
HE FINALLY RECOVERED HIS LONG-WOUNDED ARROGANCE WHEN HE BECAME A SUPER SAIYAN...
AND THEN HE GOT HIS INSIDES KICKED OUT BY A WOMAN. OR AT LEAST AN ANDROID THAT LOOKS LIKE ONE. HE WON'T BE IN THE BEST MOOD.
I...I'M SORRY... I GOT SCARED AND COULDN'T EVEN FACE THEM...
FORGET ABOUT IT. TRUNKS WAS A SUPER SAIYAN AND *HE* WAS FELLED IN ONE BLOW... YOU WOULD'VE MADE NO DIFFERENCE.
THIS IS THE BEING WHO KILLED *FREEZA*...
AND EVEN *HE* WAS POWERLESS AGAINST THE ANDROIDS...
WE'VE GOT TO FACE FACTS! GOKU IS POWERFUL...
BUT HE'S NOT SO DIFFERENT FROM TRUNKS OR VEGETA! WE CAN'T WIN!! NOT EVEN WITH GOKU...
...THEY WERE... A...A LITTLE DIFFERENT FROM THE ANDROIDS I KNEW...
THOSE ONES WEREN'T... **THAT** TERRIBLY STRONG... I...I COULD PUT UP A DECENT FIGHT BY MYSELF...

READ THIS WAY

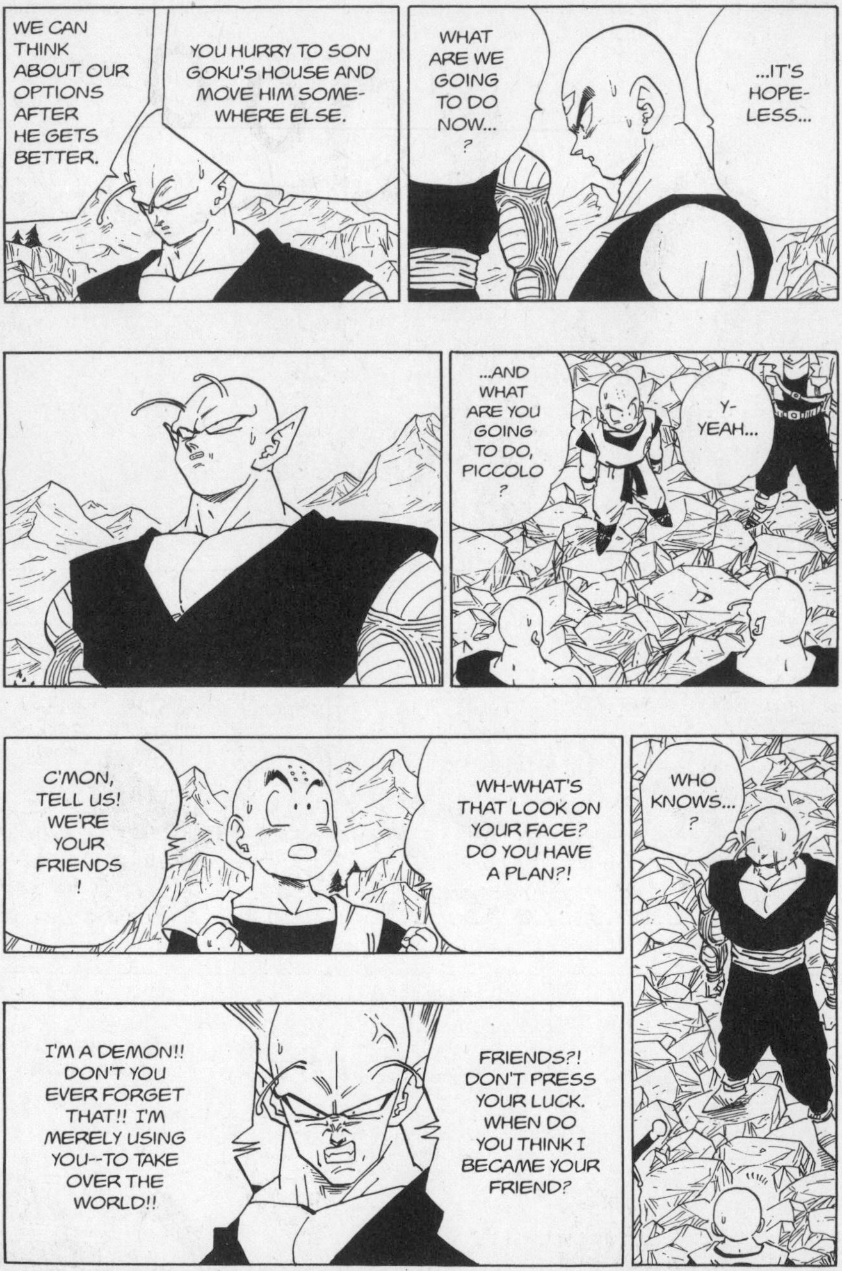
WHAT ARE WE GOING TO DO NOW...?
...IT'S HOPELESS...
YOU HURRY TO SON GOKU'S HOUSE AND MOVE HIM SOME-WHERE ELSE.
WE CAN THINK ABOUT OUR OPTIONS AFTER HE GETS BETTER.
Y-YEAH...
...AND WHAT ARE YOU GOING TO DO, PICCOLO?
WHO KNOWS...?
WH-WHAT'S THAT LOOK ON YOUR FACE? DO YOU HAVE A PLAN?!
C'MON, TELL US! WE'RE YOUR FRIENDS!
FRIENDS?! DON'T PRESS YOUR LUCK. WHEN DO YOU THINK I BECAME YOUR FRIEND?
I'M A DEMON!! DON'T YOU EVER FORGET THAT!! I'M MERELY USING YOU--TO TAKE OVER THE WORLD!!

READ THIS WAY

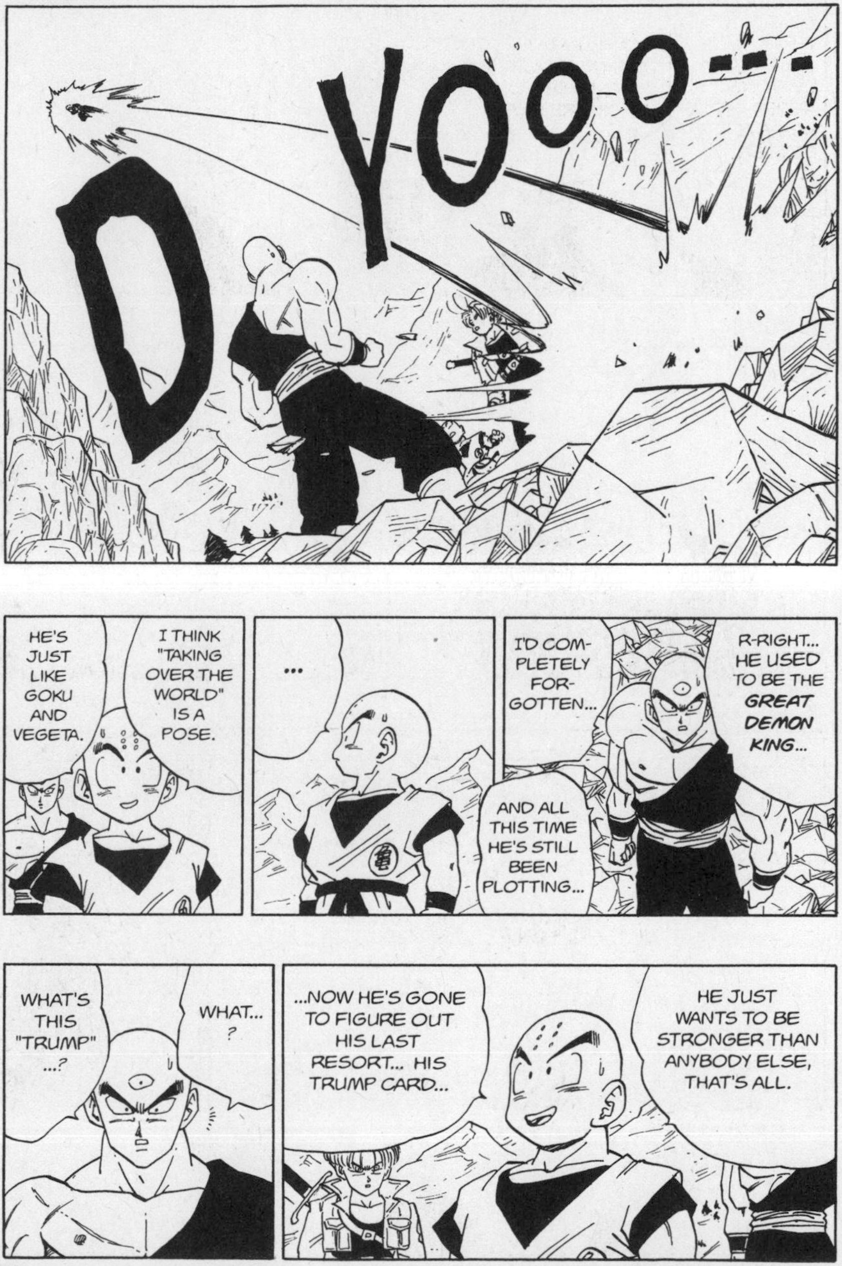

DYOOO...
R-RIGHT... HE USED TO BE THE GREAT DEMON KING...
I'D COMPLETELY FORGOTTEN...
AND ALL THIS TIME HE'S STILL BEEN PLOTTING...
...
I THINK "TAKING OVER THE WORLD" IS A POSE.
HE'S JUST LIKE GOKU AND VEGETA.
HE JUST WANTS TO BE STRONGER THAN ANYBODY ELSE, THAT'S ALL.
...NOW HE'S GONE TO FIGURE OUT HIS LAST RESORT... HIS TRUMP CARD...
WHAT... ?
WHAT'S THIS "TRUMP" ...?

READ THIS WAY

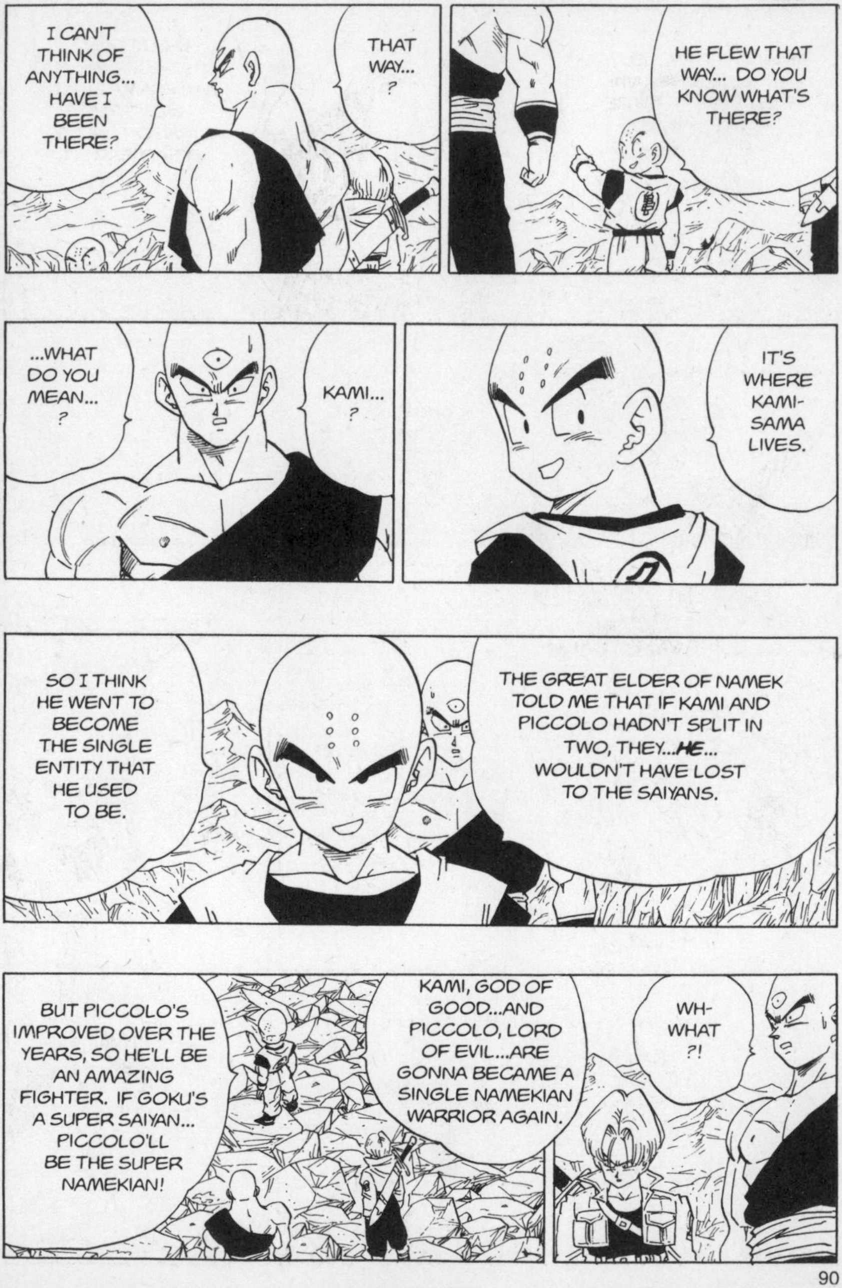

HE FLEW THAT WAY... DO YOU KNOW WHAT'S THERE?
THAT WAY... ?
I CAN'T THINK OF ANYTHING... HAVE I BEEN THERE?
IT'S WHERE KAMI-SAMA LIVES.
KAMI... ?
...WHAT DO YOU MEAN... ?
THE GREAT ELDER OF NAMEK TOLD ME THAT IF KAMI AND PICCOLO HADN'T SPLIT IN TWO, THEY...**HE**... WOULDN'T HAVE LOST TO THE SAIYANS.
SO I THINK HE WENT TO BECOME THE SINGLE ENTITY THAT HE USED TO BE.
WH-WHAT ?!
KAMI, GOD OF GOOD...AND PICCOLO, LORD OF EVIL...ARE GONNA BECAME A SINGLE NAMEKIAN WARRIOR AGAIN.
BUT PICCOLO'S IMPROVED OVER THE YEARS, SO HE'LL BE AN AMAZING FIGHTER. IF GOKU'S A SUPER SAIYAN... PICCOLO'LL BE THE SUPER NAMEKIAN!

READ THIS WAY

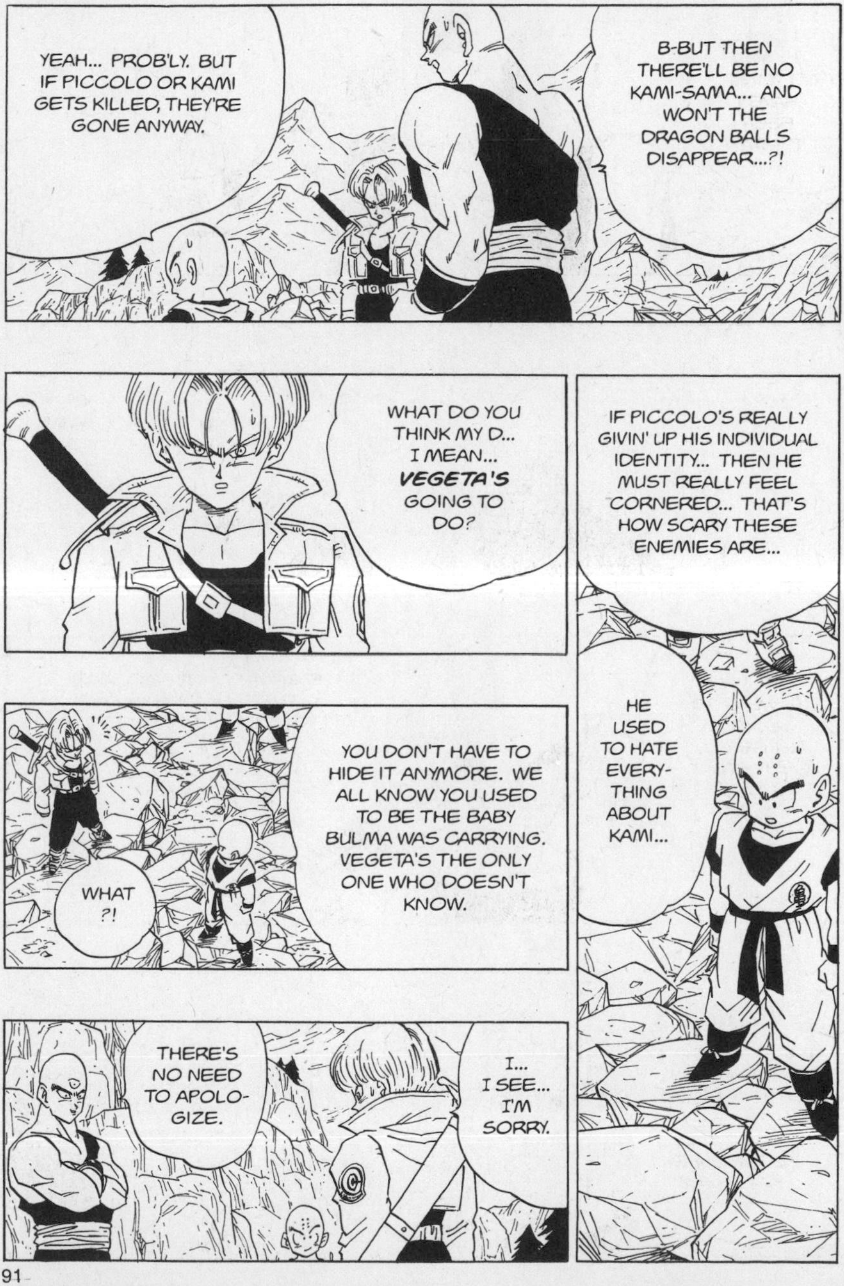

B-BUT THEN THERE'LL BE NO KAMI-SAMA... AND WON'T THE DRAGON BALLS DISAPPEAR...?!
YEAH... PROB'LY. BUT IF PICCOLO OR KAMI GETS KILLED, THEY'RE GONE ANYWAY.
IF PICCOLO'S REALLY GIVIN' UP HIS INDIVIDUAL IDENTITY... THEN HE MUST REALLY FEEL CORNERED... THAT'S HOW SCARY THESE ENEMIES ARE...
HE USED TO HATE EVERY-THING ABOUT KAMI...
WHAT DO YOU THINK MY D... I MEAN... VEGETA'S GOING TO DO?
YOU DON'T HAVE TO HIDE IT ANYMORE. WE ALL KNOW YOU USED TO BE THE BABY BULMA WAS CARRYING. VEGETA'S THE ONLY ONE WHO DOESN'T KNOW.
WHAT ?!
I... I SEE... I'M SORRY.
THERE'S NO NEED TO APOLO-GIZE.

READ THIS WAY

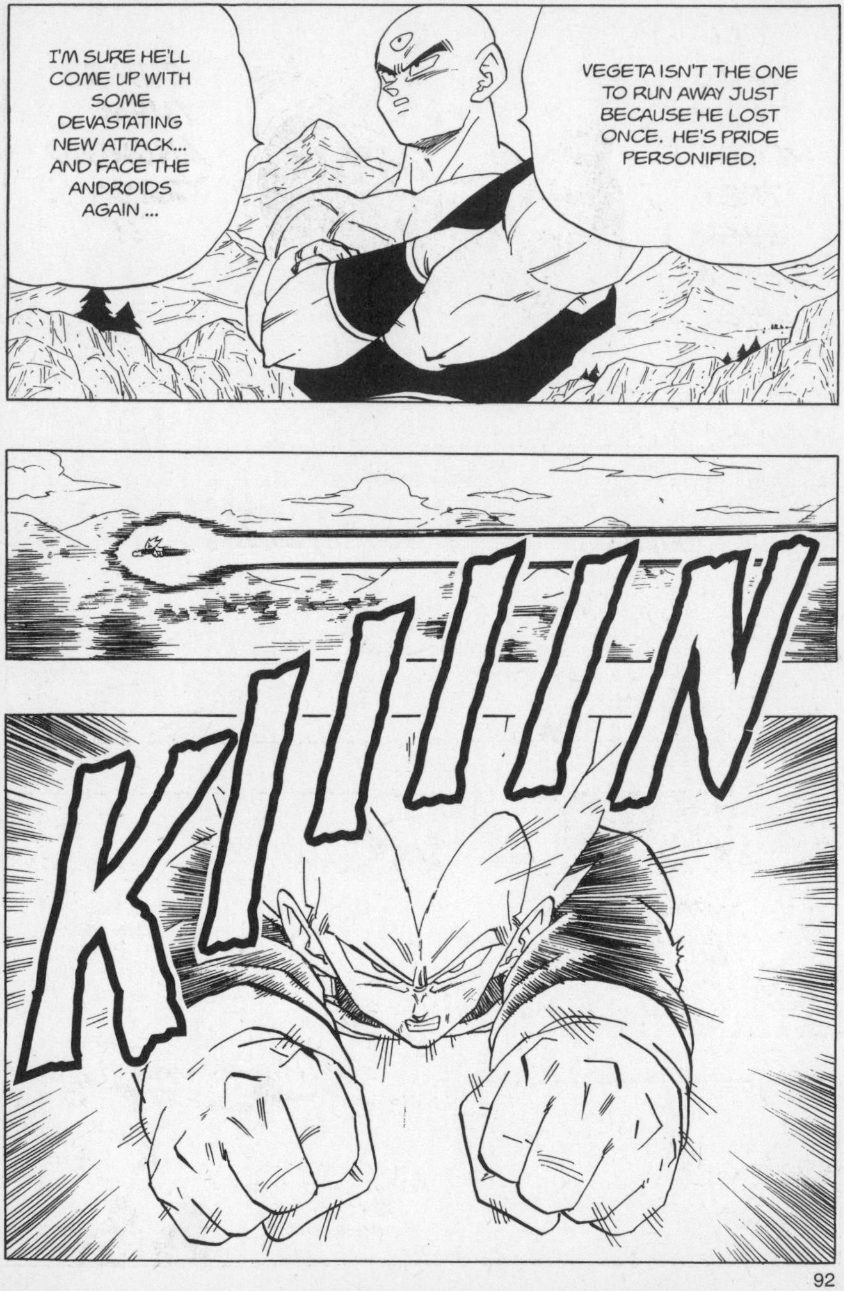
VEGETA ISN'T THE ONE TO RUN AWAY JUST BECAUSE HE LOST ONCE. HE'S PRIDE PERSONIFIED.
I'M SURE HE'LL COME UP WITH SOME DEVASTATING NEW ATTACK... AND FACE THE ANDROIDS AGAIN ...
KIIIIN

READ THIS WAY

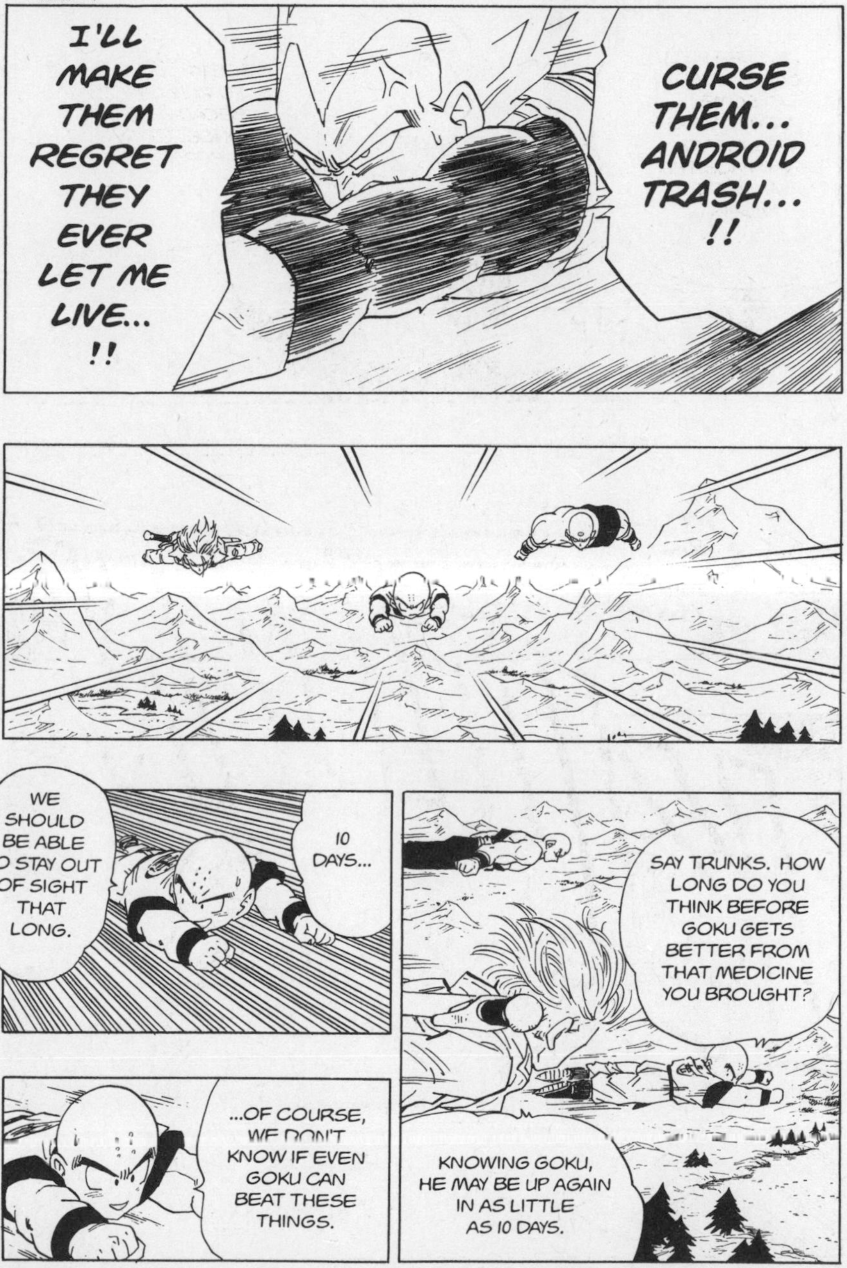
CURSE THEM... ANDROID TRASH... !!
I'LL MAKE THEM REGRET THEY EVER LET ME LIVE... !!
SAY TRUNKS. HOW LONG DO YOU THINK BEFORE GOKU GETS BETTER FROM THAT MEDICINE YOU BROUGHT?
KNOWING GOKU, HE MAY BE UP AGAIN IN AS LITTLE AS 10 DAYS.
10 DAYS...
WE SHOULD BE ABLE TO STAY OUT OF SIGHT THAT LONG.
...OF COURSE, WE DON'T KNOW IF EVEN GOKU CAN BEAT THESE THINGS.

READ THIS WAY

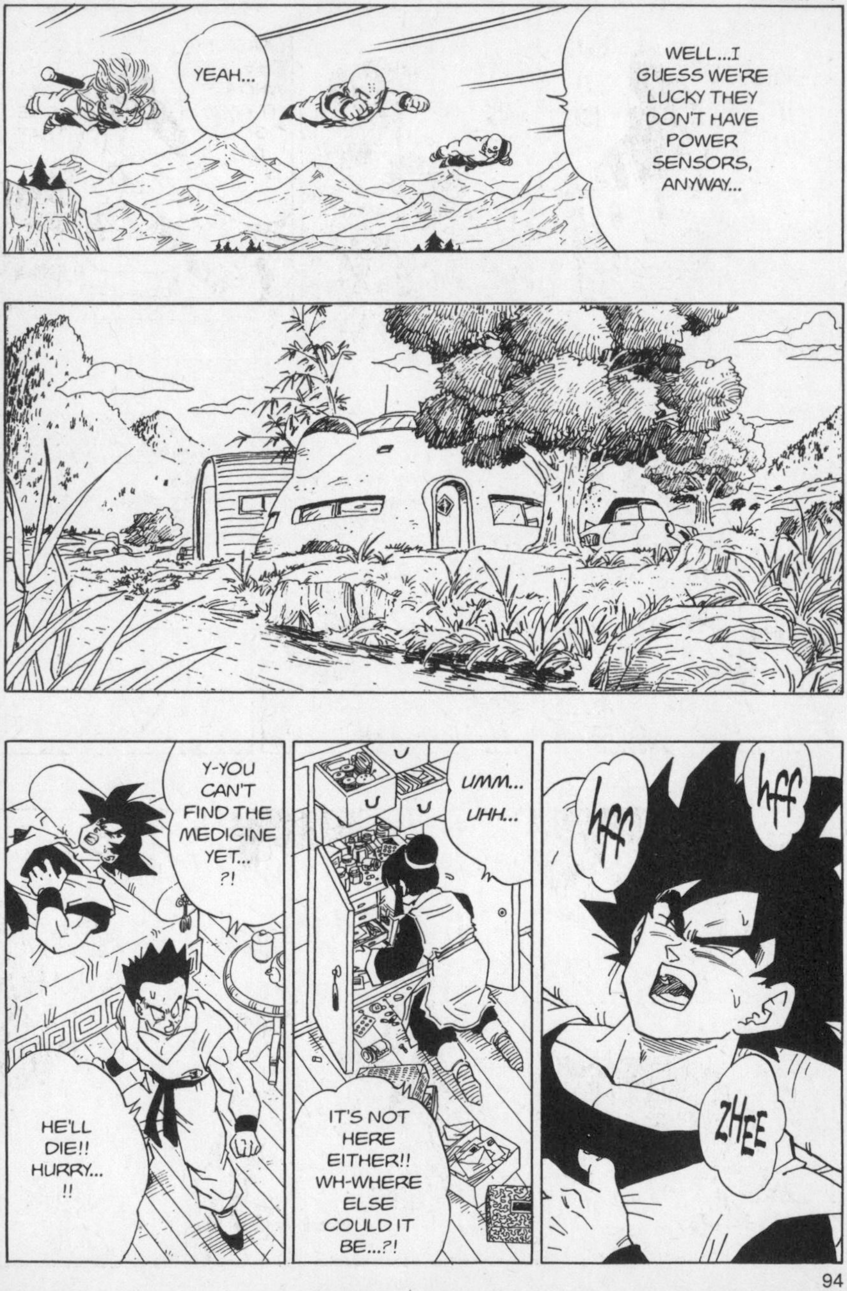

WELL...I GUESS WE'RE LUCKY THEY DON'T HAVE POWER SENSORS, ANYWAY...
YEAH...
hff
hff
ZHEE
UMM... UHH...
IT'S NOT HERE EITHER!! WH-WHERE ELSE COULD IT BE...?!
Y-YOU CAN'T FIND THE MEDICINE YET... ?!
HE'LL DIE!! HURRY... !!

READ THIS WAY

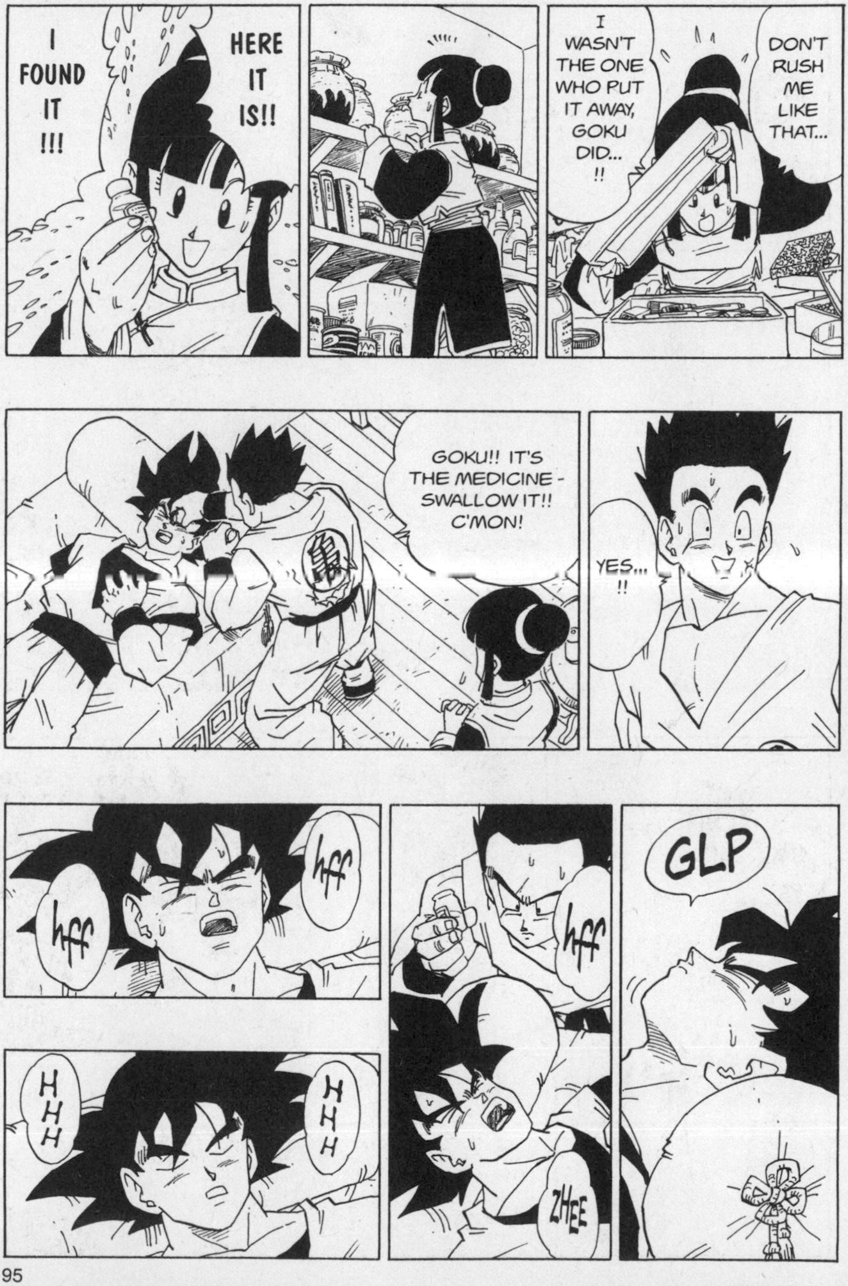

DON'T RUSH ME LIKE THAT...
I WASN'T THE ONE WHO PUT IT AWAY, GOKU DID... !!
HERE IT IS!!
I FOUND IT !!!
YES... !!
GOKU!! IT'S THE MEDICINE - SWALLOW IT!! C'MON!
GLP
hff
ZHEE
hff
hff
HHH
HHH

READ THIS WAY

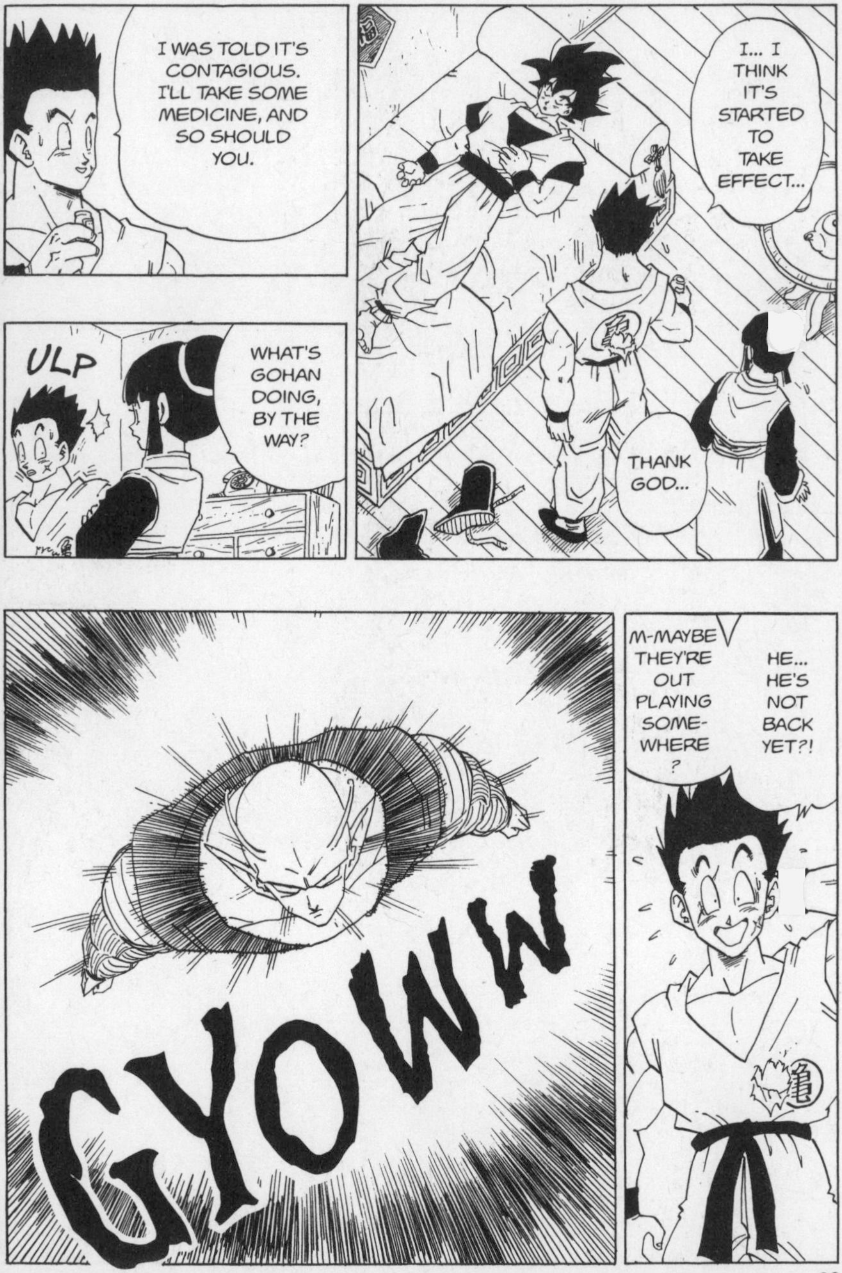
I... I THINK IT'S STARTED TO TAKE EFFECT...
THANK GOD...
I WAS TOLD IT'S CONTAGIOUS. I'LL TAKE SOME MEDICINE, AND SO SHOULD YOU.
ULP
WHAT'S GOHAN DOING, BY THE WAY?
HE... HE'S NOT BACK YET?!
M-MAYBE THEY'RE OUT PLAYING SOME-WHERE?
GYOWW

READ THIS WAY

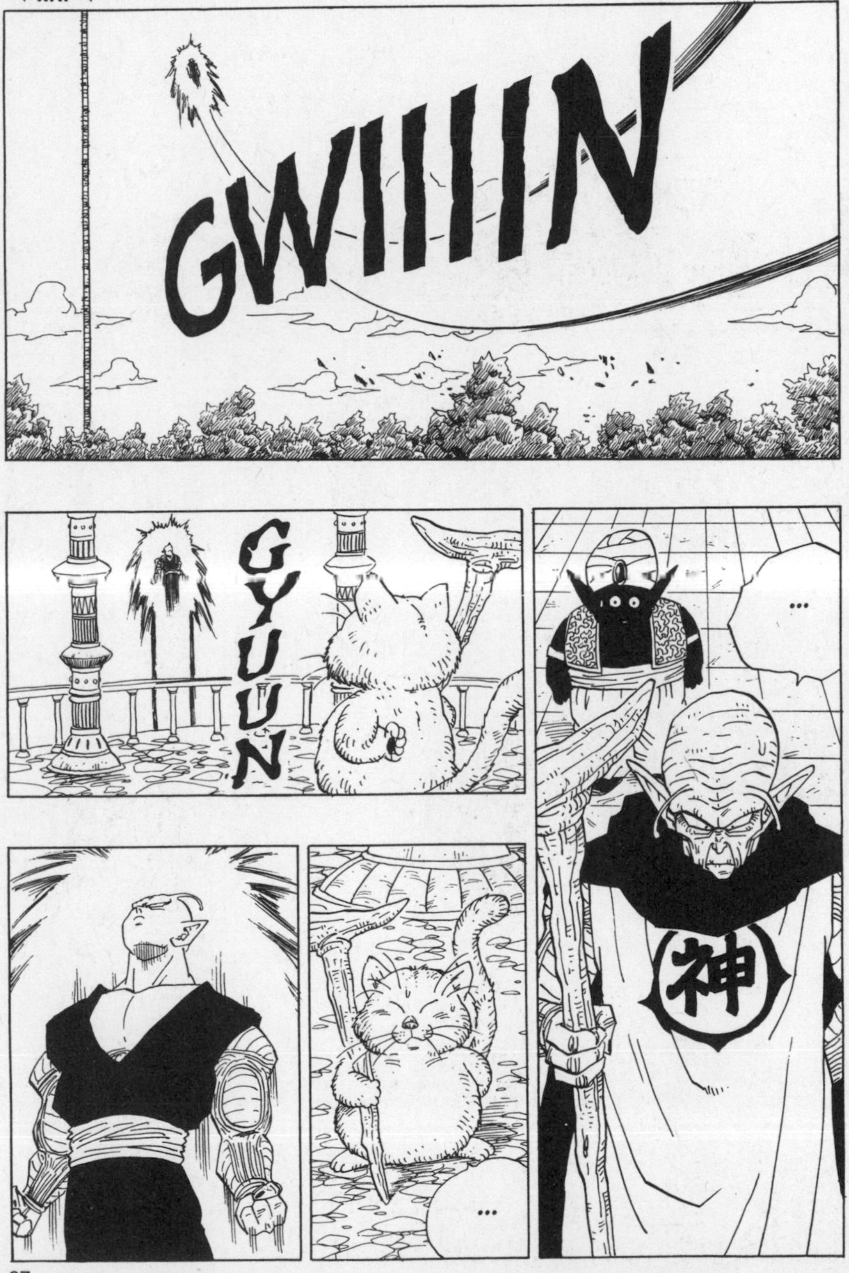
GWIIIN
...
GYUUN
...

READ THIS WAY

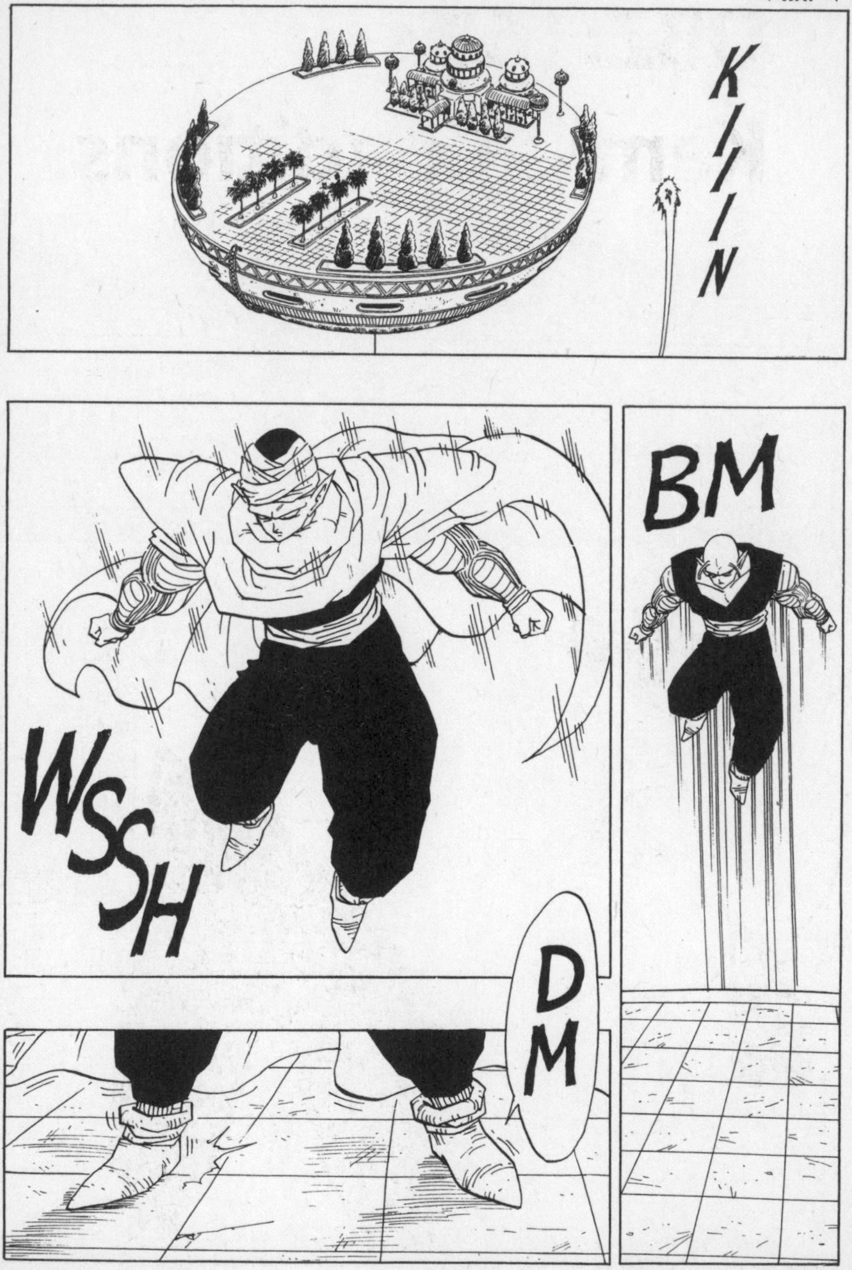

DBZ:162 • Kami's Conditions

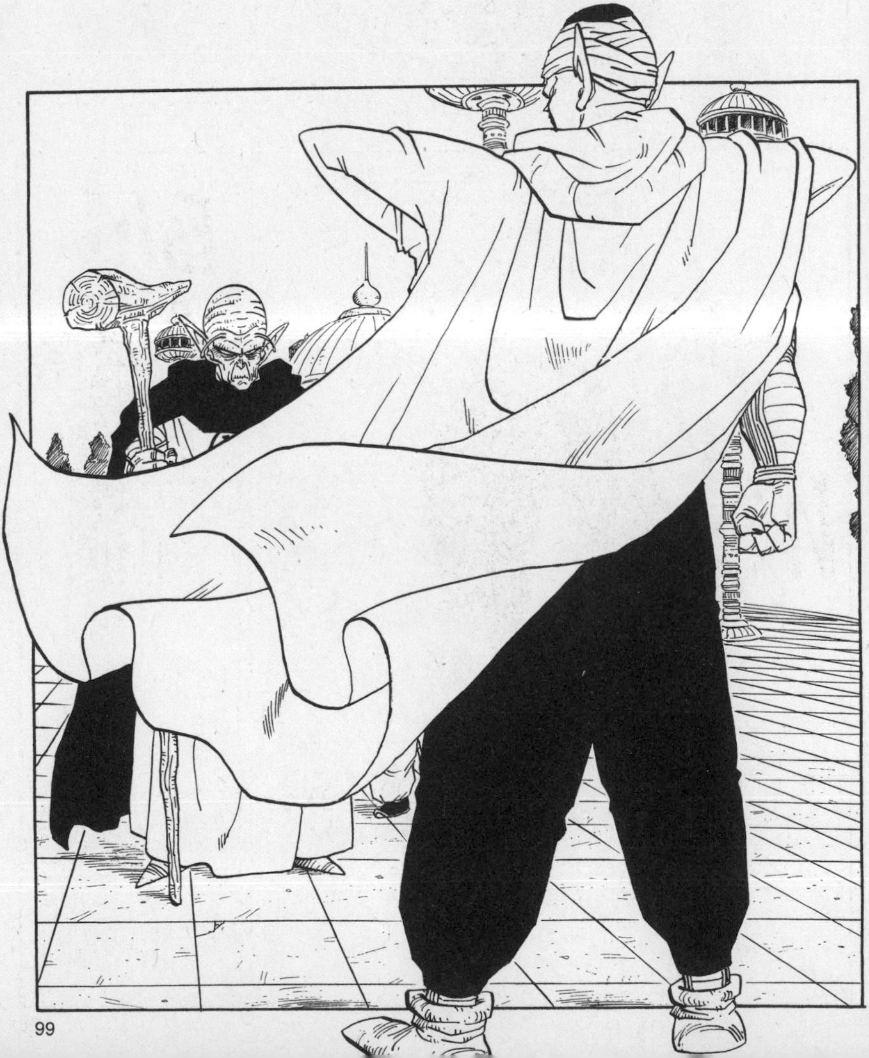

READ THIS WAY

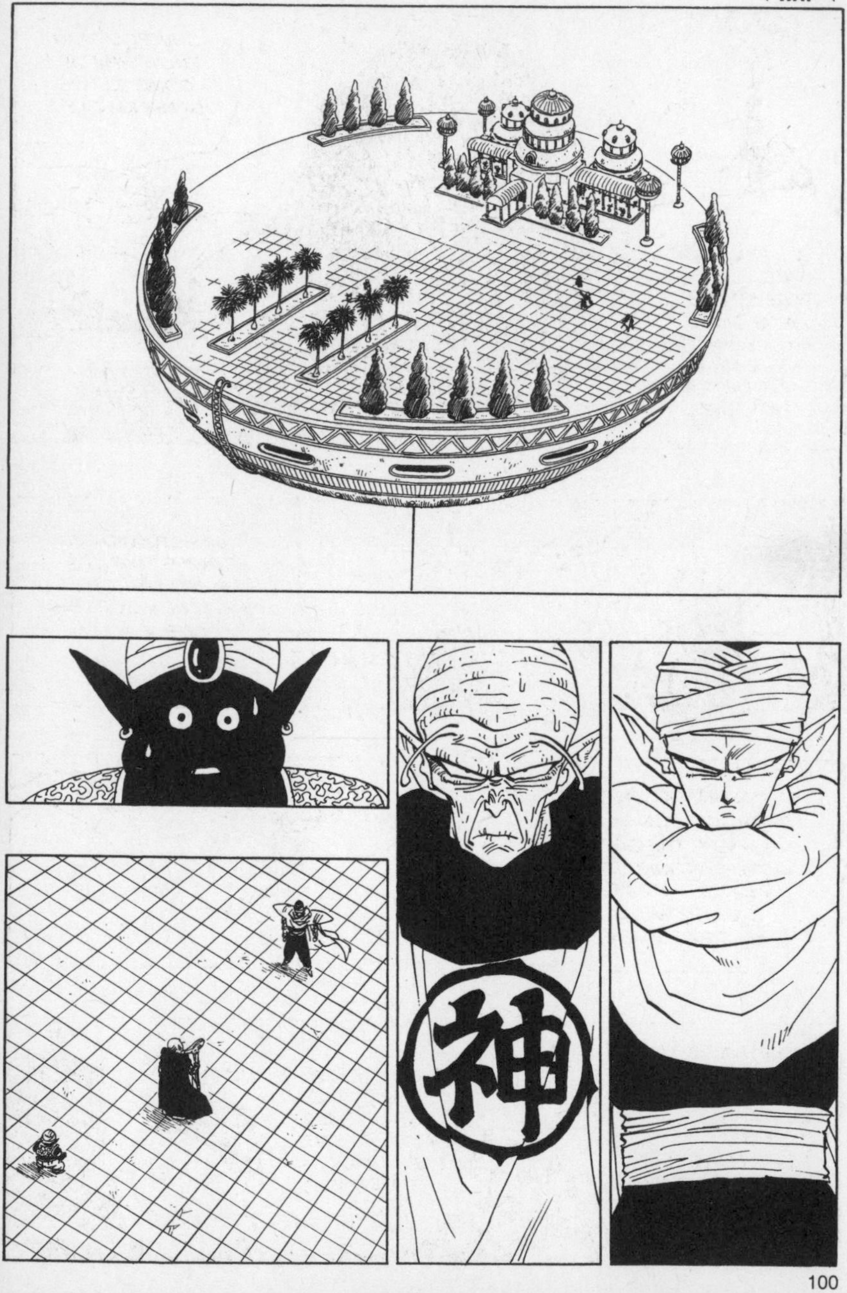
神

READ THIS WAY

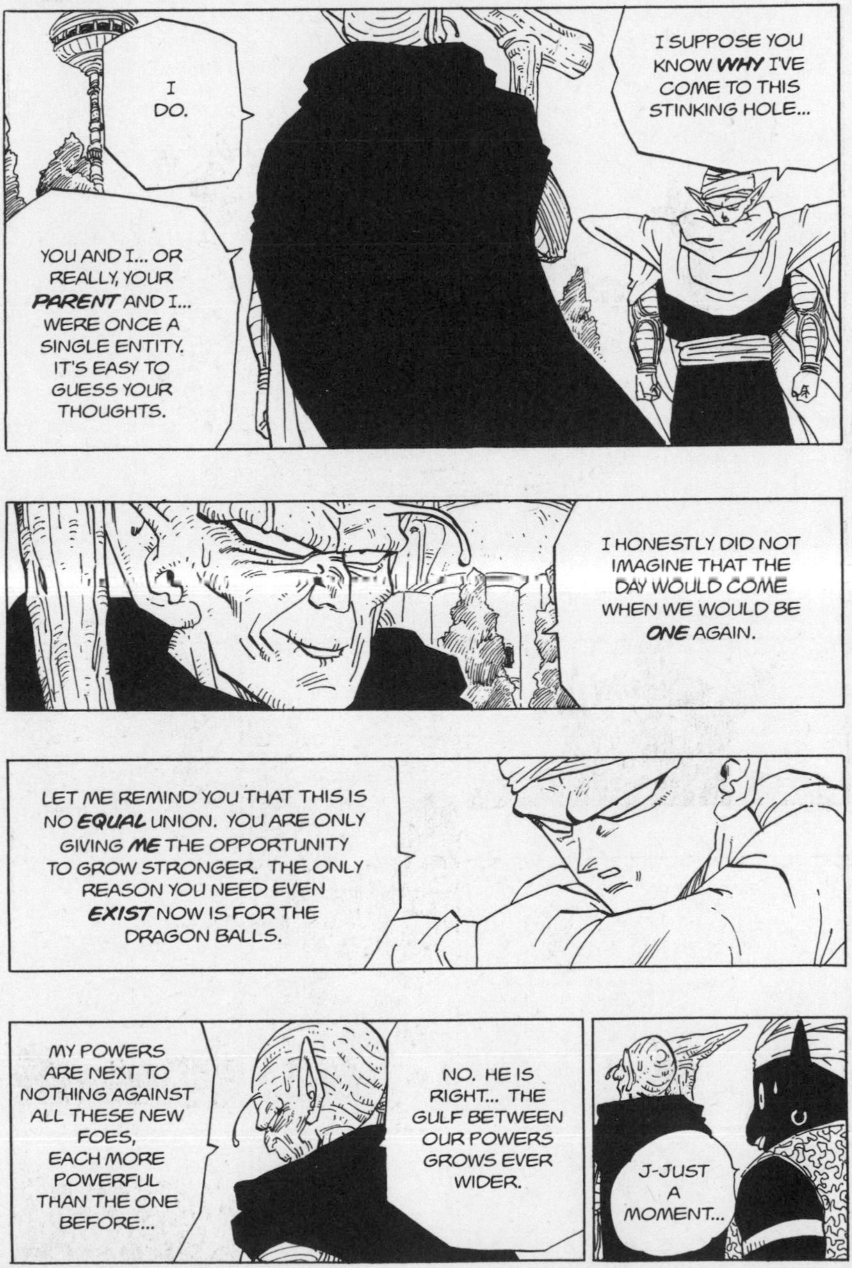
I SUPPOSE YOU KNOW WHY I'VE COME TO THIS STINKING HOLE...
I DO.
YOU AND I... OR REALLY, YOUR PARENT AND I... WERE ONCE A SINGLE ENTITY. IT'S EASY TO GUESS YOUR THOUGHTS.
I HONESTLY DID NOT IMAGINE THAT THE DAY WOULD COME WHEN WE WOULD BE ONE AGAIN.
LET ME REMIND YOU THAT THIS IS NO EQUAL UNION. YOU ARE ONLY GIVING ME THE OPPORTUNITY TO GROW STRONGER. THE ONLY REASON YOU NEED EVEN EXIST NOW IS FOR THE DRAGON BALLS.
J-JUST A MOMENT...
NO. HE IS RIGHT... THE GULF BETWEEN OUR POWERS GROWS EVER WIDER.
MY POWERS ARE NEXT TO NOTHING AGAINST ALL THESE NEW FOES, EACH MORE POWERFUL THAN THE ONE BEFORE...

READ THIS WAY

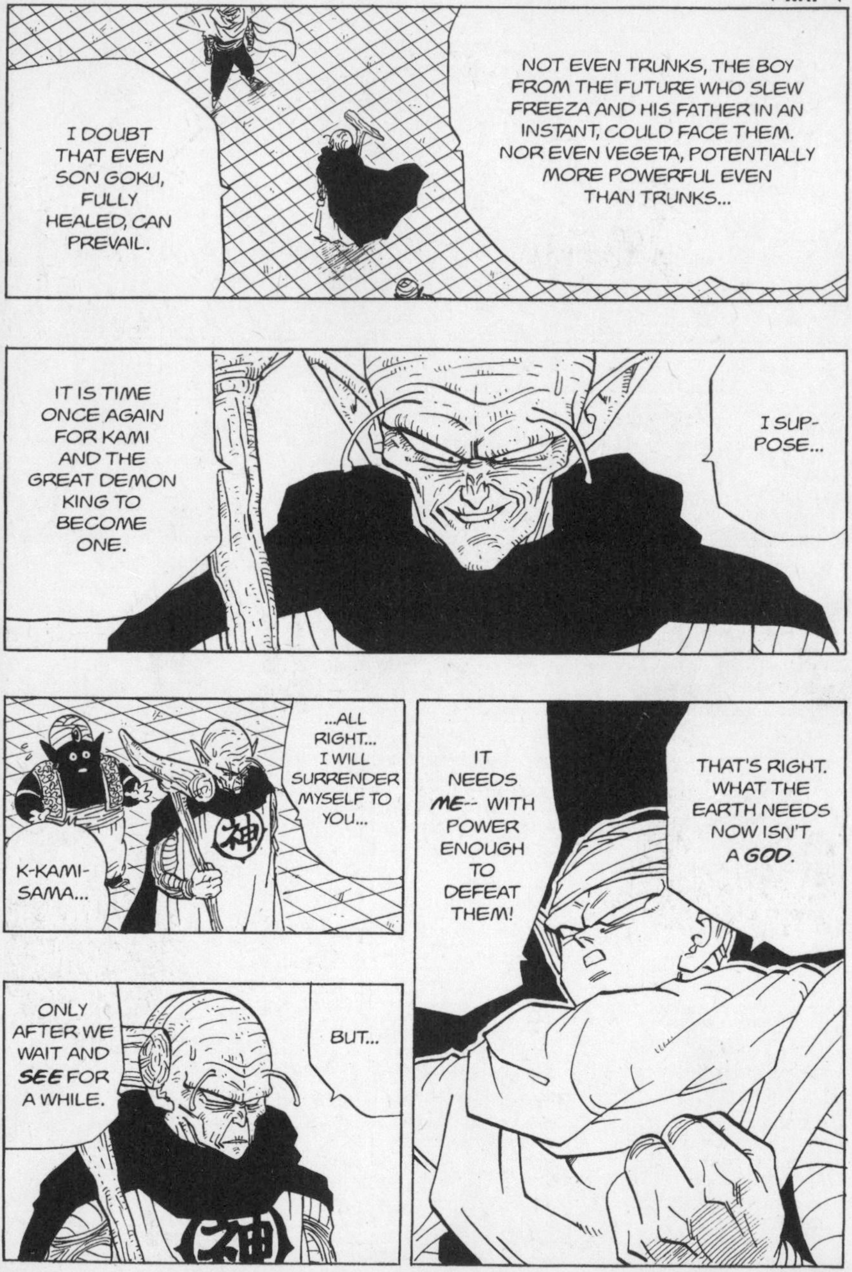

NOT EVEN TRUNKS, THE BOY FROM THE FUTURE WHO SLEW FREEZA AND HIS FATHER IN AN INSTANT, COULD FACE THEM. NOR EVEN VEGETA, POTENTIALLY MORE POWERFUL EVEN THAN TRUNKS...
I DOUBT THAT EVEN SON GOKU, FULLY HEALED, CAN PREVAIL.
I SUP-POSE...
IT IS TIME ONCE AGAIN FOR KAMI AND THE GREAT DEMON KING TO BECOME ONE.
THAT'S RIGHT. WHAT THE EARTH NEEDS NOW ISN'T A **GOD**.
IT NEEDS **ME**-- WITH POWER ENOUGH TO DEFEAT THEM!
...ALL RIGHT... I WILL SURRENDER MYSELF TO YOU...
K-KAMI-SAMA...
BUT...
ONLY AFTER WE WAIT AND **SEE** FOR A WHILE.

READ THIS WAY

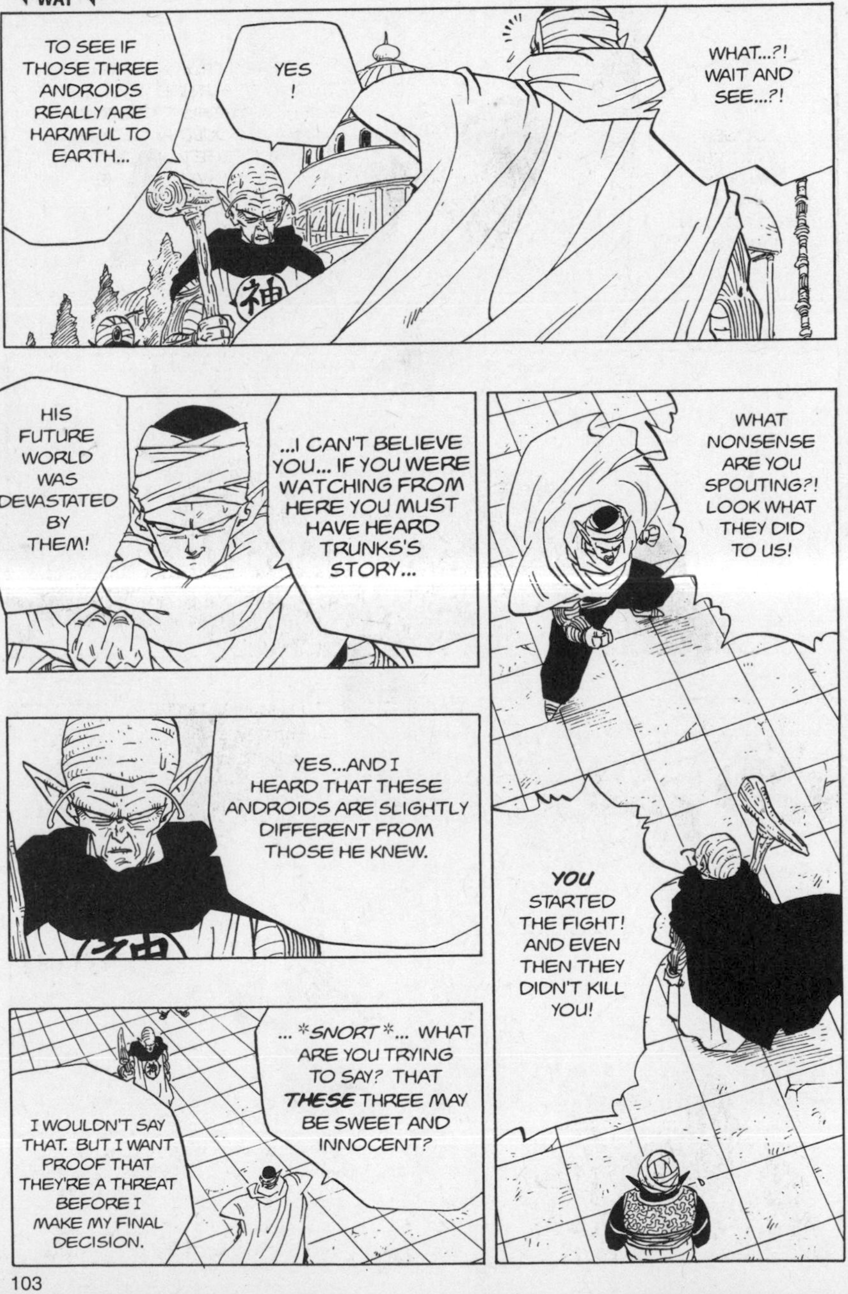

WHAT...?! WAIT AND SEE...?!
YES !
TO SEE IF THOSE THREE ANDROIDS REALLY ARE HARMFUL TO EARTH...
WHAT NONSENSE ARE YOU SPOUTING?! LOOK WHAT THEY DID TO US!
YOU STARTED THE FIGHT! AND EVEN THEN THEY DIDN'T KILL YOU!
...I CAN'T BELIEVE YOU... IF YOU WERE WATCHING FROM HERE YOU MUST HAVE HEARD TRUNKS'S STORY...
HIS FUTURE WORLD WAS DEVASTATED BY THEM!
YES...AND I HEARD THAT THESE ANDROIDS ARE SLIGHTLY DIFFERENT FROM THOSE HE KNEW.
... *SNORT*... WHAT ARE YOU TRYING TO SAY? THAT THESE THREE MAY BE SWEET AND INNOCENT?
I WOULDN'T SAY THAT. BUT I WANT PROOF THAT THEY'RE A THREAT BEFORE I MAKE MY FINAL DECISION.

READ THIS WAY

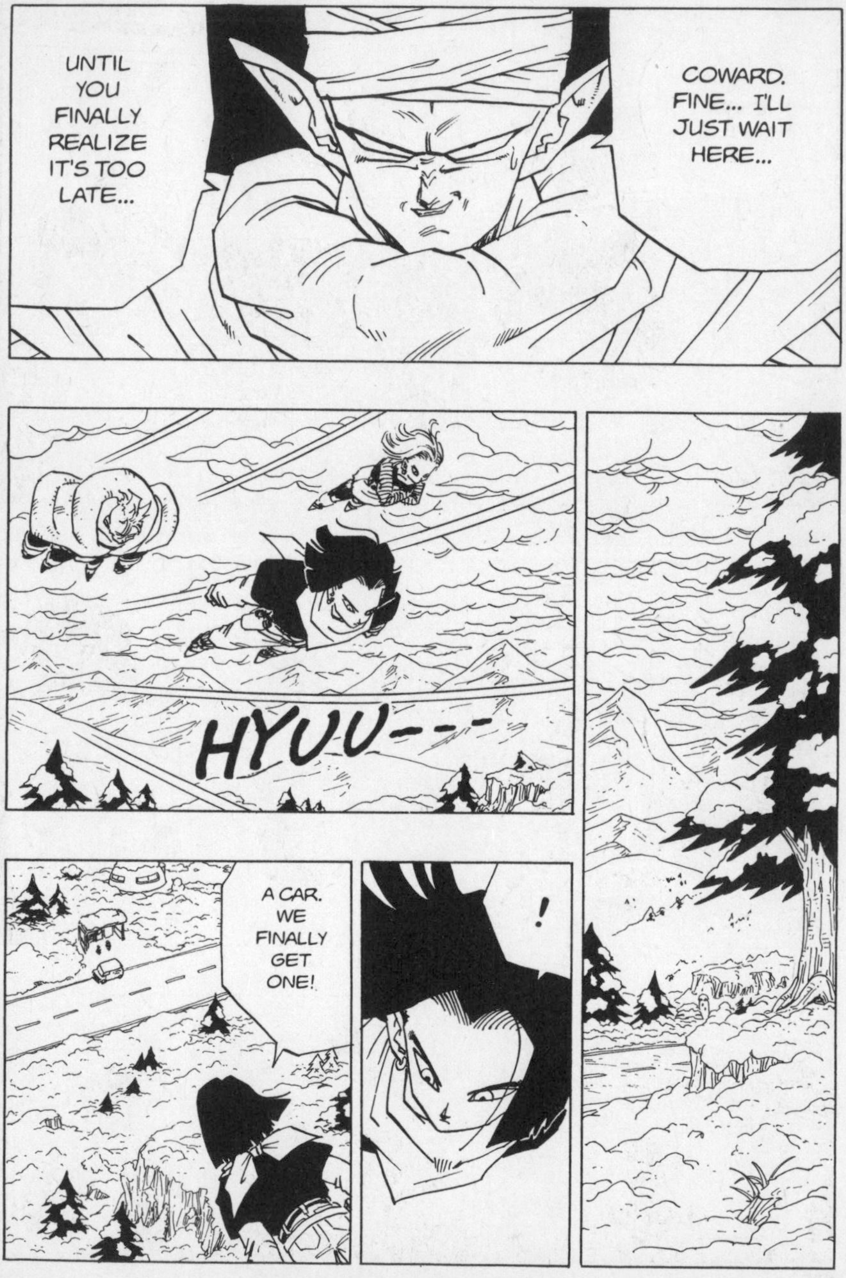

COWARD. FINE... I'LL JUST WAIT HERE...
UNTIL YOU FINALLY REALIZE IT'S TOO LATE...
HYUU---
!
A CAR. WE FINALLY GET ONE!

READ THIS WAY

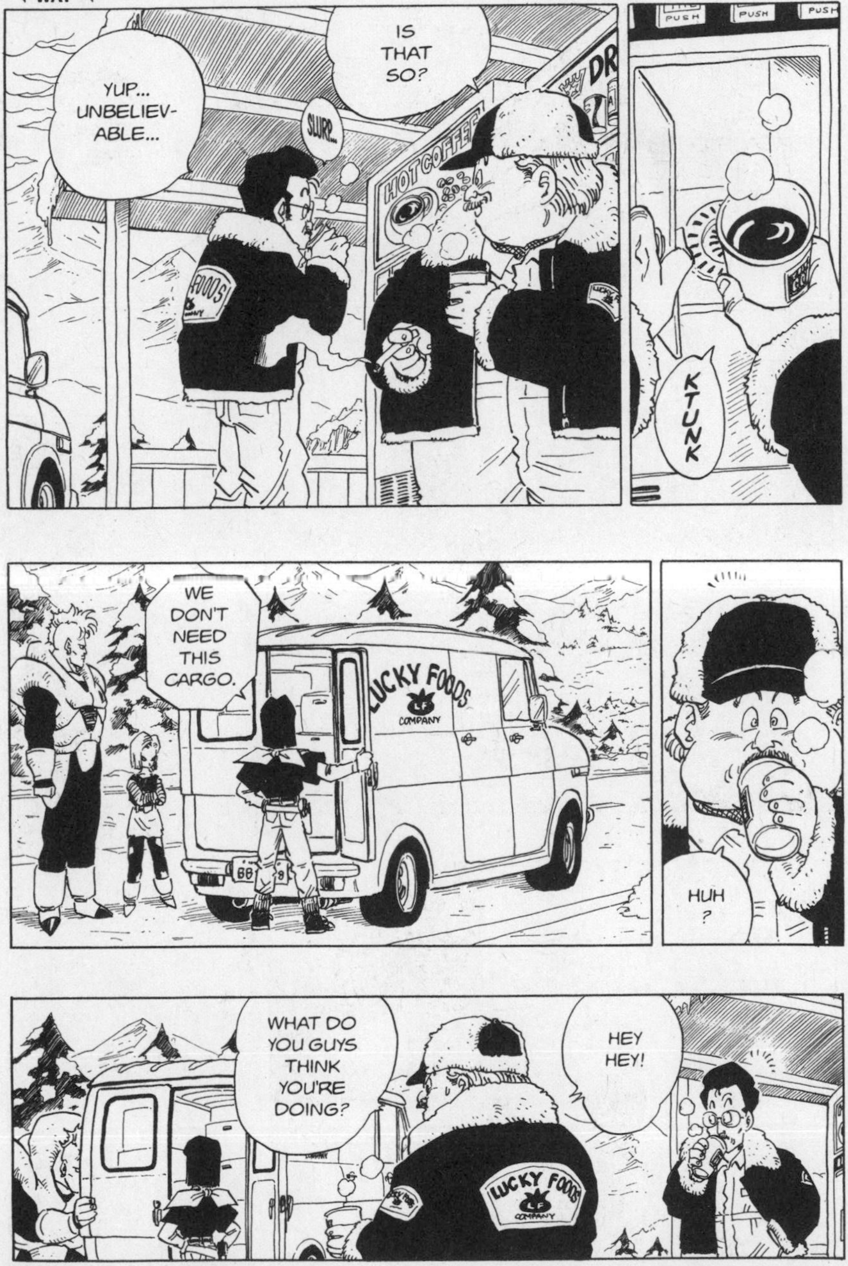
KTUNK
IS THAT SO?
YUP... UNBELIEVABLE...
SLURP...
HUH ?
WE DON'T NEED THIS CARGO.
HEY HEY!
WHAT DO YOU GUYS THINK YOU'RE DOING?

READ THIS WAY

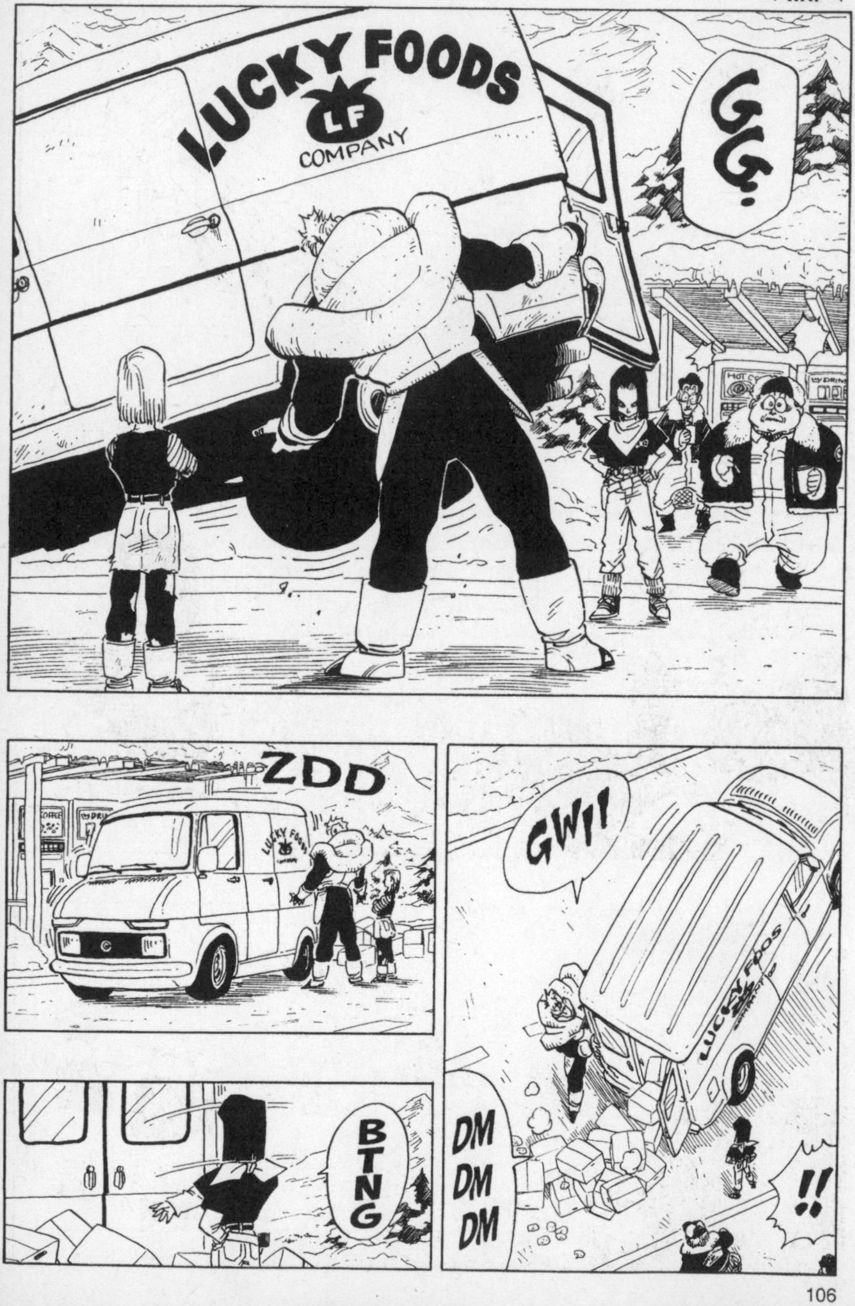
LUCKY FOODS
LF
COMPANY
GG
GWII
DM
DM
DM
!!
ZDD
BTNG

READ THIS WAY

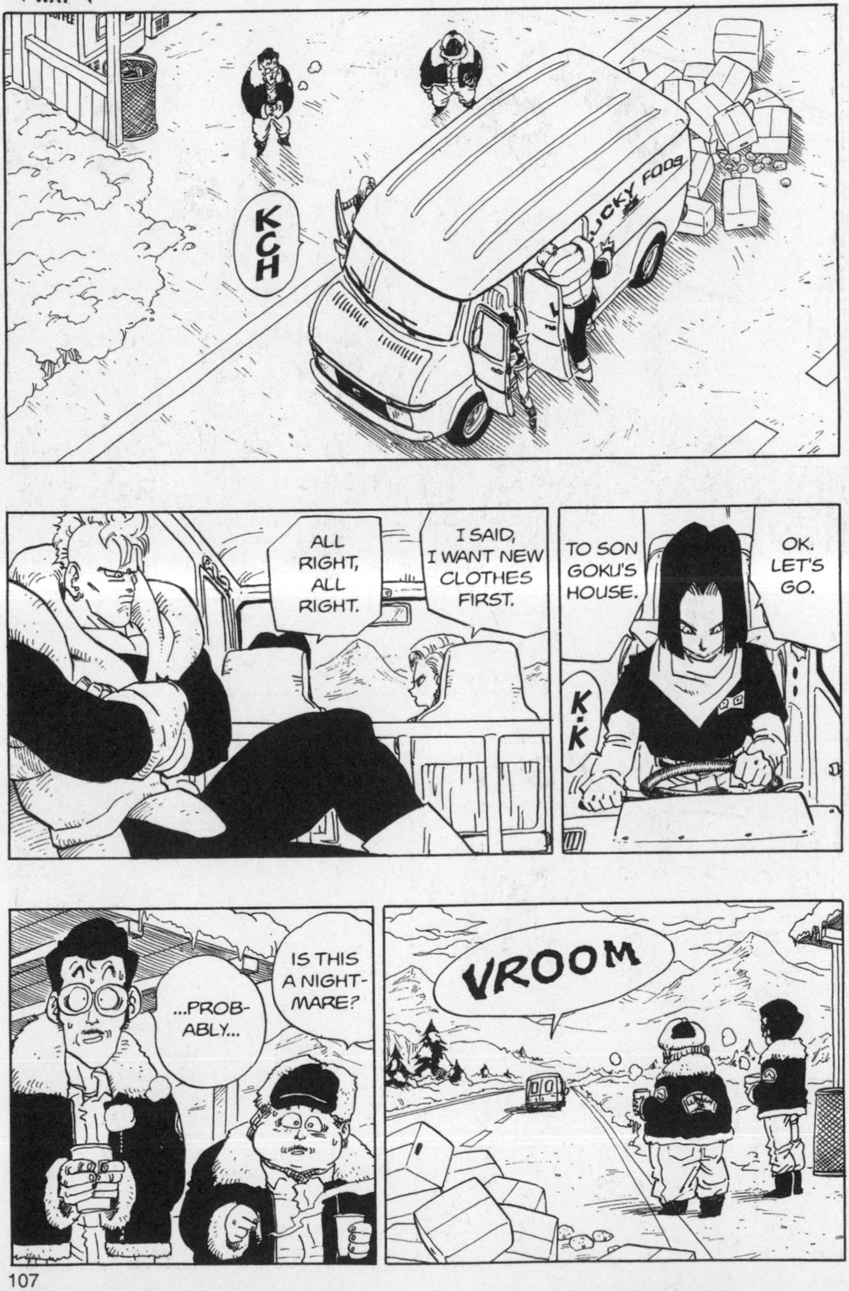

KCH
OK. LET'S GO.
TO SON GOKU'S HOUSE.
K-K
I SAID, I WANT NEW CLOTHES FIRST.
ALL RIGHT, ALL RIGHT.
VROOM
IS THIS A NIGHTMARE?
...PROBABLY...

READ THIS WAY

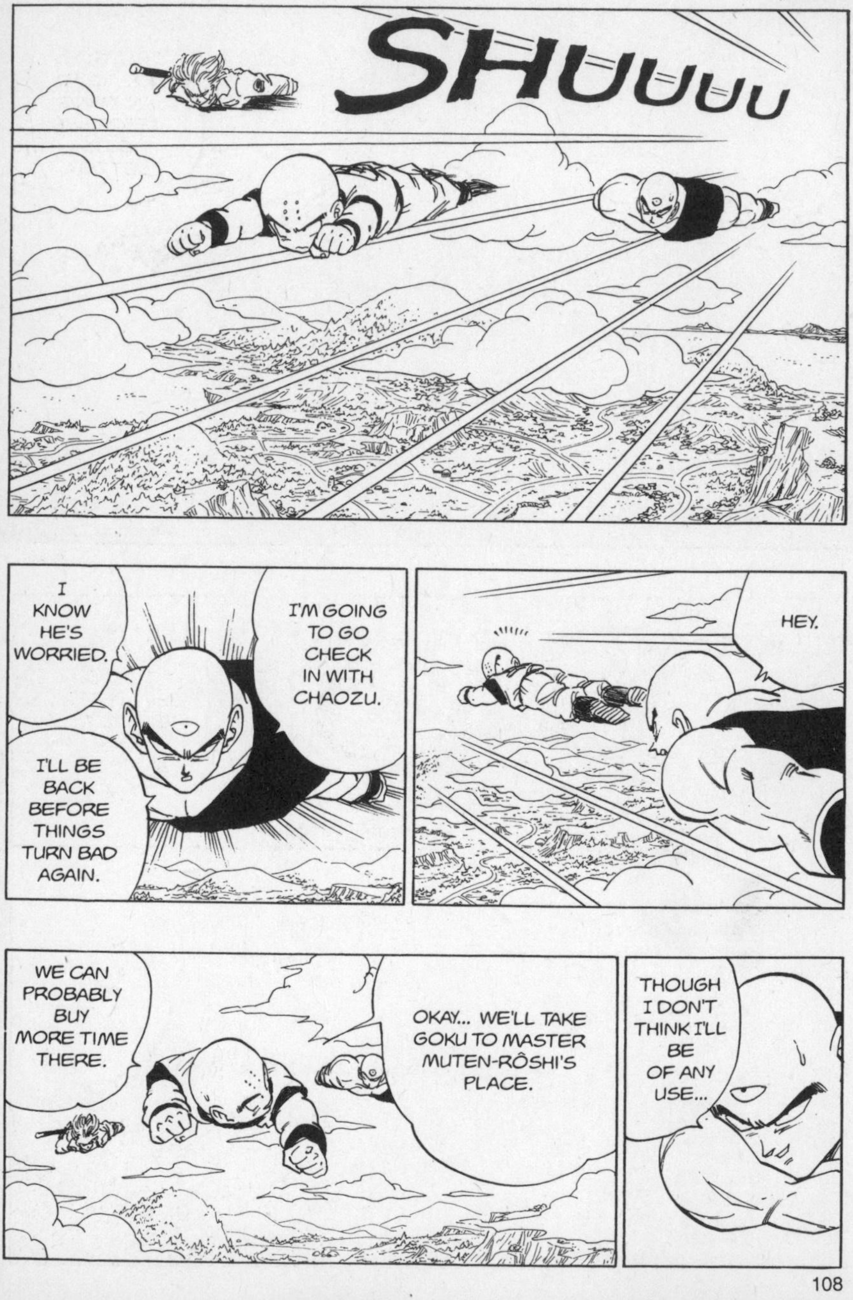

SHUUUUU
HEY.
I'M GOING TO GO CHECK IN WITH CHAOZU.
I KNOW HE'S WORRIED.
I'LL BE BACK BEFORE THINGS TURN BAD AGAIN.
THOUGH I DON'T THINK I'LL BE OF ANY USE...
OKAY... WE'LL TAKE GOKU TO MASTER MUTEN-RÔSHI'S PLACE.
WE CAN PROBABLY BUY MORE TIME THERE.

READ THIS WAY

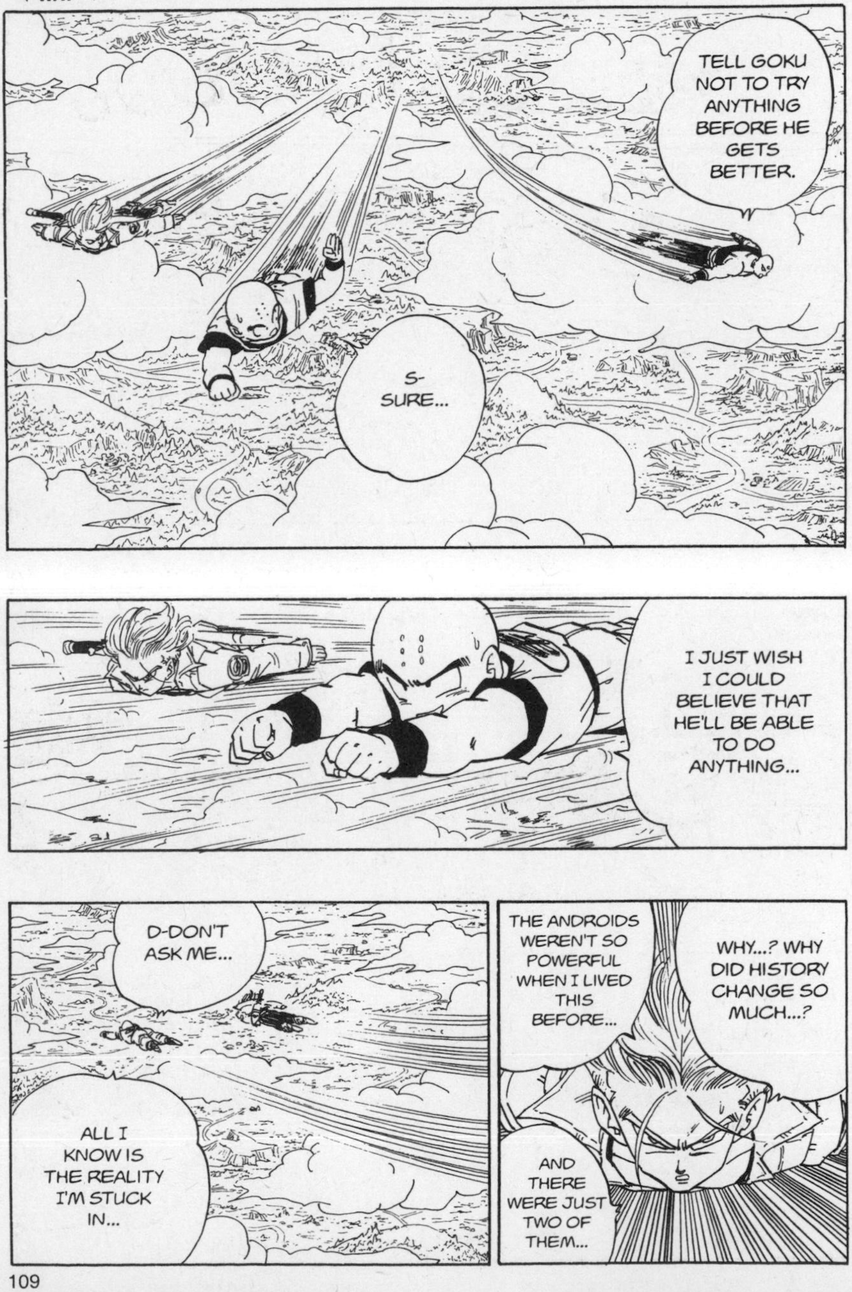

TELL GOKU NOT TO TRY ANYTHING BEFORE HE GETS BETTER.
S-SURE...
I JUST WISH I COULD BELIEVE THAT HE'LL BE ABLE TO DO ANYTHING...
WHY...? WHY DID HISTORY CHANGE SO MUCH...?
THE ANDROIDS WEREN'T SO POWERFUL WHEN I LIVED THIS BEFORE...
AND THERE WERE JUST TWO OF THEM...
D-DON'T ASK ME...
ALL I KNOW IS THE REALITY I'M STUCK IN...

READ THIS WAY

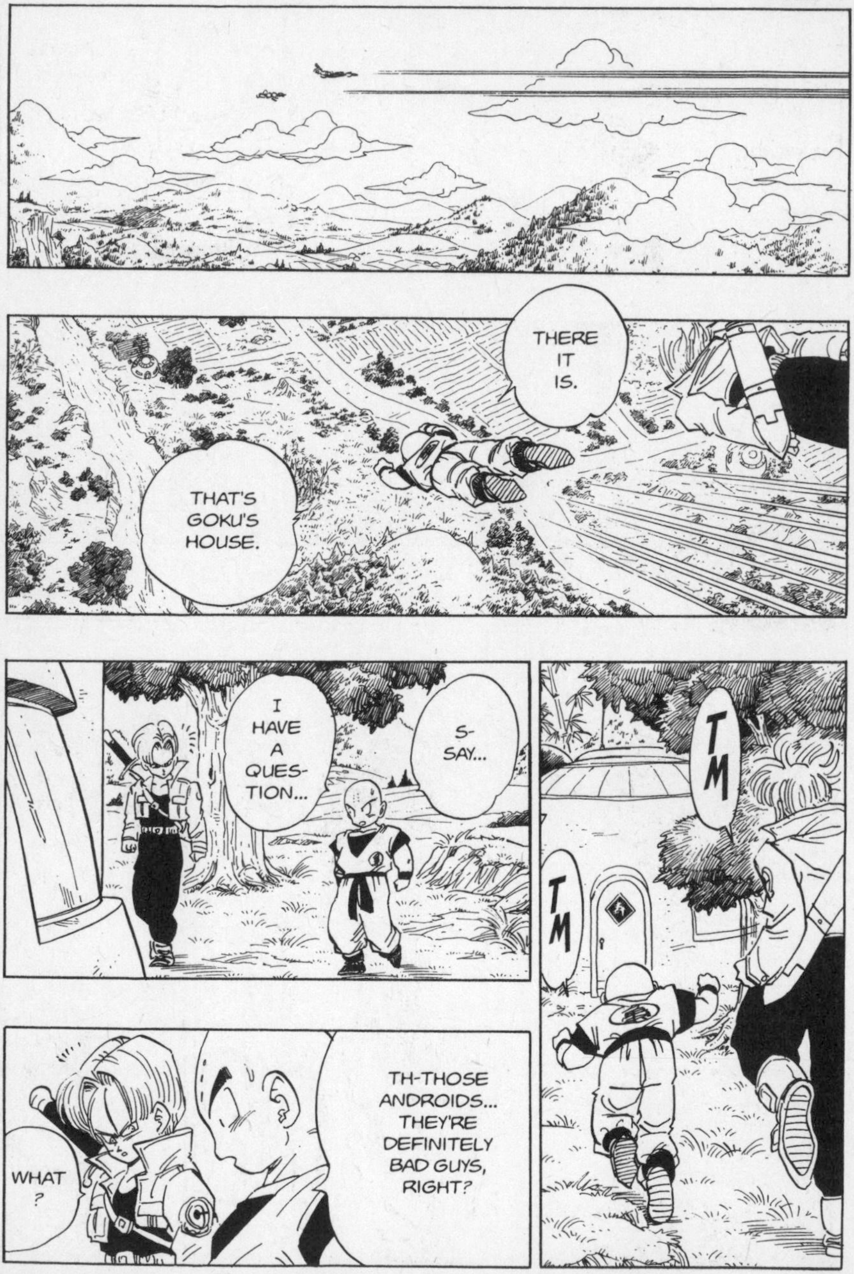
THERE IT IS.
THAT'S GOKU'S HOUSE.
TM
TM
S-SAY...
I HAVE A QUESTION...
TH-THOSE ANDROIDS... THEY'RE DEFINITELY BAD GUYS, RIGHT?
WHAT?

READ THIS WAY

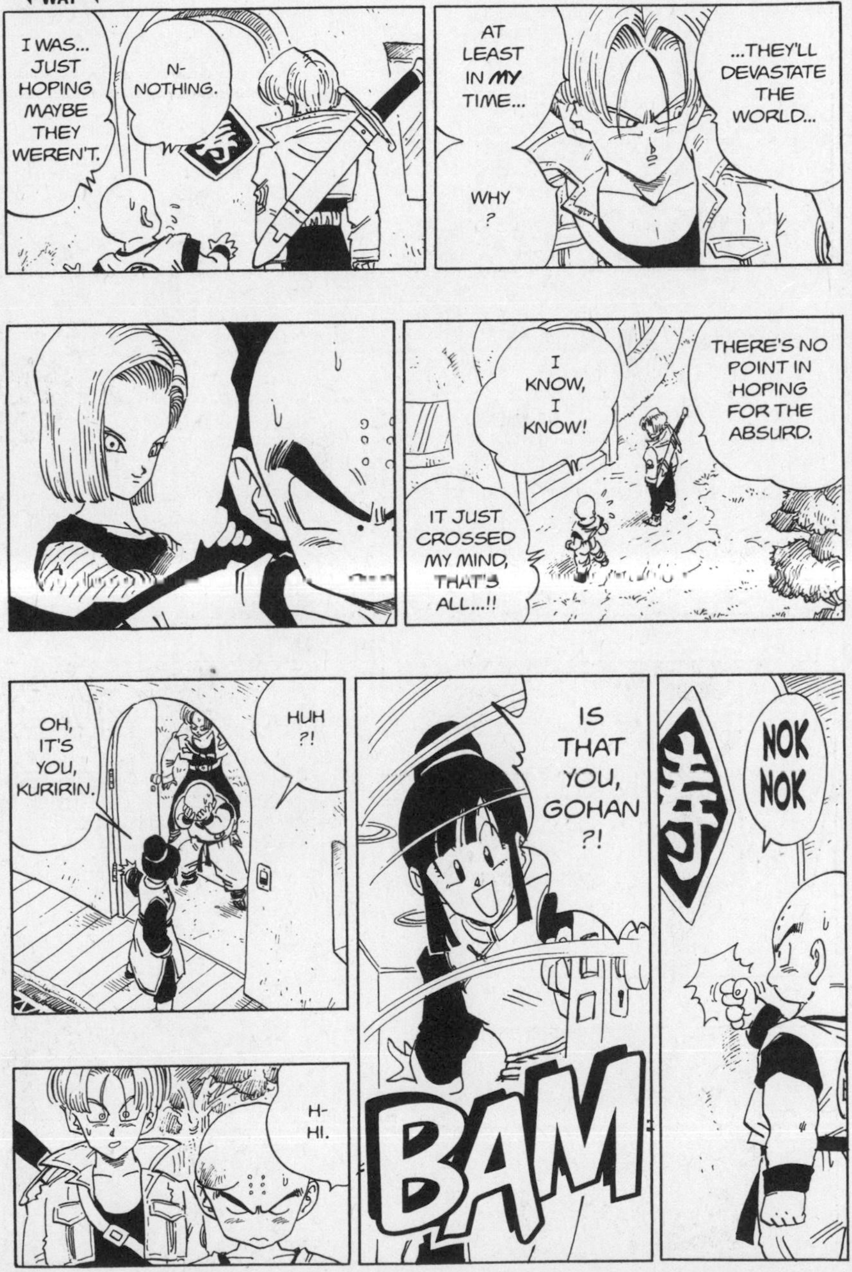
AT LEAST IN MY TIME...
...THEY'LL DEVASTATE THE WORLD...
WHY?
N- NOTHING.
I WAS... JUST HOPING MAYBE THEY WEREN'T.
THERE'S NO POINT IN HOPING FOR THE ABSURD.
I KNOW, I KNOW!
IT JUST CROSSED MY MIND, THAT'S ALL...!!
NOK NOK
IS THAT YOU, GOHAN?!
BAM
HUH?!
OH, IT'S YOU, KURIRIN.
H- HI.

READ THIS WAY

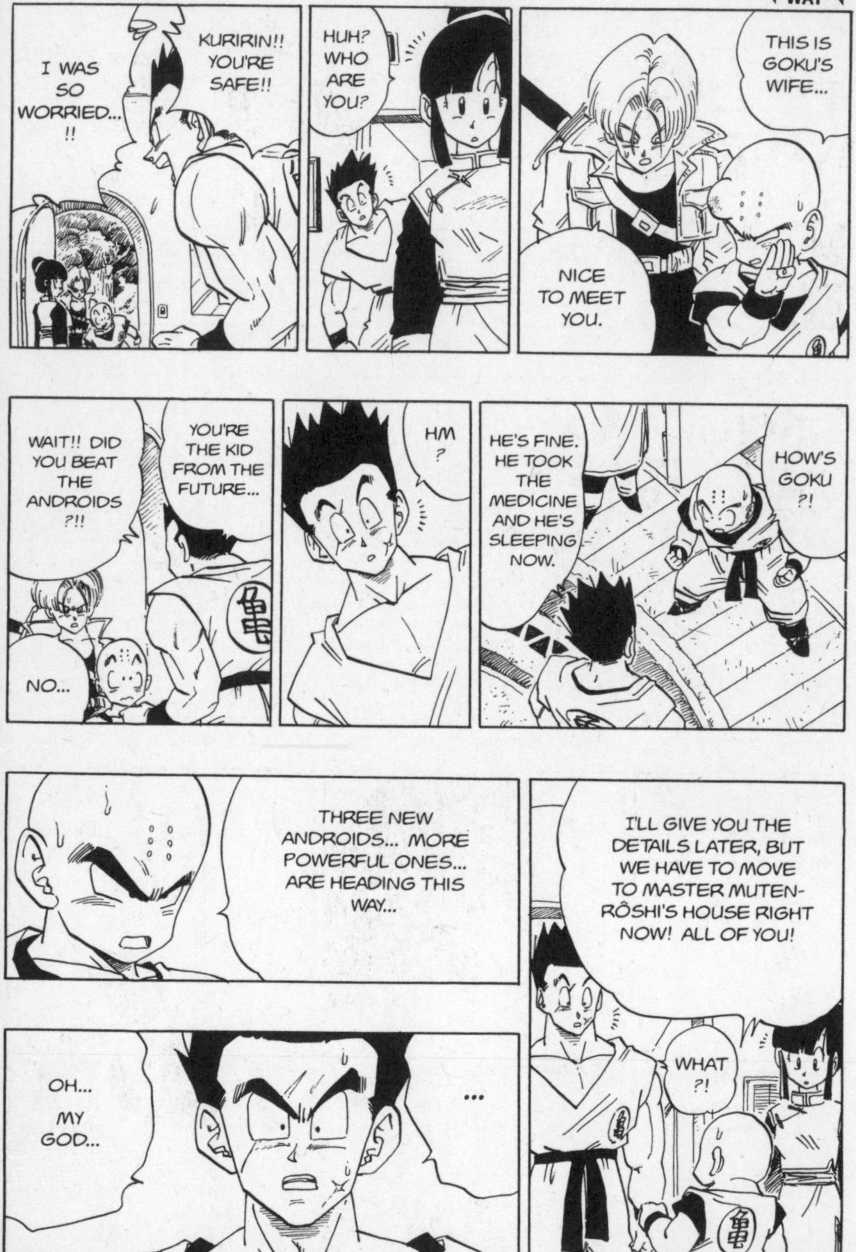
THIS IS GOKU'S WIFE...
NICE TO MEET YOU.
HUH? WHO ARE YOU?
KURIRIN!! YOU'RE SAFE!!
I WAS SO WORRIED... !!
HOW'S GOKU ?!
HE'S FINE. HE TOOK THE MEDICINE AND HE'S SLEEPING NOW.
HM ?
YOU'RE THE KID FROM THE FUTURE...
WAIT!! DID YOU BEAT THE ANDROIDS ?!!
NO...
I'LL GIVE YOU THE DETAILS LATER, BUT WE HAVE TO MOVE TO MASTER MUTEN-RÔSHI'S HOUSE RIGHT NOW! ALL OF YOU!
WHAT ?!
THREE NEW ANDROIDS... MORE POWERFUL ONES... ARE HEADING THIS WAY...
...
OH... MY GOD...

READ THIS WAY

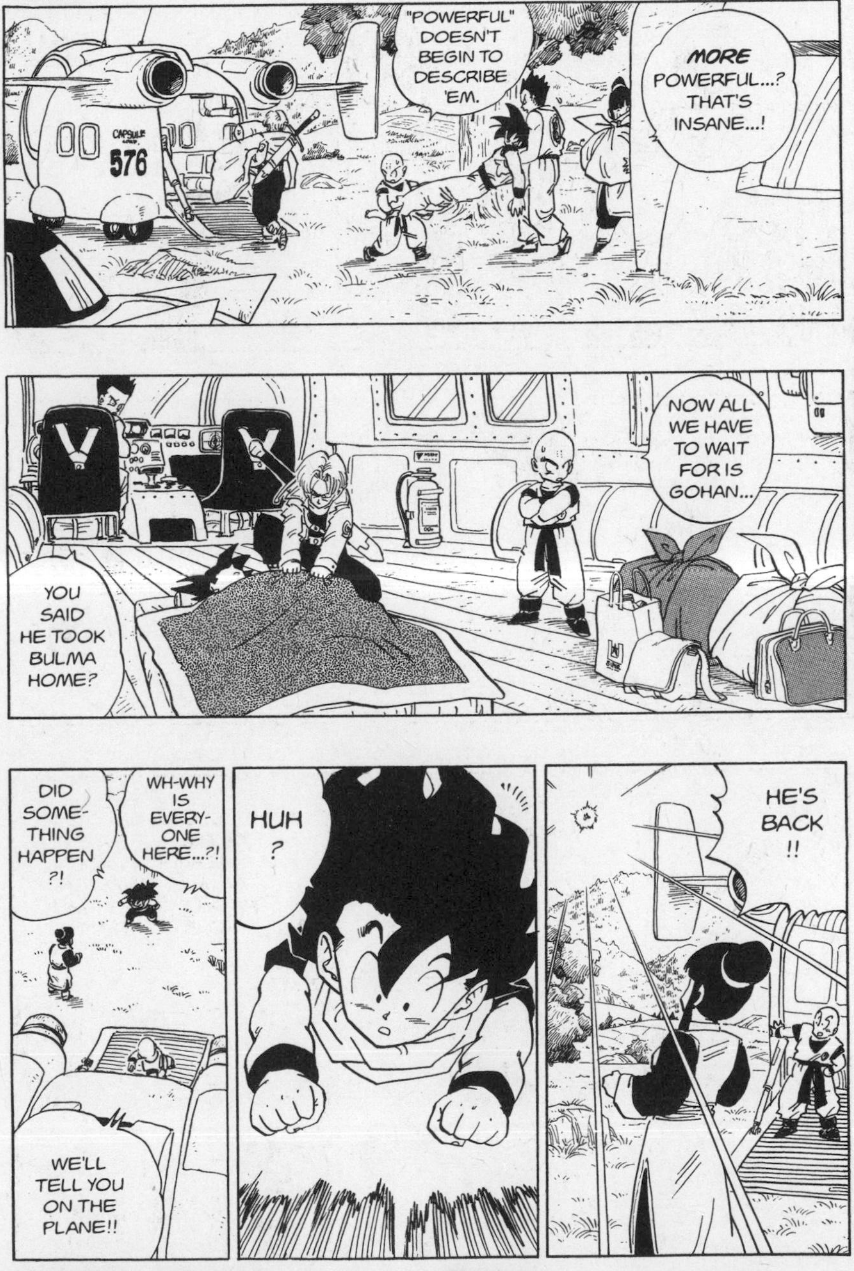
MORE POWERFUL...? THAT'S INSANE...!
"POWERFUL" DOESN'T BEGIN TO DESCRIBE 'EM.
NOW ALL WE HAVE TO WAIT FOR IS GOHAN...
YOU SAID HE TOOK BULMA HOME?
HE'S BACK!!
HUH?
WH-WHY IS EVERY-ONE HERE...?!
DID SOME-THING HAPPEN?!
WE'LL TELL YOU ON THE PLANE!!

NEXT: The News From Bulma

DBZ:163 • A Discovery

READ THIS WAY

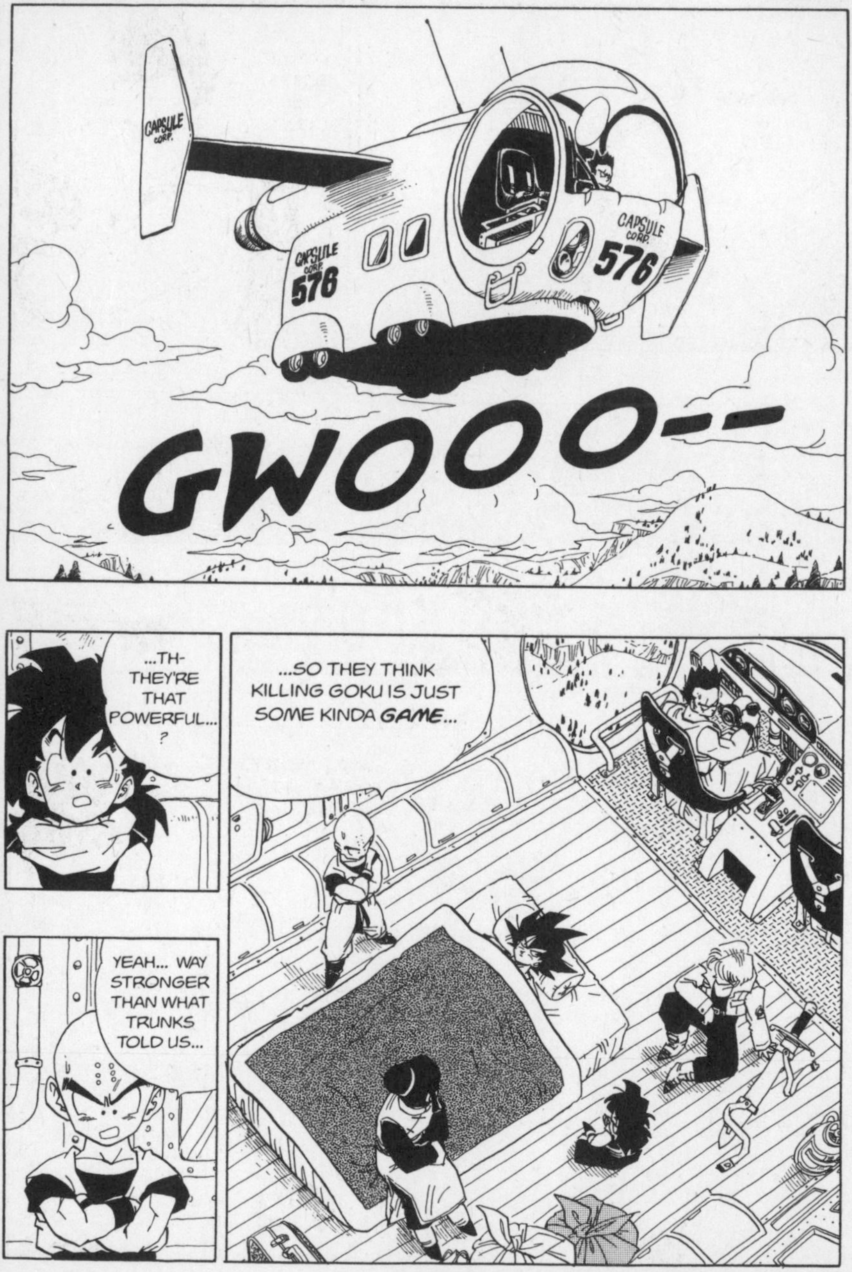
CAPSULE CORP.
CAPSULE CORP. 576
CAPSULE CORP. 576
GWOOO--
...SO THEY THINK KILLING GOKU IS JUST SOME KINDA *GAME*...
...TH-THEY'RE THAT POWERFUL...?
YEAH... WAY STRONGER THAN WHAT TRUNKS TOLD US...

READ THIS WAY

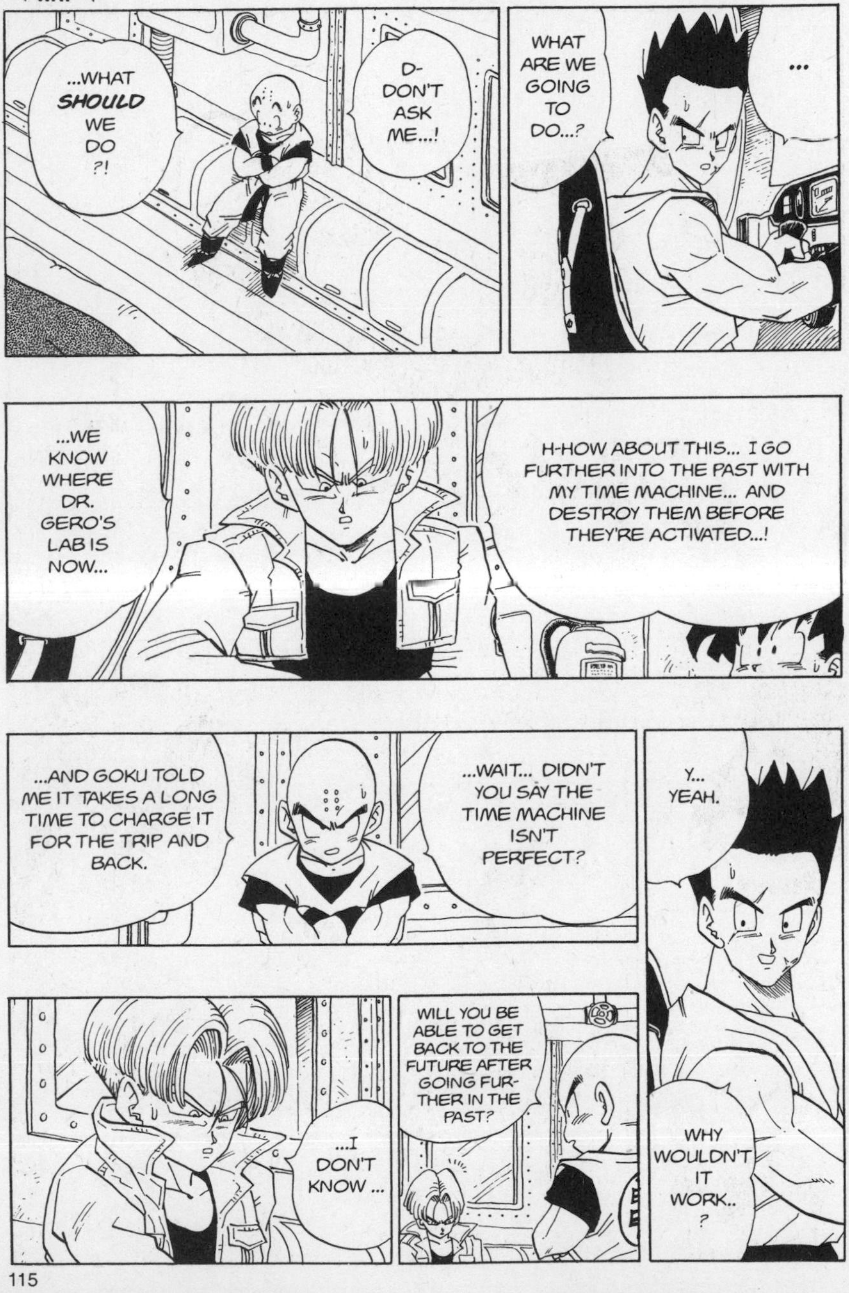
...
WHAT ARE WE GOING TO DO...?
D-DON'T ASK ME...!
...WHAT **SHOULD** WE DO ?!
H-HOW ABOUT THIS... I GO FURTHER INTO THE PAST WITH MY TIME MACHINE... AND DESTROY THEM BEFORE THEY'RE ACTIVATED...!
...WE KNOW WHERE DR. GERO'S LAB IS NOW...
Y... YEAH.
WHY WOULDN'T IT WORK.. ?
...WAIT... DIDN'T YOU SAY THE TIME MACHINE ISN'T PERFECT?
...AND GOKU TOLD ME IT TAKES A LONG TIME TO CHARGE IT FOR THE TRIP AND BACK.
WILL YOU BE ABLE TO GET BACK TO THE FUTURE AFTER GOING FUR-THER IN THE PAST?
...I DON'T KNOW ...

READ THIS WAY

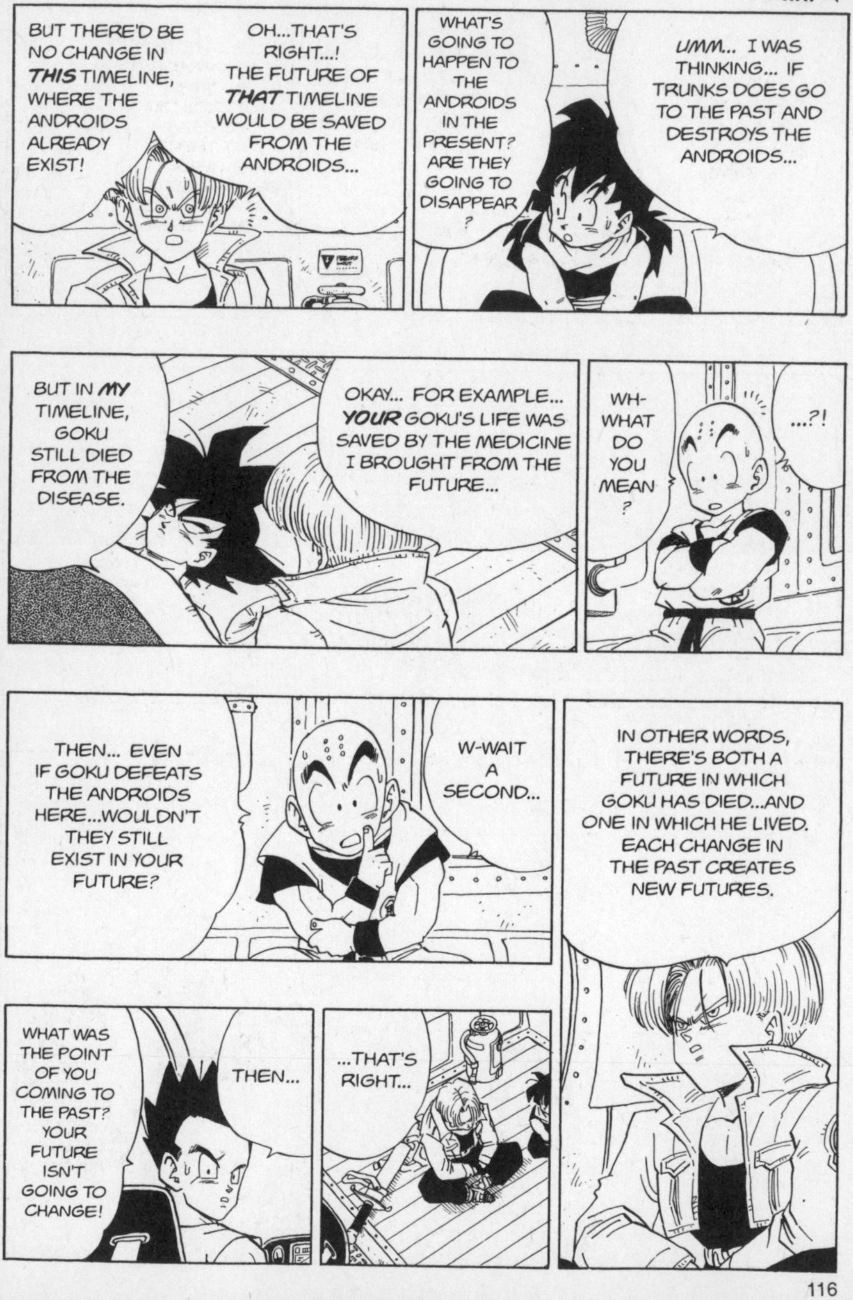
UMM... I WAS THINKING... IF TRUNKS DOES GO TO THE PAST AND DESTROYS THE ANDROIDS...
WHAT'S GOING TO HAPPEN TO THE ANDROIDS IN THE PRESENT? ARE THEY GOING TO DISAPPEAR?
OH...THAT'S RIGHT...! THE FUTURE OF THAT TIMELINE WOULD BE SAVED FROM THE ANDROIDS...
BUT THERE'D BE NO CHANGE IN THIS TIMELINE, WHERE THE ANDROIDS ALREADY EXIST!
...?!
WH-WHAT DO YOU MEAN?
OKAY... FOR EXAMPLE... YOUR GOKU'S LIFE WAS SAVED BY THE MEDICINE I BROUGHT FROM THE FUTURE...
BUT IN MY TIMELINE, GOKU STILL DIED FROM THE DISEASE.
IN OTHER WORDS, THERE'S BOTH A FUTURE IN WHICH GOKU HAS DIED...AND ONE IN WHICH HE LIVED. EACH CHANGE IN THE PAST CREATES NEW FUTURES.
W-WAIT A SECOND...
THEN... EVEN IF GOKU DEFEATS THE ANDROIDS HERE...WOULDN'T THEY STILL EXIST IN YOUR FUTURE?
...THAT'S RIGHT...
THEN...
WHAT WAS THE POINT OF YOU COMING TO THE PAST? YOUR FUTURE ISN'T GOING TO CHANGE!

READ THIS WAY

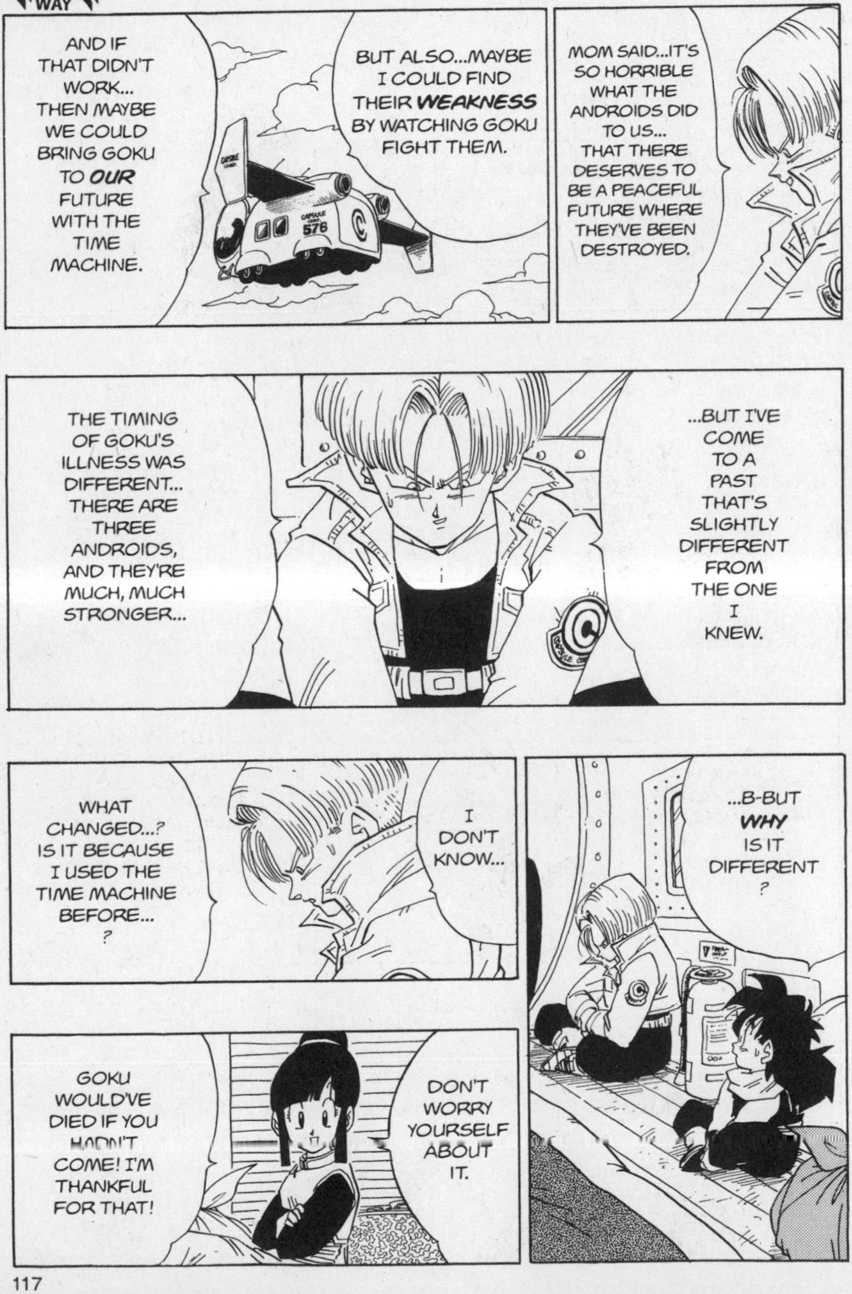

MOM SAID...IT'S SO HORRIBLE WHAT THE ANDROIDS DID TO US... THAT THERE DESERVES TO BE A PEACEFUL FUTURE WHERE THEY'VE BEEN DESTROYED.
BUT ALSO...MAYBE I COULD FIND THEIR ***WEAKNESS*** BY WATCHING GOKU FIGHT THEM.
AND IF THAT DIDN'T WORK... THEN MAYBE WE COULD BRING GOKU TO ***OUR*** FUTURE WITH THE TIME MACHINE.
...BUT I'VE COME TO A PAST THAT'S SLIGHTLY DIFFERENT FROM THE ONE I KNEW.
THE TIMING OF GOKU'S ILLNESS WAS DIFFERENT... THERE ARE THREE ANDROIDS, AND THEY'RE MUCH, MUCH STRONGER...
...B-BUT ***WHY*** IS IT DIFFERENT?
I DON'T KNOW...
WHAT CHANGED...? IS IT BECAUSE I USED THE TIME MACHINE BEFORE...?
DON'T WORRY YOURSELF ABOUT IT.
GOKU WOULD'VE DIED IF YOU HADN'T COME! I'M THANKFUL FOR THAT!

READ THIS WAY

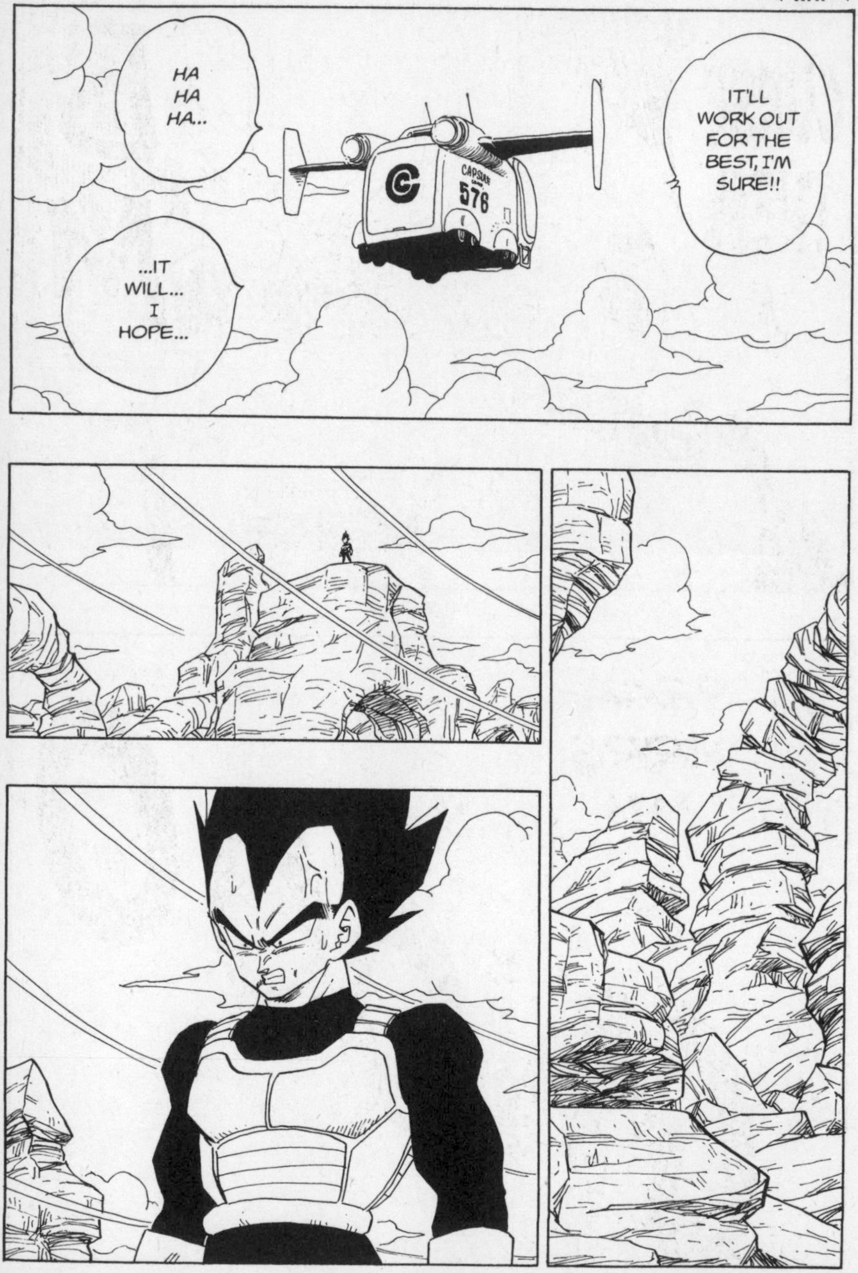
IT'LL WORK OUT FOR THE BEST, I'M SURE!!
HA HA HA...
...IT WILL... I HOPE...
CAPSULE
576

READ THIS WAY

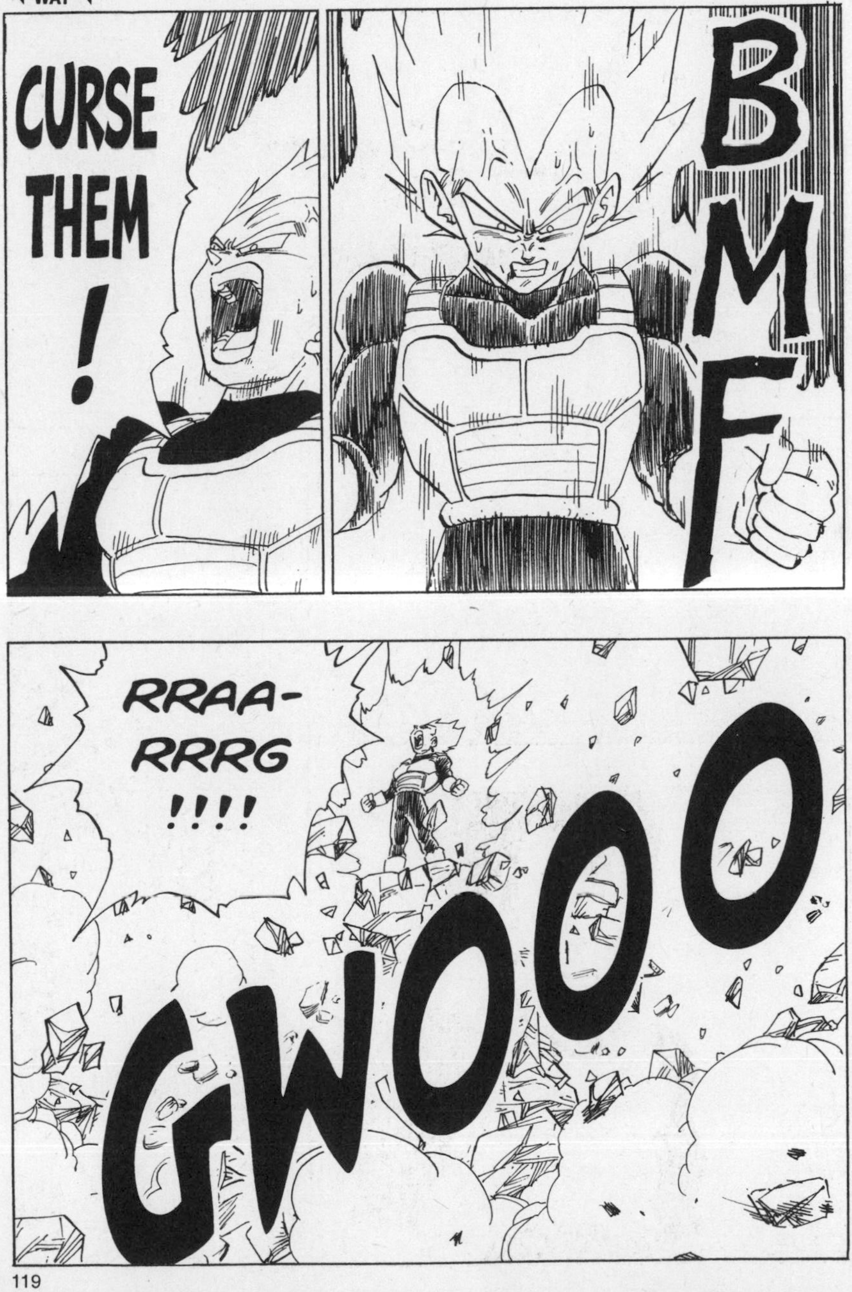
BMF
CURSE THEM!
RRAA-RRRG!!!!
GWOOOO

READ THIS WAY

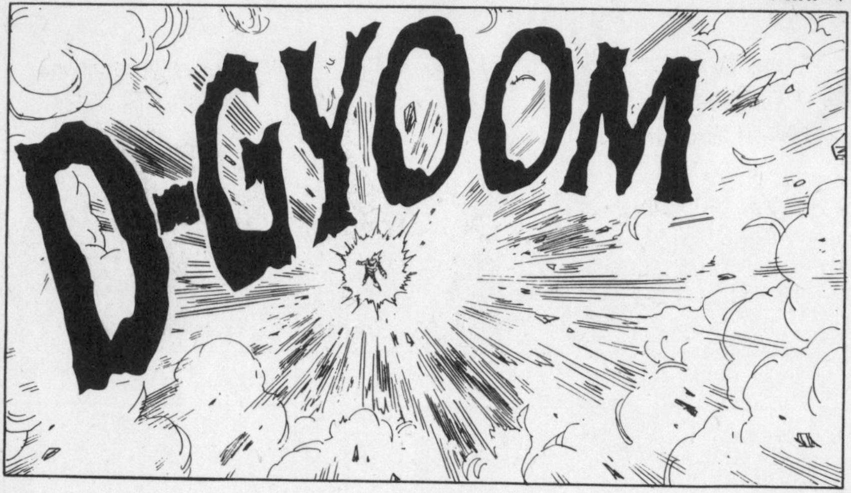
D-GYOOM

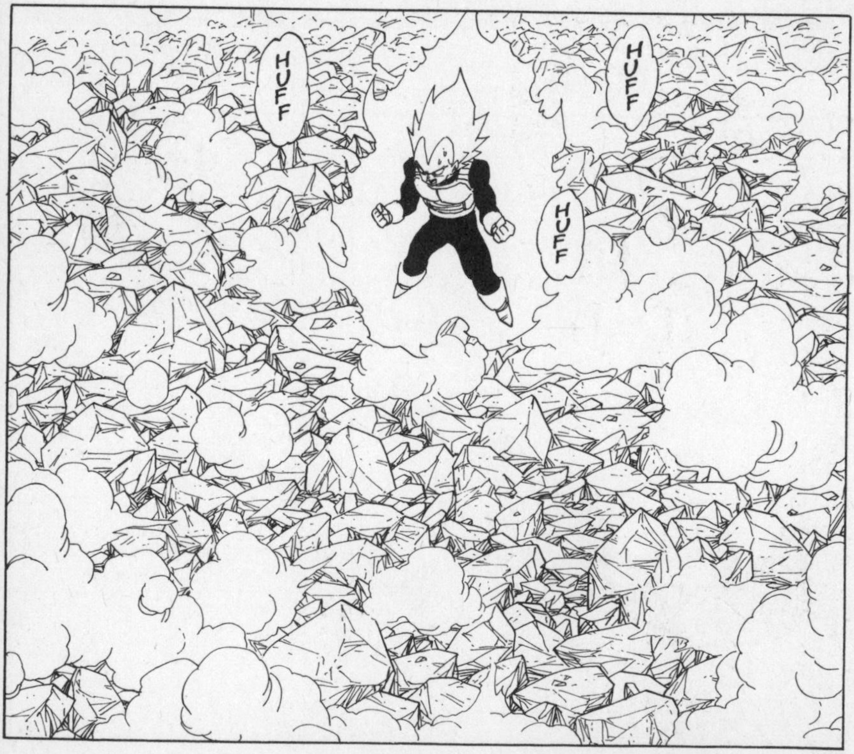
HUFF
HUFF
HUFF

READ THIS WAY

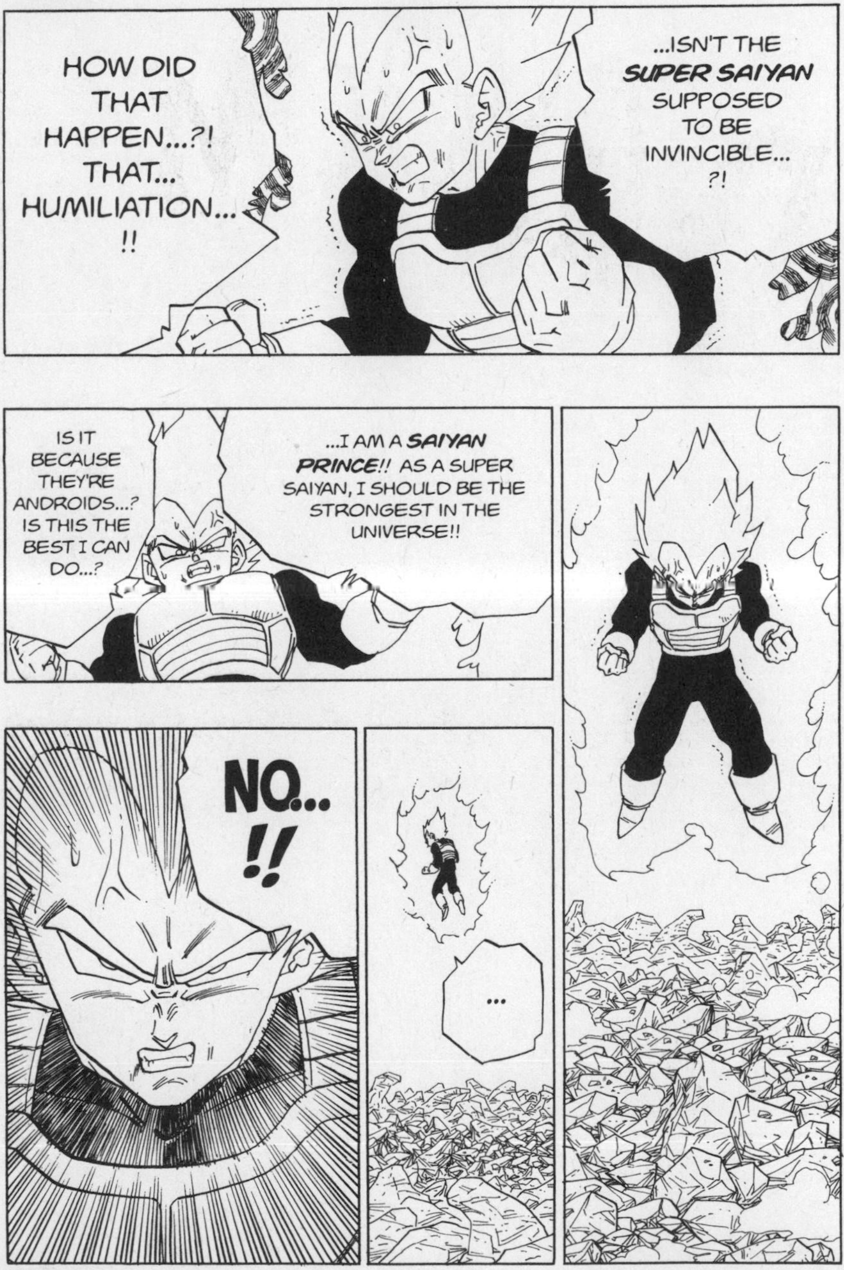
...ISN'T THE SUPER SAIYAN SUPPOSED TO BE INVINCIBLE...?!
HOW DID THAT HAPPEN...?! THAT... HUMILIATION...!!
...I AM A SAIYAN PRINCE!! AS A SUPER SAIYAN, I SHOULD BE THE STRONGEST IN THE UNIVERSE!!
IS IT BECAUSE THEY'RE ANDROIDS...? IS THIS THE BEST I CAN DO...?
...
NO...!!

READ THIS WAY

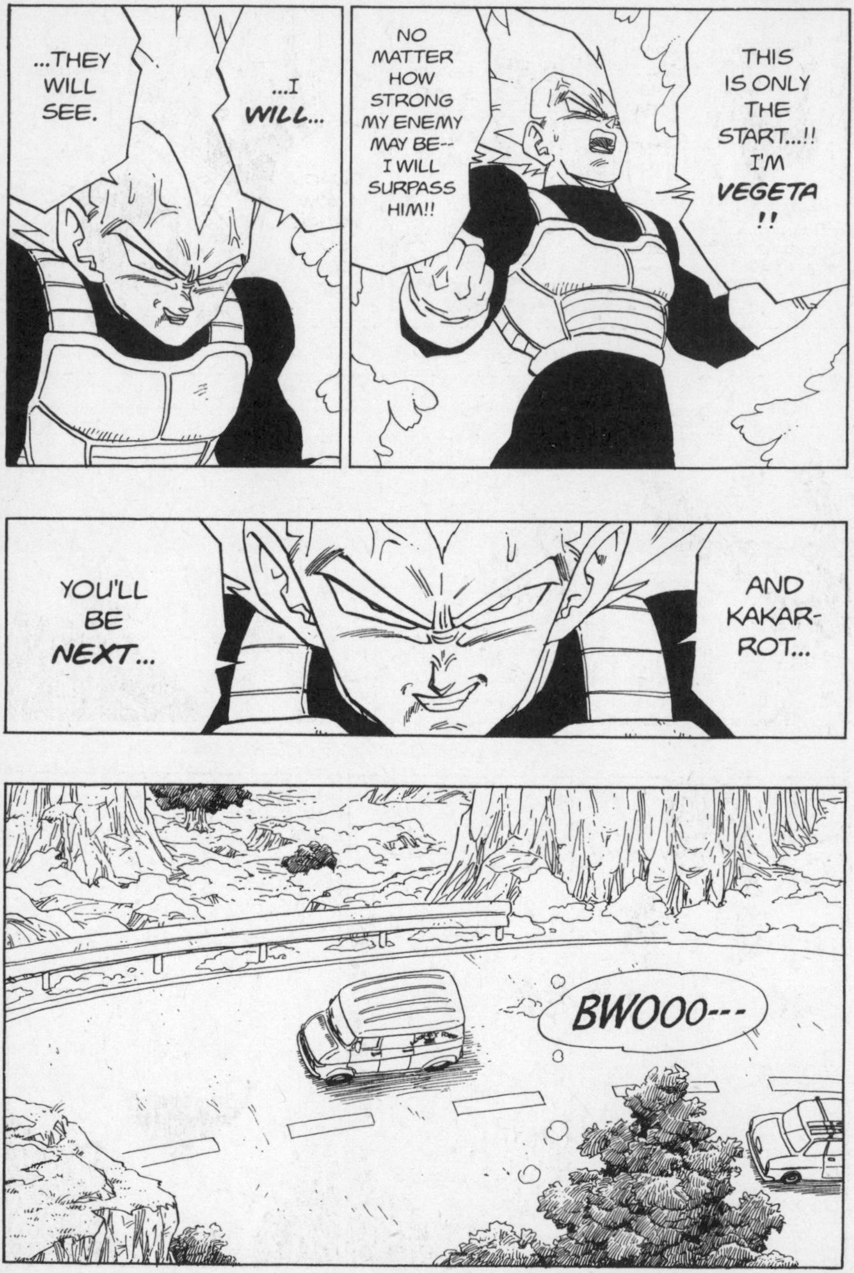
THIS IS ONLY THE START...!! I'M VEGETA !!
NO MATTER HOW STRONG MY ENEMY MAY BE-- I WILL SURPASS HIM!!
...I WILL...
...THEY WILL SEE.
AND KAKAR-ROT...
YOU'LL BE NEXT...
BWOOO---

READ THIS WAY

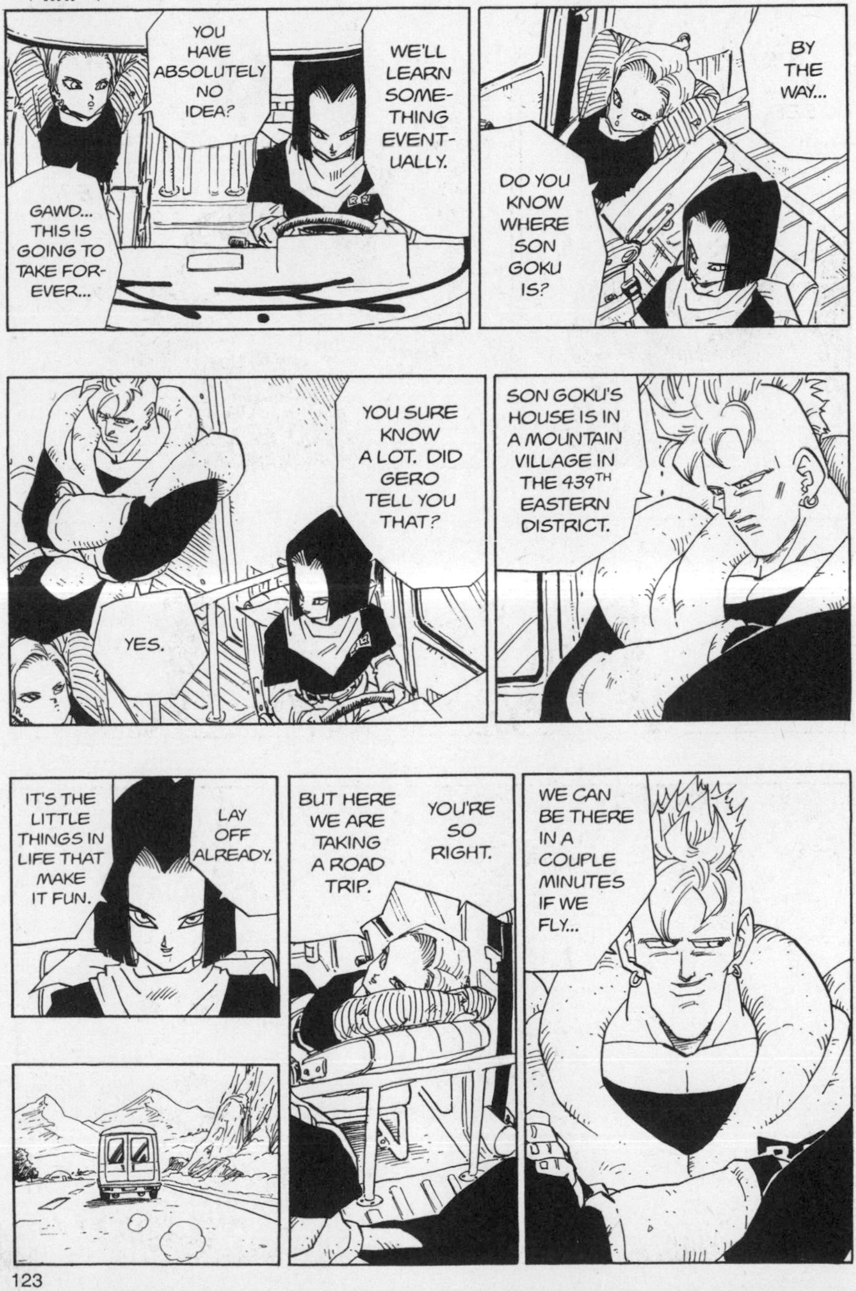
BY THE WAY...
DO YOU KNOW WHERE SON GOKU IS?
YOU HAVE ABSOLUTELY NO IDEA?
WE'LL LEARN SOMETHING EVENTUALLY.
GAWD... THIS IS GOING TO TAKE FOREVER...
SON GOKU'S HOUSE IS IN A MOUNTAIN VILLAGE IN THE 439TH EASTERN DISTRICT.
YOU SURE KNOW A LOT. DID GERO TELL YOU THAT?
YES.
WE CAN BE THERE IN A COUPLE MINUTES IF WE FLY...
YOU'RE SO RIGHT.
BUT HERE WE ARE TAKING A ROAD TRIP.
IT'S THE LITTLE THINGS IN LIFE THAT MAKE IT FUN.
LAY OFF ALREADY.

READ THIS WAY

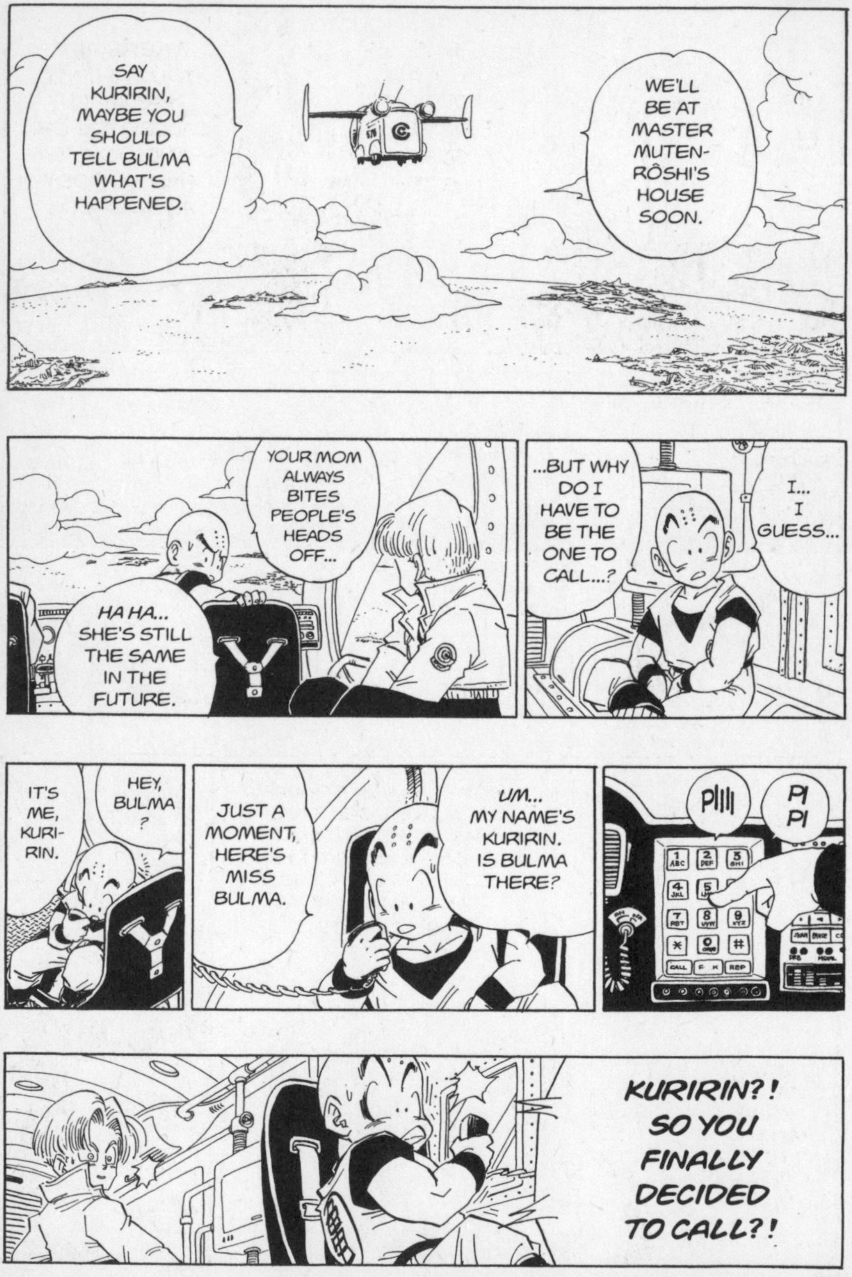

WE'LL BE AT MASTER MUTEN-RÔSHI'S HOUSE SOON.
SAY KURIRIN, MAYBE YOU SHOULD TELL BULMA WHAT'S HAPPENED.
I... I GUESS...
...BUT WHY DO I HAVE TO BE THE ONE TO CALL...?
YOUR MOM ALWAYS BITES PEOPLE'S HEADS OFF...
HA HA... SHE'S STILL THE SAME IN THE FUTURE.
PI PI
PI
UM... MY NAME'S KURIRIN. IS BULMA THERE?
JUST A MOMENT, HERE'S MISS BULMA.
HEY, BULMA?
IT'S ME, KURIRIN.
KURIRIN?! SO YOU FINALLY DECIDED TO CALL?!

READ THIS WAY

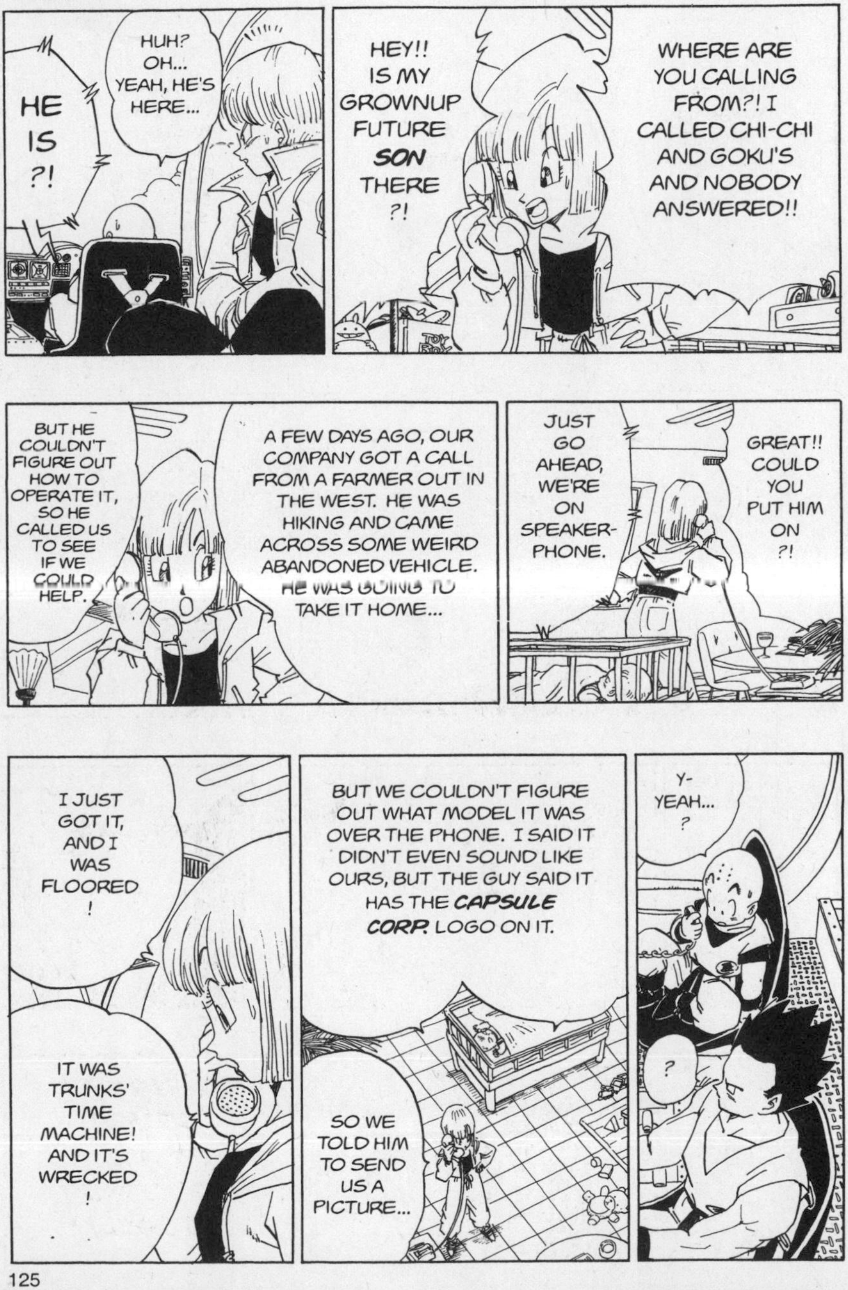

WHERE ARE YOU CALLING FROM?! I CALLED CHI-CHI AND GOKU'S AND NOBODY ANSWERED!!
HEY!! IS MY GROWNUP FUTURE SON THERE?!
HUH? OH... YEAH, HE'S HERE...
HE IS?!
GREAT!! COULD YOU PUT HIM ON?!
JUST GO AHEAD, WE'RE ON SPEAKER-PHONE.
A FEW DAYS AGO, OUR COMPANY GOT A CALL FROM A FARMER OUT IN THE WEST. HE WAS HIKING AND CAME ACROSS SOME WEIRD ABANDONED VEHICLE. HE WAS GOING TO TAKE IT HOME...
BUT HE COULDN'T FIGURE OUT HOW TO OPERATE IT, SO HE CALLED US TO SEE IF WE COULD HELP.
Y-YEAH...?
?
BUT WE COULDN'T FIGURE OUT WHAT MODEL IT WAS OVER THE PHONE. I SAID IT DIDN'T EVEN SOUND LIKE OURS, BUT THE GUY SAID IT HAS THE CAPSULE CORP. LOGO ON IT.
SO WE TOLD HIM TO SEND US A PICTURE...
I JUST GOT IT, AND I WAS FLOORED!
IT WAS TRUNKS' TIME MACHINE! AND IT'S WRECKED!

READ THIS WAY

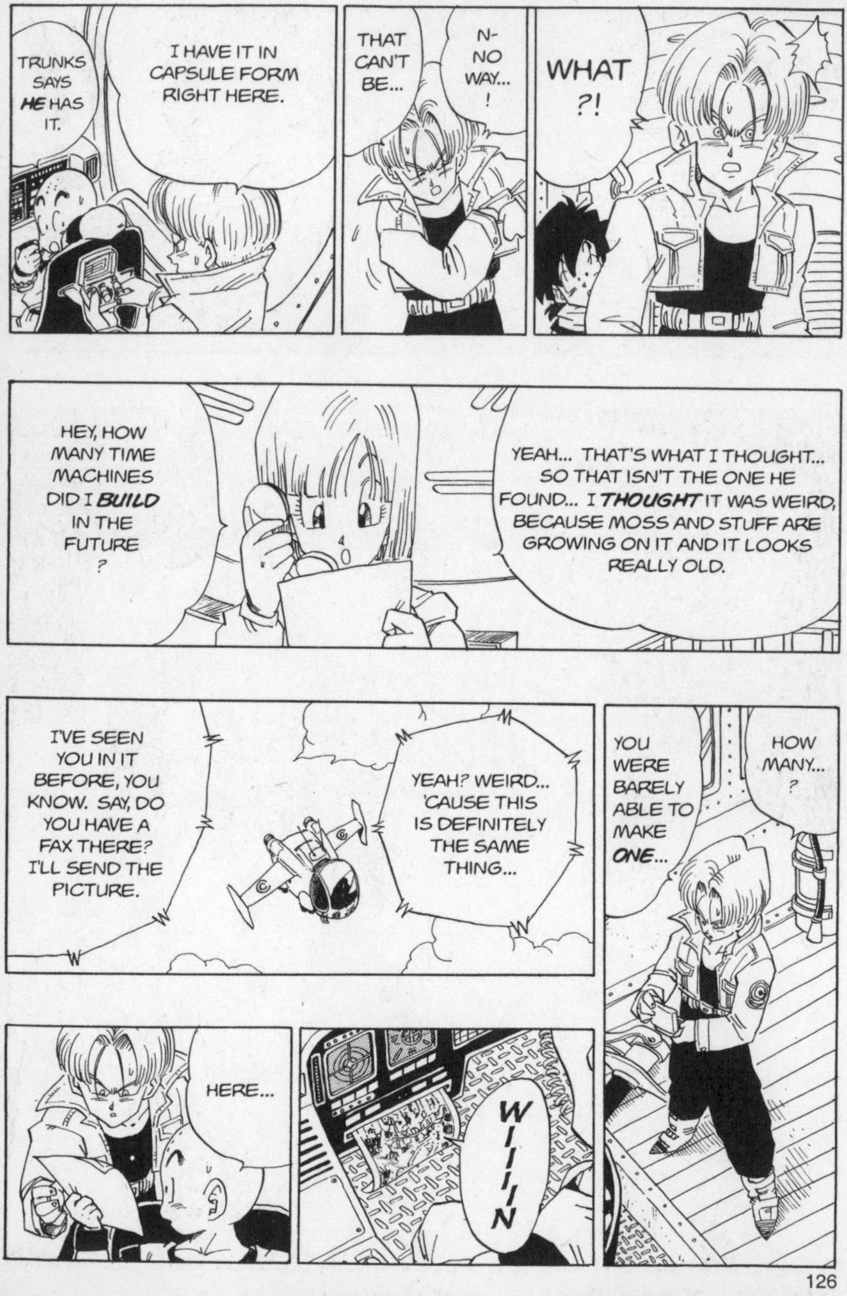

WHAT ?!
N- NO WAY... !
THAT CAN'T BE...
I HAVE IT IN CAPSULE FORM RIGHT HERE.
TRUNKS SAYS **HE** HAS IT.
YEAH... THAT'S WHAT I THOUGHT... SO THAT ISN'T THE ONE HE FOUND... I **THOUGHT** IT WAS WEIRD, BECAUSE MOSS AND STUFF ARE GROWING ON IT AND IT LOOKS REALLY OLD.
HEY, HOW MANY TIME MACHINES DID I **BUILD** IN THE FUTURE ?
HOW MANY... ?
YOU WERE BARELY ABLE TO MAKE **ONE**...
YEAH? WEIRD... 'CAUSE THIS IS DEFINITELY THE SAME THING...
I'VE SEEN YOU IN IT BEFORE, YOU KNOW. SAY, DO YOU HAVE A FAX THERE? I'LL SEND THE PICTURE.
WIIIIN
HERE...

READ THIS WAY

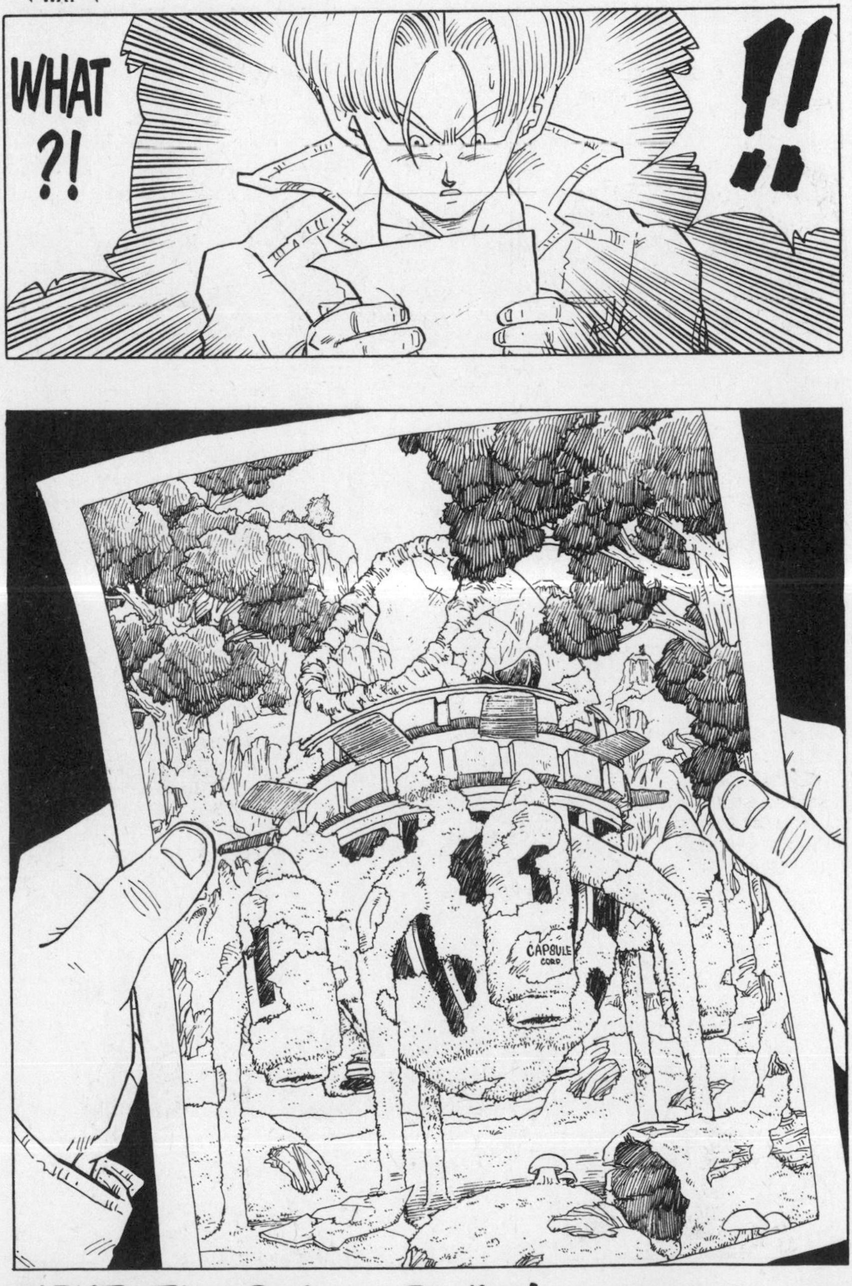
WHAT ?!
!!
CAPSULE CORP.

NEXT: That Ominous Feeling!

DBZ:164 • The Time Machine

READ THIS WAY

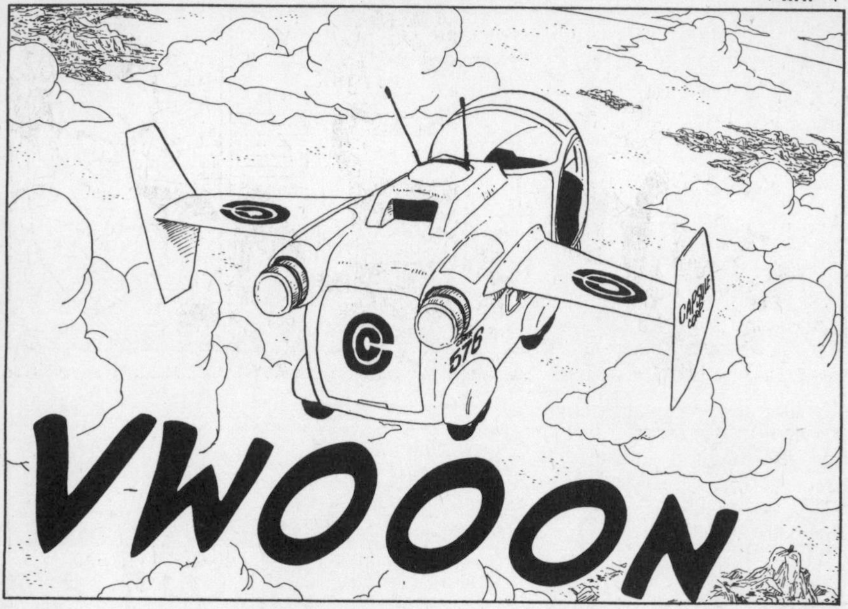
CAPSULE CORP.
576
VWOOON

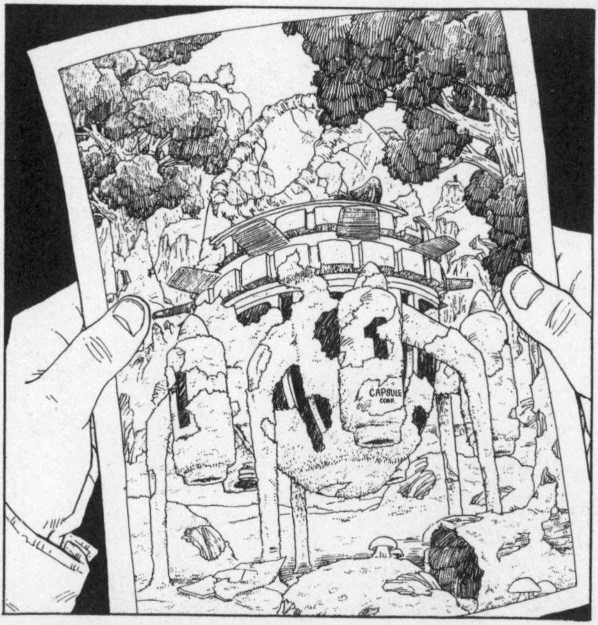
CAPSULE CORP.

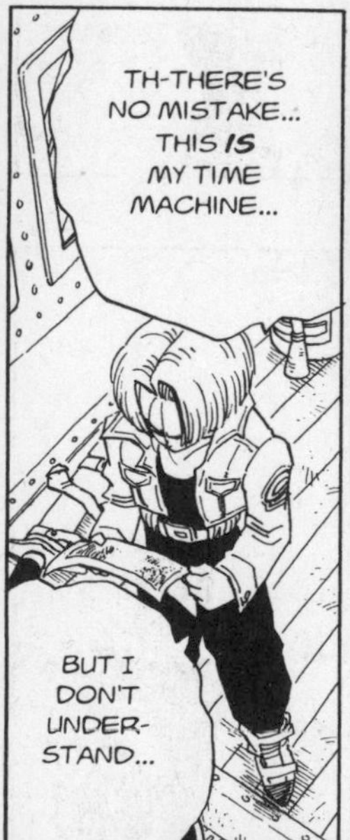
TH-THERE'S NO MISTAKE... THIS *IS* MY TIME MACHINE...
BUT I DON'T UNDER-STAND...

READ THIS WAY

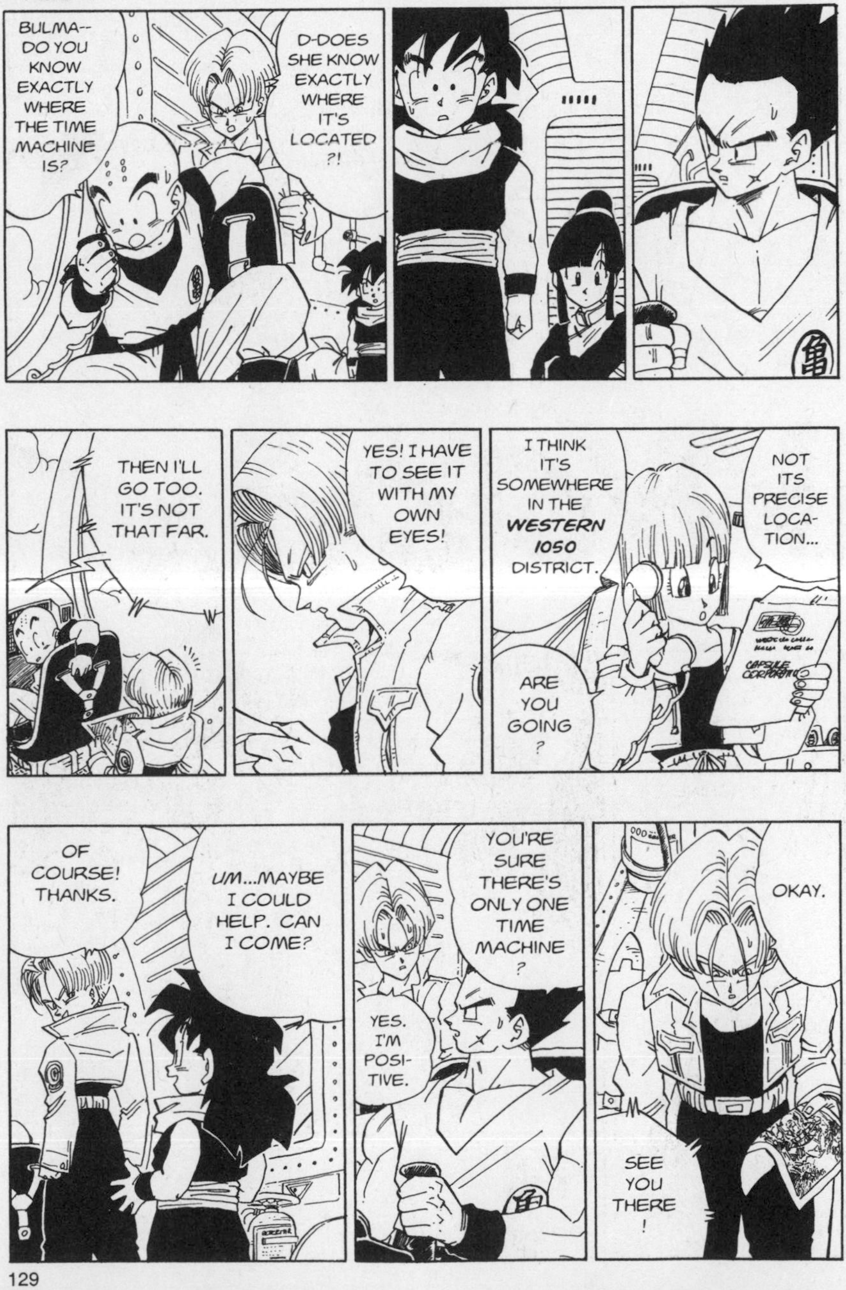
D-DOES SHE KNOW EXACTLY WHERE IT'S LOCATED ?!
BULMA-- DO YOU KNOW EXACTLY WHERE THE TIME MACHINE IS?
NOT ITS PRECISE LOCATION...
I THINK IT'S SOMEWHERE IN THE **WESTERN 1050** DISTRICT.
ARE YOU GOING ?
YES! I HAVE TO SEE IT WITH MY OWN EYES!
THEN I'LL GO TOO. IT'S NOT THAT FAR.
OKAY.
SEE YOU THERE !
YOU'RE SURE THERE'S ONLY ONE TIME MACHINE ?
YES. I'M POSITIVE.
UM...MAYBE I COULD HELP. CAN I COME?
OF COURSE! THANKS.

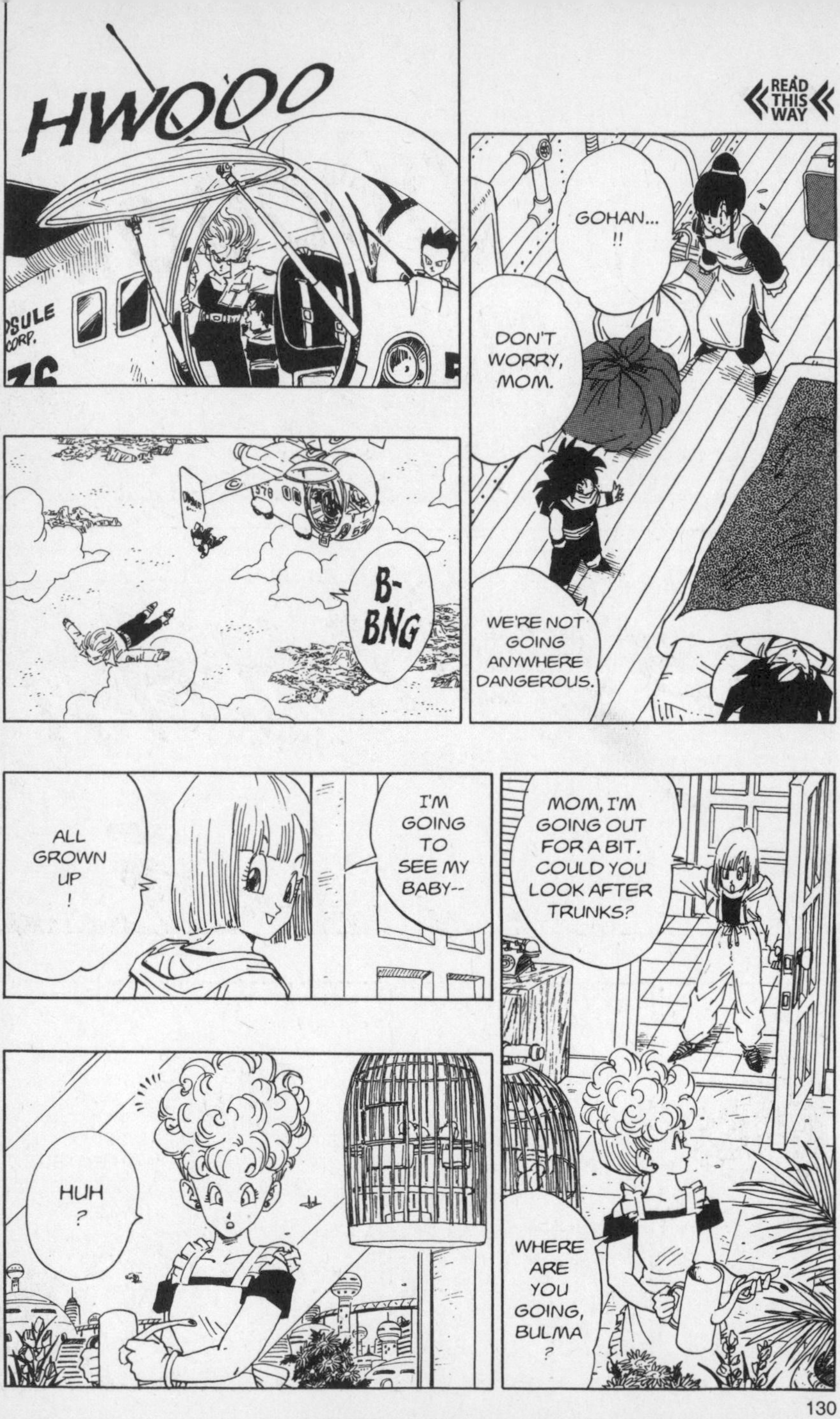
READ THIS WAY
GOHAN... !!
DON'T WORRY, MOM.
WE'RE NOT GOING ANYWHERE DANGEROUS.
HWOOO
B-BNG
MOM, I'M GOING OUT FOR A BIT. COULD YOU LOOK AFTER TRUNKS?
I'M GOING TO SEE MY BABY--
ALL GROWN UP !
WHERE ARE YOU GOING, BULMA ?
HUH ?

READ THIS WAY

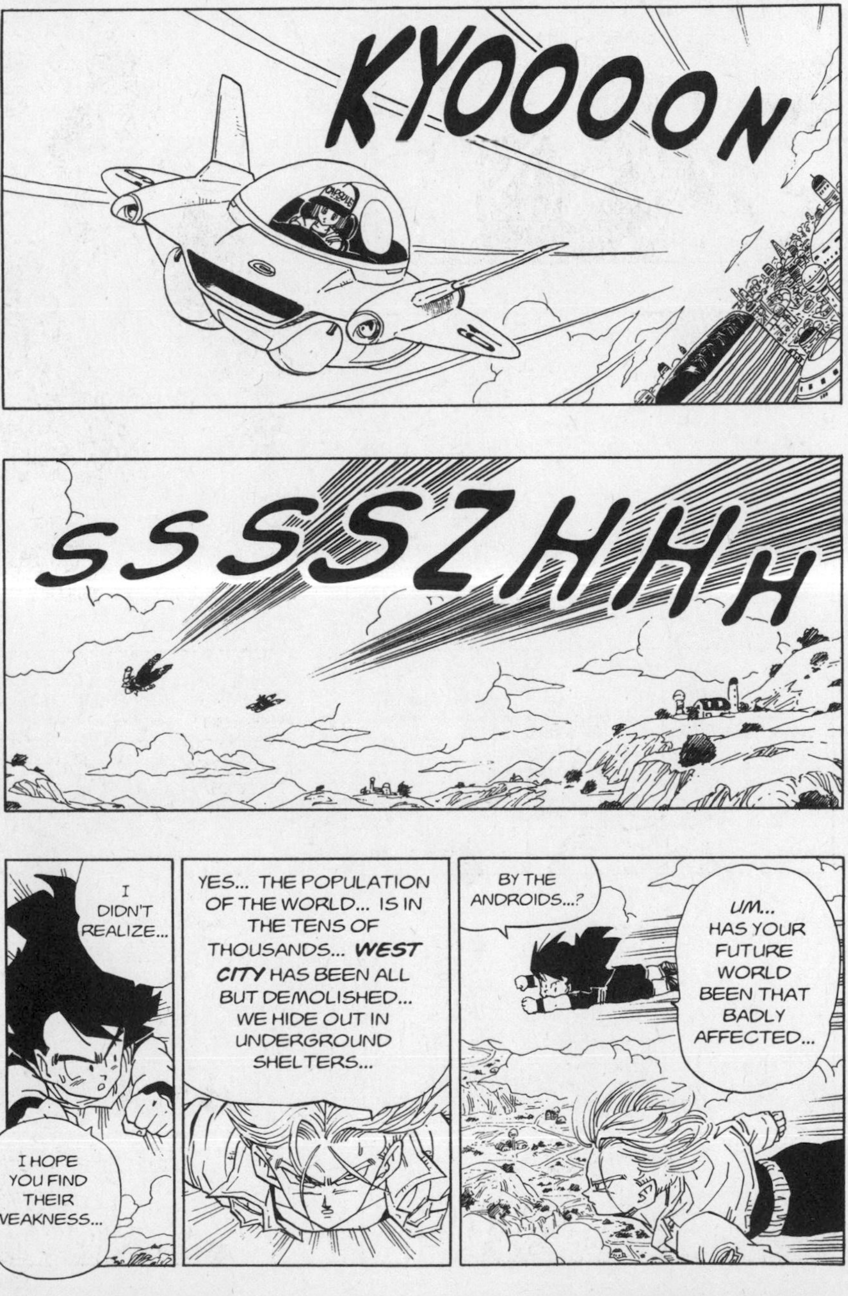
KYOOOON
SSSZHHH
UM... HAS YOUR FUTURE WORLD BEEN THAT BADLY AFFECTED...
BY THE ANDROIDS...?
YES... THE POPULATION OF THE WORLD... IS IN THE TENS OF THOUSANDS... **WEST CITY** HAS BEEN ALL BUT DEMOLISHED... WE HIDE OUT IN UNDERGROUND SHELTERS...
I DIDN'T REALIZE...
I HOPE YOU FIND THEIR WEAKNESS...

READ THIS WAY

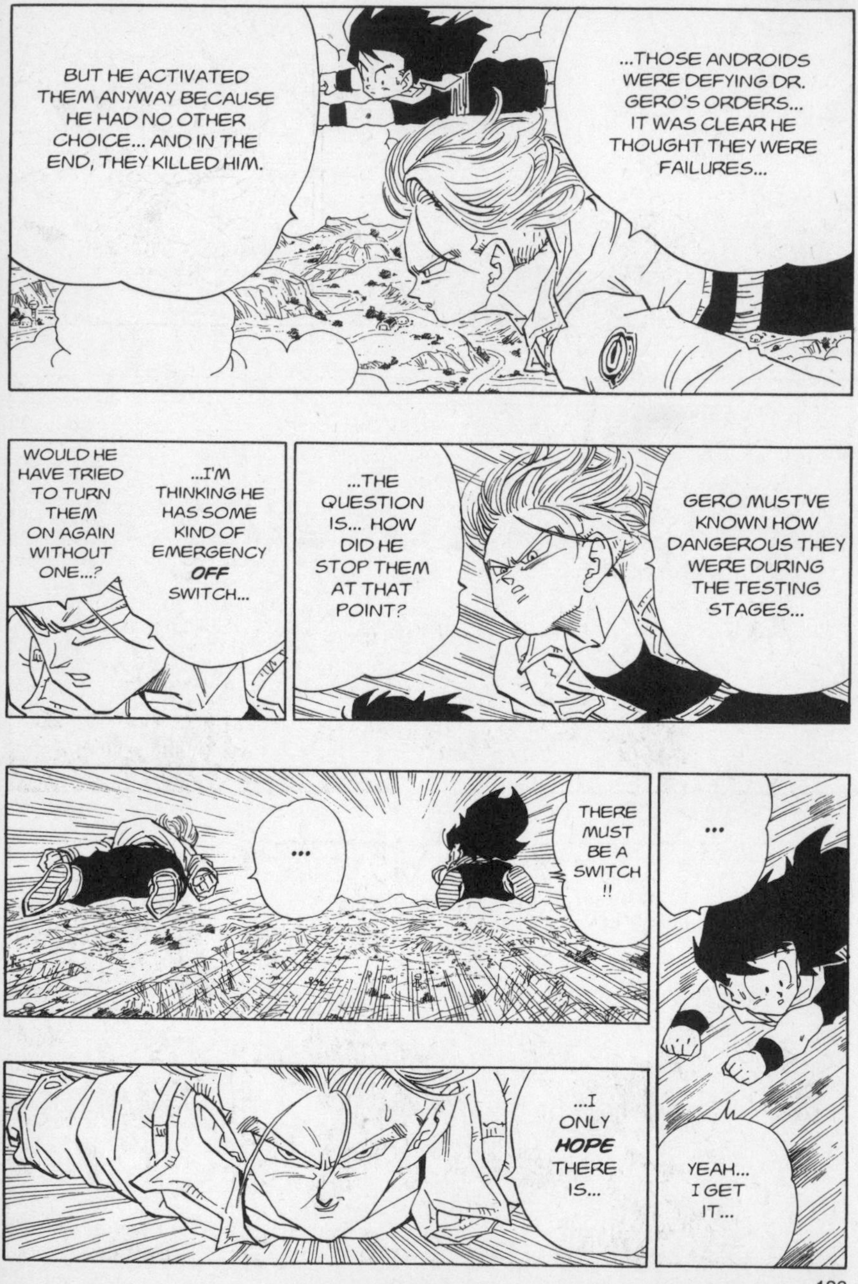

...THOSE ANDROIDS WERE DEFYING DR. GERO'S ORDERS... IT WAS CLEAR HE THOUGHT THEY WERE FAILURES...
BUT HE ACTIVATED THEM ANYWAY BECAUSE HE HAD NO OTHER CHOICE... AND IN THE END, THEY KILLED HIM.
GERO MUST'VE KNOWN HOW DANGEROUS THEY WERE DURING THE TESTING STAGES...
...THE QUESTION IS... HOW DID HE STOP THEM AT THAT POINT?
...I'M THINKING HE HAS SOME KIND OF EMERGENCY ***OFF*** SWITCH...
WOULD HE HAVE TRIED TO TURN THEM ON AGAIN WITHOUT ONE...?
...
YEAH... I GET IT...
THERE MUST BE A SWITCH !!
...
...I ONLY ***HOPE*** THERE IS...

READ THIS WAY

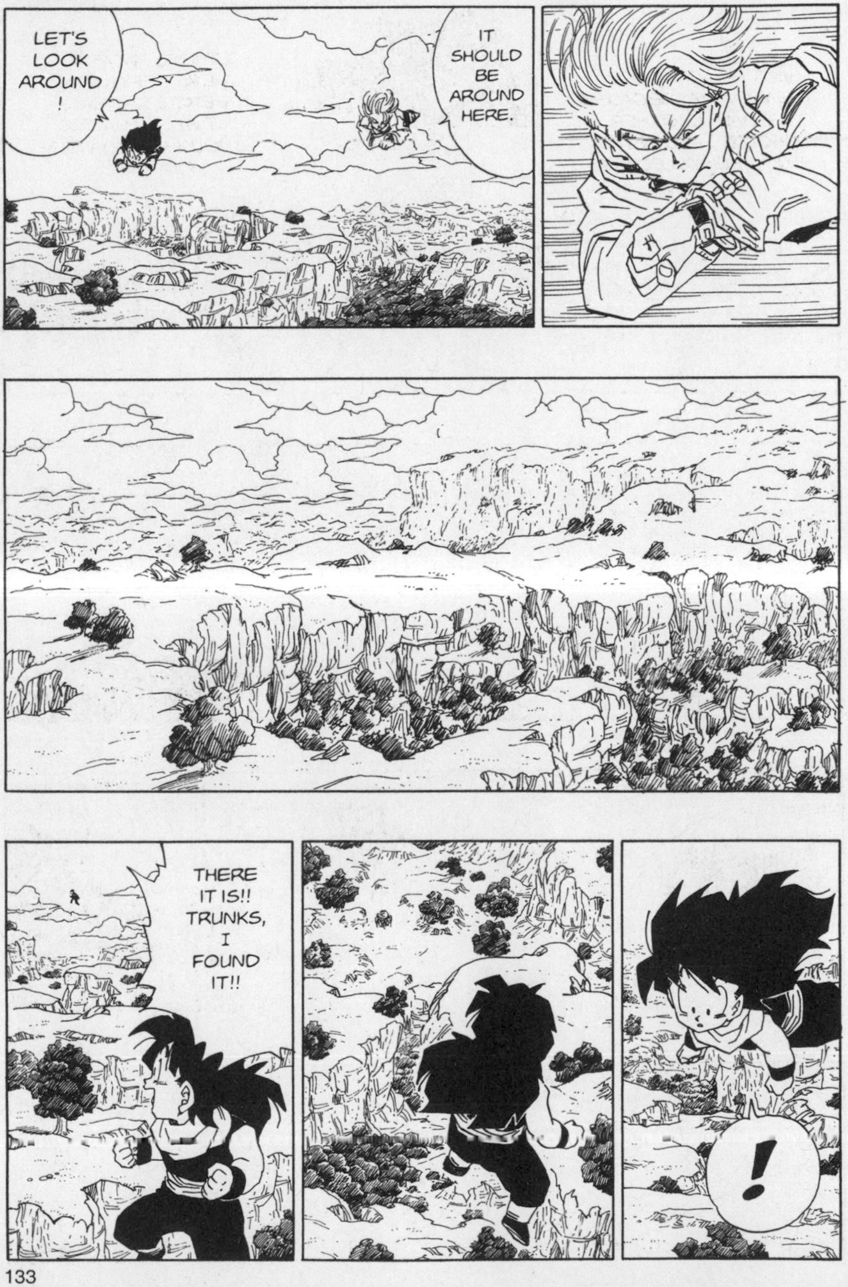
IT SHOULD BE AROUND HERE.
LET'S LOOK AROUND!
!
THERE IT IS!! TRUNKS, I FOUND IT!!

READ THIS WAY

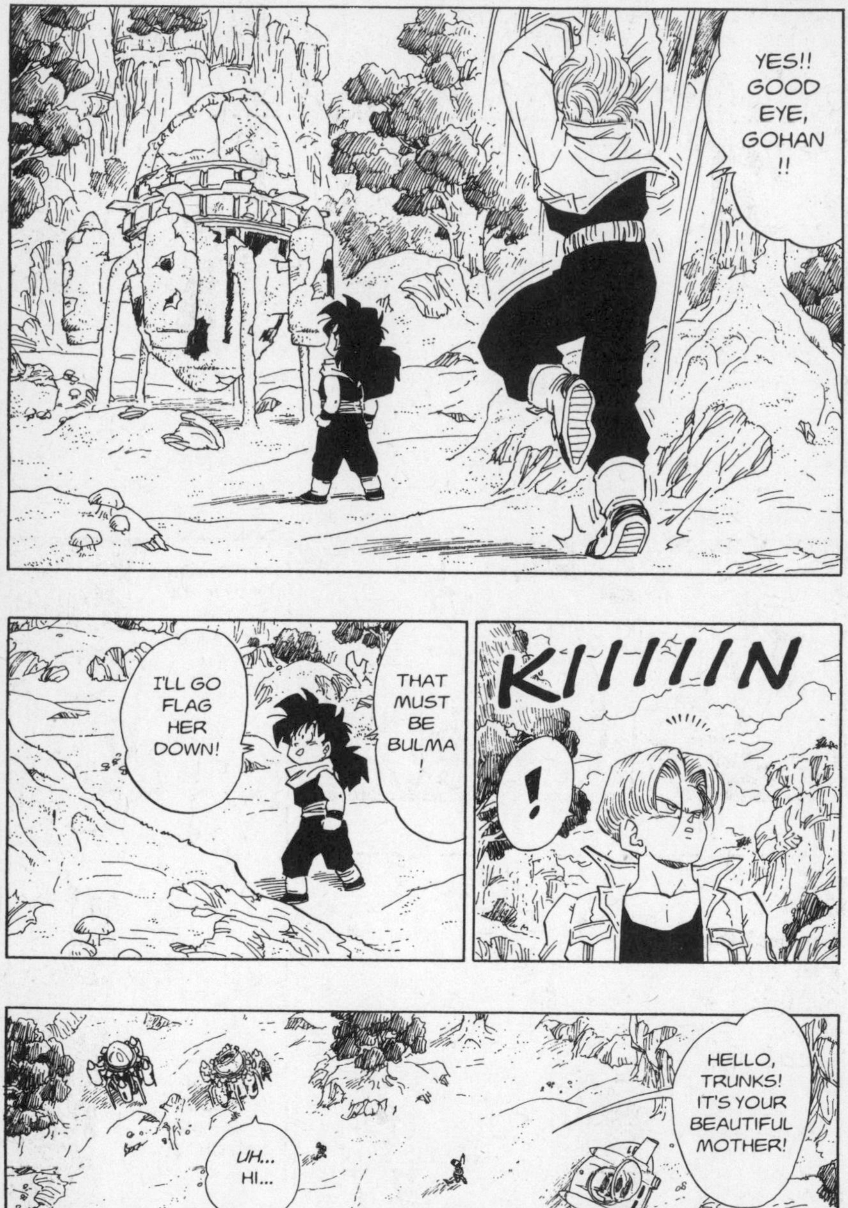
YES!! GOOD EYE, GOHAN!!
KIIIIIN
!
THAT MUST BE BULMA!
I'LL GO FLAG HER DOWN!
HELLO, TRUNKS! IT'S YOUR BEAUTIFUL MOTHER!
UH... HI...

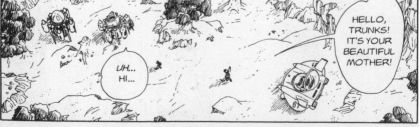

READ THIS WAY

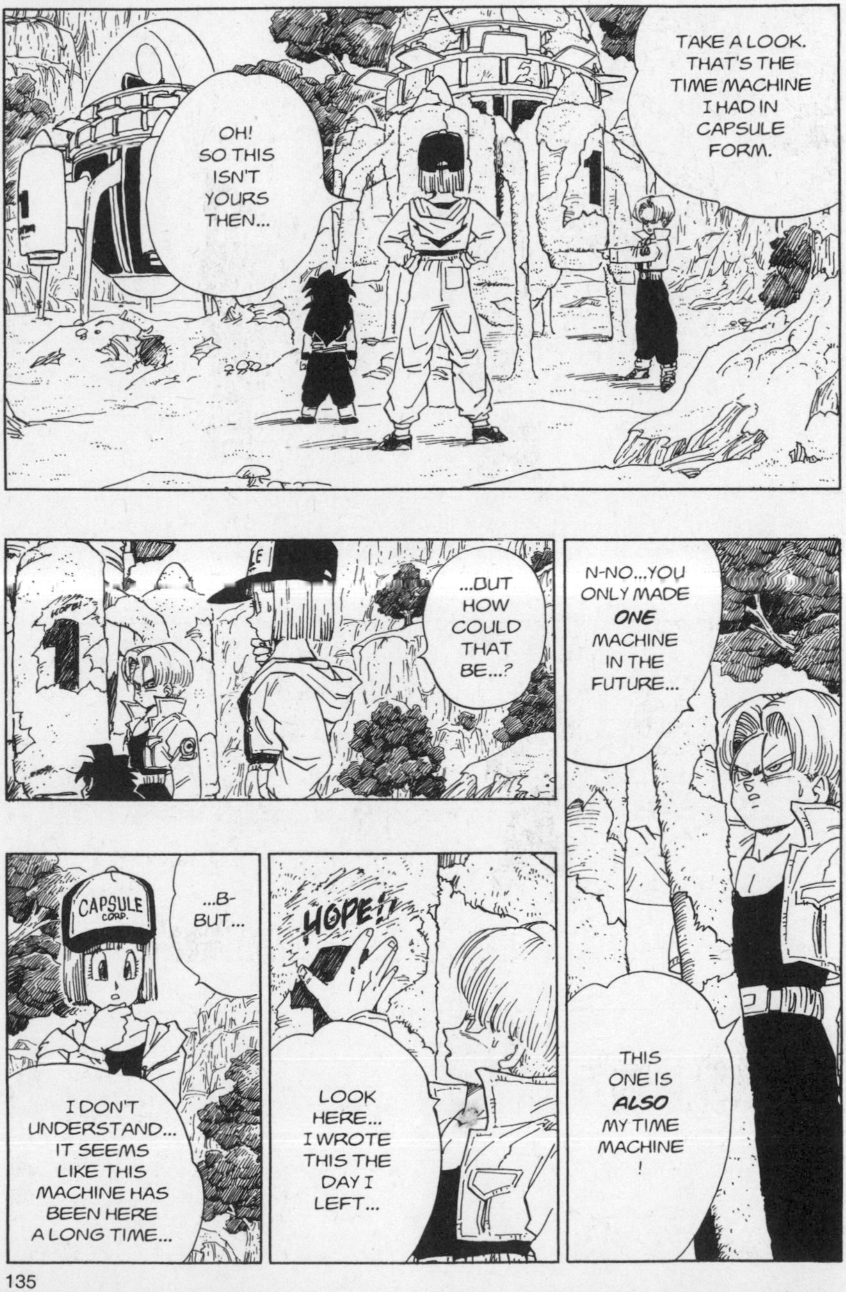
TAKE A LOOK. THAT'S THE TIME MACHINE I HAD IN CAPSULE FORM.
OH! SO THIS ISN'T YOURS THEN...
N-NO...YOU ONLY MADE ***ONE*** MACHINE IN THE FUTURE...
THIS ONE IS ***ALSO*** MY TIME MACHINE!
...BUT HOW COULD THAT BE...?
HOPE!!
LOOK HERE... I WROTE THIS THE DAY I LEFT...
CAPSULE CORP.
...B-BUT...
I DON'T UNDERSTAND... IT SEEMS LIKE THIS MACHINE HAS BEEN HERE A LONG TIME...

READ THIS WAY

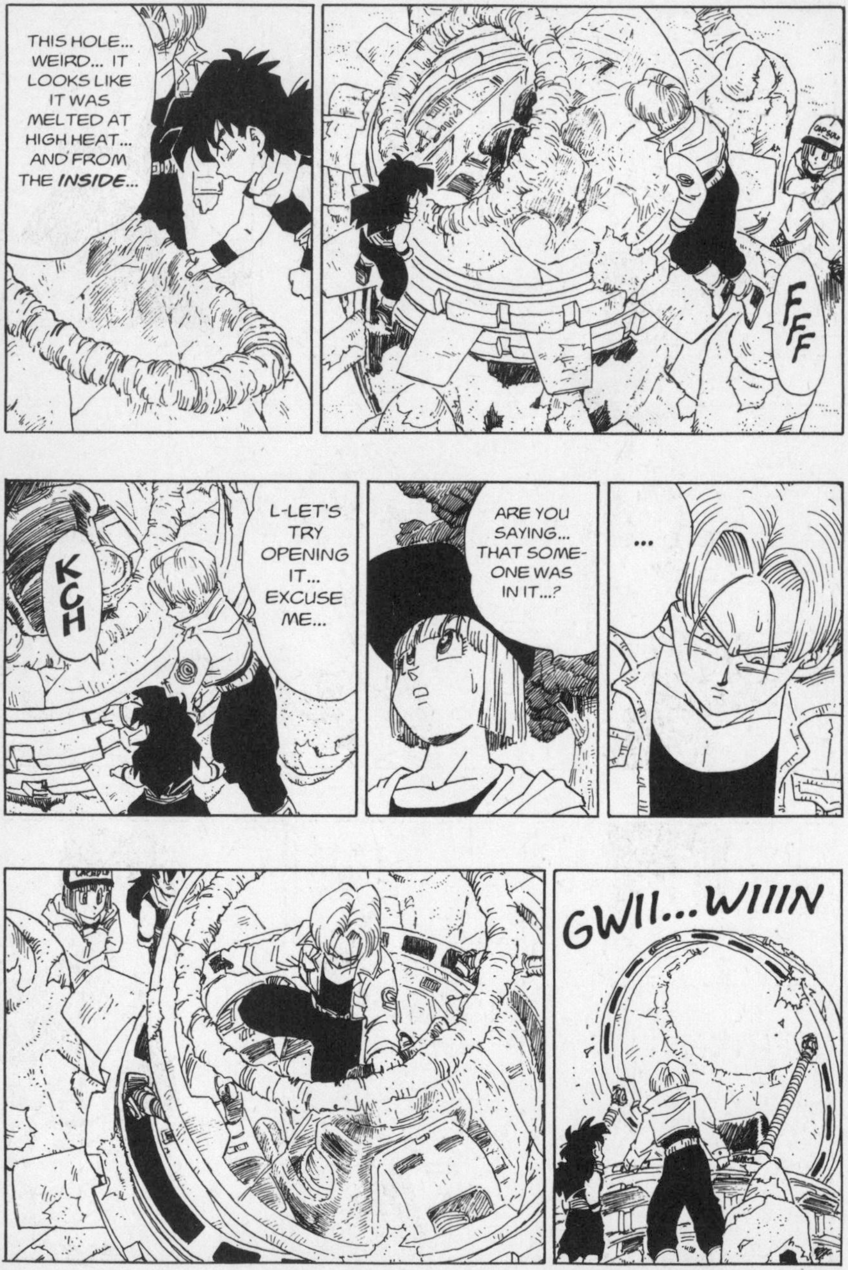

FFF
THIS HOLE... WEIRD... IT LOOKS LIKE IT WAS MELTED AT HIGH HEAT... AND FROM THE *INSIDE*...
...
ARE YOU SAYING... THAT SOME-ONE WAS IN IT...?
L-LET'S TRY OPENING IT... EXCUSE ME...
KCH
GWII...WIIIN

READ THIS WAY

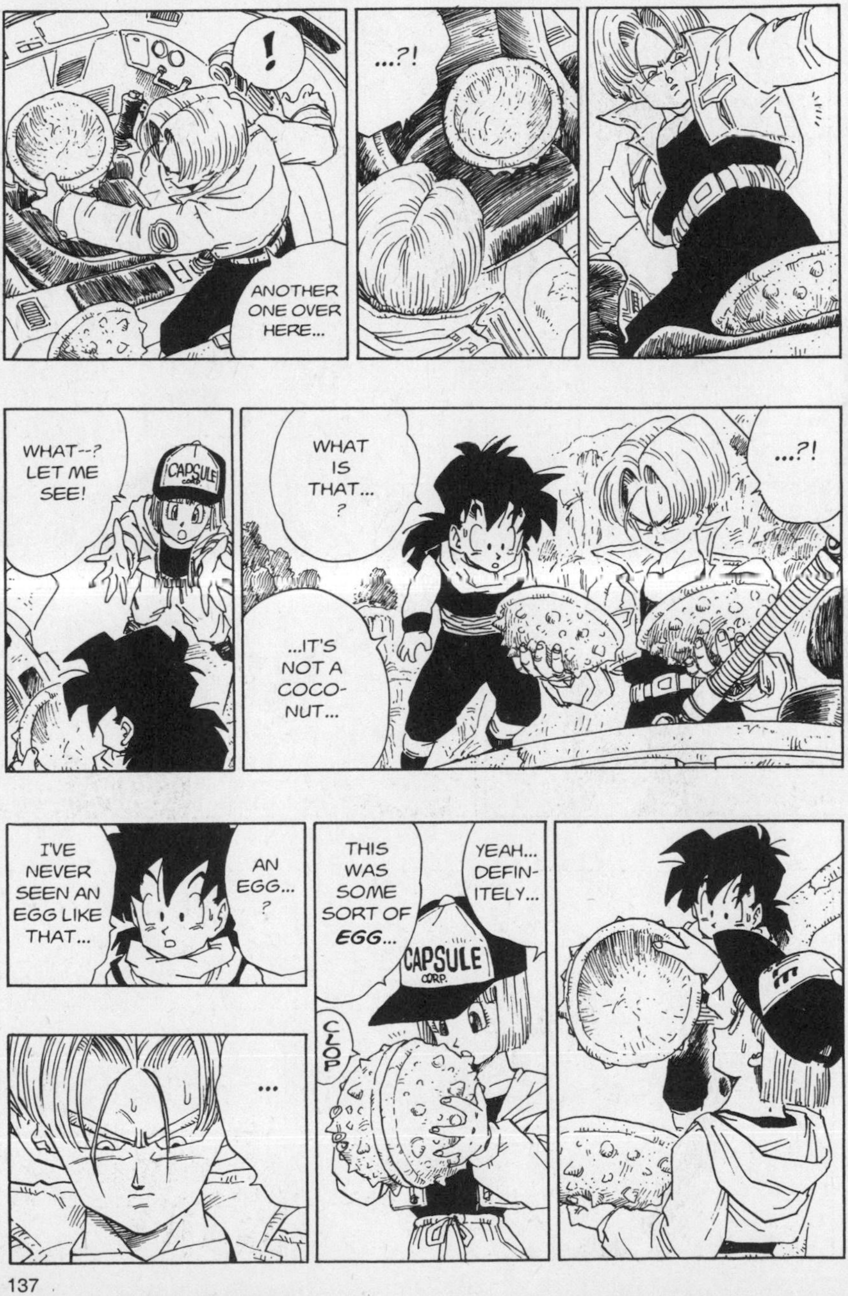
...?!
!
ANOTHER ONE OVER HERE...
...?!
WHAT IS THAT...?
...IT'S NOT A COCONUT...
WHAT--? LET ME SEE!
CAPSULE CORP.
YEAH... DEFINITELY...
THIS WAS SOME SORT OF *EGG*...
CAPSULE CORP.
CLOP
AN EGG...?
I'VE NEVER SEEN AN EGG LIKE THAT...
...

READ THIS WAY

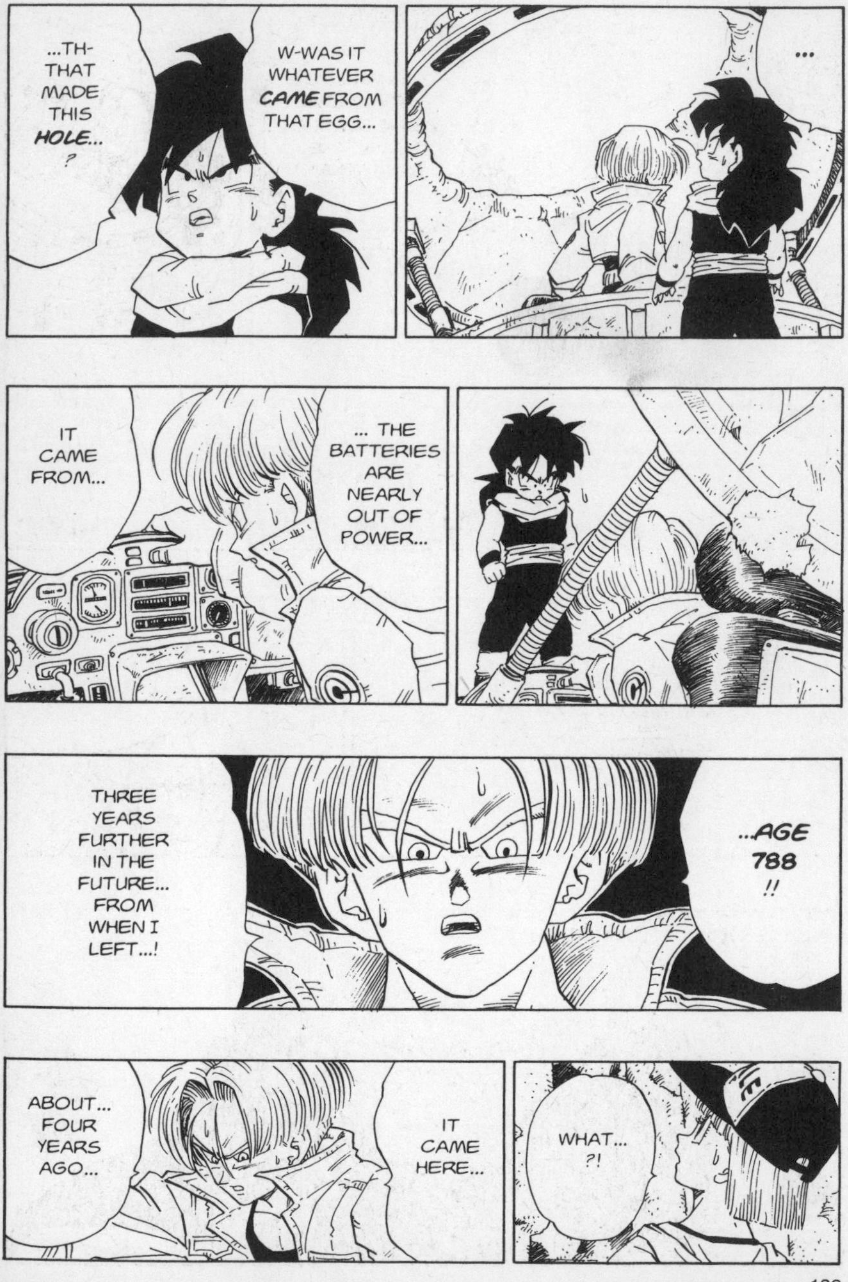
...
W-WAS IT WHATEVER CAME FROM THAT EGG...
...TH-THAT MADE THIS HOLE...?
... THE BATTERIES ARE NEARLY OUT OF POWER...
IT CAME FROM...
...AGE 788!!
THREE YEARS FURTHER IN THE FUTURE... FROM WHEN I LEFT...!
WHAT...?!
IT CAME HERE...
ABOUT... FOUR YEARS AGO...

READ THIS WAY

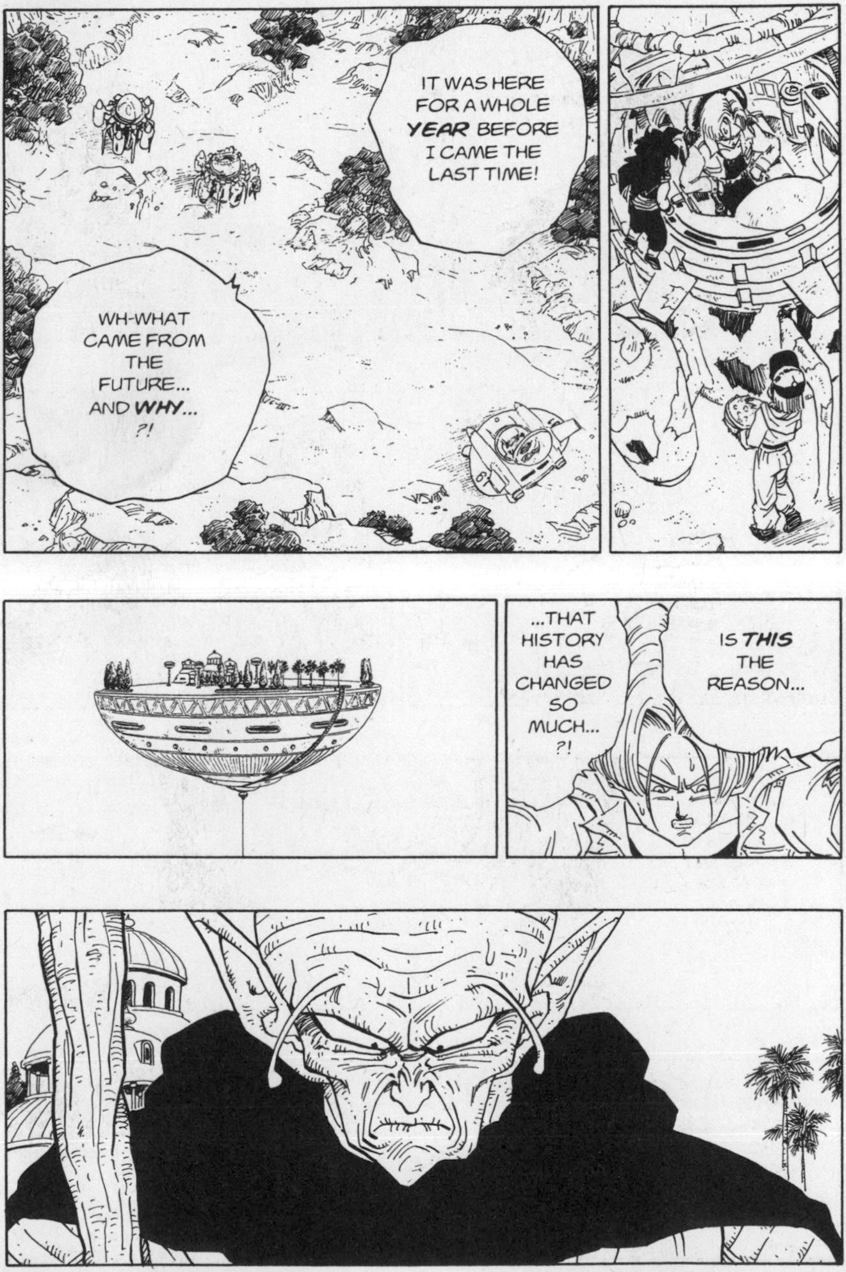
IT WAS HERE FOR A WHOLE **YEAR** BEFORE I CAME THE LAST TIME!
WH-WHAT CAME FROM THE FUTURE... AND **WHY**...?!
IS **THIS** THE REASON...
...THAT HISTORY HAS CHANGED SO MUCH...?!

READ THIS WAY

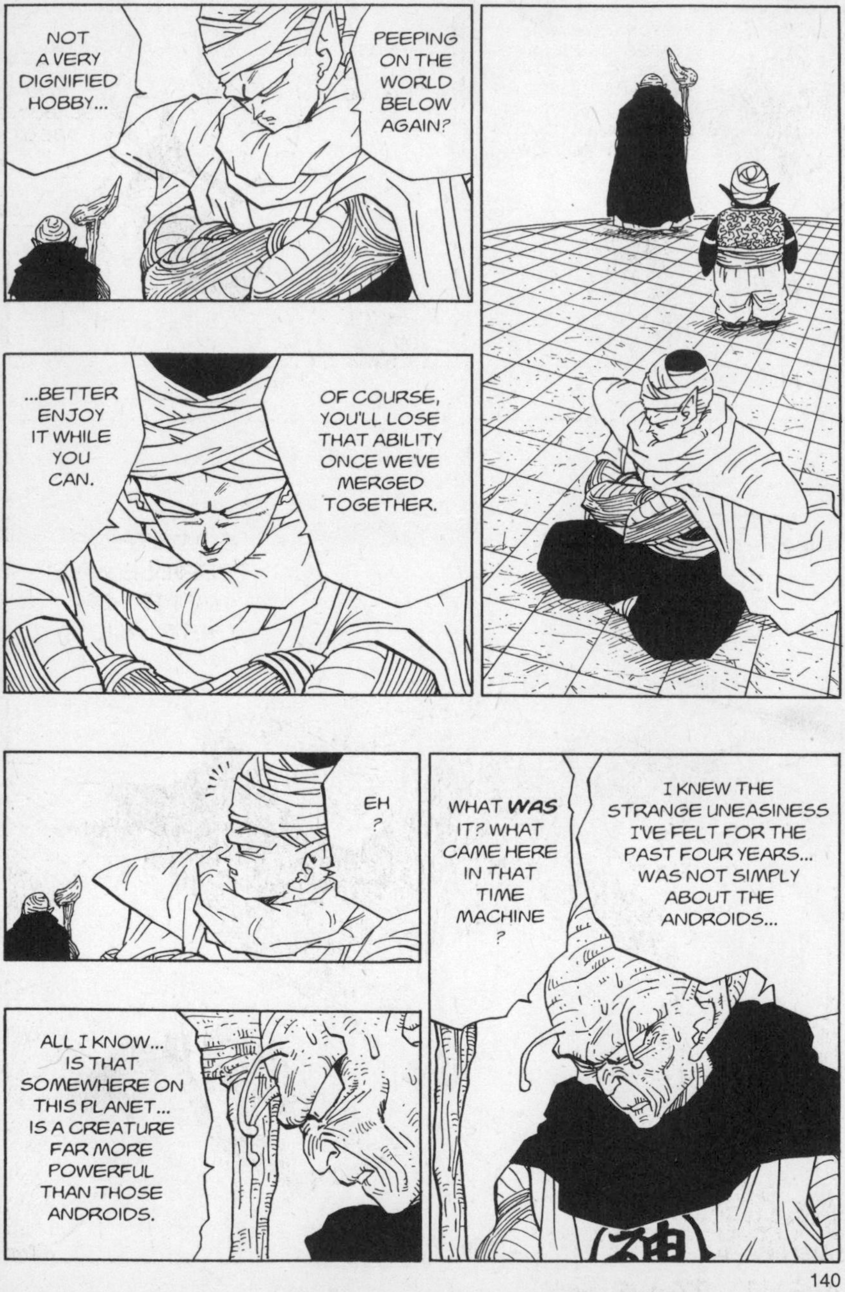
PEEPING ON THE WORLD BELOW AGAIN?
NOT A VERY DIGNIFIED HOBBY...
OF COURSE, YOU'LL LOSE THAT ABILITY ONCE WE'VE MERGED TOGETHER.
...BETTER ENJOY IT WHILE YOU CAN.
I KNEW THE STRANGE UNEASINESS I'VE FELT FOR THE PAST FOUR YEARS... WAS NOT SIMPLY ABOUT THE ANDROIDS...
WHAT **WAS** IT? WHAT CAME HERE IN THAT TIME MACHINE?
EH?
ALL I KNOW... IS THAT SOMEWHERE ON THIS PLANET... IS A CREATURE FAR MORE POWERFUL THAN THOSE ANDROIDS.

READ THIS WAY

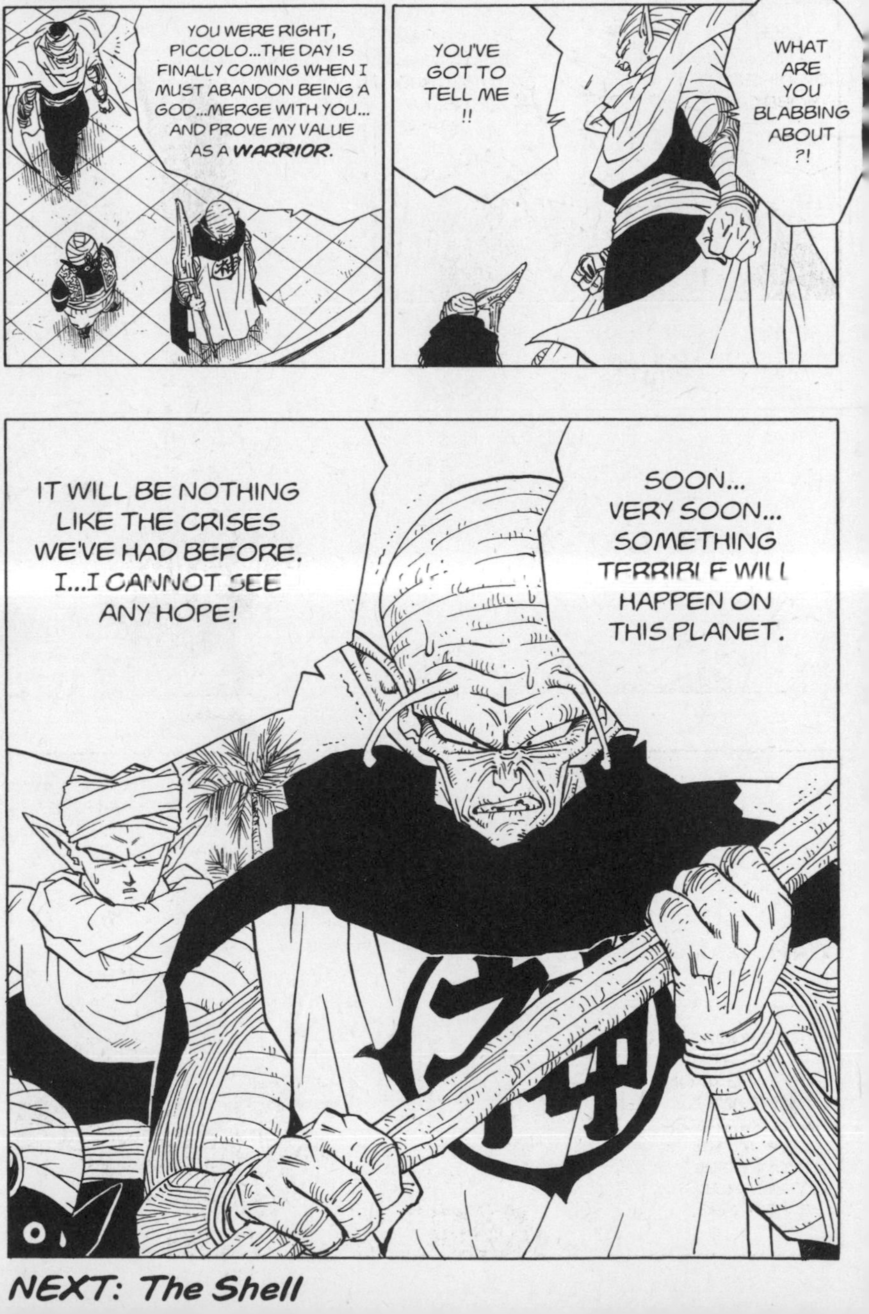
WHAT ARE YOU BLABBING ABOUT ?!
YOU'VE GOT TO TELL ME !!
YOU WERE RIGHT, PICCOLO...THE DAY IS FINALLY COMING WHEN I MUST ABANDON BEING A GOD...MERGE WITH YOU... AND PROVE MY VALUE AS A WARRIOR.
SOON... VERY SOON... SOMETHING TERRIBLE WILL HAPPEN ON THIS PLANET.
IT WILL BE NOTHING LIKE THE CRISES WE'VE HAD BEFORE. I...I CANNOT SEE ANY HOPE!

NEXT: The Shell

DBZ:165 • Kami-sama's Vision

READ THIS WAY

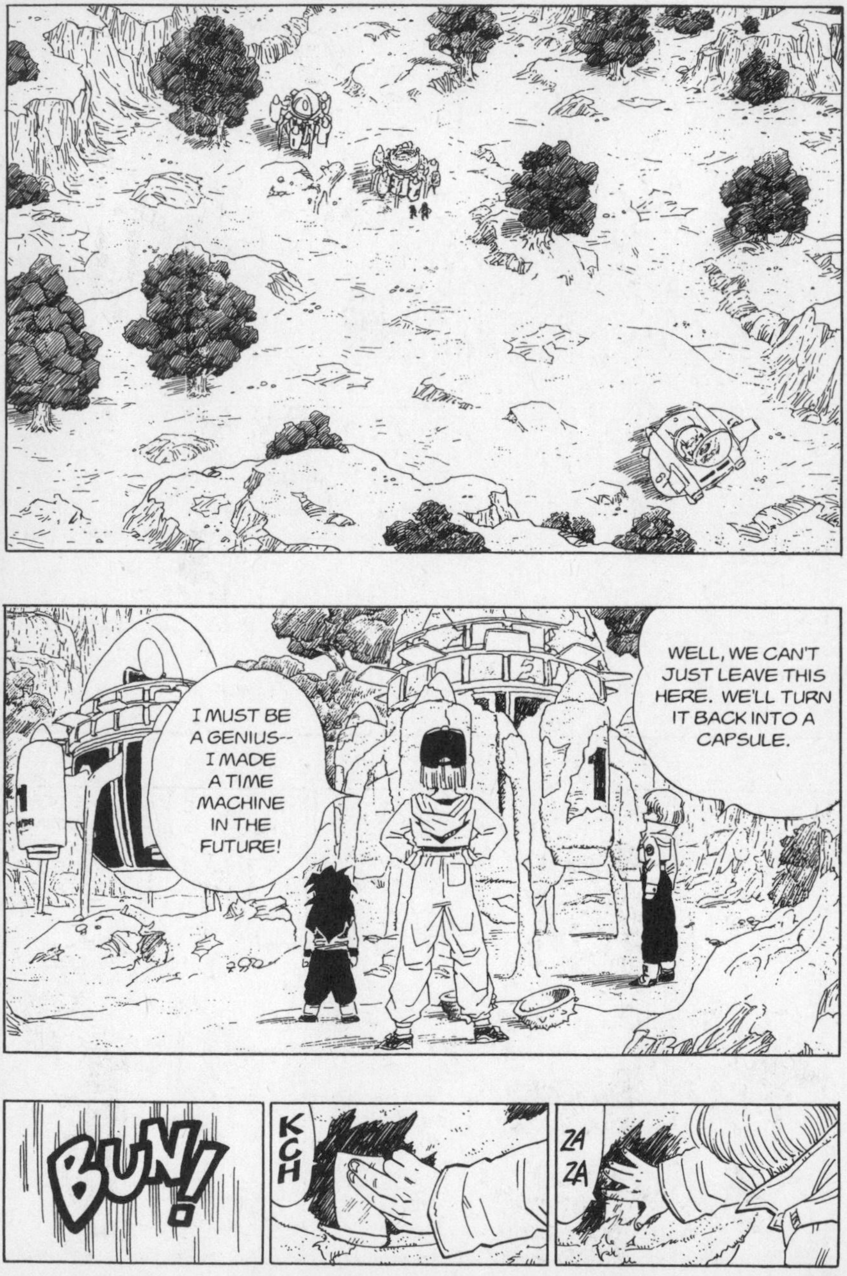

WELL, WE CAN'T JUST LEAVE THIS HERE. WE'LL TURN IT BACK INTO A CAPSULE.
I MUST BE A GENIUS-- I MADE A TIME MACHINE IN THE FUTURE!
ZA ZA
KCH
BUN!

READ THIS WAY

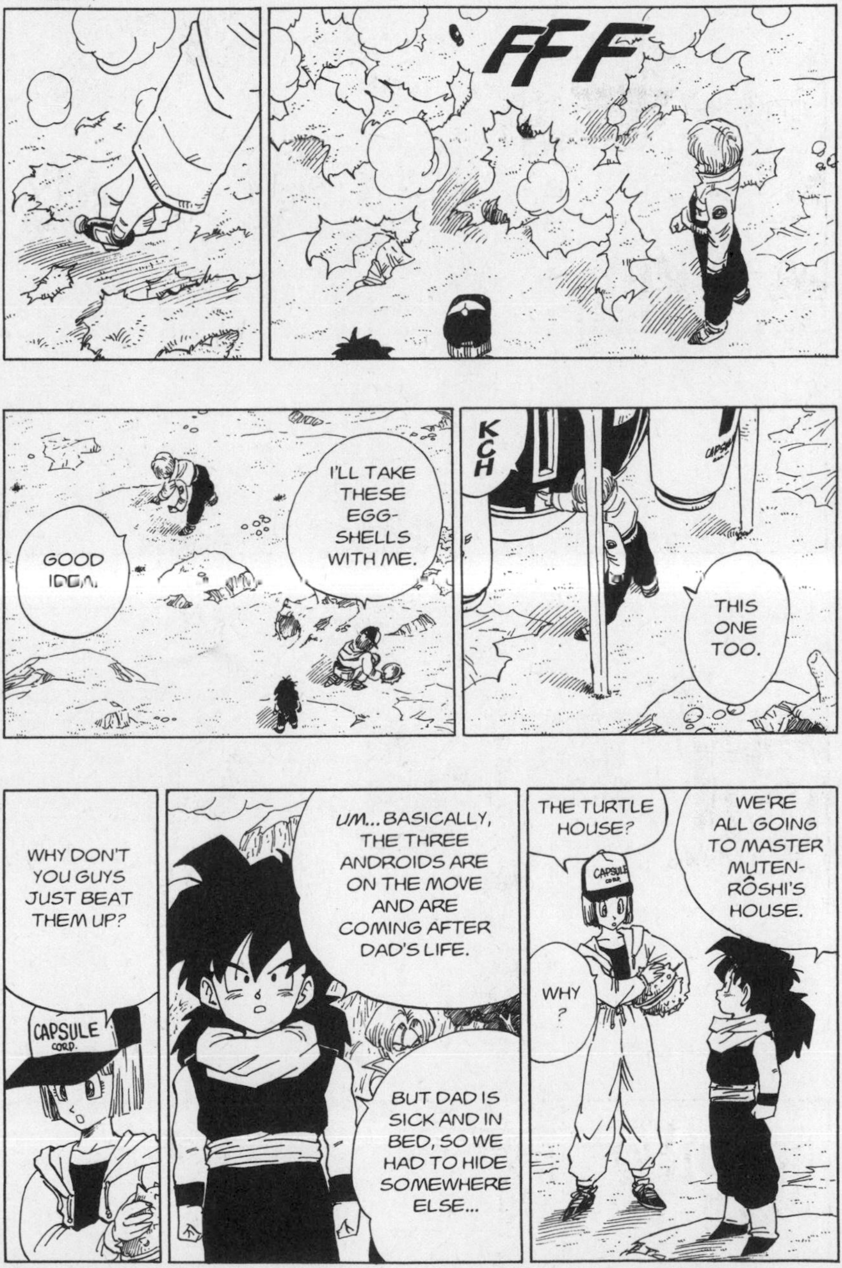
FFF
KCH
THIS ONE TOO.
I'LL TAKE THESE EGG-SHELLS WITH ME.
GOOD IDEA.
WE'RE ALL GOING TO MASTER MUTEN-RÔSHI'S HOUSE.
THE TURTLE HOUSE?
WHY?
UM... BASICALLY, THE THREE ANDROIDS ARE ON THE MOVE AND ARE COMING AFTER DAD'S LIFE.
BUT DAD IS SICK AND IN BED, SO WE HAD TO HIDE SOMEWHERE ELSE...
WHY DON'T YOU GUYS JUST BEAT THEM UP?

READ THIS WAY

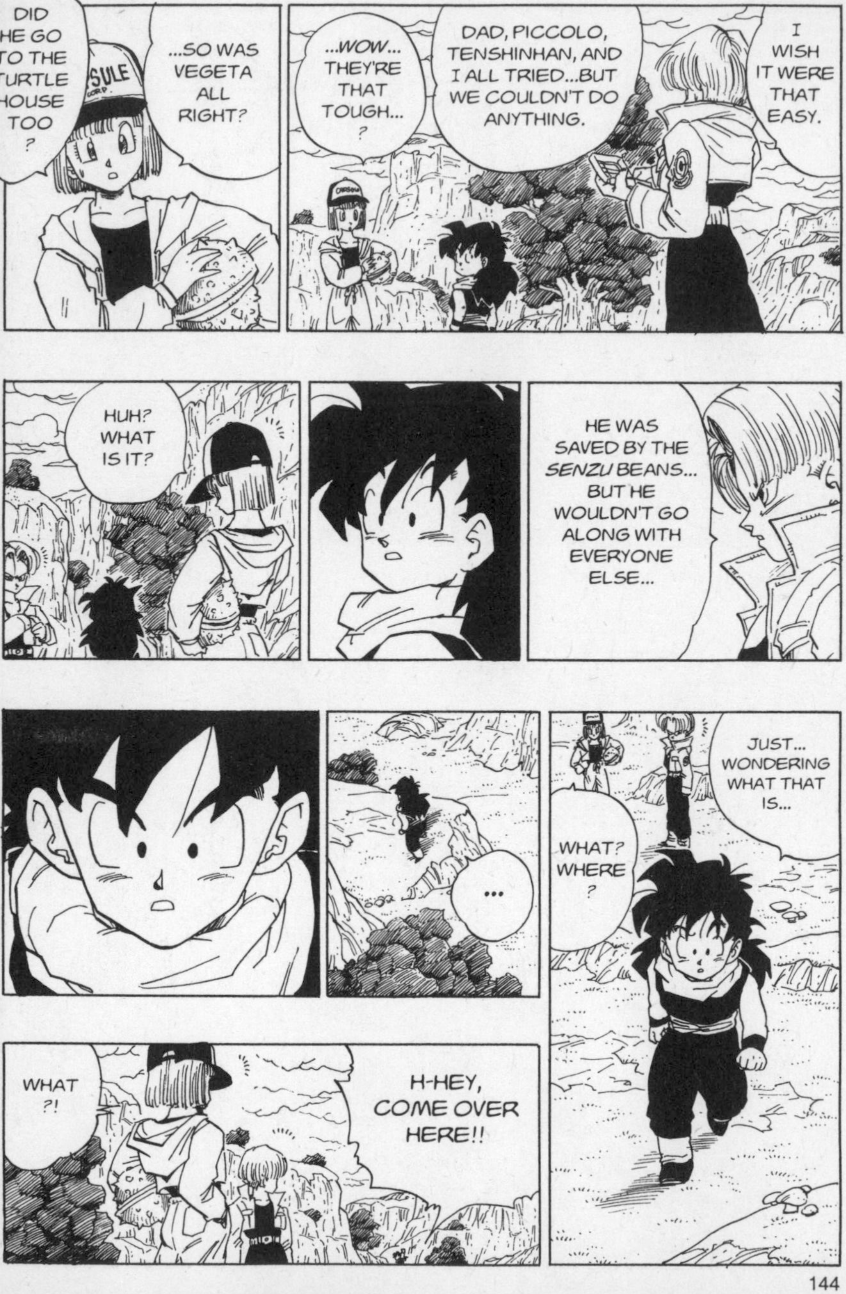
I WISH IT WERE THAT EASY.
DAD, PICCOLO, TENSHINHAN, AND I ALL TRIED...BUT WE COULDN'T DO ANYTHING.
...WOW... THEY'RE THAT TOUGH...?
...SO WAS VEGETA ALL RIGHT?
DID HE GO TO THE TURTLE HOUSE TOO?
HE WAS SAVED BY THE *SENZU* BEANS... BUT HE WOULDN'T GO ALONG WITH EVERYONE ELSE...
HUH? WHAT IS IT?
JUST... WONDERING WHAT THAT IS...
WHAT? WHERE?
...
H-HEY, COME OVER HERE!!
WHAT?!

READ THIS WAY

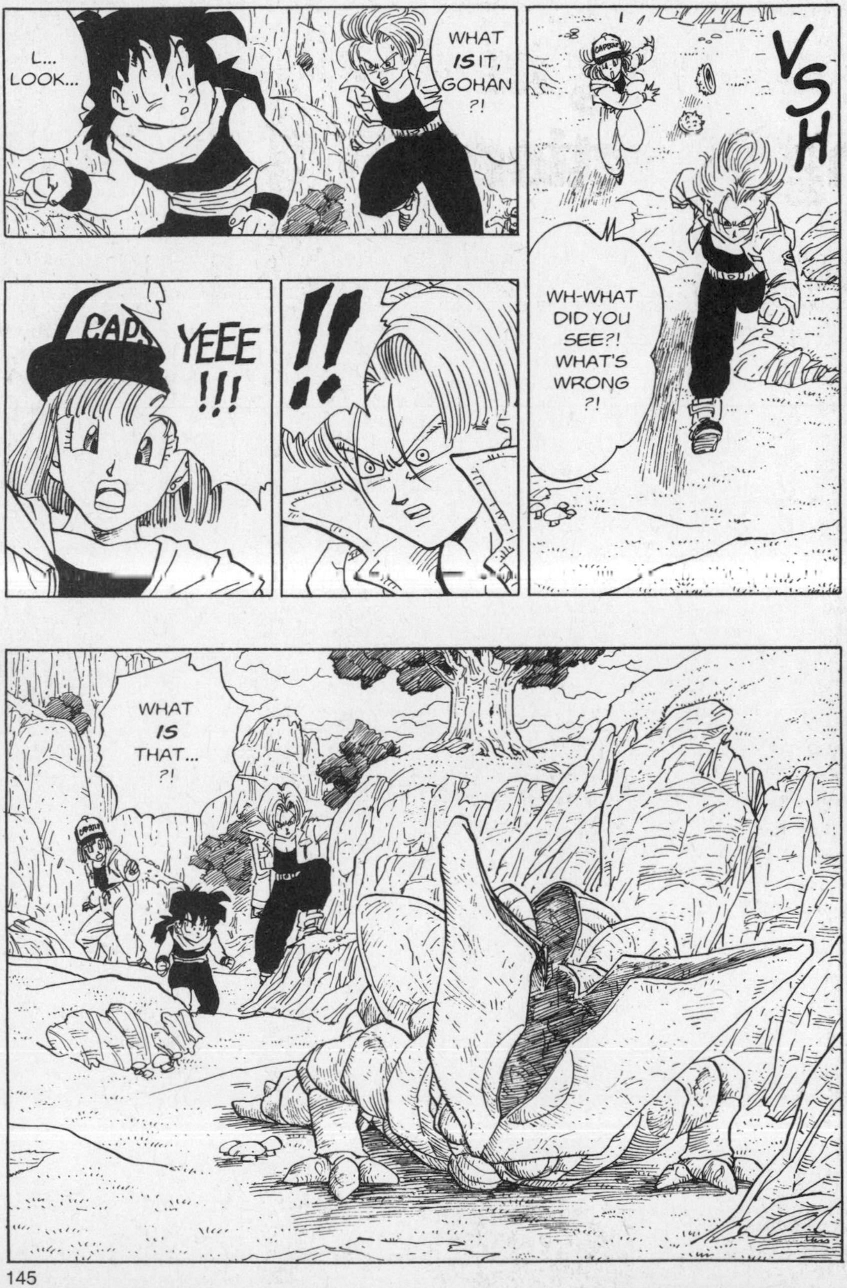
VSH
WH-WHAT DID YOU SEE?! WHAT'S WRONG ?!
WHAT *IS* IT, GOHAN ?!
L... LOOK...
!!
YEEE !!!
WHAT *IS* THAT... ?!

READ THIS WAY

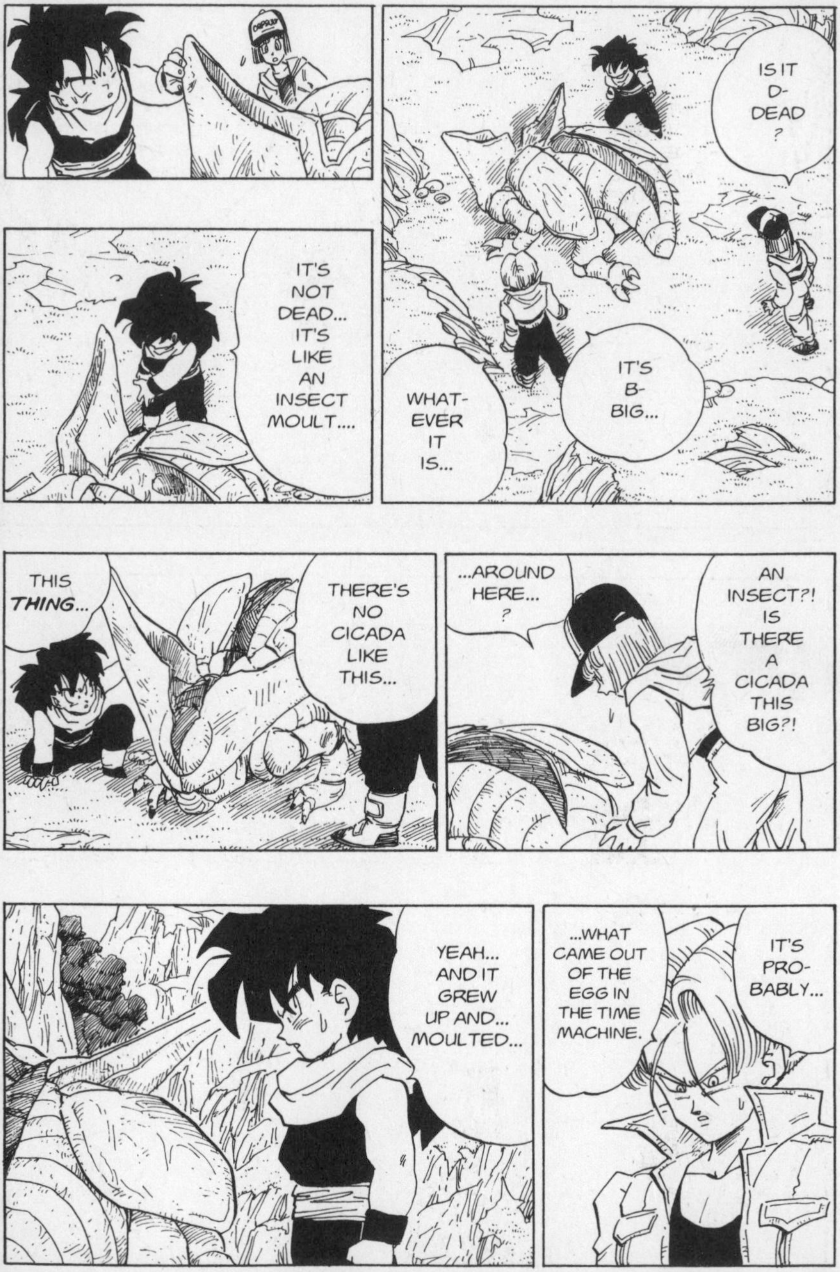
IS IT D-DEAD?
IT'S B-BIG...
WHAT-EVER IT IS...
IT'S NOT DEAD... IT'S LIKE AN INSECT MOULT....
AN INSECT?! IS THERE A CICADA THIS BIG?!
...AROUND HERE...?
THERE'S NO CICADA LIKE THIS...
THIS *THING*...
IT'S PRO-BABLY...
...WHAT CAME OUT OF THE EGG IN THE TIME MACHINE.
YEAH... AND IT GREW UP AND... MOULTED...

READ THIS WAY

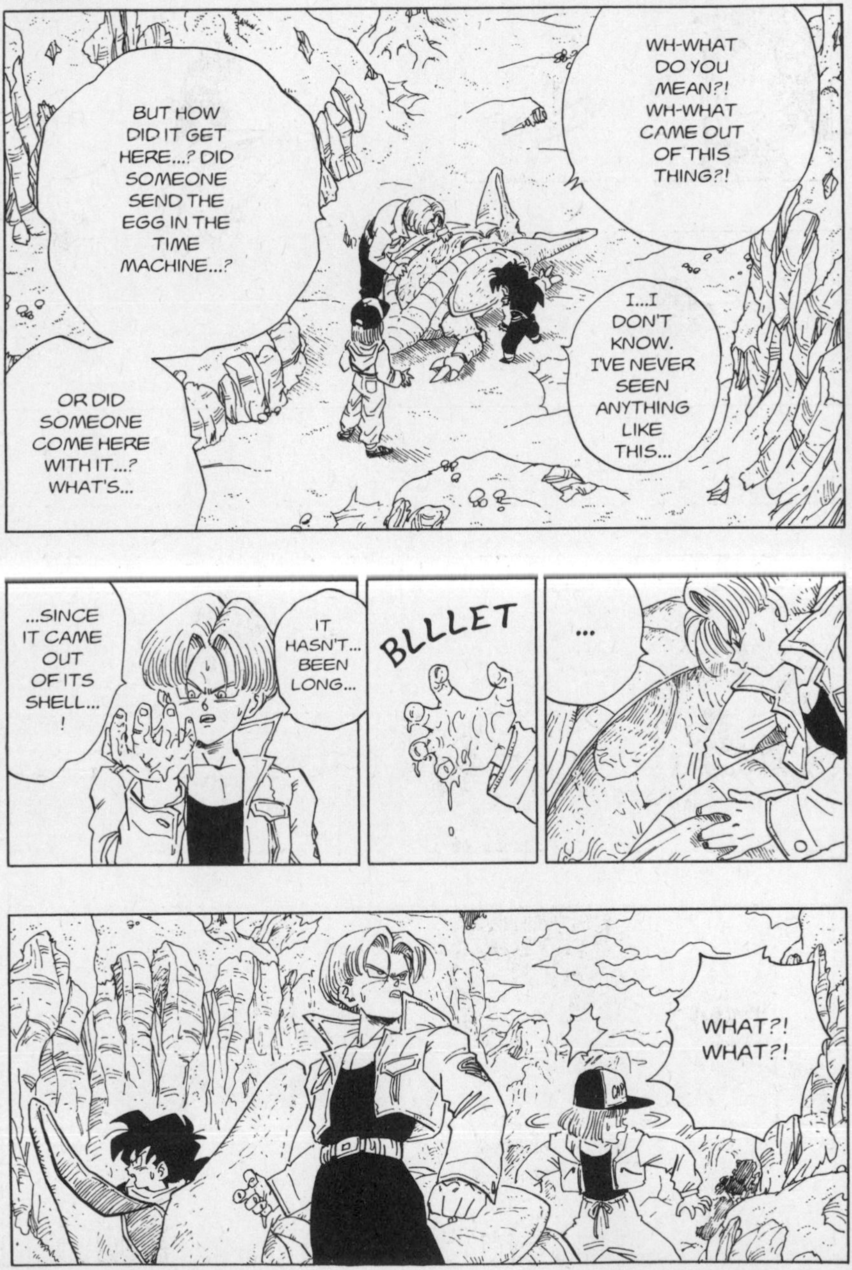
WH-WHAT DO YOU MEAN?! WH-WHAT CAME OUT OF THIS THING?!
BUT HOW DID IT GET HERE...? DID SOMEONE SEND THE EGG IN THE TIME MACHINE...?
I...I DON'T KNOW. I'VE NEVER SEEN ANYTHING LIKE THIS...
OR DID SOMEONE COME HERE WITH IT...? WHAT'S...
...
BLLLET
IT HASN'T... BEEN LONG...
...SINCE IT CAME OUT OF ITS SHELL...!
WHAT?! WHAT?!

READ THIS WAY

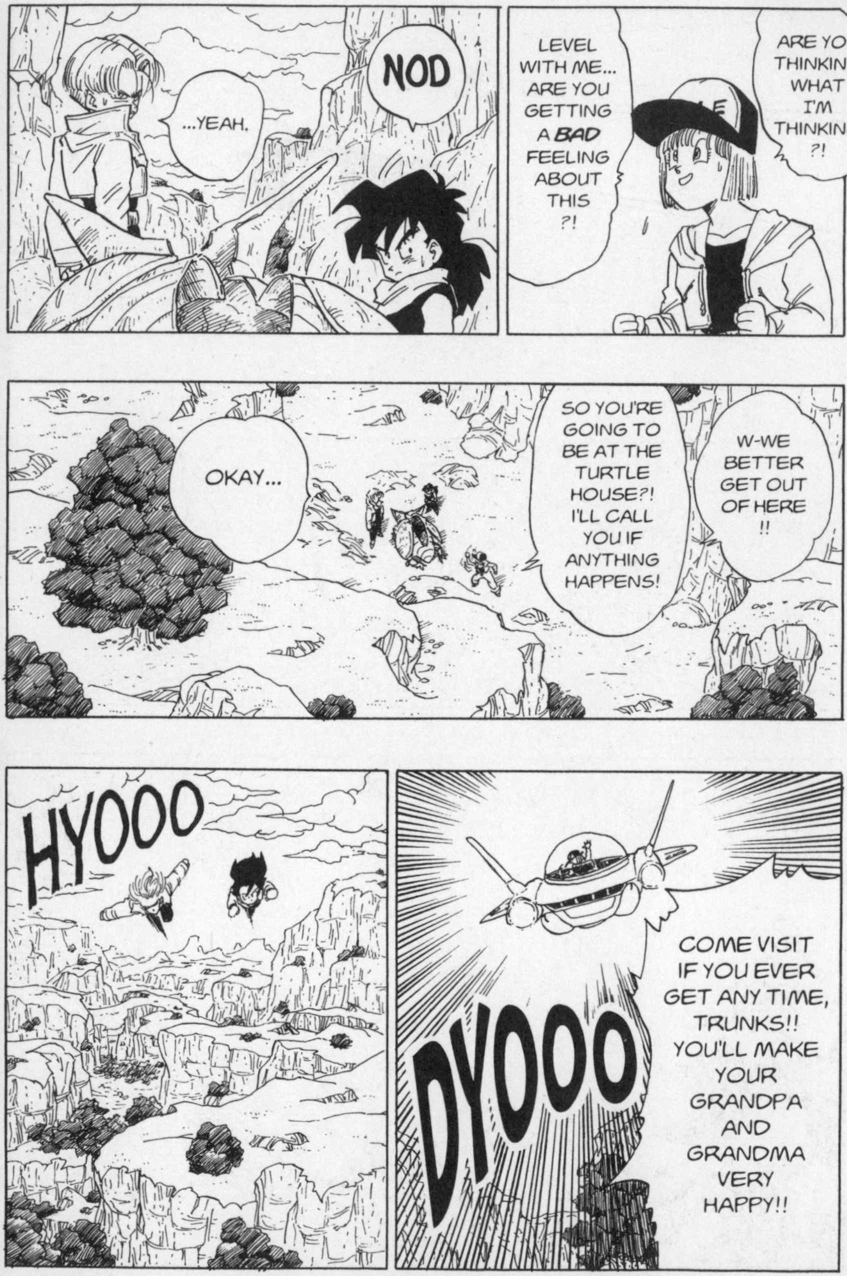

ARE YOU THINKING WHAT I'M THINKING ?!
LEVEL WITH ME... ARE YOU GETTING A **BAD** FEELING ABOUT THIS ?!
NOD
...YEAH.
W-WE BETTER GET OUT OF HERE !!
SO YOU'RE GOING TO BE AT THE TURTLE HOUSE?! I'LL CALL YOU IF ANYTHING HAPPENS!
OKAY...
COME VISIT IF YOU EVER GET ANY TIME, TRUNKS!! YOU'LL MAKE YOUR GRANDPA AND GRANDMA VERY HAPPY!!
DYOOO
HYOOO

READ THIS WAY

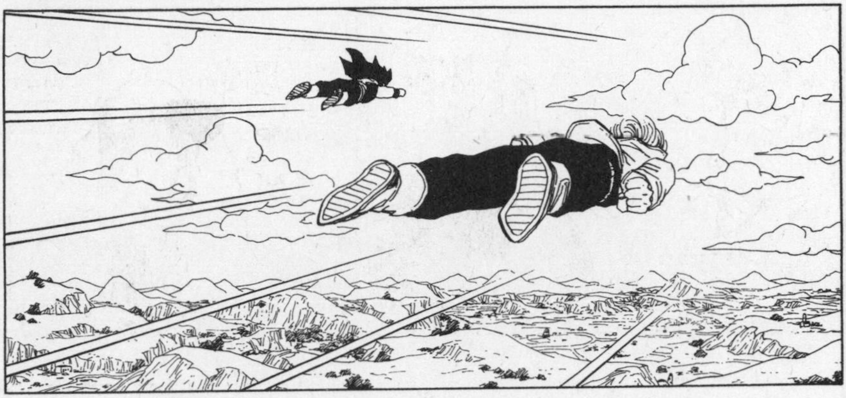

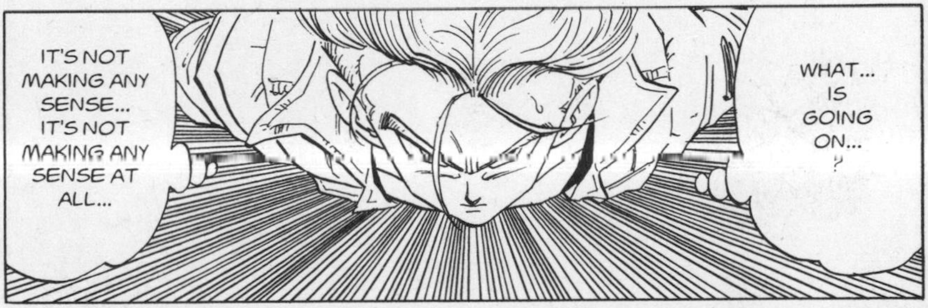
WHAT... IS GOING ON...?
IT'S NOT MAKING ANY SENSE... IT'S NOT MAKING ANY SENSE AT ALL...

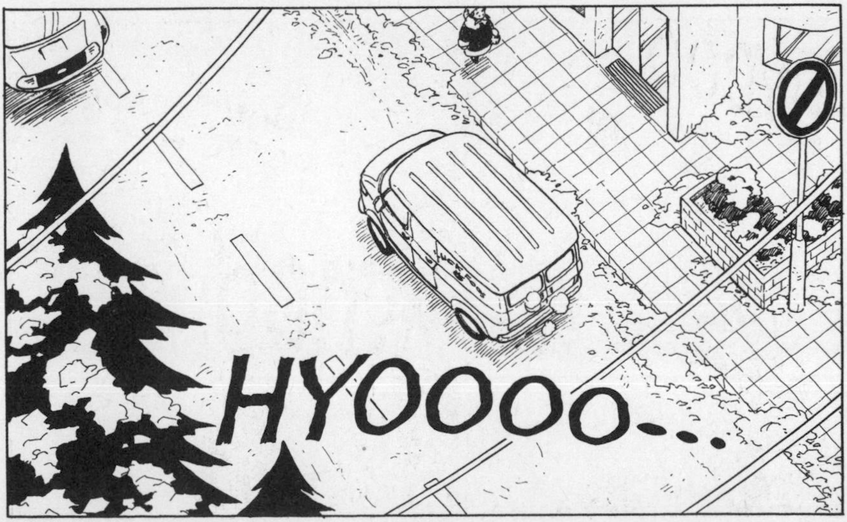
HYOOOO...

READ THIS WAY

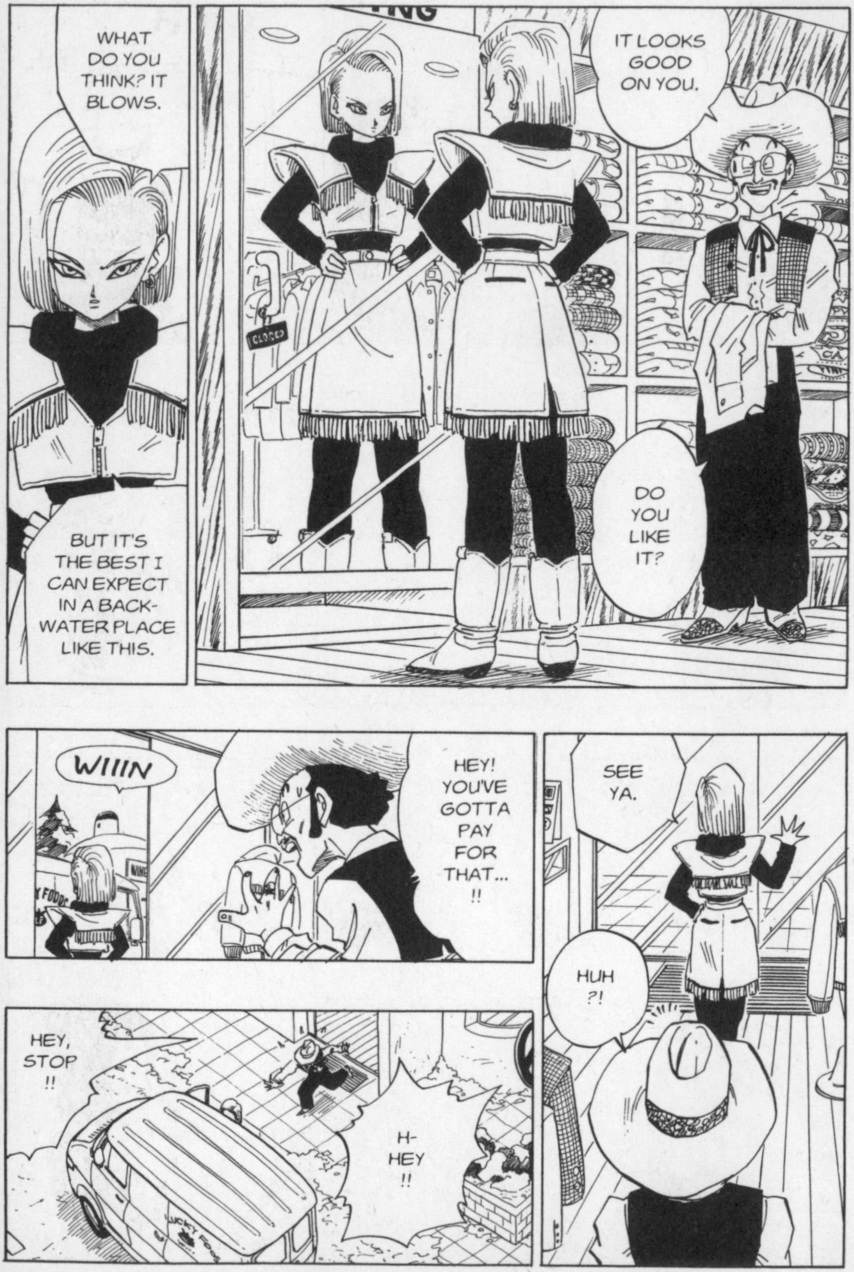
IT LOOKS GOOD ON YOU.
DO YOU LIKE IT?
WHAT DO YOU THINK? IT BLOWS.
BUT IT'S THE BEST I CAN EXPECT IN A BACK-WATER PLACE LIKE THIS.
CLOSED
SEE YA.
HUH ?!
HEY! YOU'VE GOTTA PAY FOR THAT... !!
WIIIN
H- HEY !!
HEY, STOP !!

READ THIS WAY

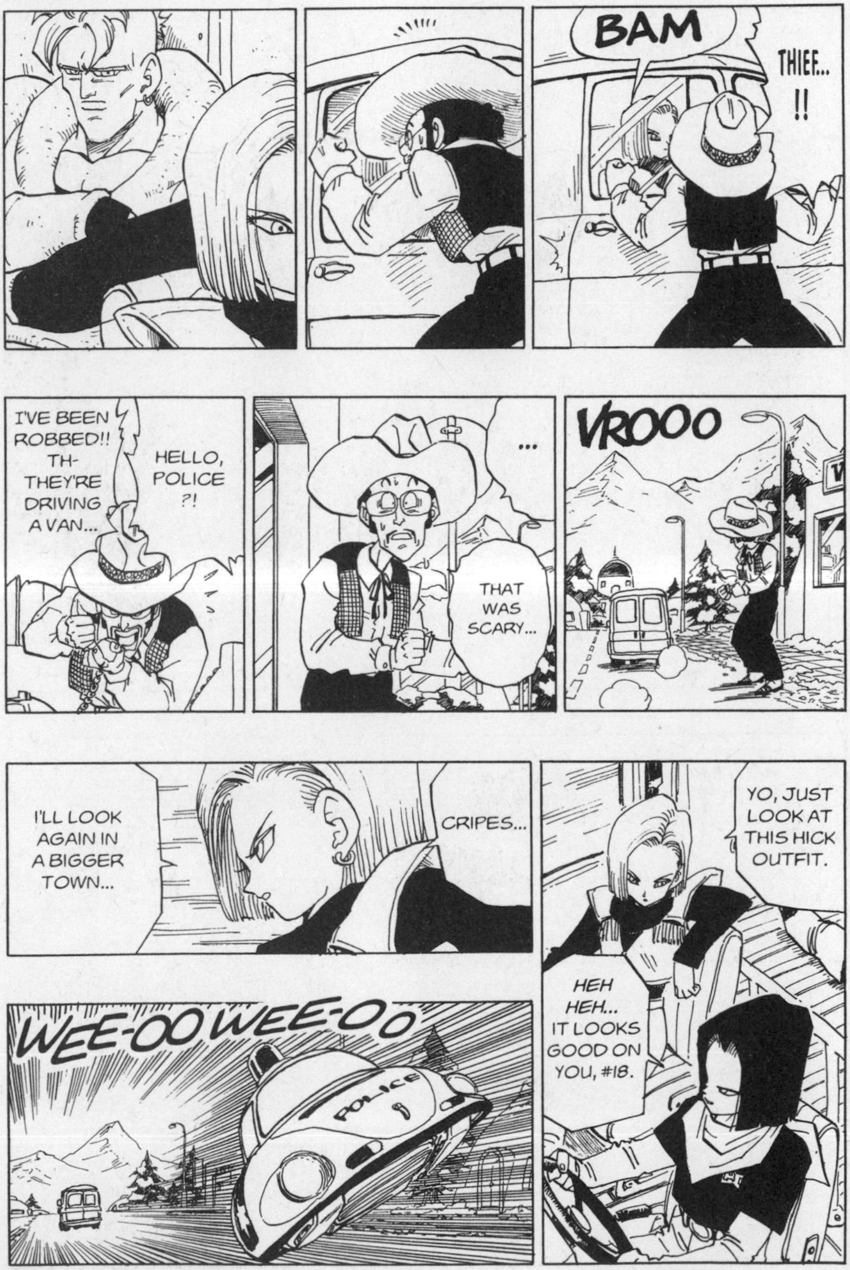
BAM
THIEF... !!
VROOO
...
THAT WAS SCARY...
HELLO, POLICE ?!
I'VE BEEN ROBBED!! TH- THEY'RE DRIVING A VAN...
YO, JUST LOOK AT THIS HICK OUTFIT.
HEH HEH... IT LOOKS GOOD ON YOU, #18.
CRIPES...
I'LL LOOK AGAIN IN A BIGGER TOWN...
WEE-OO WEE-OO
POLICE

READ THIS WAY

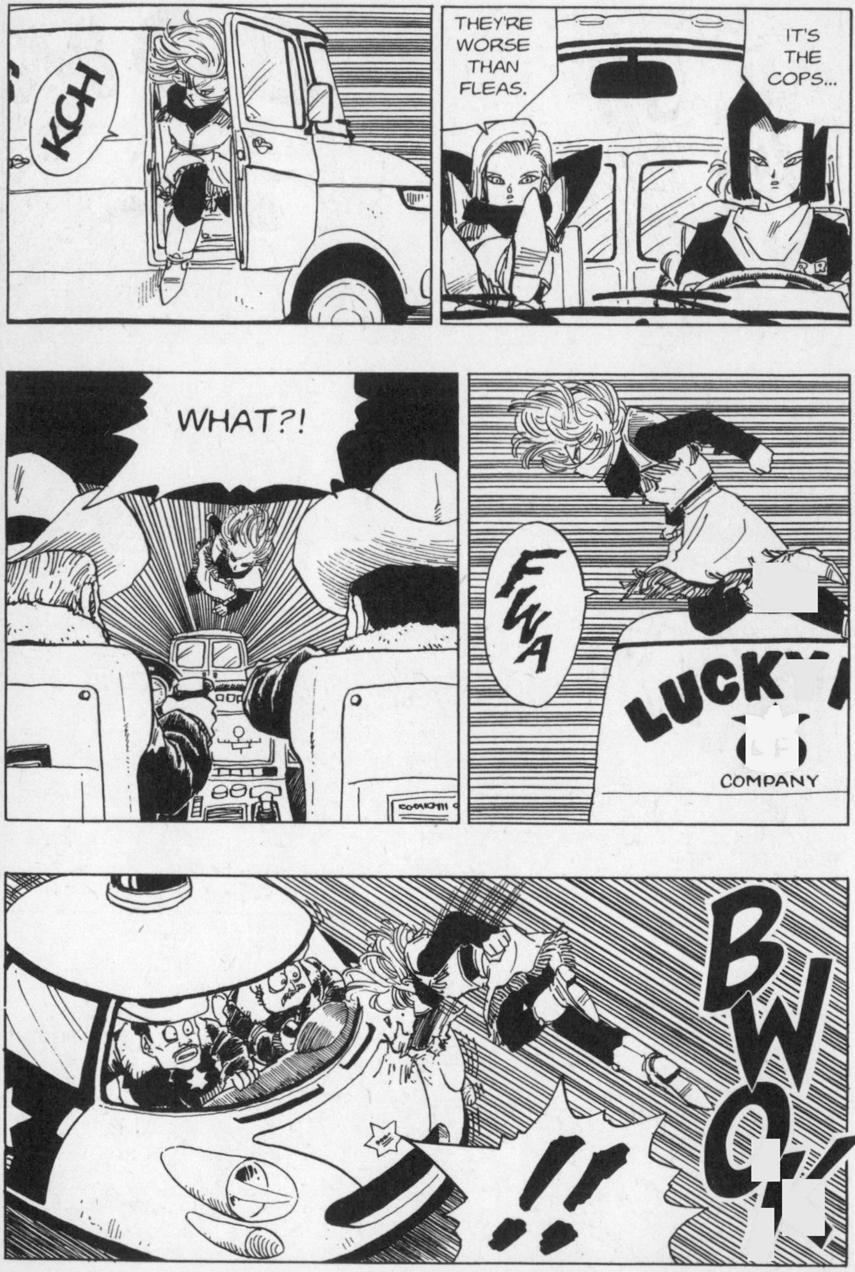

IT'S THE COPS...
THEY'RE WORSE THAN FLEAS.
KCH
FWA
LUCKY
COMPANY
WHAT?!
BWOK
!!

READ THIS WAY

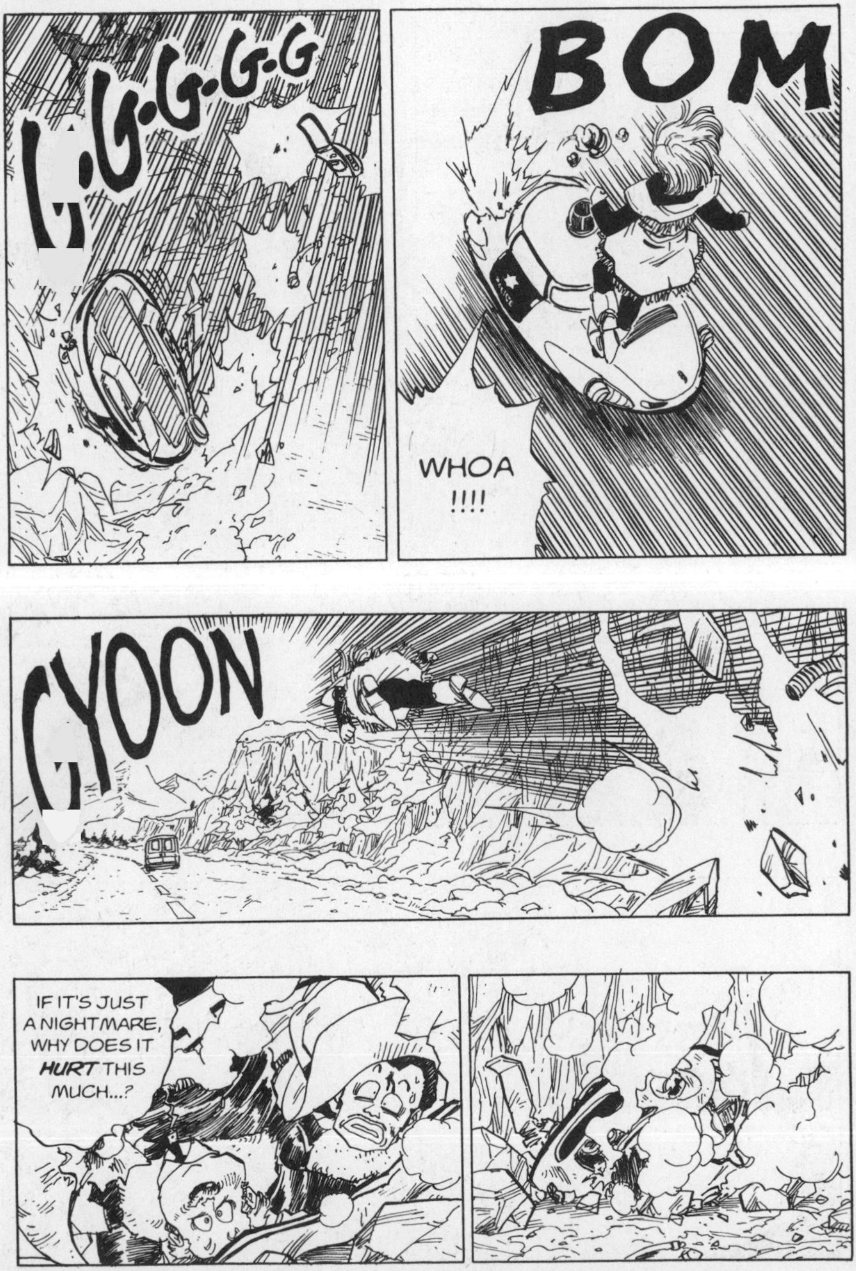
BOM
WHOA !!!!
G-G-G-G
CYOON
IF IT'S JUST A NIGHTMARE, WHY DOES IT ***HURT*** THIS MUCH...?

WHAT?! WHAT HAPPENED?!

...!!

K-KAMI-SAMA...

BWA

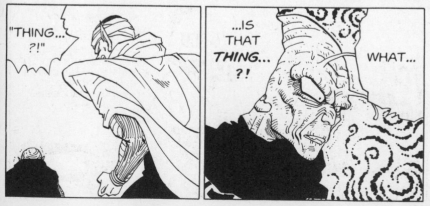

"THING...?!"

...IS THAT *THING*...?!

WHAT...

READ THIS WAY

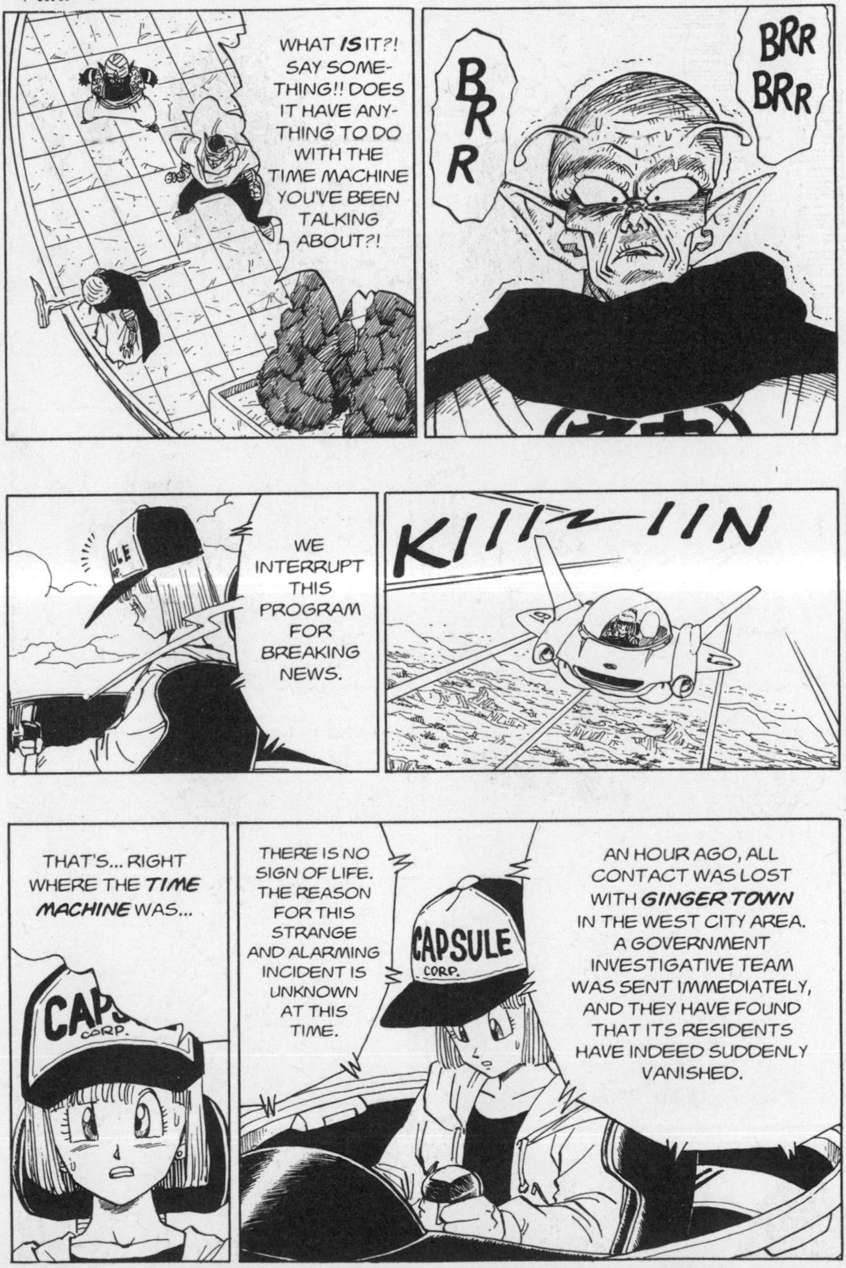
BRR BRR
BRR
WHAT IS IT?! SAY SOMETHING!! DOES IT HAVE ANYTHING TO DO WITH THE TIME MACHINE YOU'VE BEEN TALKING ABOUT?!
KIIIIIN
WE INTERRUPT THIS PROGRAM FOR BREAKING NEWS.
CAPSULE CORP.
AN HOUR AGO, ALL CONTACT WAS LOST WITH GINGER TOWN IN THE WEST CITY AREA. A GOVERNMENT INVESTIGATIVE TEAM WAS SENT IMMEDIATELY, AND THEY HAVE FOUND THAT ITS RESIDENTS HAVE INDEED SUDDENLY VANISHED.
THERE IS NO SIGN OF LIFE. THE REASON FOR THIS STRANGE AND ALARMING INCIDENT IS UNKNOWN AT THIS TIME.
THAT'S... RIGHT WHERE THE TIME MACHINE WAS...

NEXT: The Terror of Ginger Town

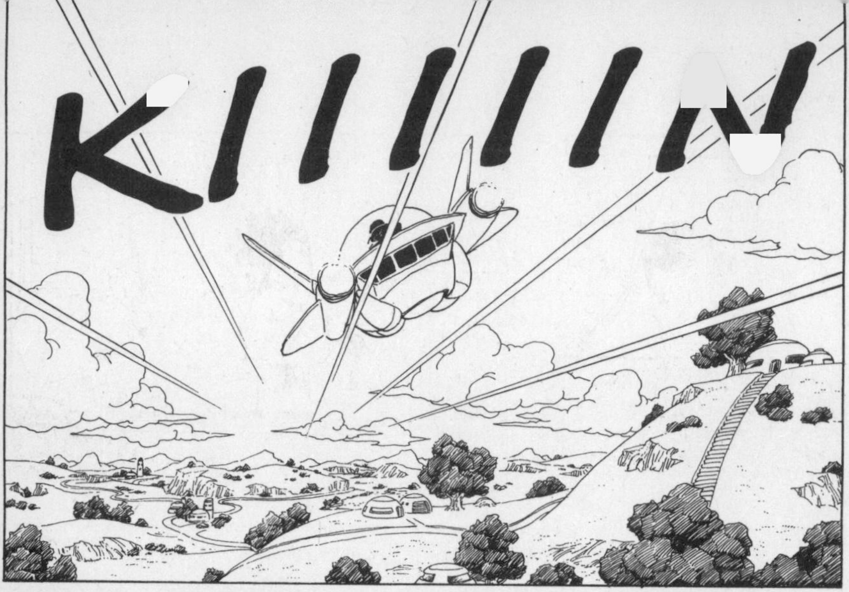
KIIIIIN

DBZ:166 • Kami-sama and the Demon King Become One

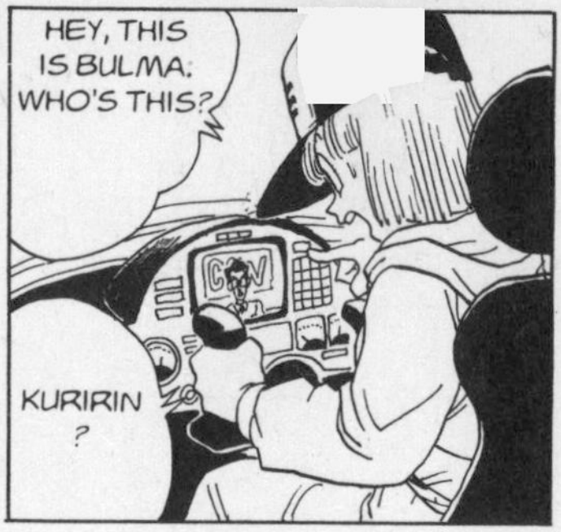
HEY, THIS IS BULMA: WHO'S THIS?
KURIRIN ?

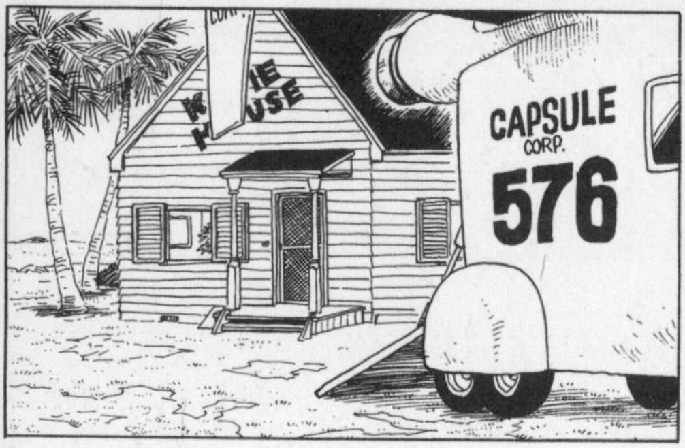
CAPSULE CORP. 576

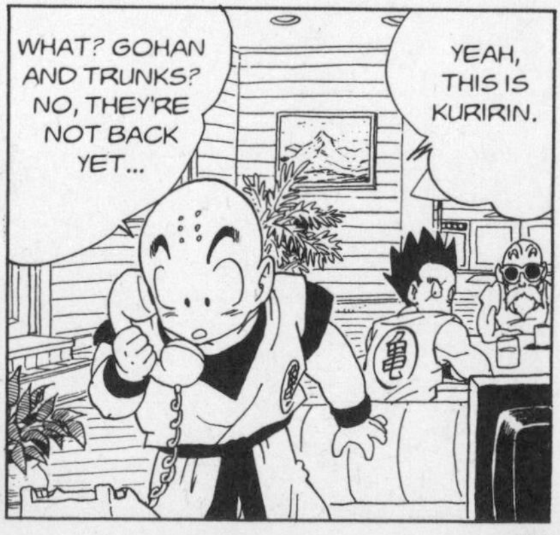
YEAH, THIS IS KURIRIN.
WHAT? GOHAN AND TRUNKS? NO, THEY'RE NOT BACK YET...

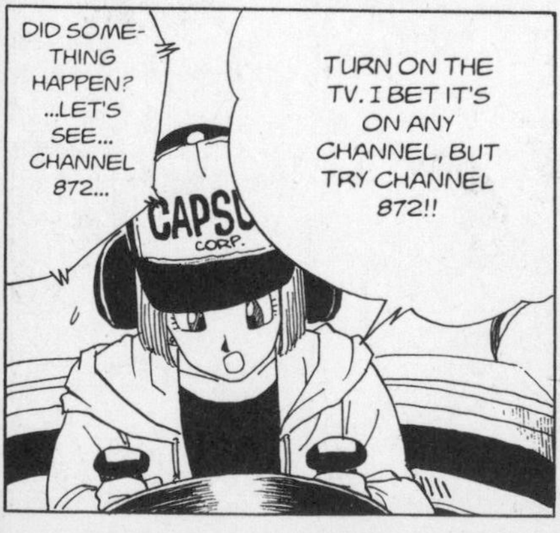
TURN ON THE TV. I BET IT'S ON ANY CHANNEL, BUT TRY CHANNEL 872!!
DID SOME-THING HAPPEN? ...LET'S SEE... CHANNEL 872...

READ THIS WAY

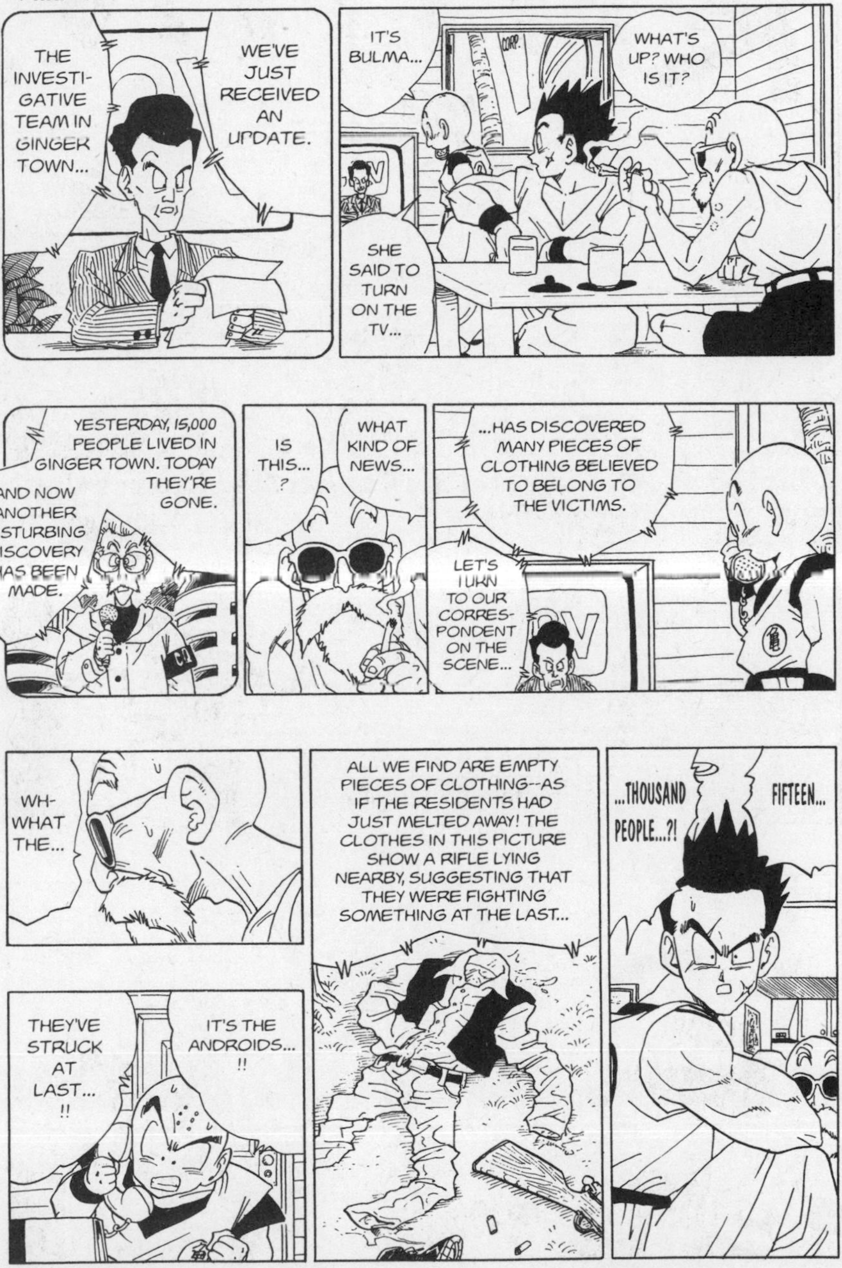
WHAT'S UP? WHO IS IT?
IT'S BULMA...
SHE SAID TO TURN ON THE TV...
WE'VE JUST RECEIVED AN UPDATE.
THE INVESTI-GATIVE TEAM IN GINGER TOWN...
...HAS DISCOVERED MANY PIECES OF CLOTHING BELIEVED TO BELONG TO THE VICTIMS.
LET'S TURN TO OUR CORRES-PONDENT ON THE SCENE...
WHAT KIND OF NEWS...
IS THIS...?
YESTERDAY, 15,000 PEOPLE LIVED IN GINGER TOWN. TODAY THEY'RE GONE.
AND NOW ANOTHER DISTURBING DISCOVERY HAS BEEN MADE.
FIFTEEN...
...THOUSAND PEOPLE...?!
ALL WE FIND ARE EMPTY PIECES OF CLOTHING--AS IF THE RESIDENTS HAD JUST MELTED AWAY! THE CLOTHES IN THIS PICTURE SHOW A RIFLE LYING NEARBY, SUGGESTING THAT THEY WERE FIGHTING SOMETHING AT THE LAST...
WH- WHAT THE...
IT'S THE ANDROIDS... !!
THEY'VE STRUCK AT LAST... !!

READ THIS WAY

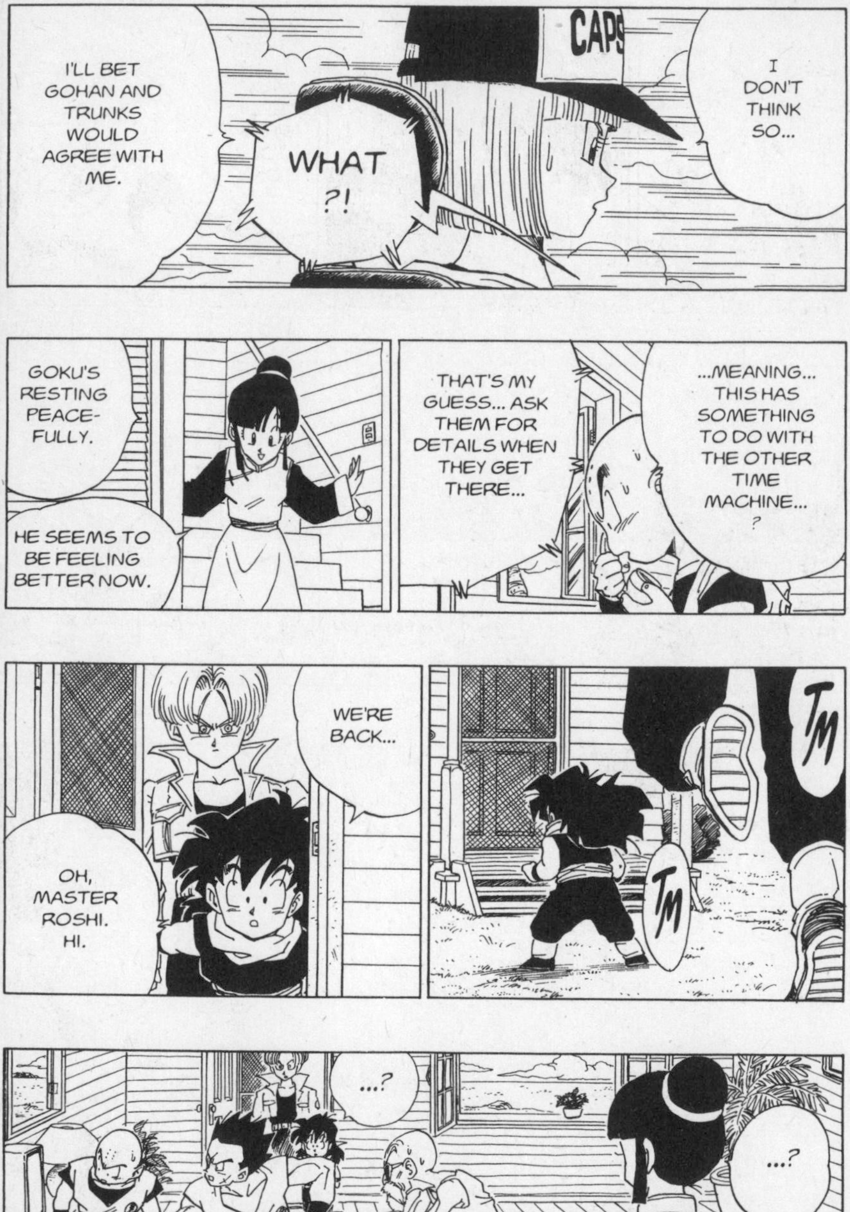
I DON'T THINK SO...
WHAT?!
I'LL BET GOHAN AND TRUNKS WOULD AGREE WITH ME.
...MEANING... THIS HAS SOMETHING TO DO WITH THE OTHER TIME MACHINE...?
THAT'S MY GUESS... ASK THEM FOR DETAILS WHEN THEY GET THERE...
GOKU'S RESTING PEACE-FULLY.
HE SEEMS TO BE FEELING BETTER NOW.
TM
TM
WE'RE BACK...
OH, MASTER ROSHI. HI.
...?
...?

READ THIS WAY

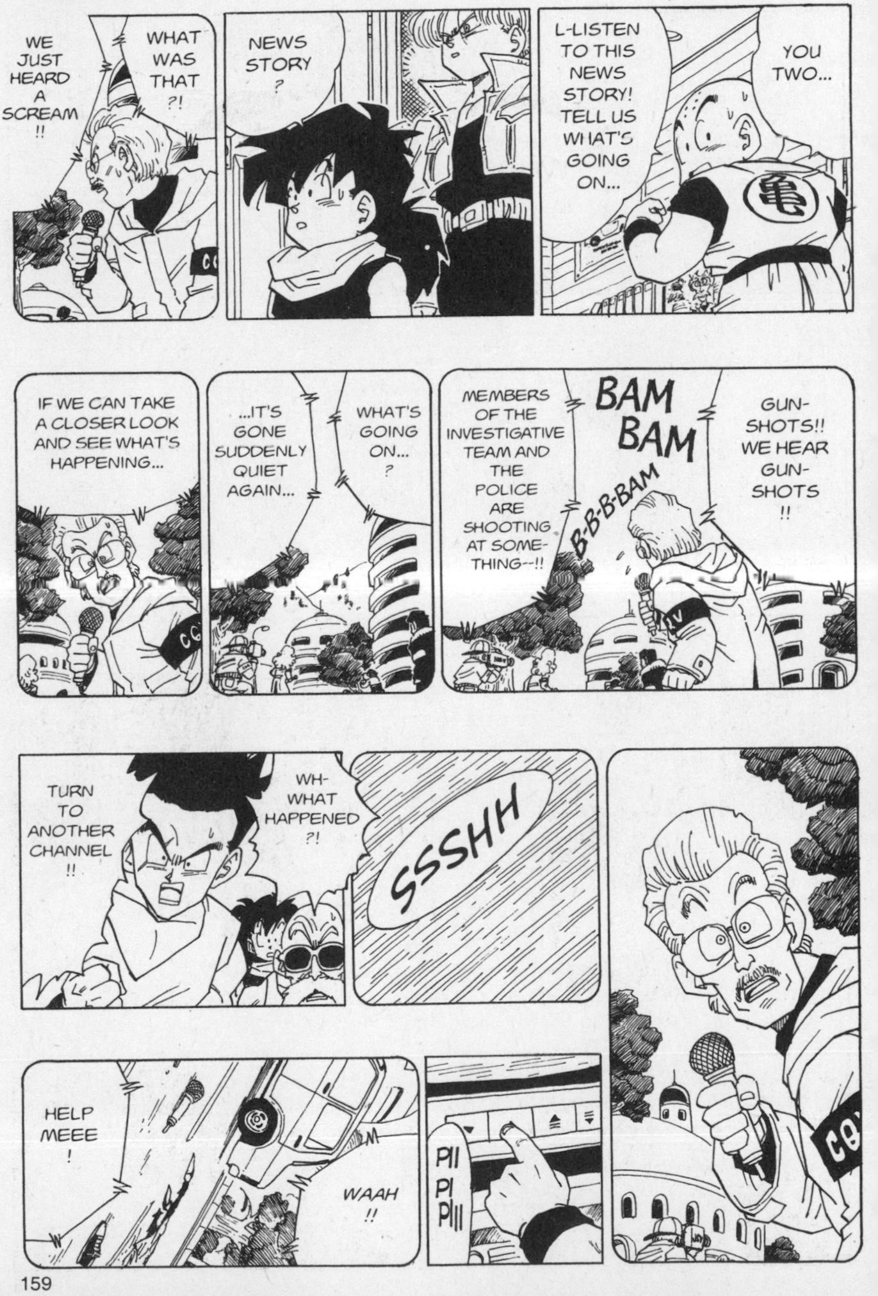

YOU TWO...
L-LISTEN TO THIS NEWS STORY! TELL US WHAT'S GOING ON...
NEWS STORY ?
WHAT WAS THAT ?!
WE JUST HEARD A SCREAM !!
GUN-SHOTS!! WE HEAR GUN-SHOTS !!
BAM BAM
B-B-B-BAM
MEMBERS OF THE INVESTIGATIVE TEAM AND THE POLICE ARE SHOOTING AT SOME-THING--!!
WHAT'S GOING ON... ?
...IT'S GONE SUDDENLY QUIET AGAIN...
IF WE CAN TAKE A CLOSER LOOK AND SEE WHAT'S HAPPENING...
SSSHH
WH-WHAT HAPPENED ?!
TURN TO ANOTHER CHANNEL !!
PI PI PI
WAAH !!
HELP MEEE !

READ THIS WAY

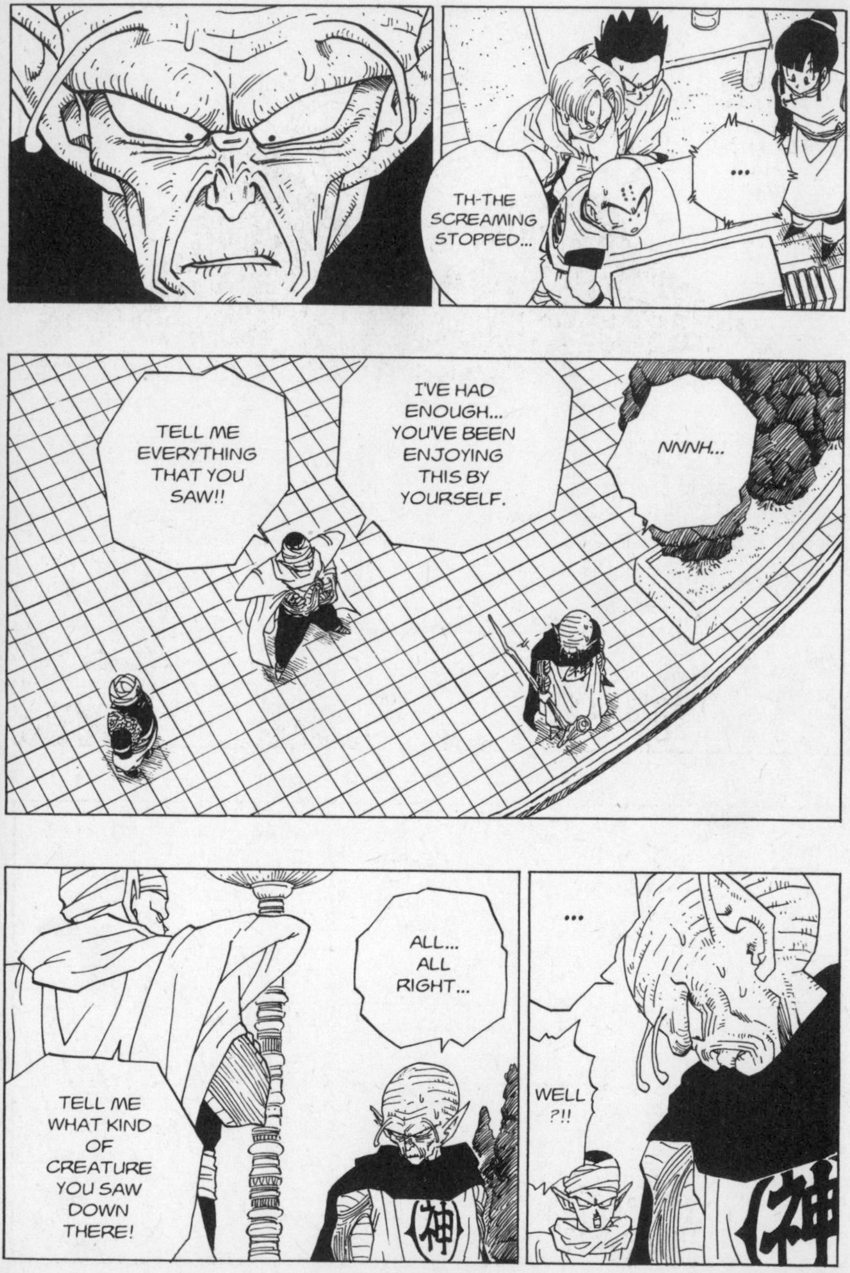
...
TH-THE SCREAMING STOPPED...
NNNH...
I'VE HAD ENOUGH... YOU'VE BEEN ENJOYING THIS BY YOURSELF.
TELL ME EVERYTHING THAT YOU SAW!!
...
WELL ?!!
ALL... ALL RIGHT...
TELL ME WHAT KIND OF CREATURE YOU SAW DOWN THERE!

READ THIS WAY

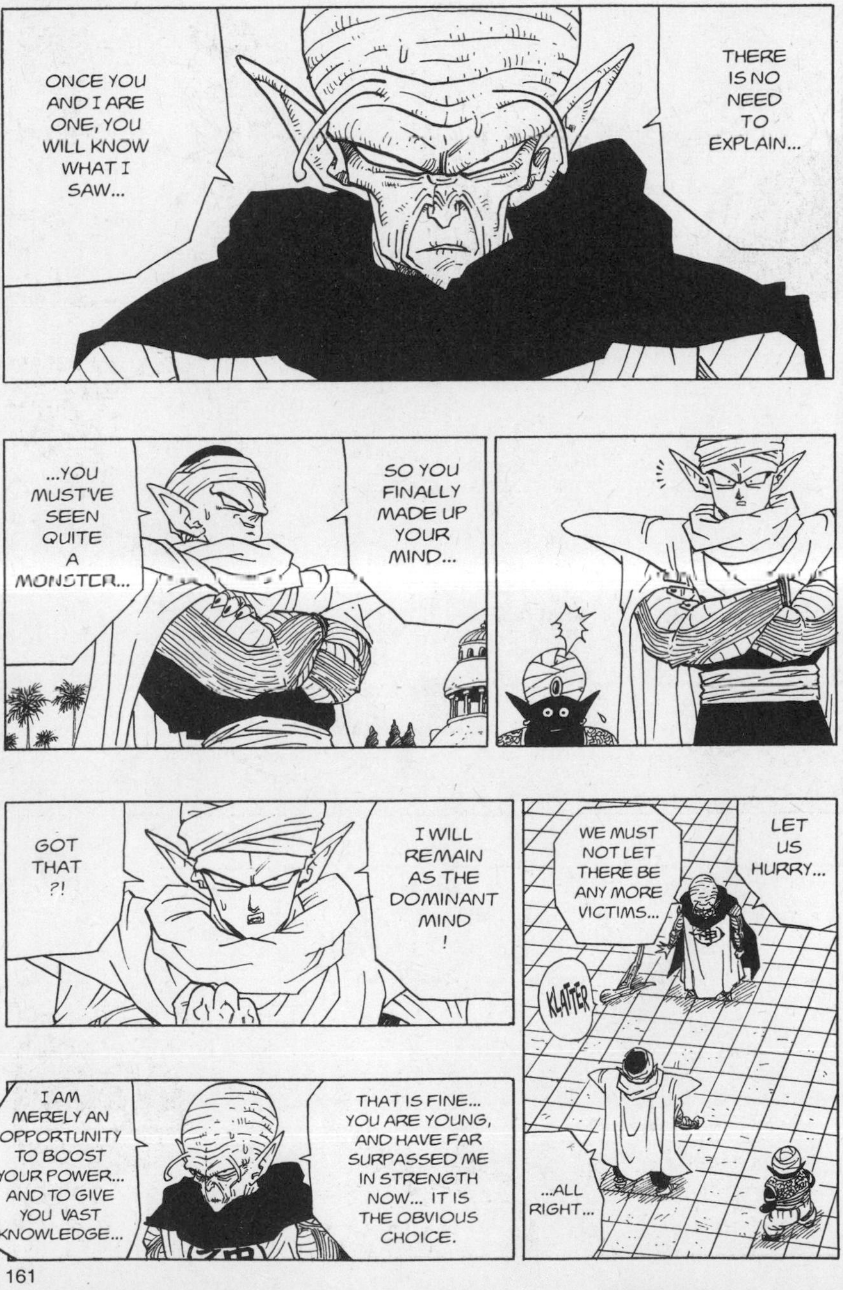

THERE IS NO NEED TO EXPLAIN...
ONCE YOU AND I ARE ONE, YOU WILL KNOW WHAT I SAW...
SO YOU FINALLY MADE UP YOUR MIND...
...YOU MUST'VE SEEN QUITE A MONSTER...
LET US HURRY...
WE MUST NOT LET THERE BE ANY MORE VICTIMS...
KLATTER
...ALL RIGHT...
I WILL REMAIN AS THE DOMINANT MIND!
GOT THAT?!
THAT IS FINE... YOU ARE YOUNG, AND HAVE FAR SURPASSED ME IN STRENGTH NOW... IT IS THE OBVIOUS CHOICE.
I AM MERELY AN OPPORTUNITY TO BOOST YOUR POWER... AND TO GIVE YOU VAST KNOWLEDGE...

READ THIS WAY

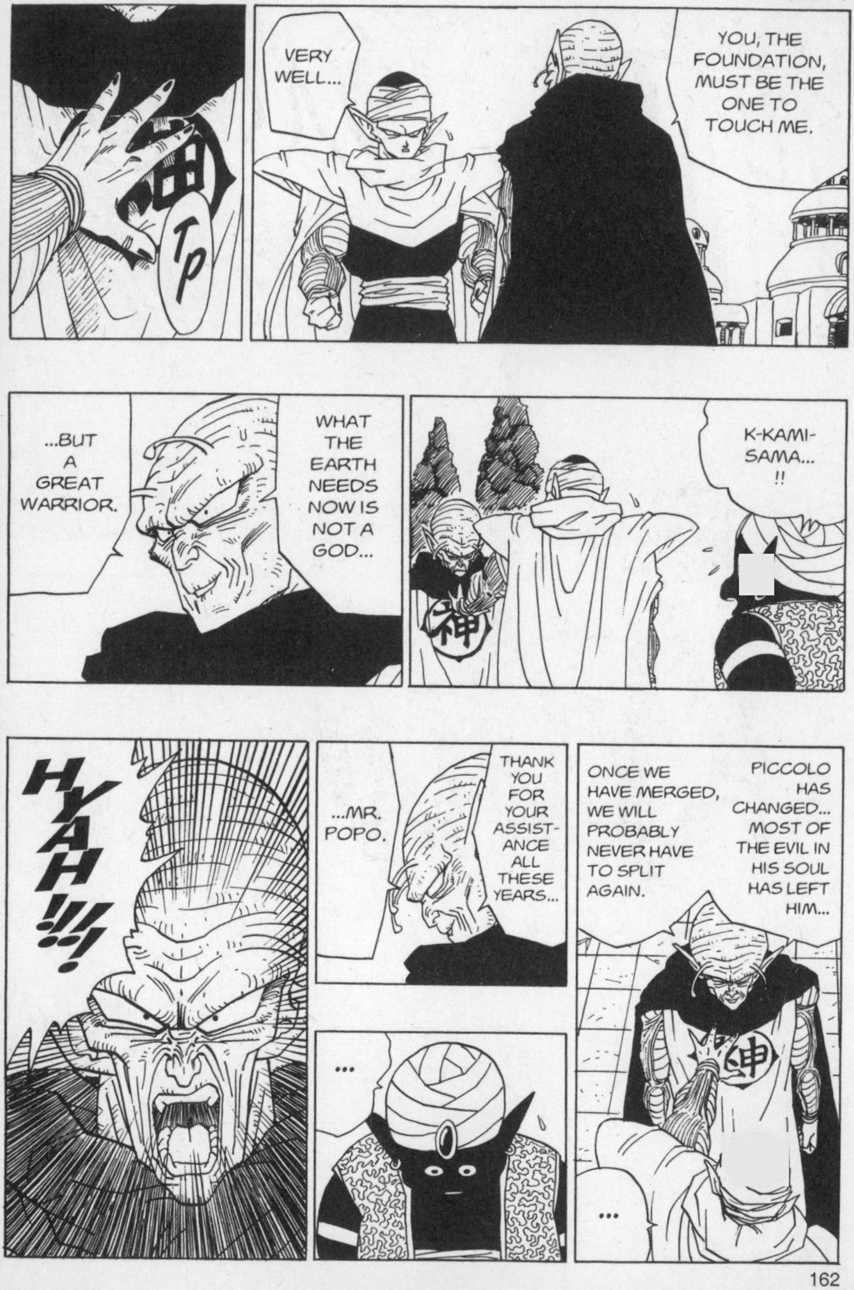
YOU, THE FOUNDATION, MUST BE THE ONE TO TOUCH ME.
VERY WELL...
Tp
K-KAMI-SAMA... !!
WHAT THE EARTH NEEDS NOW IS NOT A GOD...
...BUT A GREAT WARRIOR.
PICCOLO HAS CHANGED... MOST OF THE EVIL IN HIS SOUL HAS LEFT HIM...
ONCE WE HAVE MERGED, WE WILL PROBABLY NEVER HAVE TO SPLIT AGAIN.
...
THANK YOU FOR YOUR ASSISTANCE ALL THESE YEARS...
...MR. POPO.
...
HYAH!!!!

READ THIS WAY

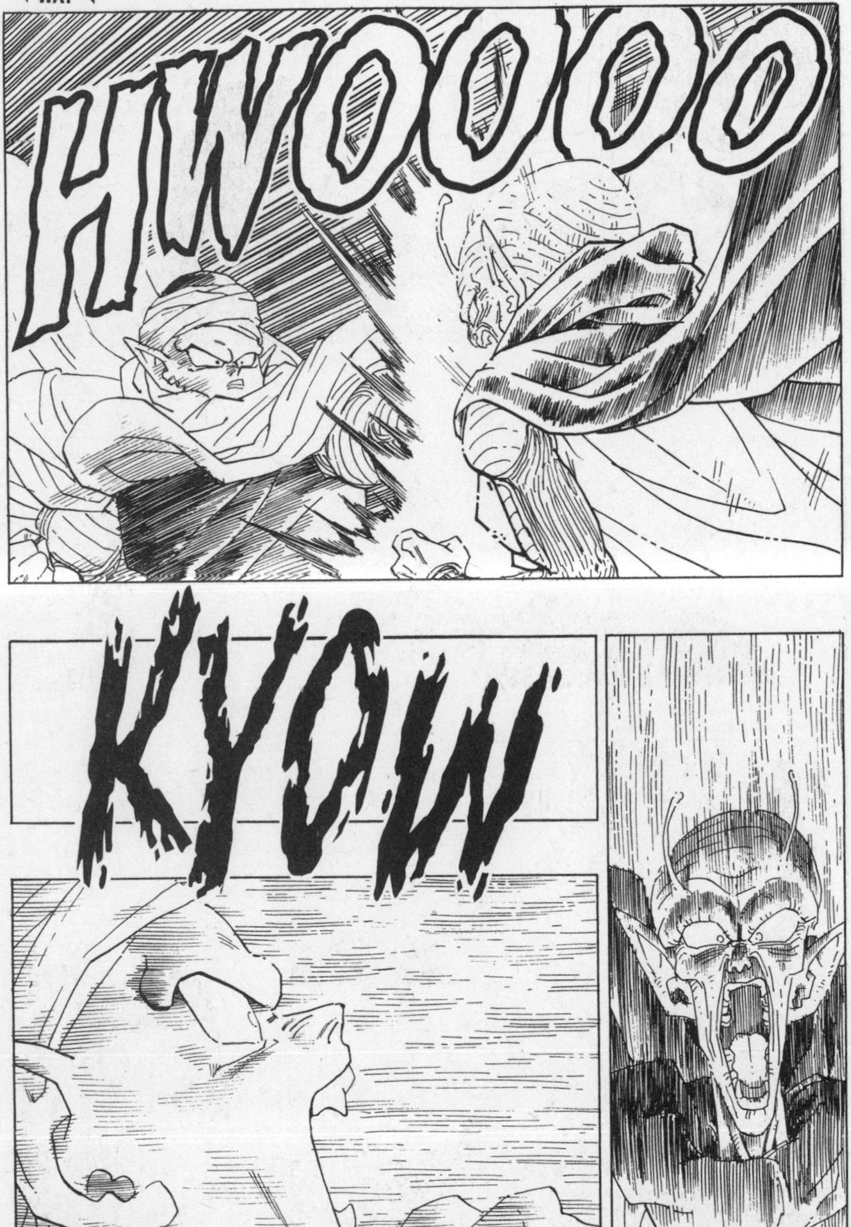
HWOOOOO
KYOW

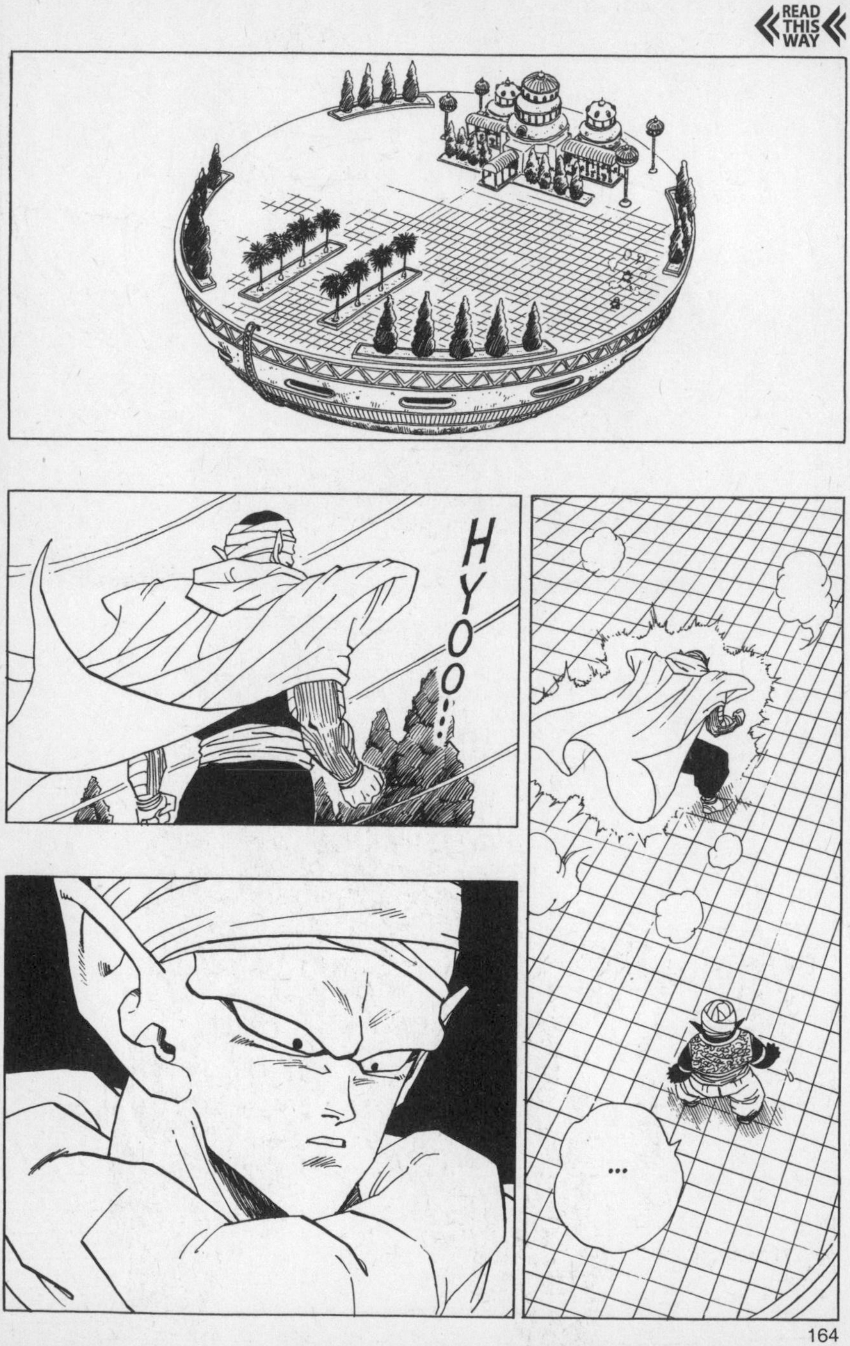

READ THIS WAY
HYOOO...
...

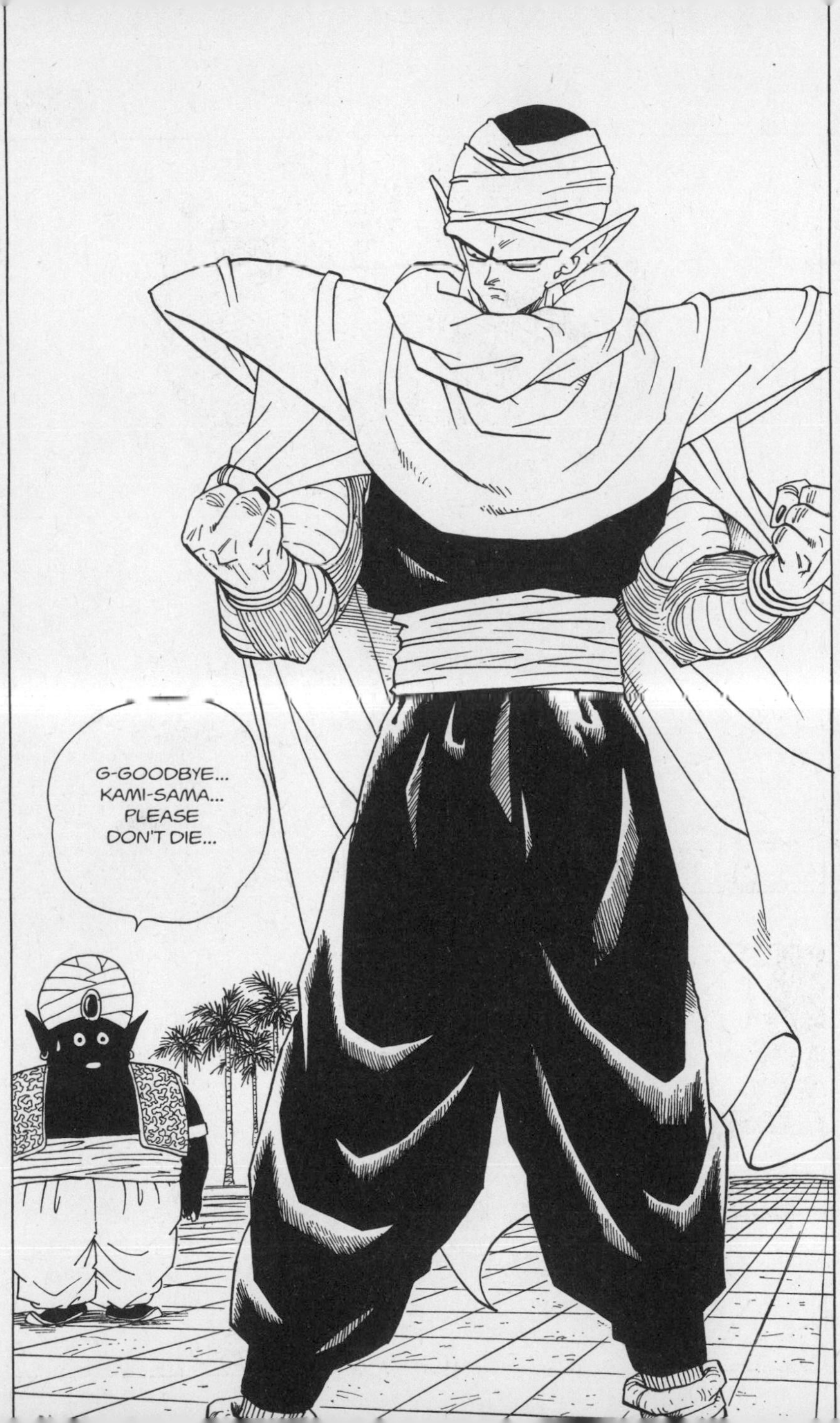
G-GOODBYE... KAMI-SAMA... PLEASE DON'T DIE...

READ THIS WAY

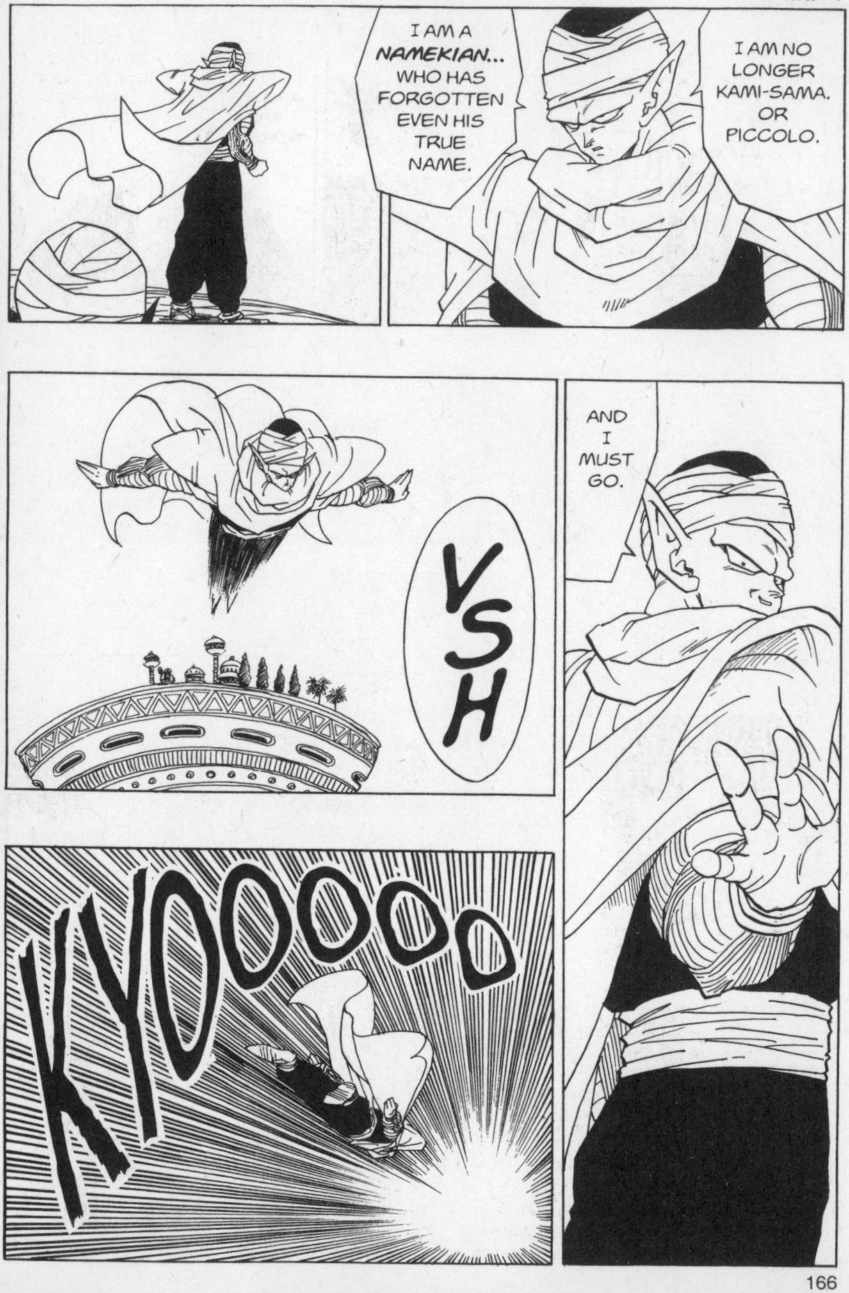
I AM NO LONGER KAMI-SAMA. OR PICCOLO.
I AM A **NAMEKIAN...** WHO HAS FORGOTTEN EVEN HIS TRUE NAME.
AND I MUST GO.
VSH
KYOOOOO

READ THIS WAY

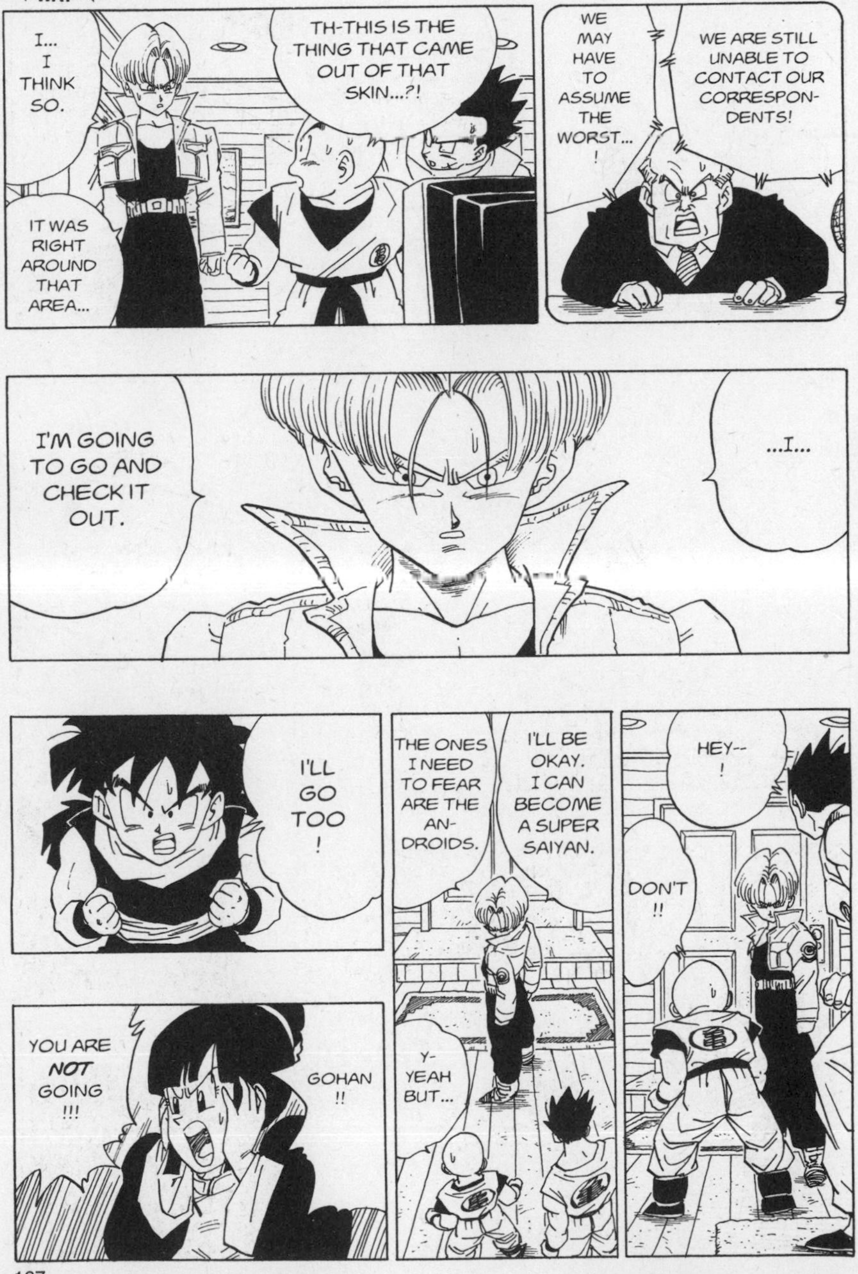
WE ARE STILL UNABLE TO CONTACT OUR CORRESPON-DENTS!
WE MAY HAVE TO ASSUME THE WORST...!
TH-THIS IS THE THING THAT CAME OUT OF THAT SKIN...?!
I... I THINK SO.
IT WAS RIGHT AROUND THAT AREA...
...I...
I'M GOING TO GO AND CHECK IT OUT.
HEY--!
DON'T!!
I'LL BE OKAY. I CAN BECOME A SUPER SAIYAN.
THE ONES I NEED TO FEAR ARE THE AN-DROIDS.
Y-YEAH BUT...
I'LL GO TOO!
GOHAN!!
YOU ARE NOT GOING!!!

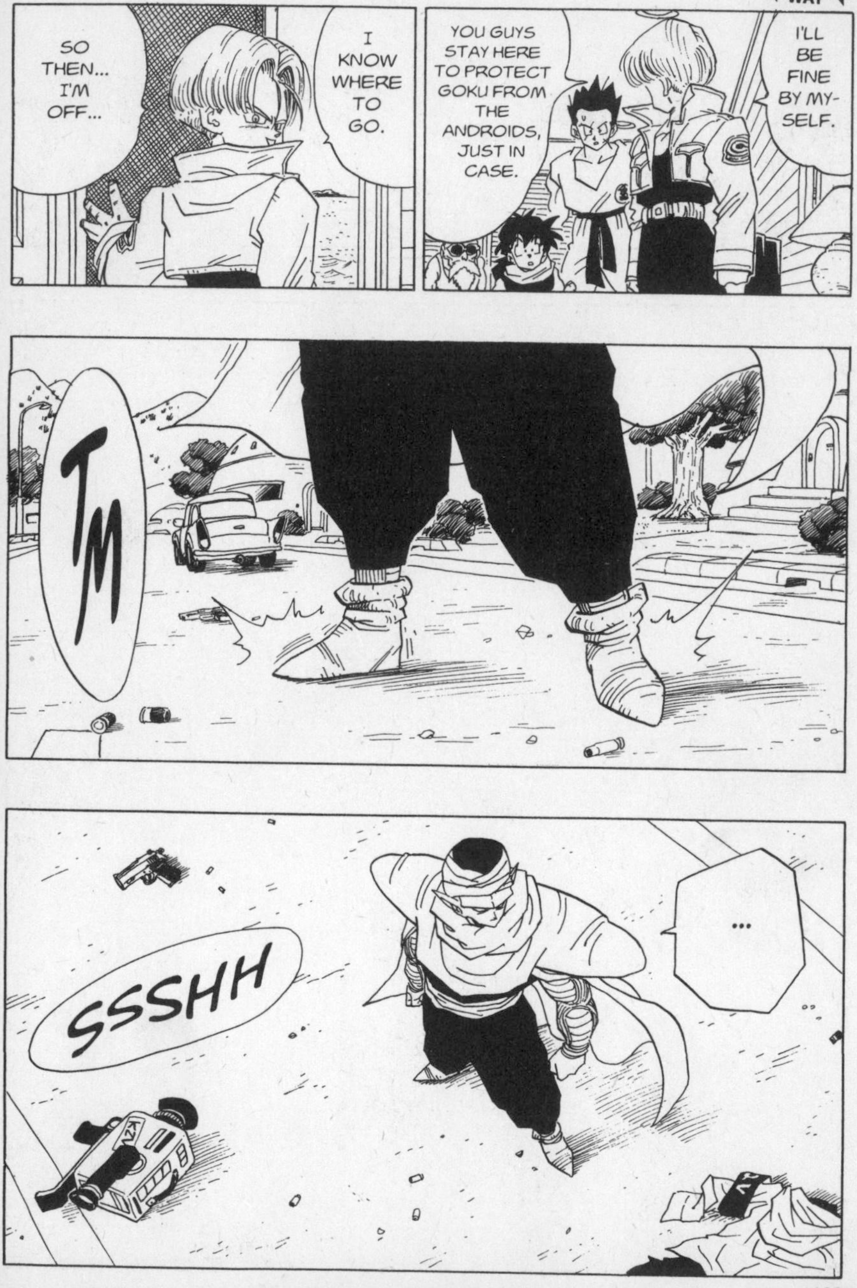
I'LL BE FINE BY MY-SELF.
YOU GUYS STAY HERE TO PROTECT GOKU FROM THE ANDROIDS, JUST IN CASE.
I KNOW WHERE TO GO.
SO THEN... I'M OFF...
TM
...
SSSHH

READ THIS WAY

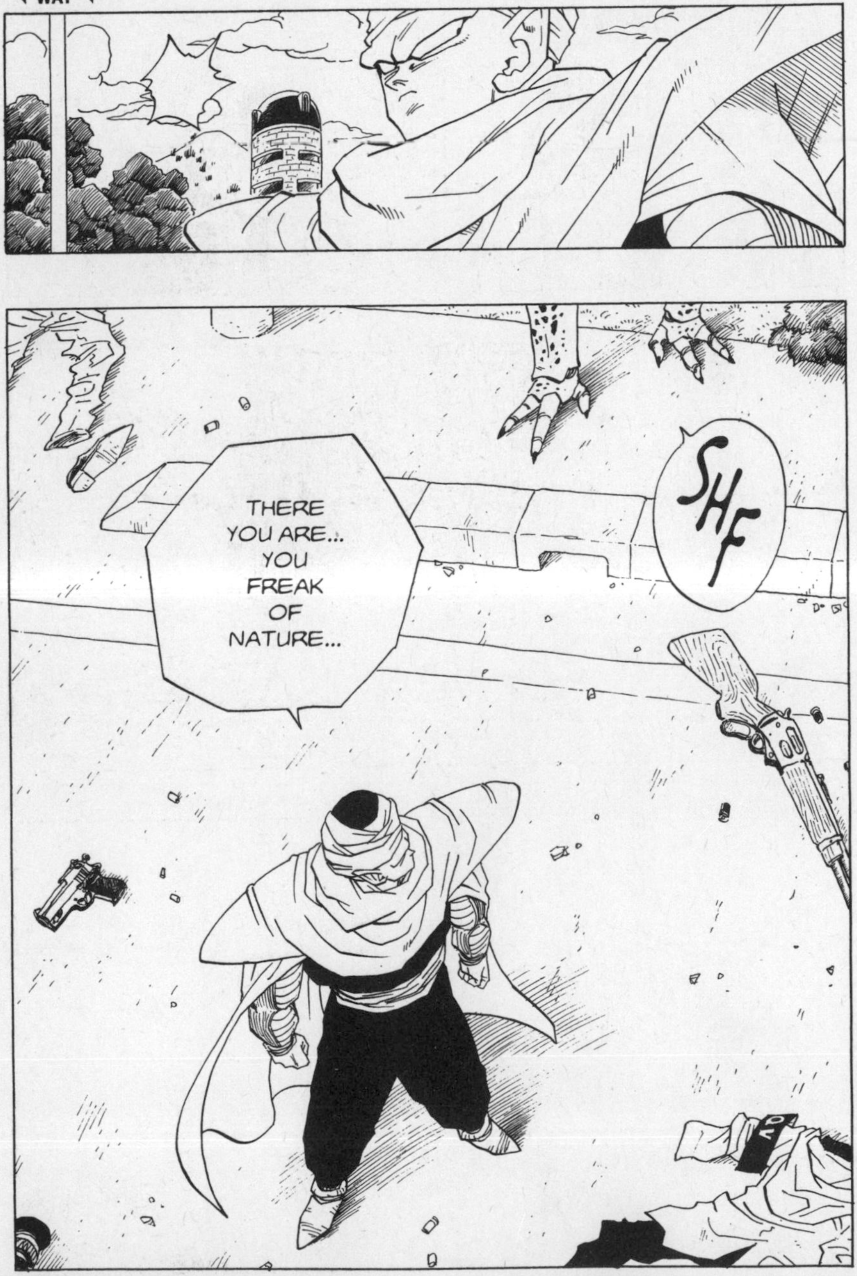
SHF
THERE YOU ARE... YOU FREAK OF NATURE...

NEXT: The Monster Shows Itself!!

DBZ:167 • Cell

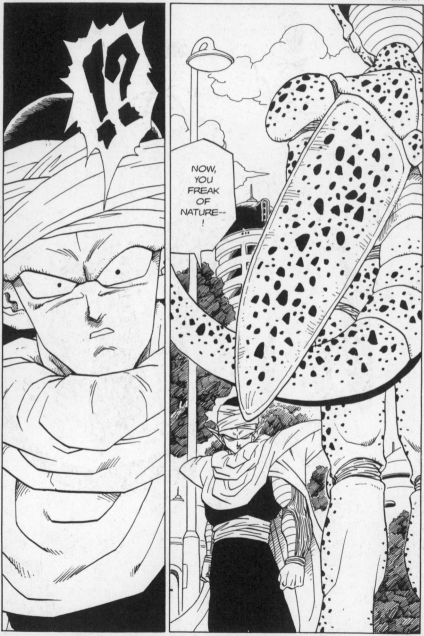

NOW, YOU FREAK OF NATURE--!

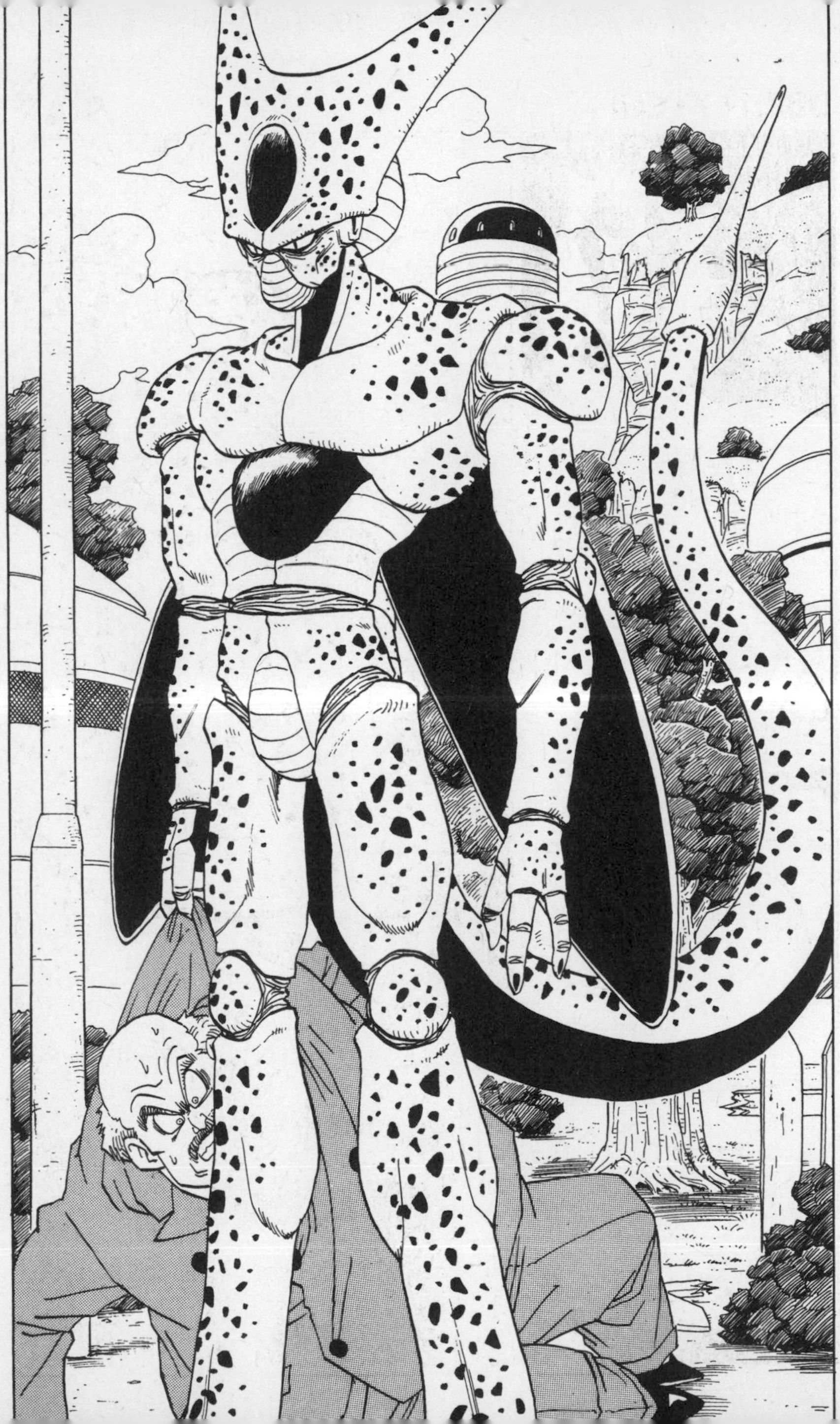

READ THIS WAY

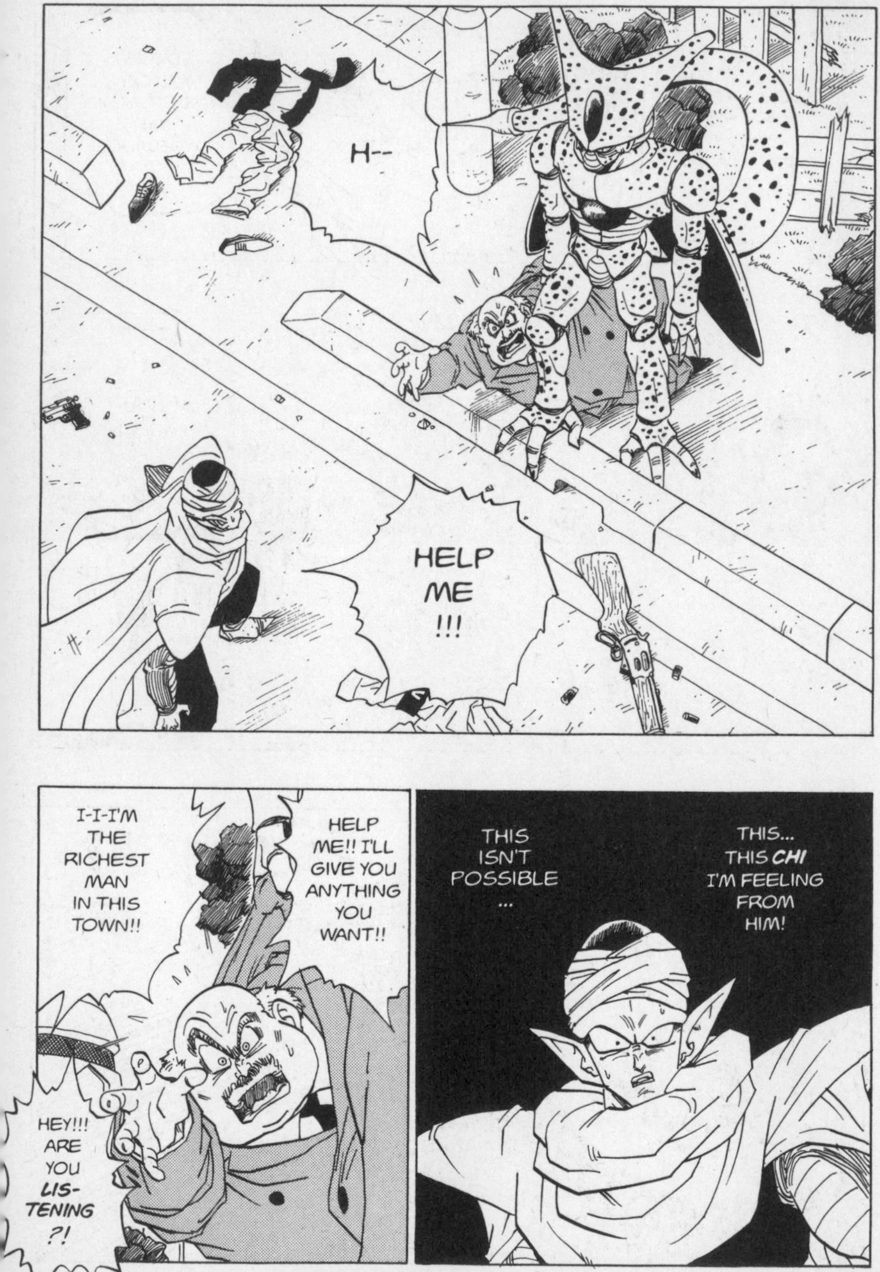
H--
HELP ME !!!
THIS... THIS ***CHI*** I'M FEELING FROM HIM!
THIS ISN'T POSSIBLE ...
HELP ME!! I'LL GIVE YOU ANYTHING YOU WANT!!
I-I-I'M THE RICHEST MAN IN THIS TOWN!!
HEY!!! ARE YOU ***LIS-TENING*** ?!

READ THIS WAY

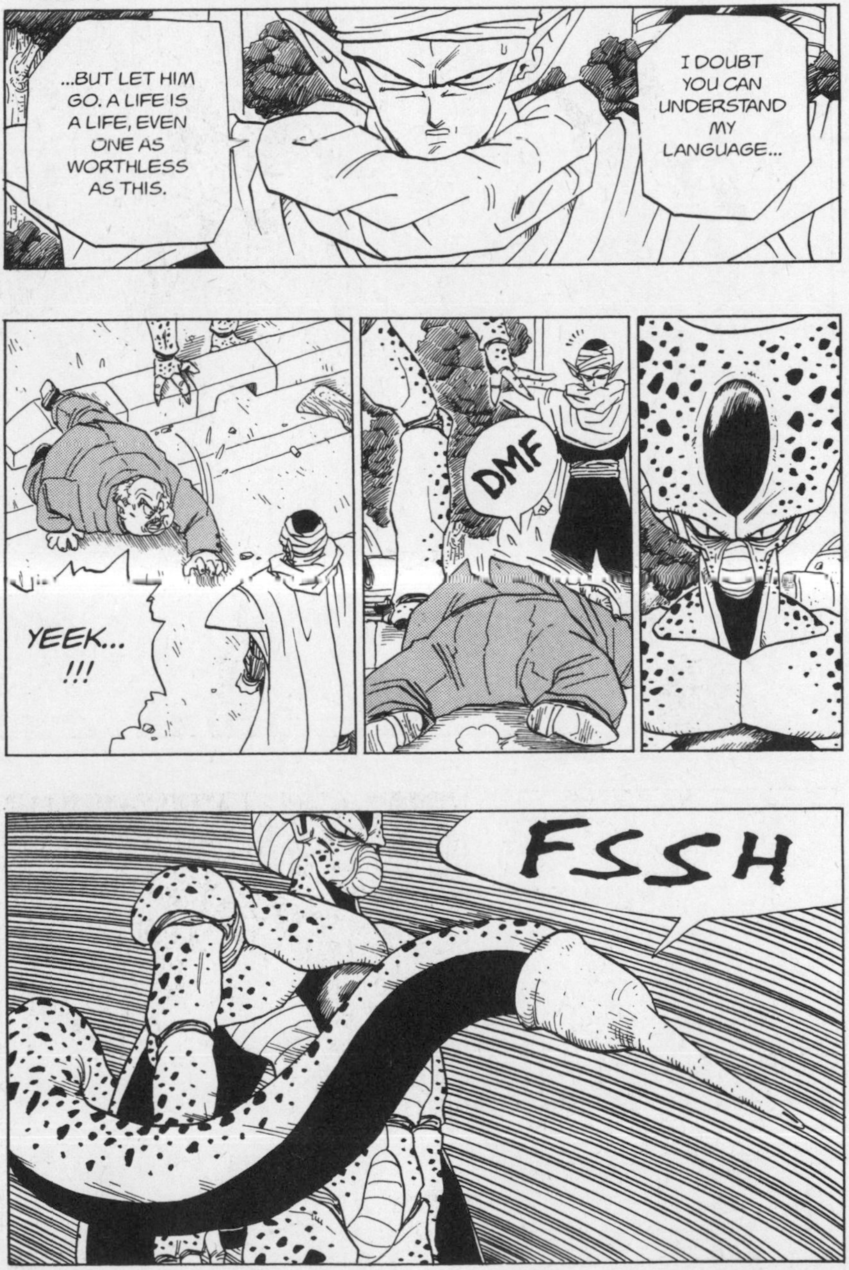
I DOUBT YOU CAN UNDERSTAND MY LANGUAGE...
...BUT LET HIM GO. A LIFE IS A LIFE, EVEN ONE AS WORTHLESS AS THIS.
DMF
YEEK... !!!
FSSH

READ THIS WAY

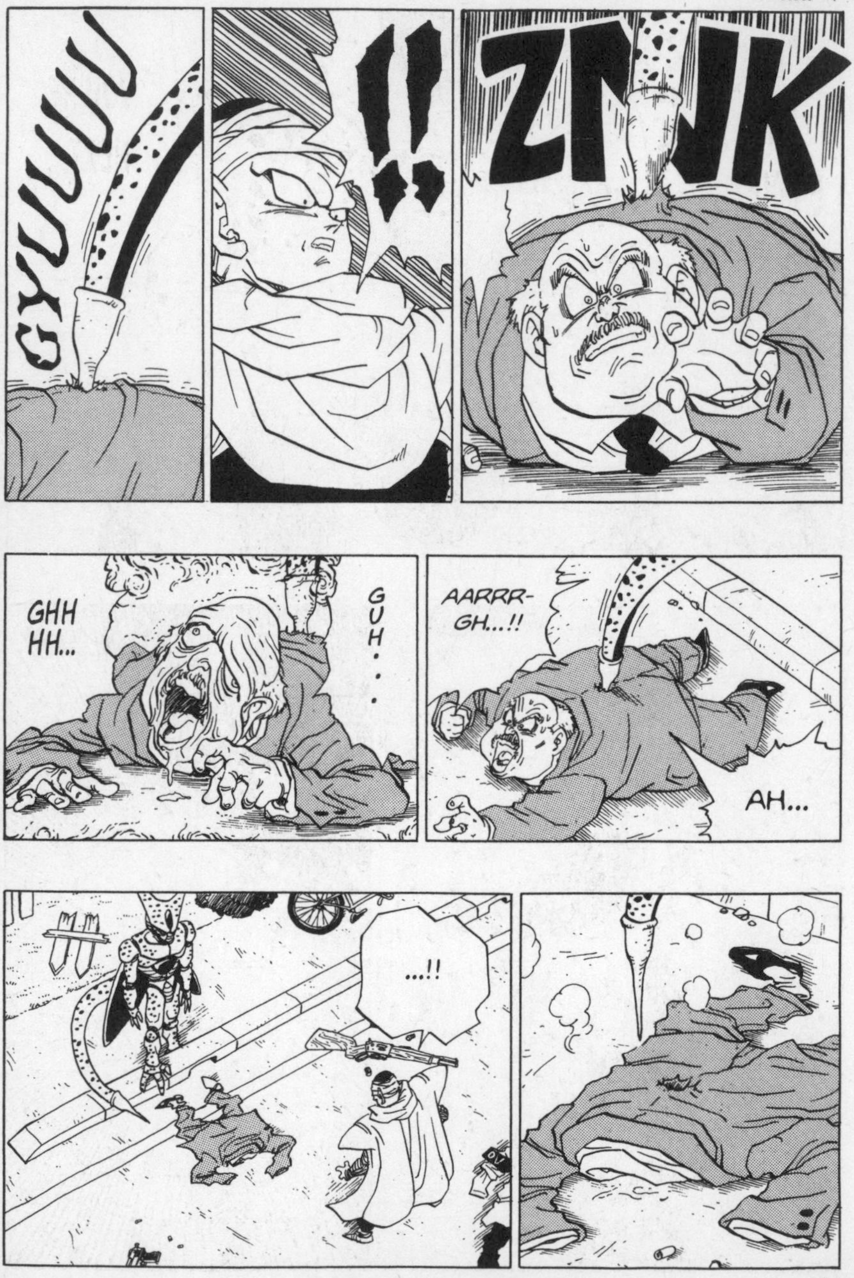
ZNK
!!
GYUUUU
AARRR-GH...!!
AH...
GUH...
GHHHH...
...!!

READ THIS WAY

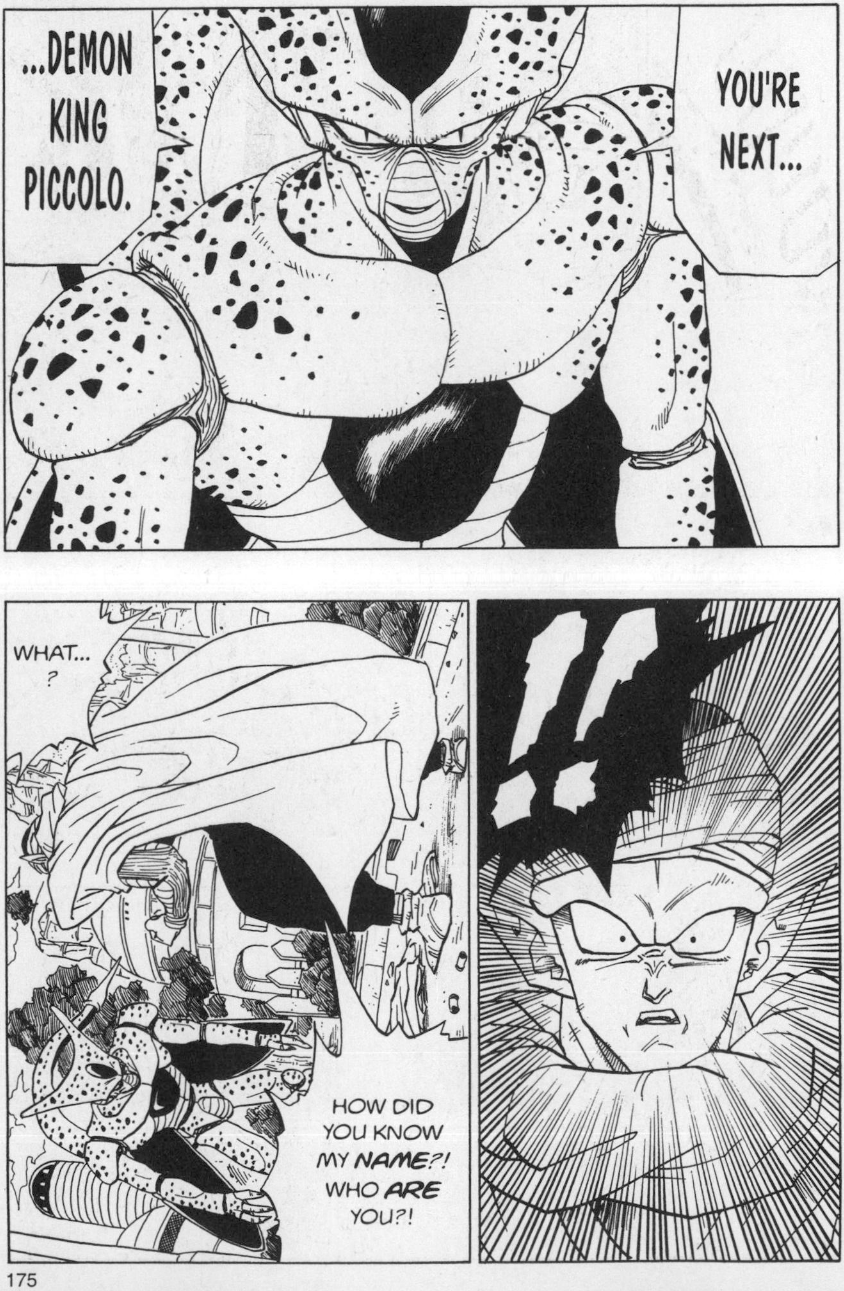
YOU'RE NEXT...
...DEMON KING PICCOLO.
WHAT...?
HOW DID YOU KNOW MY *NAME*?! WHO *ARE* YOU?!

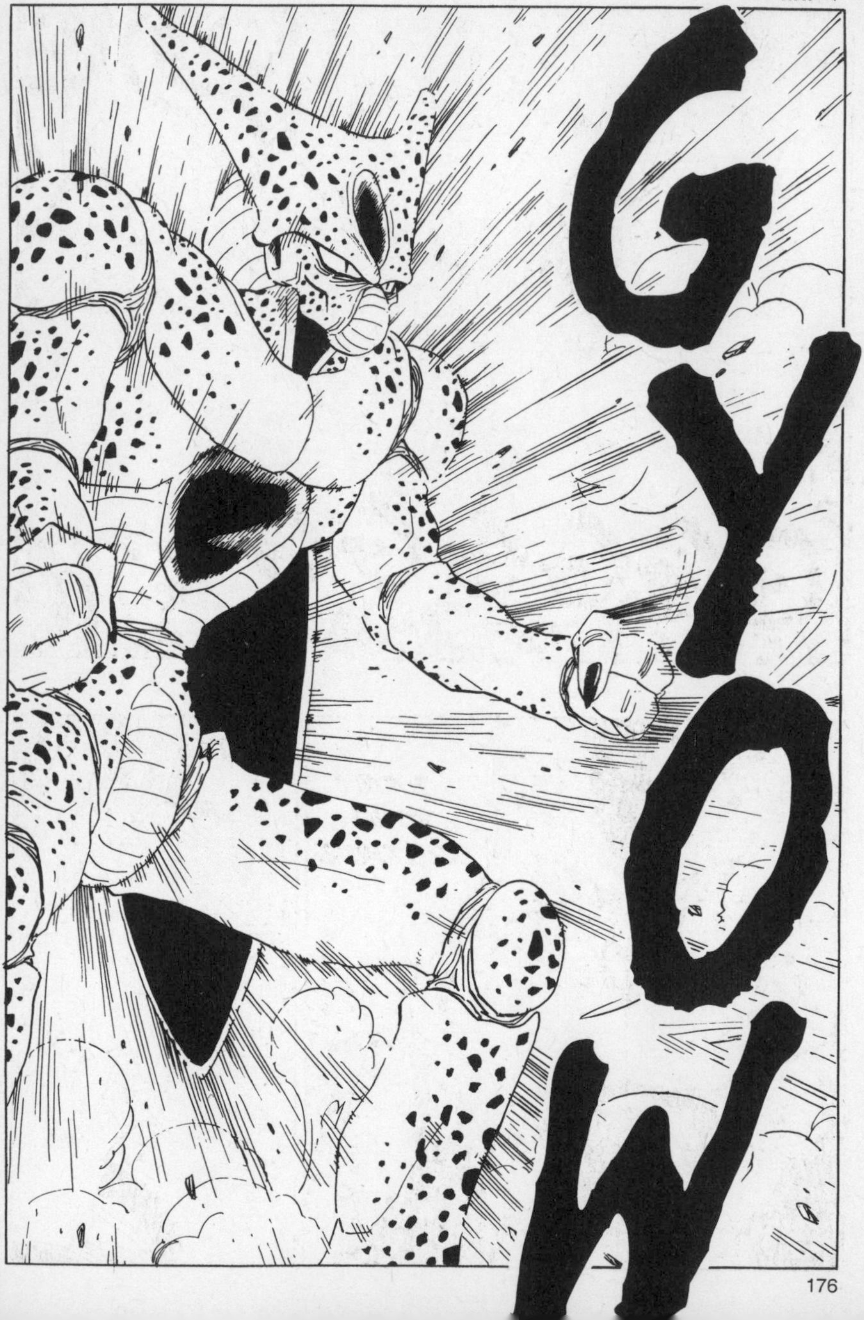

READ THIS WAY
GYOW

READ THIS WAY

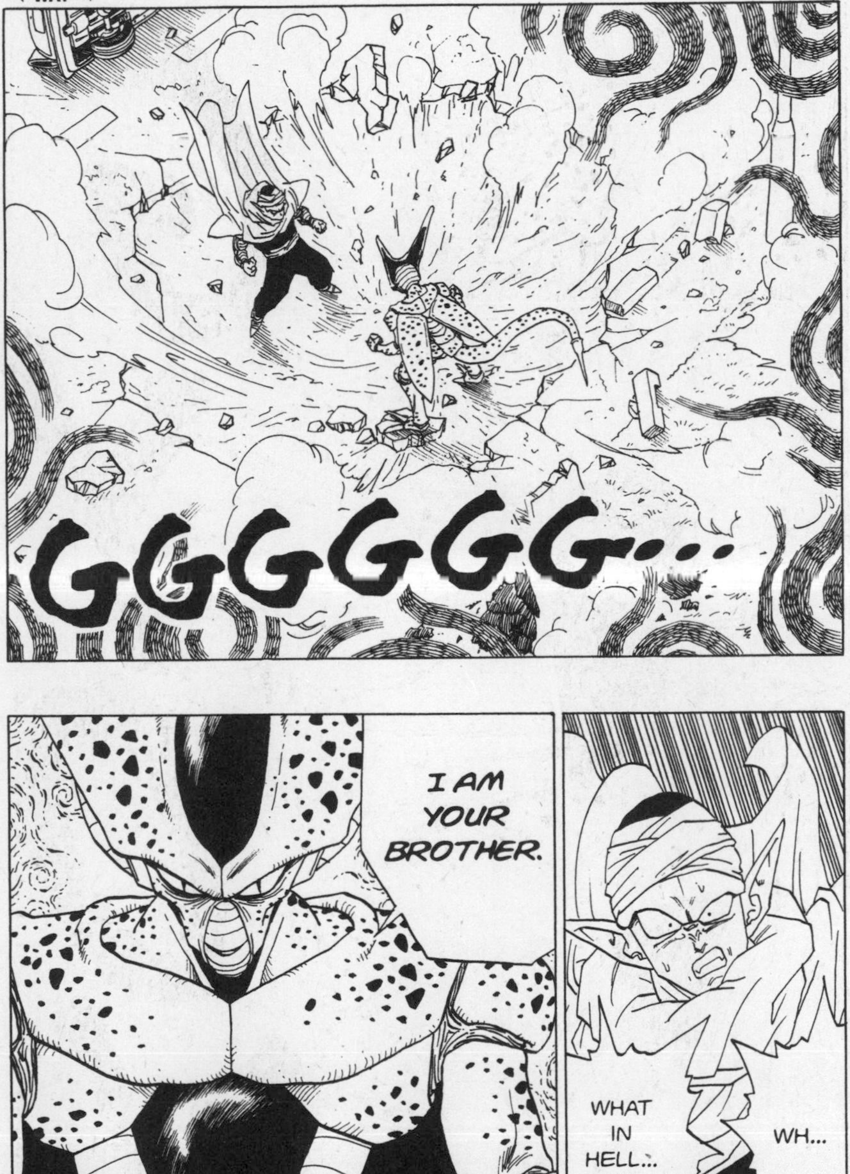
GGGGGG...
WH...
WHAT IN HELL... ?!!
I AM YOUR BROTHER.

READ THIS WAY

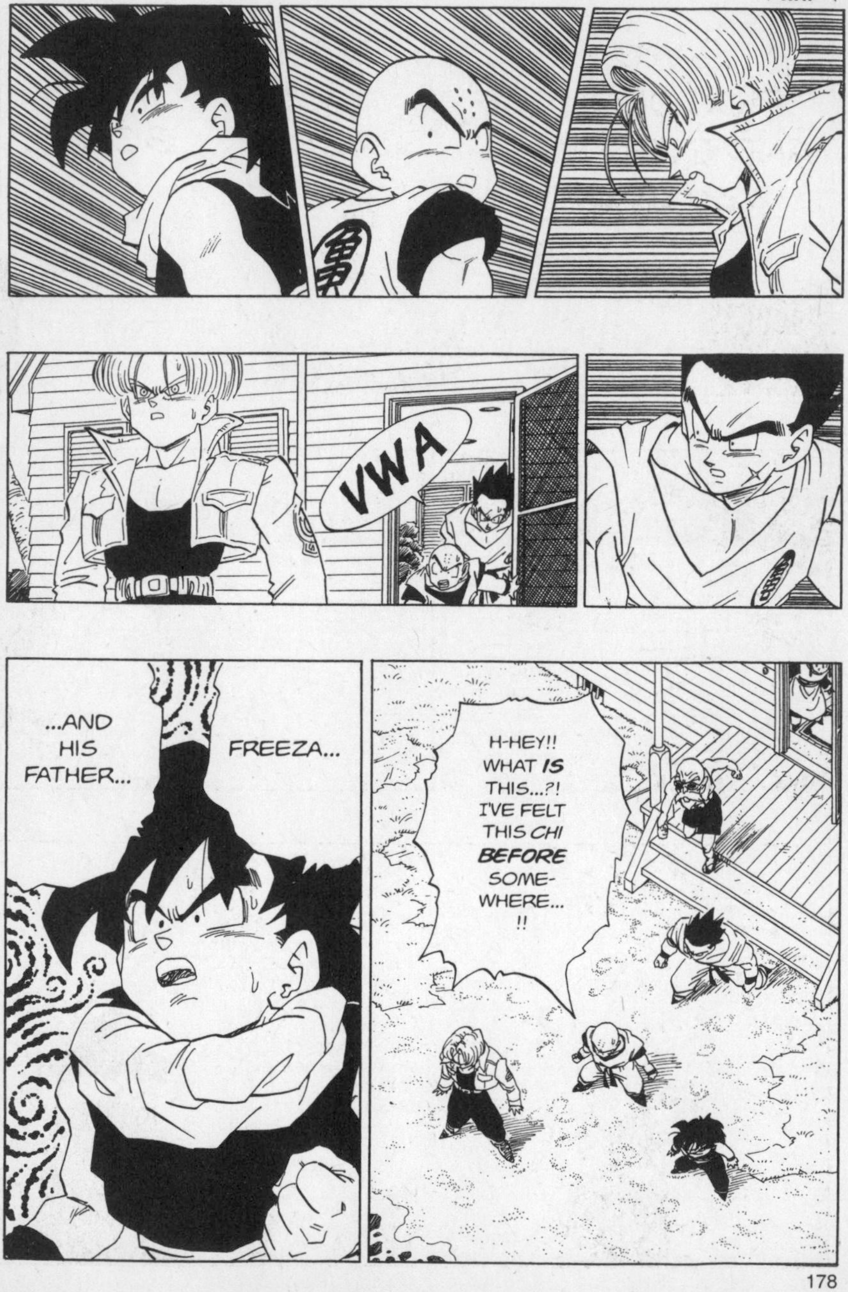
VWA
H-HEY!! WHAT *IS* THIS...?! I'VE FELT THIS *CHI* **BEFORE** SOME-WHERE... !!
FREEZA...
...AND HIS FATHER...

READ THIS WAY

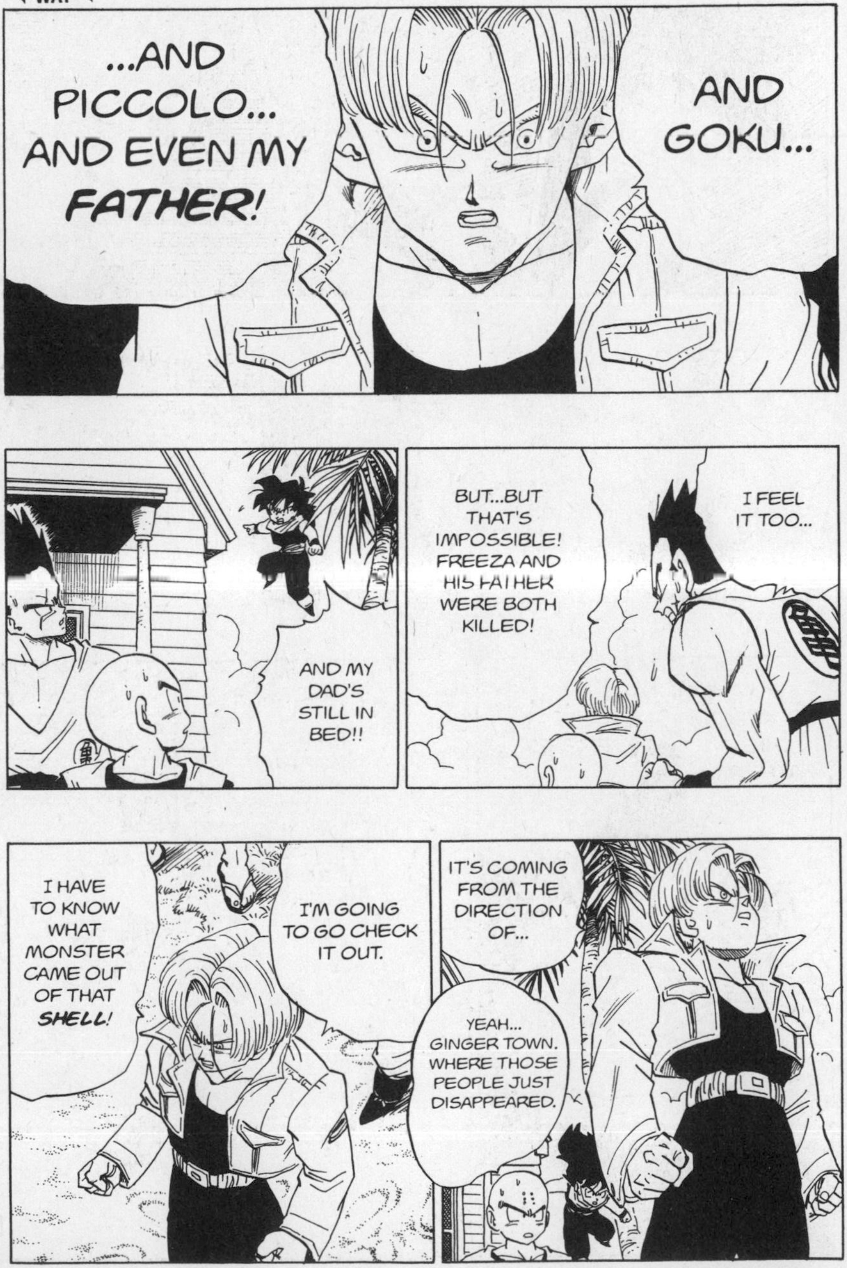
AND GOKU...
...AND PICCOLO... AND EVEN MY FATHER!
I FEEL IT TOO...
BUT...BUT THAT'S IMPOSSIBLE! FREEZA AND HIS FATHER WERE BOTH KILLED!
AND MY DAD'S STILL IN BED!!
IT'S COMING FROM THE DIRECTION OF...
YEAH... GINGER TOWN. WHERE THOSE PEOPLE JUST DISAPPEARED.
I'M GOING TO GO CHECK IT OUT.
I HAVE TO KNOW WHAT MONSTER CAME OUT OF THAT SHELL!

READ THIS WAY

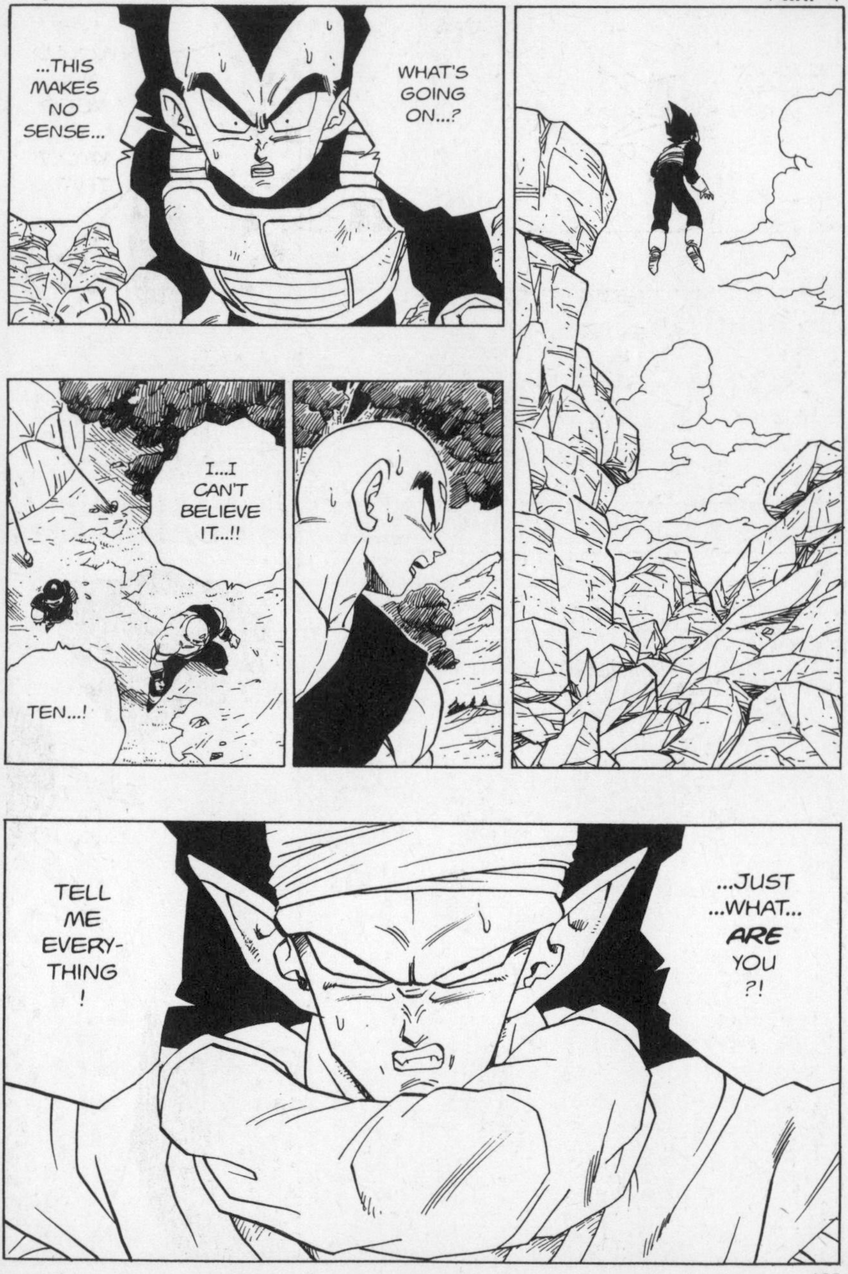
WHAT'S GOING ON...?
...THIS MAKES NO SENSE...
I...I CAN'T BELIEVE IT...!!
TEN...!
...JUST ...WHAT... ARE YOU ?!
TELL ME EVERY-THING !

READ THIS WAY

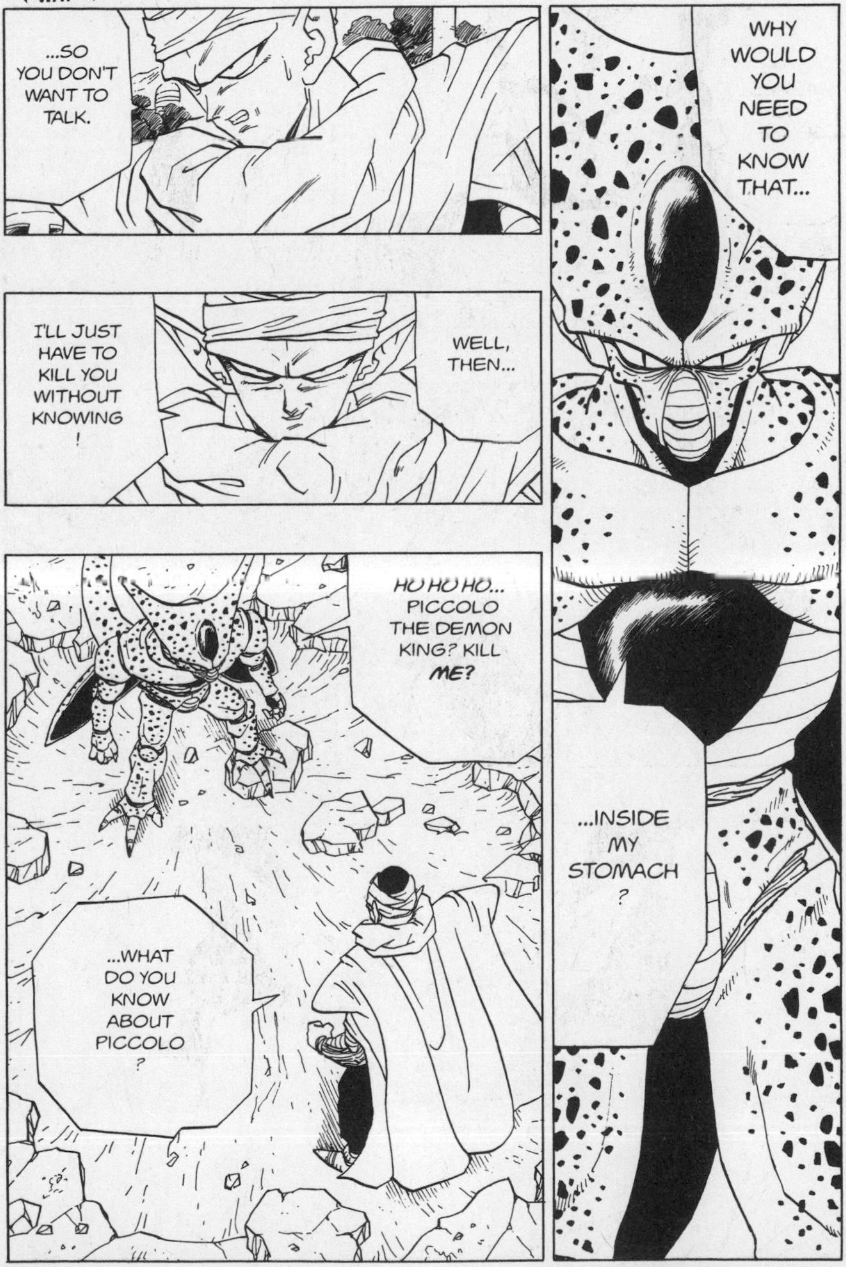
WHY WOULD YOU NEED TO KNOW THAT...
...INSIDE MY STOMACH?
...SO YOU DON'T WANT TO TALK.
WELL, THEN...
I'LL JUST HAVE TO KILL YOU WITHOUT KNOWING!
HO HO HO... PICCOLO THE DEMON KING? KILL *ME?*
...WHAT DO YOU KNOW ABOUT PICCOLO?

READ THIS WAY

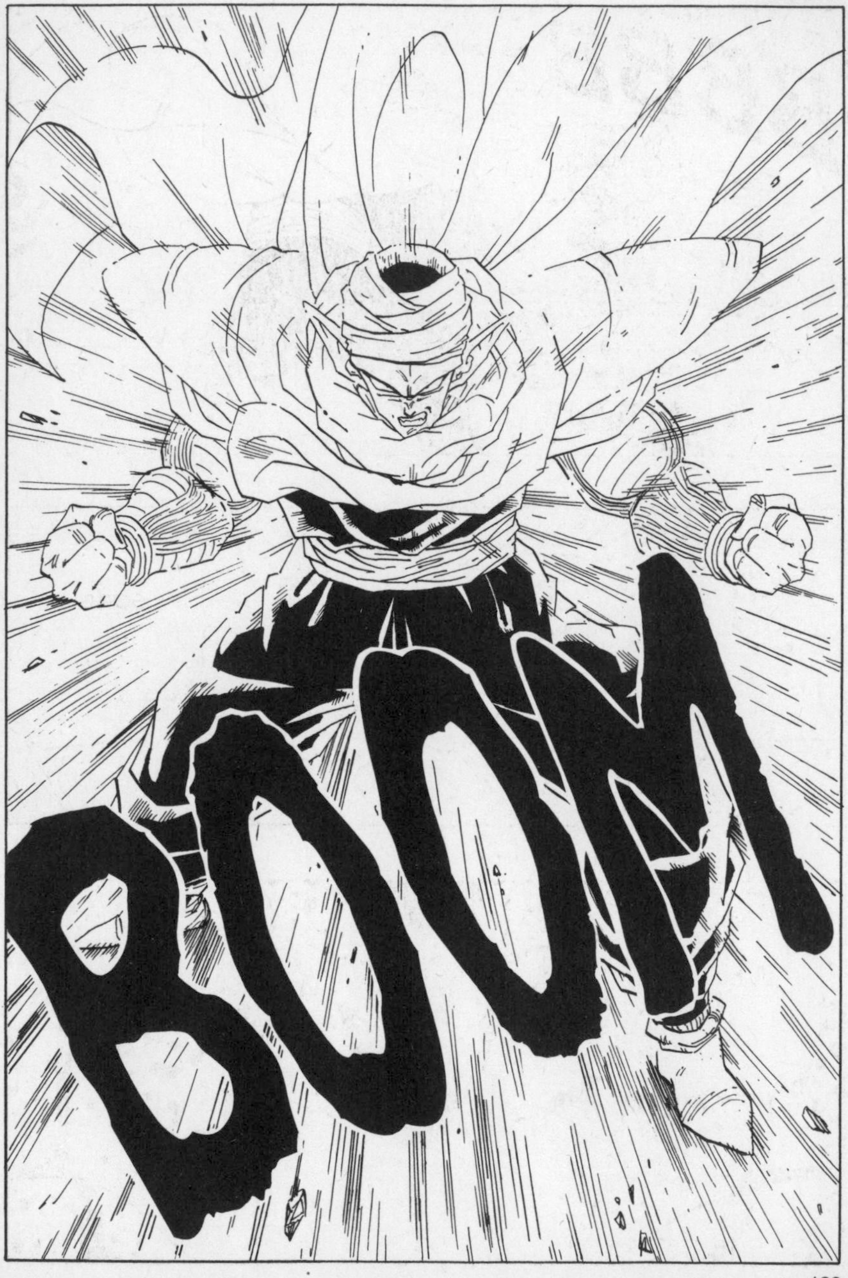
BOOM

READ THIS WAY

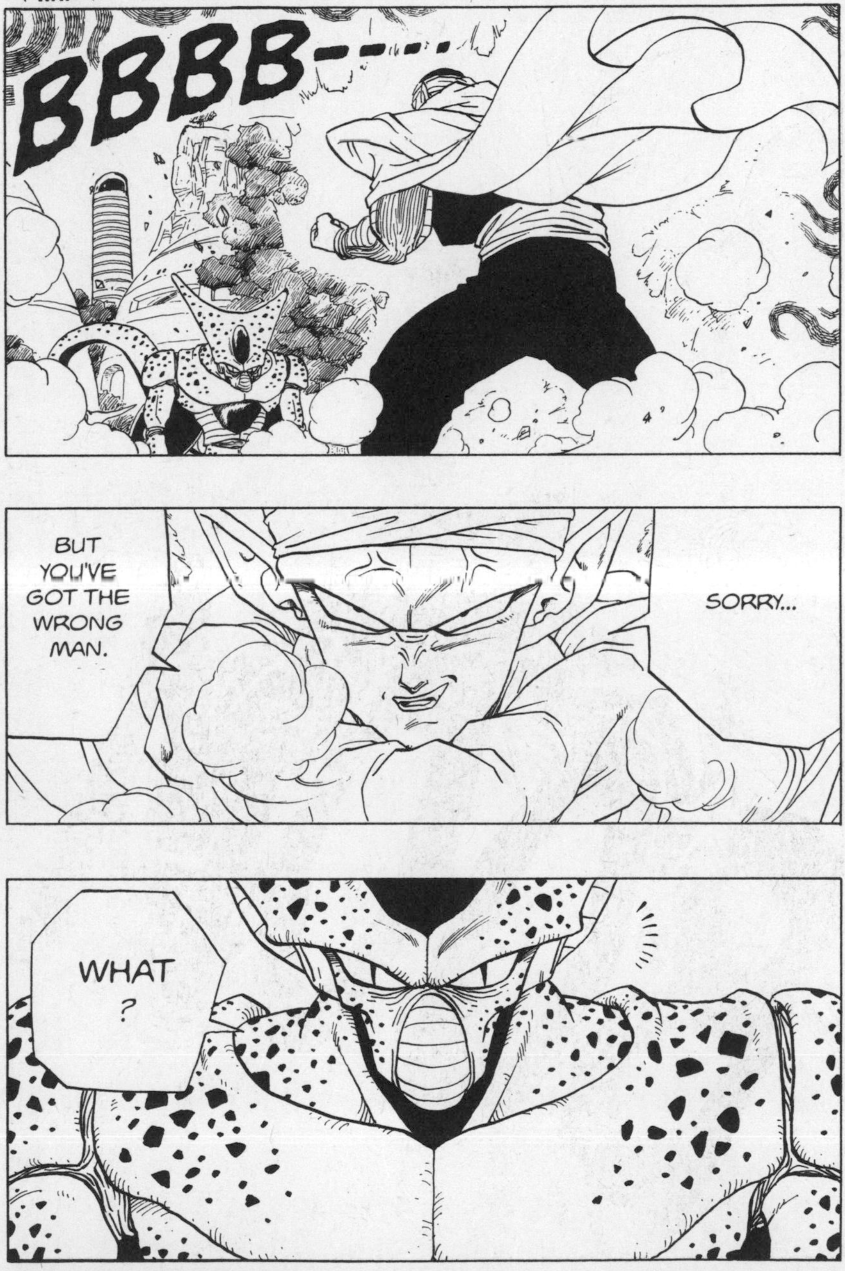
BBBB----
SORRY...
BUT YOU'VE GOT THE WRONG MAN.
WHAT ?

NEXT: Battle of the Monsters

TITLE PAGE GALLERY

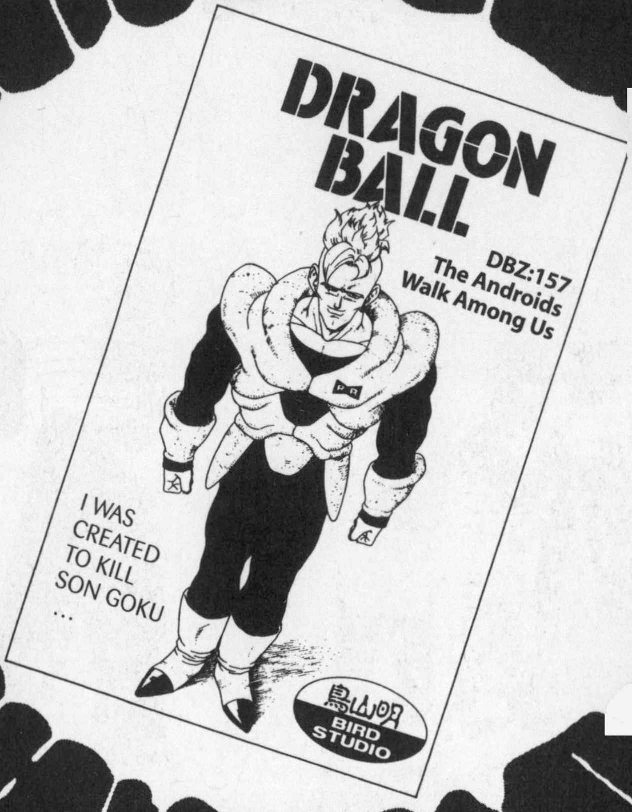
DRAGON BALL
DBZ:157
The Androids Walk Among Us
I WAS CREATED TO KILL SON GOKU ...
鳥山明
BIRD STUDIO

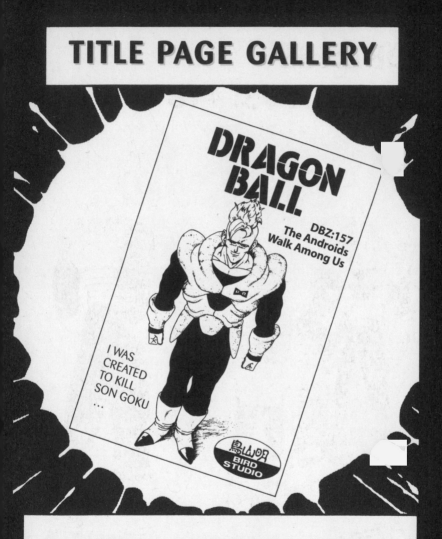

These title pages were used when these chapters of **Dragon Ball** were originally published in Japan in 1992 in **Weekly Shonen Jump** magazine.

DBZ:158
VEGETA VS. #18

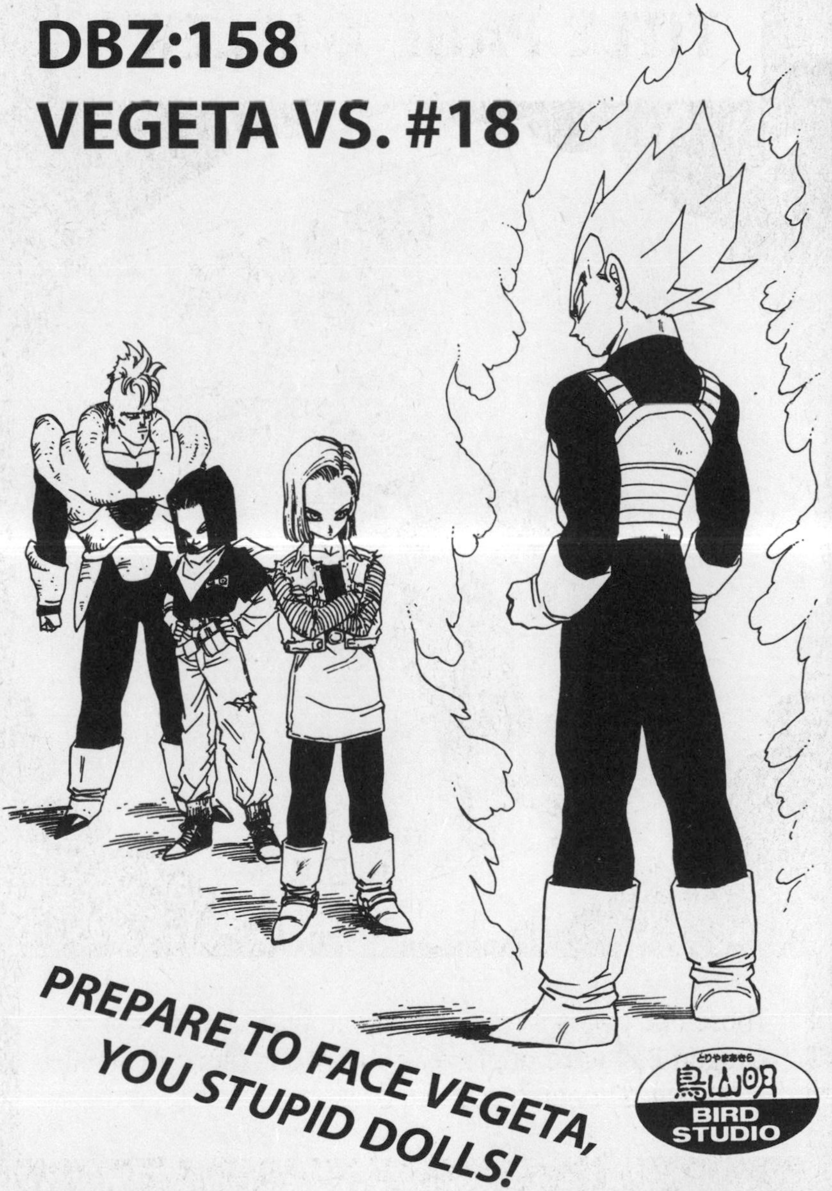

PREPARE TO FACE VEGETA,
YOU STUPID DOLLS!

とりやまあきら
鳥山明
BIRD
STUDIO

DBZ:159

Vegeta vs. #18,

Round Two

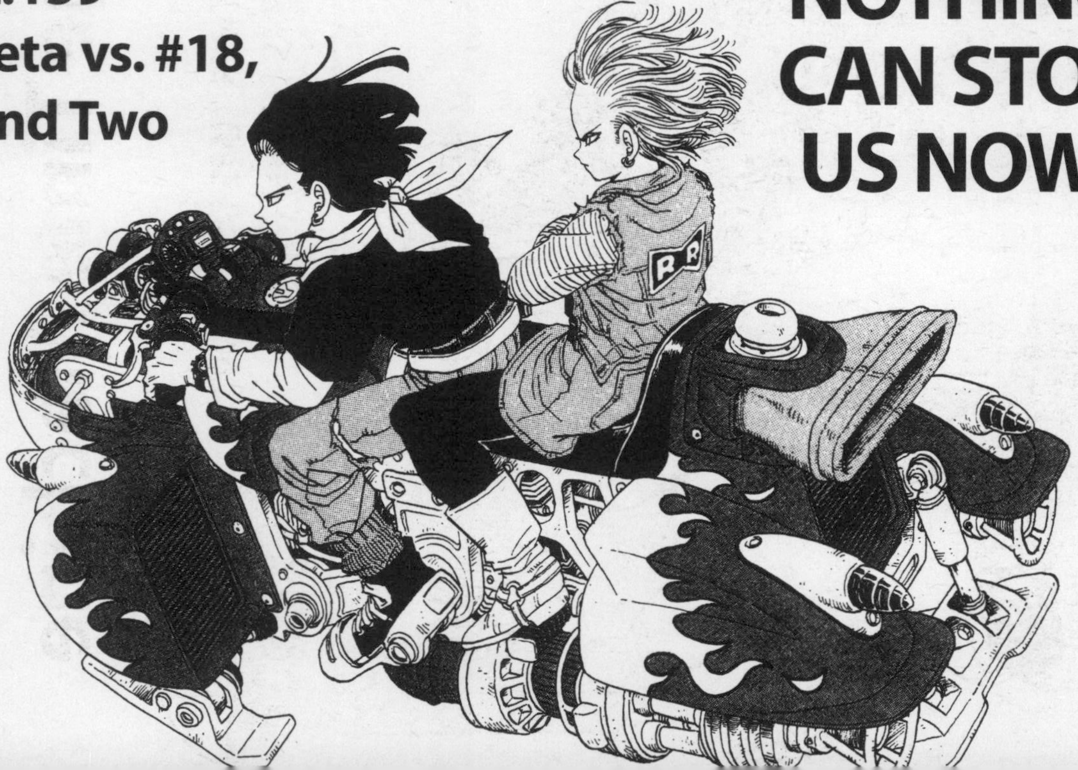

NOTHING CAN STOP US NOW!

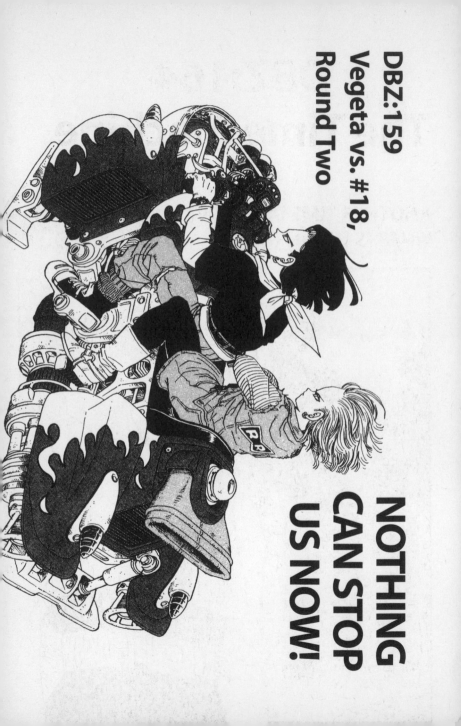

DBZ:164
The Time Machine

鳥山明
BIRD STUDIO

**ANOTHER TIME MACHINE?
WHAT IS GOING ON...?!**

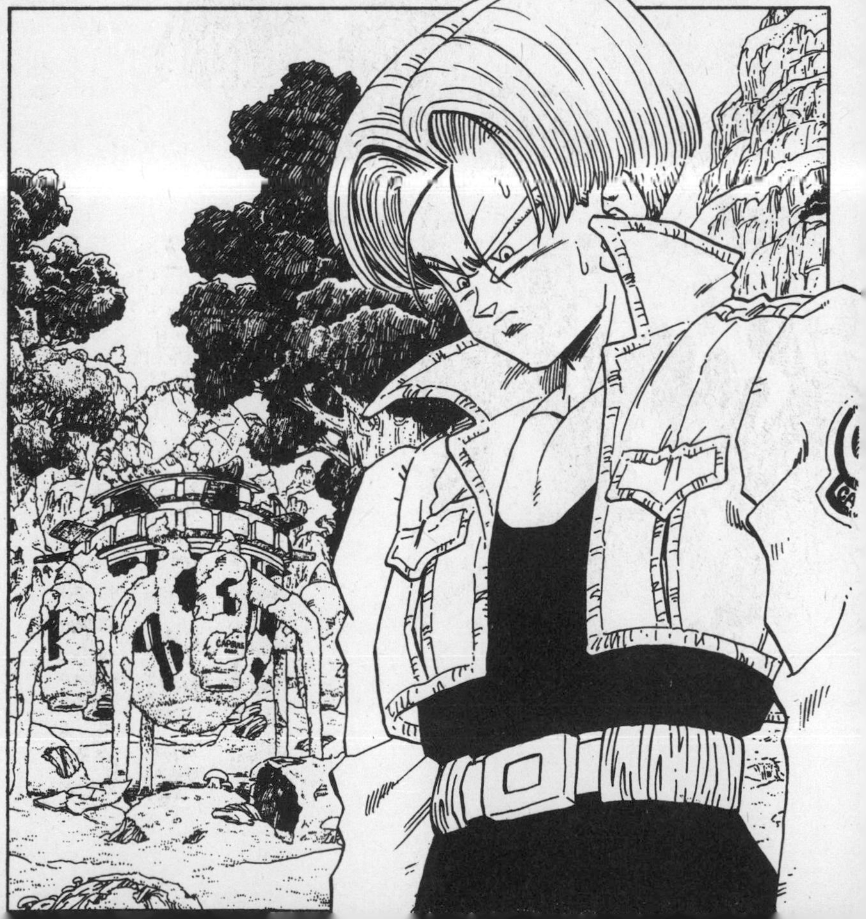

IN THE NEXT VOLUME...

Cell has been awakened – a bio-engineered monstrosity designed to become the ultimate weapon, a being that eats whole cities to drain the life energy from their inhabitants and grow stronger. While Piccolo challenges the monster, the Super Saiyans undergo unimaginable training in a room where one year passes for every day outside. But Cell's true goal is to merge with Androids #17 and #18, which will increase its strength exponentially! Can it be stopped before it fuses with the androids and becomes the strongest creature on Earth?

AVAILABLE NOW!